CURRENT AFFAIRS ATLAS

CURRENT AFFAIRS ATLAS

Edited by Donald Paneth

Special article by Nathan O. Abelson
Map Librarian, United Nations Library

Maps by George Buctel
Art Direction by Patrick R. Smith

Facts On File, Inc.
119 W. 57 Street, New York, N.Y. 10019

CURRENT AFFAIRS ATLAS

Library of Congress Cataloging in Publication Data
Main entry under title:

Current Affairs Atlas.

    Includes index.
    1.   History, Modern—20th century.   I. Paneth, Donald.
II.   Facts On File, Inc., New York.
D421.C87   909.82   79-11004
ISBN 0-87196-306-X

9 8 7 6 5 4 3 2 1

PRINTED IN THE UNITED STATES OF AMERICA

Photo Credits: National Oceanic & Atmospheric Administration Pages vi, 42; U.S. Geological Survey 4, 6; United Nations Educational, Scientific & Cultural Organization 10, 36; United Nations 11, 46, 85, 144, 148, 153, 172, 175, 177; Princeton University 27; U.S. Department of Energy 28; World Health Organization 33, 54, 121; U.S. Navy 63, 75; U.S. Air Force 65, 71, 163; Wide World 112, 126, 162; U.S. Energy Research & Development Administration 114, 115; U.S. Bureau of Reclamation 120; U.N. High Commissioner for Refugees 151, 181; National Aeronautics & Space Administration 164

Map Credits: British Aerospace, Inc. 35; U.S. Bureau of Reclamation 121

Contents

The Northern Hemisphere, as photographed by a polar-orbiting satellite. Countries and continents are outlined. The U.S., Mexico and Central America, for example, are in the center foreground, while North Africa and the Arabian Peninsula are highlighted at the right. Such photos provide additional data for map-makers or confirm information already derived from ground or aircraft observation.

Introduction

By Donald Paneth

". . . [A]ll knowledge is naturally agreeable to us. . . ."
—Matthew Arnold, 1853

The journalist is a trained observer. To a degree, he can record, explain and interpret events and issues, situations and problems. This book is an exploratory effort, in which the author has attempted to look at the world and see what is going on as a whole.

It is a thematic atlas in which the nature of diverse international and national issues is assessed. The aim is to make sense out of questions that concern everyone's humanity, despite all the differences that separate people into nations, clans, rich, poor and so on. The approach is interdisciplinary (knowledge from a large number of fields is brought together) and holistic (problems are viewed as a complex of interacting causes and effects).

". . . Essentially," as Dr. K. Soedjatmoko of Indonesia recently told a meeting of scholars and scientists at United Nations University in Tokyo, "what we are trying to do is put an end to the fragmentation of knowledge. . . ."

As an atlas, this volume covers a lot of ground, so to speak. Many of its maps conceptualize world and regional questions. Man can fly from any point in the world to any other point within twelve hours; a series of maps demonstrates this significant development. Global and regional maps illustrate the nuclear standoff; each of the superpowers, having deployed aircraft and submarines with strategic capabilities, can destroy the other. Geoeconomical problems such as commodity prices, multinational influence, energy sources are depicted in world maps.

To these are joined climatological, environmental, medical issues. The medical issues are particularly interesting from the viewpoint of public health. For example, how many of us are aware that in Africa south of the Sahara each year one million children die of malaria? Is there a remedy? What is the strategy of the World Health Organization in relation to this extremely difficult control problem? Equally significant is the reported relationship between environment and the incidence of cancer; 80 to 90 per cent of the cases of cancer in the United States may be traced to environmental or occupational causes, scientists say. Aspects of the epidemiology of both diseases are illuminated cartographically.

Dangerous political issues are clarified in maps that range the world. "Conflict in the Middle East is the most imminent and troublesome risk of all," warn Henry Owen and Charles L. Schultze, editors of the survey *Setting National Priorities.* The struggle is defined in maps of Israel and the occupied Arab territories as well as the oil-producing states of the Persian Gulf. The bitter racial conflicts in southern Africa and Africa's largely unknown refugee problem are set forth. The clash of regional interests in Southeast Asia and its overtones are charted. Communal warfare in Northern Ireland, the military regimes of Latin America, the human rights contretemps in East Europe—each is outlined on regional maps.

U.S. affairs from political mood to the dollar crisis, Indian land claims, nuclear power, organized crime are taken up within a global, national or sectional focus, as the case may be.

The maps themselves are by turn dramatic, precise, interestingly projected. Most of them have been specially drawn for this volume by the cartographer George Buctel, who has prepared maps for the U.S. government and for periodicals, books and encyclopedias. They are accompanied by text, photographs, graphs, charts and tables, the result of a year's work at the United Nations, research in such specialized libraries as that at the Carnegie Endowment for International Peace in addition to the research divisions of the New York Public Library, and a reading of newspapers from several countries and a very wide-reaching selection of current periodicals and books. U.N. headquarters in New York proved to be an excellent source of information for many of the subjects that were to be mapped and discussed. Among the sources at the U.N. were the members of the Secretariat, the liaison offices of the specialized agencies, and the reference services of the Dag Hammarskjold library.

What did the author conclude from his year of study? He concluded that the world is a continuum, fluid and unfolding; that it is not going to blow itself up; and that many problems might give way to a calm, cheerful, disinterestedly objective orientation, an exploratory rather than an adversary approach. The former approach came to seem of particular relevance since he encountered so many viewpoints in the course of his research. They and the work connected with each of them seemed to suggest that one might be able to balance out a huge amount of material about global events and reach some tentative conclusions about them, about worthwhile possibilities to follow up.

U.N. Secretary General Kurt Waldheim expressed the conviction in his report to the General Assembly last year that daily developments in the world show that global organization and global order, "however imperfect they may at present be, are an increasingly indispensable necessity. . . ." The development of a strong and effective U.N. system is imperative, Waldheim said, "precisely because we live in a world of nation states jealous of their sovereignty . . . a world of regional conflicts, deepening poverty, economic dislocation. . . ." He added: ". . . We can, and must, develop a sense of human solidarity . . . if our major international problems are to be contained and ultimately solved."

In an evaluation of future national and international problems, a report to the National Science Foundation in Washington, D.C. suggests that a new *type* of problem is emerging. It tends to arise as the result of continuing past trends interacting in new ways, or reaching some kind of limits, or both. As such it is systemic in nature, catching up various sectors and strata of society. Finally, it significantly involves attitudes, values and beliefs, and is, therefore, open to a multitude of interpretations and reactions. Potentially critical problems, the report observes, include unemployment and underemployment, growing conflict between central control and individual freedom, barriers to achieving large-scale technological projects, the effects of stress on individuals and society, potential use and misuse of "consciousness technologies."

How do the prospects for solving critical problems look? Responses are sanguine or gloomy, broadly or narrowly based, backgrounded in science, history, economics, or politics, depending on the authority consulted.

"We could fashion a stable human ecosystem for the earth as easily as we can put men on the moon," says Sir Macfarlane Burnet, Australian microbiologist and Nobel laureate, "if we could find the necessary good will, energy, and imagination on an international scale." Ronald Higgins, diplomat-journalist-professor, writes in *The Seventh Enemy* that "The evidence as a whole strongly suggests . . . an era of anarchy and widespread suffering is swiftly coming upon us," the most serious threat being the "human factor," blindness to the urgency of the approaching crises and the "frightening inertia of our political institutions."

In his pamphlet *Future Worlds,* Richard A. Falk contends that "It is all too easy to identify what is wrong with the present world political system. . . . It is far more difficult to depict a credible and constructive transition path. . . ." Despite his reservations, Falk asserts that a lack of political seriousness would be exhibited if the transition interval were to be ignored. He calls for the presentation of evolutionary forms of change as far as possible.

Wassily Leontief *et al.* in *The Future of the World Economy* attempt to investigate the economic and policy measures needed to create a new international economic order, employing input-output analysis, the econometric technique pioneered by Leontief. To provide a quantitative basis for the study, a global economic model of the world economy was constructed. The world economy was divided into 15 regions, each region described in terms of 45 sectors of economic activity. The different paths along which the different parts of the world economy could advance either rapidly or slowly, or indeed, along which they could be forced to retreat, were described.

The *Current Affairs Atlas* endeavors in any event to focus on the geography of a complex world and to offer clear summaries of the major issues affecting it, for as Neville Brown says in *The Future Global Challenge,* "the overriding need of Man today is...a commanding overview...."

The author wishes to acknowledge the generous assistance of the following individuals and institutions in the preparation of this book: Genichi Akatani, U.N. Under Secretary General for Public Information, and Kenneth B. Kelly of the U.N. Press & Publications Division; Amin Abdelsamad, chief, and Charlotte Bedford, Sylvie Jacque, Luciana Marulli and Tahany Wahab, librarians, U.N. Documents Reference & Collections Division; Thomas J. Prendergast, librarian, and Marvin A. Weill, Reynaldo Reyes and Joe Bottwin, U.N. Photo Library; Beryl Bernay and Lila L. Goldin of the Food & Agriculture Organization; Joan Bush of the World Health Organization; Jebon Szenttornyay of the U.N. Conference on Trade & Development; Iris Haynes of the Office of the U.N. High Commissioner for Refugees. And Nathaniel O. Abelson, U.N. map librarian, in addition to providing much advice and information, supplied the article on "The Value of Maps," which follows this introduction.

Particular thanks are extended to Vivian D. Hewitt, chief librarian, Jane E. Lowenthal, assistant librarian, and Susan Hendrickson and Barbara Perry of the library of the Carnegie Endowment for International Peace, and the librarians of the New York Public Library's Mid-Manhattan library and Fort Washington branch library. The author is indebted personally to Lester A. Sobel for his editorial astuteness and consistent encouragement and to Edward W. Knappman with whom the idea for the atlas project originated. He must gratefully note the patient, resilient, good-humored contribution of his wife, Elma, who often slept on the Chesterfield in the living room while he worked late into the night.

A first step in map-making — the aerial photograph (eastern shore of Maryland).

The Value of Maps

By Nathaniel O. Abelson

Most people will admit to loving maps, but when asked to use them, many will ask to be excused. This is because a map has dual characteristics. Primarily, it is a tool. It shows areal relationships, and with it one can make certain measurements or computations. It is also a work of art. Each cartographic agency has its own style, techniques and shades of colors. One who works with maps becomes familiar with the different styles and can usually identify the product of say the Institut Geographique National, the Touring Club Italiano, John Bartholemew, or the U.S. Geological Survey. A map user has to be aware of these two qualities. A very inaccurate map can be an exquisite work of art. Or a very crudely drawn map can be quite precise. When a highly accurate map is also beautifully rendered, then indeed, it is a superior product. And how, one may ask, can you tell whether or not a map is accurate? Unfortunately, this can only be determined by testing it on the area it represents (field checking) or by consulting an expert on the subject that it covers.

One used to be able to say that a map is not a picture, but this is no longer always true. At least back as far as World War II aerial photos have been overlayed with place-names and various physical, and, especially, cultural, features have been artistically emphasized. This is the exception to the rule. A map is almost always a representation of an area, small or large, created by the use of lines, symbols, and colors laid out on a mathematical projection of the region concerned. This may sound highly technical and complicated, and in fact, it is, but the concepts are not too difficult to understand.

A cartographer doesn't just draw a map. In most cases he compiles it, using other maps or surveys to draw his base map, and adding such data on this outline as he wishes to depict. How then do maps begin? Where does the original base information come from? It comes from the geodesists, surveyors and less accurately from the explorers who measure the actual surface of the earth.

The geodesist starts with our earth. He measures it, bit by bit, using the stars, planets, and in recent years, artificial satellites to determine with a high degree of accuracy thousands of fixed points all over the earth. Through a technique known as triangulation he moves out from his precise base-lines and determines to a high degree of accuracy the exact location of thousands of additional positions. The result is a triangulation network. He also determines the mean sea level and from this base by a process called levelling proceeds to measure the altitudes of thousands of points, including the triangulation points already computed; this process has been shortened considerably by the use of aerial photogrammetry and electronic measurements.

At this point, he has a book full of mathematical calculations, but he hasn't made a map. If the earth were a perfect sphere or ball, making a map would be much simpler than it is. Geodesists through their measurements have determined that the earth is not perfectly round. It bulges ever so slightly, and the actual shape of the earth is referred to as the geoid.

Nathaniel O. Abelson is the map librarian at the United Nations library in New York, a post he has held for the past 32 years. He is also the official U.N. vexillologist, or flag expert. A graduate of Yale University, he served in the U.S. Navy during World War II; he retired from the Navel Reserve in 1970 with the rank of commander.

5

The most difficult problem in making a map is that the irregular shaped geoid must be projected onto a flat surface. To do this the geodesists have computed spheroids which they feel represent most accurately the shape of the geoid. Many spheroids have been calculated, and each is felt to represent most accurately the true shape of part of the geoid in the area for which the spheroid was devised. In the United States, the Clarke Spheroid of 1866 is considered most representative of the true shape of the earth in that area.

After selecting a spheroid, the next step is to project it onto a flat surface. This is done geometrically by selecting one of many map projections which have been computed over hundreds of years. As in the classic example of trying to flatten a large section of orange peel, it cannot be accomplished without tearing the peel. In the same manner, the spheroid cannot be projected onto a flat surface without the creation of distortions. Each map projection possesses special properties which enables the cartographer to avoid some distortions, but it is impossible to avoid them all. The larger the area mapped, the more difficult the problem becomes. For example, one of the best known is the Mercator projection. It belongs to the family known as cylindrical projections because of the mathematical way that they are created. The area of least distortion on a standard Mercator map of the World is along the equator. As one goes farther

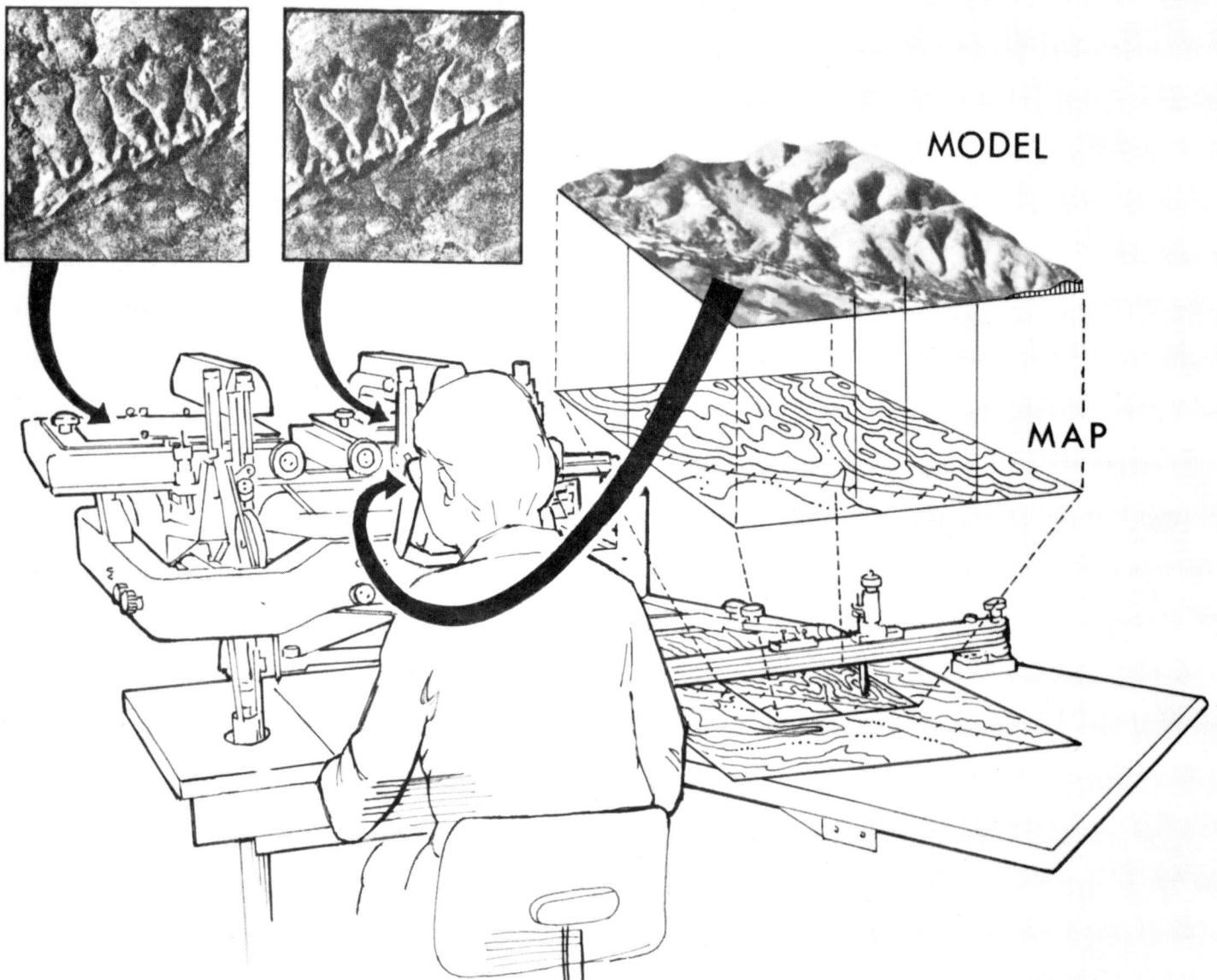

Visual model seen with stereoplotting instrument furnishes measurements needed in map construction.

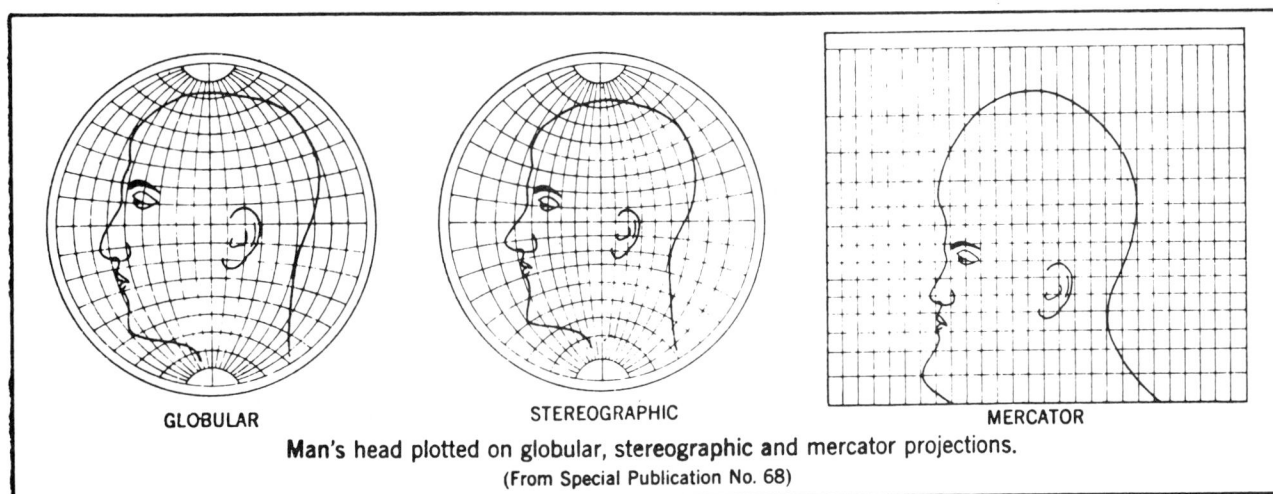

GLOBULAR   STEREOGRAPHIC   MERCATOR

Man's head plotted on globular, stereographic and mercator projections.
(From Special Publication No. 68)

Illustrations of relative distortion from *Elements of Map Projection* by Charles H. Deetz & Oscar S. Adams, U.S. Coast & Geodetic Survey. Distortion may be in directions, in distances, in shapes, in areas, or in varying combinations of all four. The distortions are manifested by the manner in which the framework of latitude and longitude lines are projected on the map.

north or south from this line the distortion increases to such an extent that the area of the island of Greenland appears to be almost as large as the continent of South America. Equal area is not a feature of that projection. The properties that make the Mercator map so valuable are those which make it useful for navigation. All compass directions are straight lines, and distances can be measured accurately along the latitude at which they are found. Thus the decision as to which projection will be used in projecting the spheroid to a flat surface will depend on which properties the cartographer wishes most to preserve.

The first maps prepared from geodetic surveys are usually of large scale. The masses of astronomically determined points, the points computed by triangulation and levelling have to be plotted on flat sheets showing nothing but the lines of latitude and longitude of the selected projection. From this plotting the coastlines and the other physical features such as terrain, rivers, lakes, etc. slowly begin to take shape. By joining together points of equal elevation, contours are drawn giving a reasonably accurate representation of such features as hills, valleys and ridges. Physical features can be shown by symbols other than contours but contours are the most accurate way of describing them. Other symbols can be used to tell whether the terrain is sandy, swampy, savan-

nah or forest. Depending upon the scale even the types of trees can be indicated as well as the vegetation.

Once the natural physical features have been depicted, the man-made features can be added. These are called cultural features and include dams, reservoirs, canals, cities, roads, railways, airports, and agricultural information such as farms, groves, and even individual crops. Most important are the areas of habitation, from farms to cities.

At this point we should have a large-scale topographic map. One important item still has to be added, the names of the places shown. Almost every physical and cultural feature probably is known by name. These names are usually learned during the process of surveying, and it is very important that they be verified and written down at that time. Later they may be considered by an official committee such as the U.S. Board on Geographic Names in Washington. They will receive this committee's approval when it is found that the name is correctly located and that it is spelled correctly. The names may be published separately as a gazetteer or index of geographical names, an invaluable tool for anyone doing geographical research.

The original manuscript may be completely drawn by hand. Today, in all likelihood, it will contain stick-on letters and symbols. There are many techniques for drawing, ranging from scribing to computer programming.

The process of transforming the original manuscripts into finished maps is generally referred to as reproduction. It is a science in itself which involves all aspects of art layout, photography, paper quality and printing. Because topographic maps are used for exact measurements, every step in the reproduction process is of great importance. Exact scale must be maintained throughout each step. Even the composition of the papers used are based on their abilities to resist shrinkage and expansion under conditions to which ordinary paper would not be subjected. The standard of the drafting, artwork and paper, the sharpness of the photo reproduction, and the choice of inks also govern the artistic quality of the map.

Up to this point I have described as briefly as possible most of the steps required in the preparation of the first or basic surveyor maps of an area. This product is usually of very large scale in many sheets. From it reductions can be made to compile smaller scale topographic maps and thematic maps. Thematic maps such as soil, geology, population, resource, transportation, etc. maps primarily show the subject of their title. Many of the symbols used on topographic maps are not used in order to emphasize the special subject. A thematic map can be prepared at any scale, but it is usually compiled at small scale on a single sheet. Groups of these thematic maps prepared at one or possibly a few different scales can be bound together to provide a thematic atlas, such as this one. There are thematic atlases of the world and of individual areas. Atlases of countries, prepared by national authorities, are known as national atlases. There are three types of atlases: those consisting of topographic maps at small scales together with a matching names index or gazetteer, the thematic atlases, and atlases which combine topographic and thematic maps.

Everyone should learn to read maps, and perhaps this article will encourage those who profess their love for maps to use them as well. There is nothing mysterious about them, and if they bear legends as all good maps should, almost every symbol that appears on each map should appear in its legend. Put them on your walls as works of art, if you will, for that they are, but never forget that first and foremost they are tools and the final product of a vast amount of research, time and technology.

CHAPTER 1

Rich World/Poor World

A multi-polar world has evolved. In the post-war, post-colonial era, 100 nations have achieved independence. Much of the world is now divided politically into East and West, capitalist and socialist countries. And largely, it is divided economically into North and South, developed and developing countries.

The North includes countries of the West and East—the 24 members of the Organization for Economic Cooperation & Development (OECD), also the Soviet Union and Eastern Europe. The South encompasses the 13 members of the Organization of Petroleum Exporting Countries (OPEC) as well as industrializing countries such as Mexico, Brazil, Taiwan and South Korea and a large number of poorer lands.

The developing countries also are known as the Third World, in reference to the division between East and West. Some of the Third World nations are "nonaligned," formally the supporters of neither Washington nor Moscow; among these are India and Yugoslavia. The poorest countries sometimes are called the Fourth World.

About a fifth of the world's population lives in the North, more than half in the South. Roughly, five-eights of the world's goods are produced in the North, one-seventh in the South.

Growth is the imperative issue in both the North and South. The countries of the South hope to provide their peoples with a decent life by increasing their output of commodities, raw materials and manufactured items that are needed the world over. On average, they have posted an annual increase in gross national product (GNP) of 5.5 per cent through the 1960s and 5.9 per cent in the first half of the 1970s.

Growth rates, however, vary widely among Third World countries. By far the greatest advance has been made by relatively well-off developing countries, the members of OPEC, which have a crucial commodity upon which to base their growth. The growth rates of the poor countries hover at 3 per cent annually. Another measure, per capita GNP, similarly varies. Oil-rich Kuwait, with a population of one million, achieved the highest per capita GNP in the world, exceeding $12,000. Mali, with a population of six million and a cattle-and-cotton economy, has a per capita GNP of about $110.

Along the East-West axis, a trio of economic ills—inflation, unemployment and a slow growth rate—troubles OECD members. The U.S. urged two of the economically strongest OECD nations, West Germany and Japan, to adopt "expansionist" policies as a stimulus to growth; that is, to consume more and export less. But the notion is resisted in both countries.

In 1977, the overall growth rate of the OECD countries declined to 3.5 per cent from 5.2 per cent in 1976. The total number of unemployed was 16.3 million, or 5.4 per cent of the workforce. Inflation ranged from 1.3 per cent annually in Switzerland to 5.6 per cent in the U.S., 15.6 per cent in Great Britain, 36.6 per cent in Turkey (the highest annual rate of inflation in any industrialized nation). Sweden ranked first in per capita income with $9,030; Switzerland second, with $8,870; Canada third, with $8,410; the U.S. fourth, with $7,910; and Norway fifth, with $7,770.

The rate of growth in the centrally planned economies of the Soviet Union and Eastern Europe declined from 5.5 per cent in 1976 to 4.3 per cent in 1977; a long-term factor contributing to a lower growth rate was the rising capital costs of raw material production.

In a global survey, the United Nations re-

9

In India, notorious for areas of abject poverty, the region surrounding Jamshedpur is rich in iron deposits and is being developed by both state and private enterprise. Yet poverty persists here despite such developments as the Tata Iron & Steel Works, shown above, which was founded as far back as the beginning of the century.

POOR WORLD
Income Disparities Between Nations
In constant 1975 U.S. $

	Population (millions)	Income per capita 1965	1975	1985
Poorest nations (below $200 per capita)	1,200	130	150	180
Middle-income developing countries (above $200 per capita)	900	630	950	1,350
Developed nations	700	4,200	5,500	8,100

The Plight of the Poor

	Population (in millions) Total	Absolute poor	Infant mortality (per 1000)	Life expectancy (years)	Mal-nourished (in millions)	Adult illiteracy
Poorest nations	1,200	750	128	50	600	62%
Developed countries	700	<20	16	72	<20	1%

Absolute Poor in the Rural and Urban Areas of Middle-Income Countries
(1975: in millions)

Region	Absolute poor Rural	Urban	Total	Absolute poor as % of population Rural	Urban	Total
Middle East and North Africa	10	30	40	25	27	27
Sub-Saharan Africa	32	8	40	29	27	29
East Asia	25	10	35	25	17	22
Latin America	20	35	55	18	18	18
	87	83	170	24	21	23

Estimates: U.N. Development Program

UNDP-AIDED AREAS
Geographic Areas Receiving the Largest Share of UNDP
Assistance (as of June 30, 1976)

Area	No. of projects	Cost to UNDP ($ millions)	Per cent of total
Africa	2,316	689.1	31
Asia and the Pacific	2,177	564.5	26
Latin America	1,670	473.0	21
Europe, Mediterranean and Middle East	1,718	434.8	20
Interregional and global	137	54.6	2
Total	8,018	$2,216.0	100

Source: U.N. Development Program

ports "widespread uncertainty and unease" about the world economic situation. "There are forces at work . . . which, if not soon reversed . . . are likely to exercise a cumulatively disruptive effect on world production and trade," the U.N. said. It cited, among disquieting trends, a slowdown in the volume of trade; instability of currency exchange rates; and the drift towards protectionist tariffs.

"In the developed market economies, a slackened pace of economic growth means the persistence of high and ever rising levels of unemployment, intensifying social tensions and undermining resistance to protectionist demands," the U.N. cautioned. The world organization urged "more affirmative action" by governments "to counter the prevailing mood." But, it added, the "restoration of confidence in

CURRENT UNDP PROJECTS
Economic & Social Fields in which U.N. Development
Program Assistance is Concentrated.

Sector	No. of projects	Cost to UNDP ($ millions)	Per cent of total
Agriculture, forestry and fisheries	1,578	618.2	28
Industry	1,840	347.1	16
Transport and communications	745	249.9	11
Economic and social planning	1,040	251.4	11
Education	531	175.0	8
Science and technology	472	130.9	6
Natural resources	290	126.6	6
Health	524	137.6	6
Other	998	179.3	8
Total	8,018	$2,216.0	100

Source: U.N. Development Program

Typical of poor countries is this scene at India's Tata Iron & Steel Works, where a woman worker transports limestone in a basket on her head. To protect themselves from industrial dust, workers mask their faces and wear goggles.

. . . rapid and sustainable growth . . . also demands firm evidence of the intent to introduce more basic and lasting changes into the international economic order."

From the North's point of view, according to the Foreign Policy Association (FPA), five key issues have emerged as primary in relations with the South. They are:

Energy. The North would need a vast flow of OPEC oil through the present "energy transition" period of a decade or so. Meanwhile, the major OPEC countries already were building or planning "downstream" industries—refineries

The multi-polar world of rich and poor, developed and developing countries is depicted here. Very rich nations, such as Sweden, the United States, Canada and West Germany, produce goods and services at an annual rate of more than $8,000 for every person in the country. Tiny Kuwait is superrich, its astonishing $12,700-per-capita Gross National Product (GNP) derived entirely from oil. Other nations have achieved an in-between status. They range from Brazil, with a per-capita GNP of $1,390 and a comparatively high growth rate of 4.8% to near-rich Japan, whose $5,640 per-capita GNP is supported by an amazing 8% growth rate. And then there are the desperately poor—such as Mali and Bangladesh with per-capita GNPs, respectively, of $110 and $90.

and petrochemical plants to process their own crude oil for export.

Trade. Commodities—unprocessed products of agriculture or mining—ranked first in value. Then, manufactured and processed goods. "So intent" were the developing countries on industrializing, the FPA recalled, that "they pushed through the U.N. in 1975 a declaration setting their target share of world manufactures at 25 per cent in the year 2000."

Aid. How much aid is enough? The only international consensus was a 1970 target: 0.7 per cent of the GNP for each developed country offering assistance. Aid from 17 developed countries had dropped from 0.42 per cent of GNP in the mid-1960s to 0.33 per cent in 1976. That of the U.S. had fallen sharply from 0.45 to 0.26. Another significant trend was the growing proportion of aid distributed through U.N. institutions; it had risen from one-sixth in 1970 to nearly a quarter by mid-decade.

Basic needs. In recent years, the World Bank and the U.S. had shifted from a strategy of aiding economic growth to meeting "basic human needs." U.S. aid now is aimed at those with a per capita income below $150 a year—an estimated 800 million people.

Private business. Mainly through the subsidiaries of multi-national corporations, hundreds of billions of dollars had been invested in the Third World. Yet, the relationship "has been tormented with cross-purposes," the FPA remarked. Complaints have been frequent that foreign companies ignore development priorities.

Discussing the South's position, economist Barbara Ward emphasized that "the basic distribution of the world's wealth has changed lit-

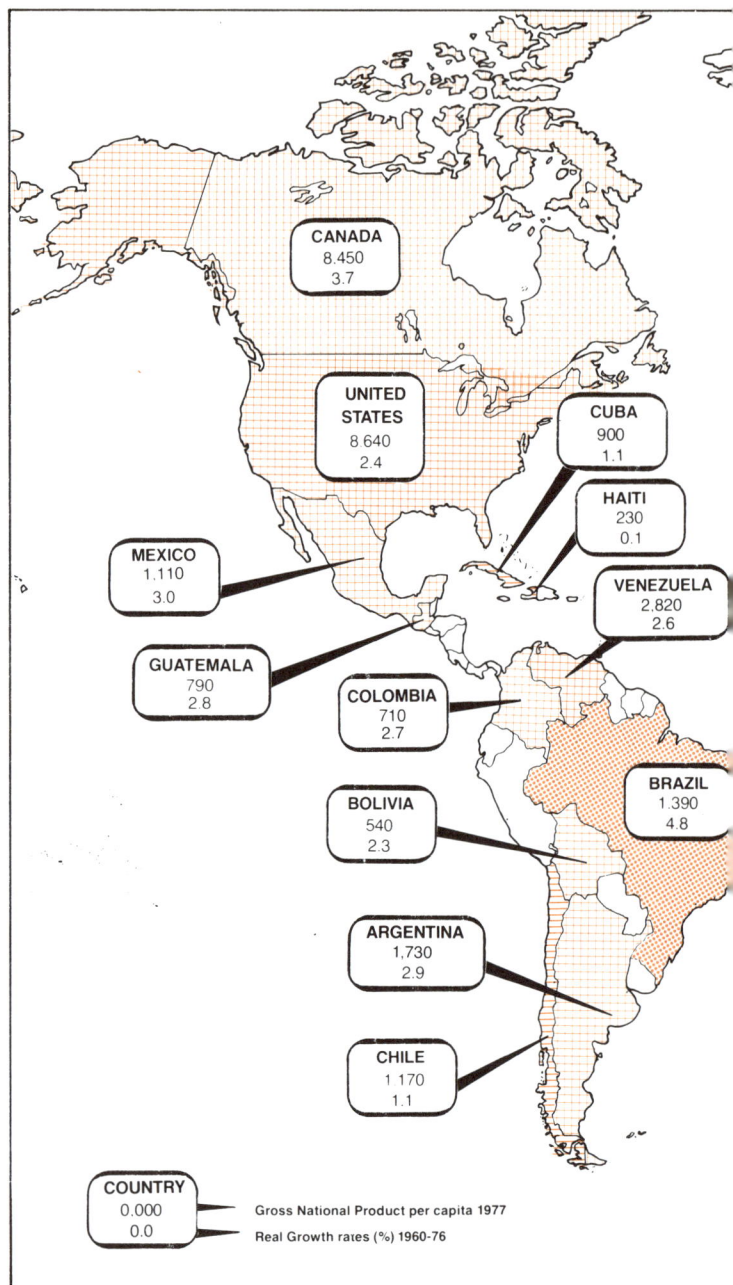

tle in the recent decades of rapid growth. In 1978 as in 1948, some 80 per cent of industry and almost 100 per cent of research, services, insurance and banking facilities are controlled by the market and planned economies of the North." Further, said a report to the 1976 U.N. Conference on Trade & Development (UNCTAD), "the underlying problems of hunger and malnutrition, even famine, of unemployment and underemployment, of rural poverty and urban degradation, are even more pressing today than they were a quarter of a century ago."

The UNCTAD report affirmed the need for a "New International Economic Order" such as

RICH WORLD/POOR WORLD

UNITED KINGDOM
4.430
2.7

SWEDEN
9.250
3.0

WEST GERMANY
8.160
3.3

EAST GERMANY
4.940
3.2

FRANCE
7.290
4.3

ITALY
3.450
3.8

BULGARIA
2.590
4.5

INDIA
150
1.2

U.S.S.R.
3.010
3.8

ISRAEL
2.920
5.1

BANGLADESH
90
−0.4

SOUTH KOREA
810
7.3

ALGERIA
1.110
1.8

CHINA
410
5.2

JAPAN
5.640
8.0

LIBYA
6.680
7.3

TAIWAN
1.180
6.2

MALI
110
0.9

KUWAIT
12.700
−3.2

PHILIPPINES
450
2.4

NIGERIA
420
3.5

SO. YEMEN
320
−5.2

SAUDI ARABIA
4.980
6.5

NEW ZEALAND
4.370
2.0

EGYPT
310
1.9

ETHIOPIA
110
1.9

AUSTRALIA
7.340
3.1

KENYA
270
2.6

SOUTH AFRICA
1.340
2.2

MALAWI
140
3.0

GNP Per Capita Growth Rate (1960–1976)

- Less than 1.0%
- 1.0% to less than 2.0%
- 2.0% to less than 4.0%
- 4.0% to less than 6.0%
- 6.0% and over

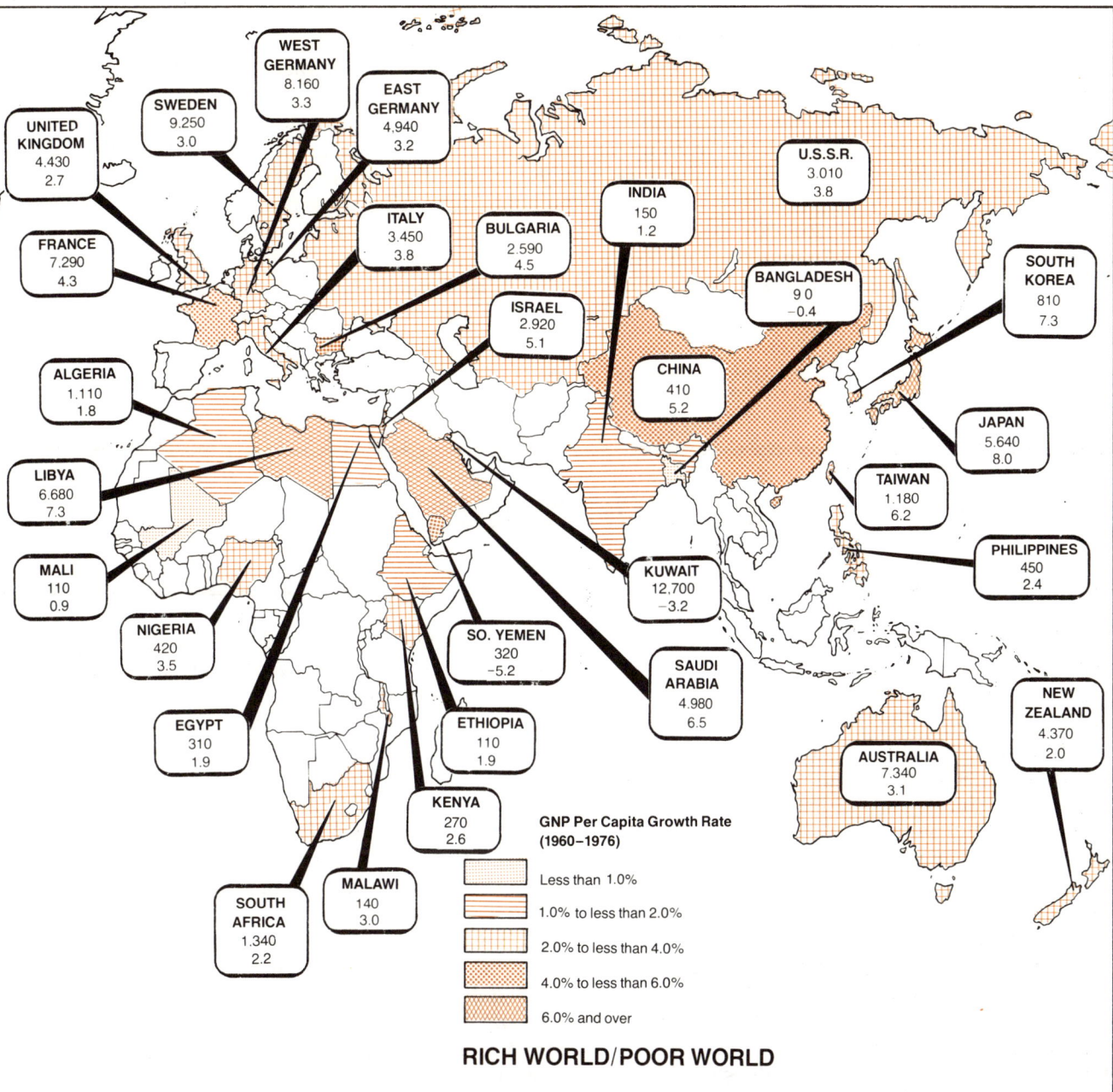

many of the poorer countries had been urging. New structures were needed to govern the commodity trade and the industrialization of developing countries, the report said. A new international monetary system is required. The conference reiterated these goals, but follow-up meetings did not accomplish much. Negotiations to establish "a common fund" to finance commodity purchases ended in deadlock. The common fund is intended to smooth out volatile price fluctuations for raw materials. A surplus commodity would be bought at low prices, held as a buffer stock, and sold at high prices in times of shortages. The industrial countries are opposed to the creation of the common fund to

which they would be the principal contributors. There also is disagreement about the scope of the fund. The developing countries want it used to finance product-diversification and market-development projects. The industrial nations contend that the World Bank and other agencies already finance these projects.

Projects of various types are aided by the U.N. Development Program (UNDP) in Asia, Africa, Latin America, the Middle East and parts of Europe. The UNDP carries out surveys to locate cultivable land, water for irrigation, industrial minerals; provides funds for investments; trains people in essential occupations; sets up research centers. UNDP funds are contributed by developed and developing countries. An international tax proposal was recommended for study by the U.N. General Assembly in 1977. Jan Tinbergen, Nobel Prize-winning economist, was among those who backed the concept. "It has been proven that the present system of voluntary contributions from the industrialized countries is inadequate," Tinbergen said. "Apparently, you cannot convince nations that they should assist others voluntarily. It is necessary to create an international system of direct taxes that makes the transfer of capital automatic."

A global strategy of development is advocated by Raul Prebisch, former UNCTAD secretary-general. "Why global?" he wrote. "For two main reasons; first, because each country, in its own strategy, must take into account all its own economic and social phenomena and, secondly, because . . . purely internal measures taken by any one country will not be very effective without full international cooperation. . . ." Prebisch added: "There are enormous possibilities. I believe that within 50 years those who look back . . . will be amazed to see how slow we were in adopting new ideas. . . ."

The Borrowers

In 1973, the aggregate foreign debt of the less developed countries (LDCs) and developing countries that do not export oil amounted to about $100 billion. Four years later, it had climbed to $250 billion. The rise paralleled (a) the increasing price of oil and imported industrial goods, (b) deteriorating terms of trade and balance-of-payments deficits, and (c) the simultaneous occurrence of world-wide inflation and recession.

The LDCs borrowed heavily from governments, international agencies, commercial banks, other private lenders. They paid huge sums annually for debt service; debt service costs added up to $15.9 billion in 1977, devouring export earnings. About 40 per cent of the debt was owed to commercial lenders.

Brazil's foreign debt, for example, reached $31.2 billion in 1977. One-third of the debt was owed to U.S. banks, including an estimated $2.5 billion to Citibank. Amortization and interest payments on the debt totaled $5.6 billion in 1977, an increase of 18 per cent over 1976. Meanwhile, to keep expanding the Brazilian economy, more loans were obtained. In 1978, the Bank of America syndicated a $300-million loan for steel, chemical, petrochemical, paper and fertilizer projects. Three European banks made a $200-million loan to the electric utility, Eletrobras, and the World Bank provided a $110-million loan to help improve São Paulo's sewage system. Bankers still regarded Brazil as

a "relatively good risk," said Christopher Roper in the *Manchester Guardian*. Brazil had resources in abundance, and its financial managers had "demonstrated considerable agility during some extremely difficult years," he explained.

However, the financial situation of Peru, another country with large foreign debts, had steadily worsened. Its troubles had taken root as the catch in its anchovetta fishing grounds declined, a new $1-billion Trans-Andean pipeline came through with a mere trickle of oil, and prices of copper, cotton and sugar collapsed. Peru's debts totaled more than $4 billion. Their servicing in 1978 cost $911 million, or 46.3 per cent of the country's export earnings. Peru requested a new financing arrangement from the International Monetary Fund (IMF). The IMF refused unless the country put its finances in order. The government adopted austerity measures, tax increases and new incentives for investment. The IMF and Peru then reached a new agreement.

Along with the debts of such countries as Peru, Zaire, Pakistan has grown the possibility of default. Different observers assess it differently. "It is the vast extent of the indebtedness which is so worrying," Lord Balogh, economic adviser to the British National Oil Corporation, says. "Any default might precipitate a serious monetary and banking crisis as people are alerted to the threat to their savings or capital."

DEVELOPING COUNTRIES' EXTERNAL PUBLIC DEBT
By region, 1970–76

In U.S. $ millions
Outstanding debt end of years:

	1970	1972	1974	1976
Africa south of the Sahara	7,327.1	9,554.9	15,957.3	21,400
East Asia and Pacific (a)	9,325.0	14,109.0	23,761.8	32,000
Latin America and the Caribbean	21,286.8	30,087.5	45,385.3	61,000
North Africa and Near East (b)	10,801.8	15,426.6	22,791.5	30,700
South Asia	15,139.2	17,821.0	23,383.8	31,400
Developed Mediterranean countries	10,348.9	14,229.0	20,119.7	27,000
Total	74,228.8	101,228.0	151,399.4	203,500

(a) Does not include publicly guaranteed private debt of the Philippines, estimated at $582.3 million as of the end of 1974.
(b) Does not include $600 million disbursed and outstanding at the end of 1974 on suppliers' credits with a maturity of 0 to 5 years of the Arab Republic of Egypt.
Source: World Bank

But there are those who are relaxed on the subject, David O. Beim, executive vice president of the U.S. Export-Import Bank, wrote in *Foreign Affairs.* They point to historical experience and case-by-case considerations showing that very few losses have been incurred up to now in LDC lending, though billions have been written off in domestic real estate, corporate and personal loans.

A solution to the debt problem has proved to be elusive. The council of ministers of the Organization of African Unity last year called for "reorganization of the entire system of debt renegotiation." Some LDCs have requested debt relief measures, including write-offs, the conversion of loans into grants. Five industrialized countries—Canada, Great Britain, the Netherlands, Sweden and Switzerland—have canceled LDC debts. In 1977, Sweden canceled more than $200 million in debts owed by Bangladesh, Botswana, Ethiopia, India, Kenya, Sri Lanka, Pakistan and Tanzania. At the same time, Sweden urged creditor nations to write off $20 billion in official loans that had been made to the world's 40 to 50 poorest countries. Last year, Britain canceled about $1.74 billion in loans due from 17 LDCs.

But the developed nations' position, as represented by a joint U.S.-European Community statement, remains essentially a case-by-case approach. They would be willing to consider debt reorganization, "as a last resort," only for LDCs facing default on debt servicing. For other LDCs, whose debt problems are of a longer-term nature, efforts should be intensified to improve their resource and financial management.

THE 29 POOREST COUNTRIES, 1975
In U.S. $ millions

	Total outstanding debt (disbursed)	Debt service	Debt service ratio*
Afghanistan	787	23	10
Bangladesh	1,622	70	16
Benin	99	9	7
Botswana	263	20	12
Bhutan	0	0	0
Burundi	15	2	6
Central African Empire	92	11	14
Chad	70	6	5
Ethiopia	387	32	9
Gambia	14	na	na
Guinea	211	24	na
Haiti	62	6	5
Laos	25	2	na
Lesotho	13	na	na
Malawi	262	17	9
Maldives	1	na	na
Mali	327	6	5
Nepal	37	5	na
Niger	114	13	na
Rwanda	22	1	2
Sikkim	na	na	na
Somalia	257	5	4
Sudan	1,191	158	30
Tanzania	839	38	8
Uganda	209	29	11
Upper Volta	63	8	6
Yemen Arab Republic	243	17	5
Yemen PDR	101	4	1
Western Samoa	16	1	5

*Total debt service as % of total exports of goods and services

Source: Organization for Economic Cooperation & Development.

Wheat is a key world commodity; its chief growing areas and producers are shown here. The price and supply of wheat and other important commodities are a global issue. In some cases, the marketing of commodities is controlled by international cartels. The most heavily cartelized industries include steel, electrical equipment, textile fibers, oil, chemicals. In a very few cases, international commodity agreements attempt to stabilize price and supply. In 1977, tin and sugar agreements were renegotiated. However, talks on two other major commodities—natural rubber and wheat—reached an impasse last year. Negotiators failed to agree on the creation of a buffer stock that would keep rubber prices within an established range. And wheat-trading nations adjourned without any agreement on how to stabilize world prices through the coordination of reserve stocks.

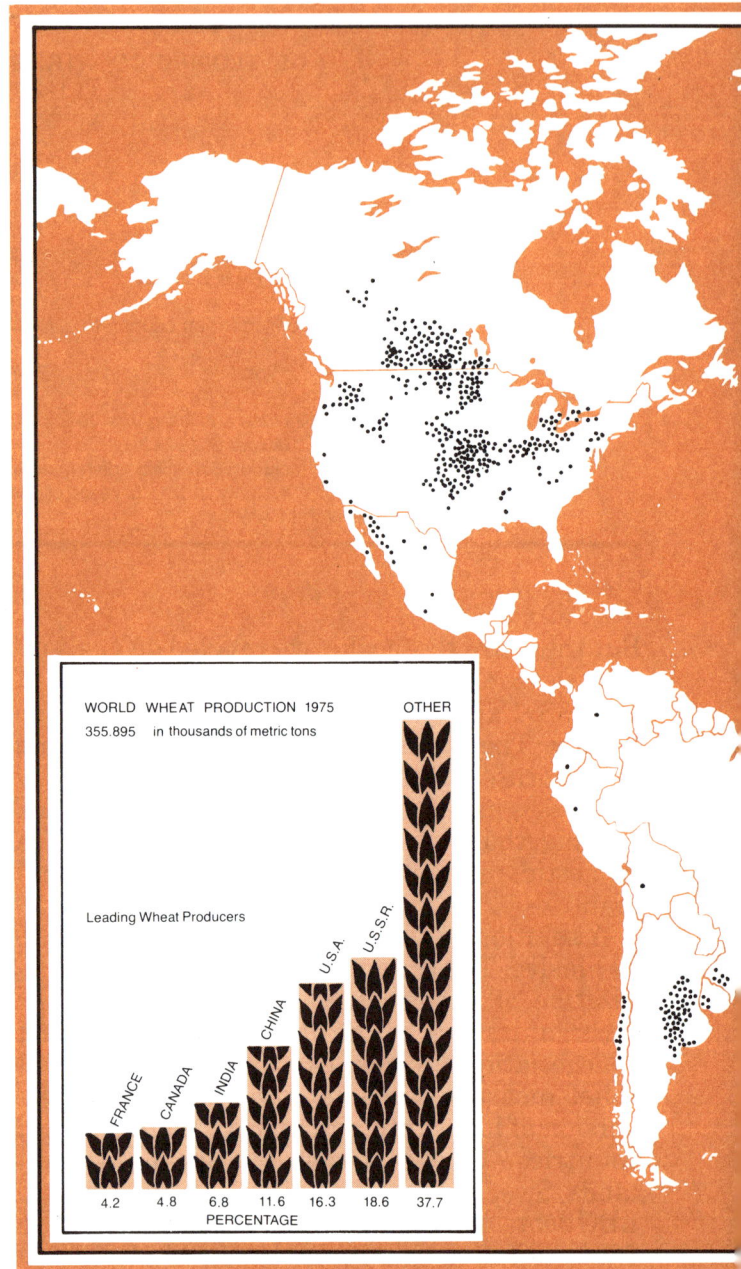

WORLD WHEAT PRODUCTION 1975
355.895   in thousands of metric tons

OTHER

Leading Wheat Producers

FRANCE   CANADA   INDIA   CHINA   U.S.A.   U.S.S.R.

4.2   4.8   6.8   11.6   16.3   18.6   37.7
PERCENTAGE

CHAPTER 2

Commodities: the Problems of Price & Supply

Key world commodities include bauxite, cocoa, coffee, copper, cotton, hard fibers, iron ore, jute, meat, oil, phosphates, rubber, sugar, tea, tropical timber, tin, vegetable oils and wheat.

Some may be bought and sold on commodity exchanges. Physical exchange of the goods in this type of sale does not take place, only the rights to ownership. Terms are usually c.i.f. (cost, insurance and freight, or charged-in-full).

PRINCIPAL WHEAT GROWING AREAS OF THE WORLD

Areas of wheat production

Source: U.S. DEPARTMENT OF COMMERCE

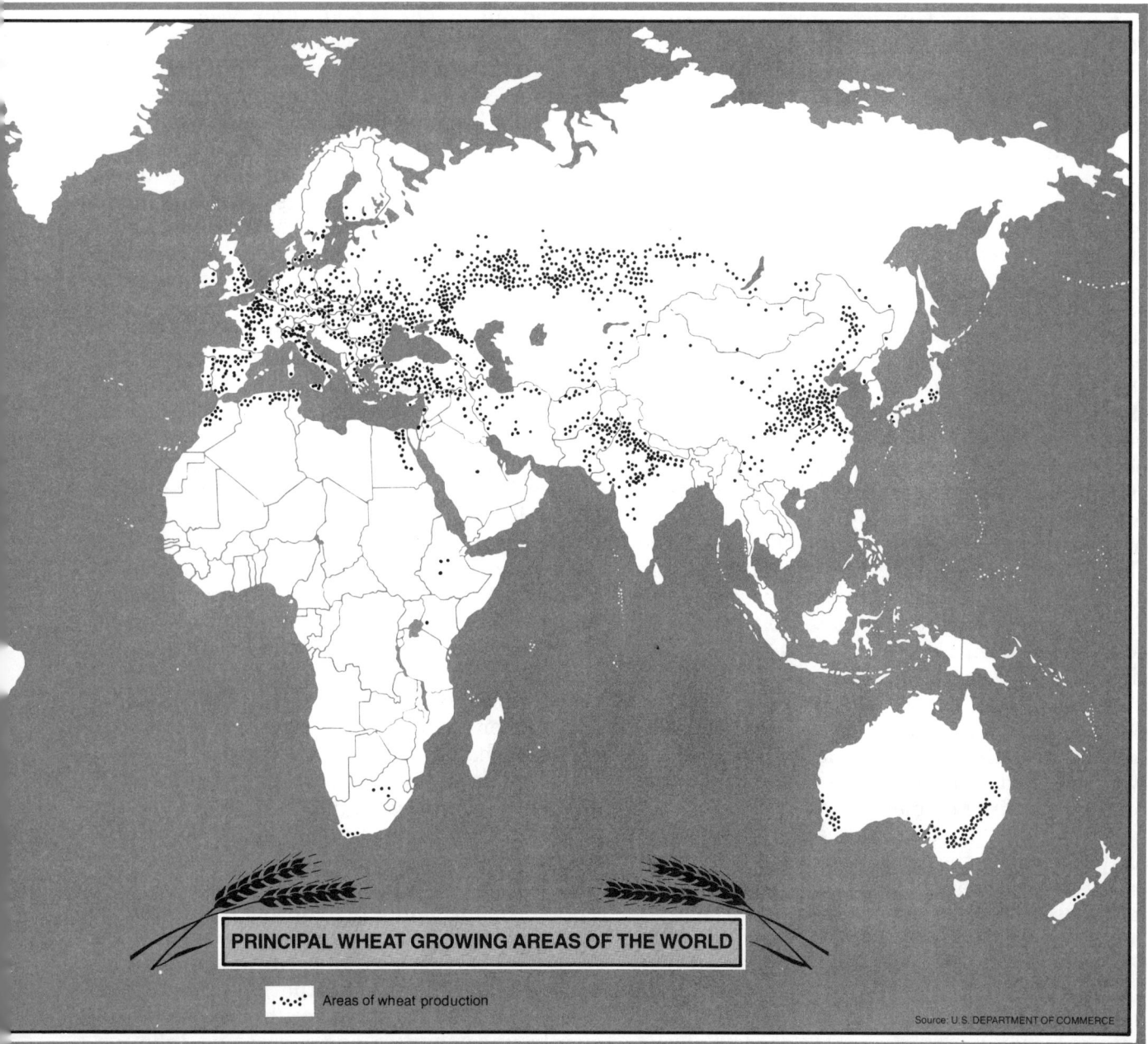

Spot prices are the prices for delivery at a particular time and place. A futures market allows purchases for forward delivery at an agreed price that will not be affected by market fluctuations.

The marketing of other commodities may be controlled by cartels or governed by international agreements.

Cartels are formed by groups of firms (occasionally countries) that fix prices, production and investment quotas. Their aim is to limit or regulate competition. International cartels are reportedly flourishing today. Data suggest that "there is a rock-bottom minimum of around 80 legal international cartels," Jean Ross-Skinner wrote recently in *Dun's Review*. Among the

most heavily cartelized industries are steel, electrical equipment, textile fibers, oil, chemicals, paper, fertilizers. International cartels, unlike domestic cartels, are legal, as long as they have no provable effect on the domestic economy of their members' countries, or groups of countries in the case of the European Community, Ross-Skinner noted. Only two countries effectively forbid their companies from joining international cartels—Japan and the U.S.

Last year, the Gulf Oil Corporation was fined $40,000 in Federal Court after pleading *nolo contendere* to charges of taking part in an international cartel that attempted to fix world uranium prices. A House subcommittee investigation had found that Gulf was among more than 20 companies that formed the cartel in 1972 under the sponsorship of Canada, France, South Africa and Australia. By 1976, uranium prices had risen from about $6 a pound to $41 a pound.

The international oil combine was unable to act as a successful cartel for more than a decade. Then war broke out Oct. 6, 1973 between Israel and the Arabs. On Oct. 17, the members of the Organization of Arab Petroleum Exporting Countries agreed to cut oil production and exports as a means of pressuring other countries to withdraw support from Israel. The cutback included a total embargo on oil exports to the U.S. and the Netherlands. At the same time, the price of oil was raised 17 per cent. The war ended Oct. 22 with a U.N. cease-fire. In December, the price of oil was doubled. The Arab countries lifted their embargo in 1974 but continued to raise prices during the following years. Prices held steady in 1978, as a glut of oil and the sluggish economy of Western Europe checked demand. Now oil prices are again rising.

Attempts to stabilize or cartelize the price of coffee have been chaotic. In 1964, an International Coffee Agreement came into force, aimed at guaranteeing export quotas and prices. Importing and exporting countries were signatories to the pact, which was later renegotiated with the participation of the U.N. Conference on Trade & Development (UNCTAD).

With coffee market changes in the middle 1970s, however, the agreement became inoperative. At first, coffee prices were pushed up by crop losses. Then, prices declined, apparently as consumer resistance developed. Brazil and Colombia, the chief coffee-exporting nations, adopted conflicting strategies during the price drop. Colombia chose an aggressive marketing policy, making extensive sales abroad at the lower prices. Brazil took the opposite approach. The government decided to withhold its coffee crop from the world market in hopes of sending the price back up. Brazil's strategy was supported by ten other coffee-producing nations in Central and South America. Then, following secret negotiations with Colombia, Brazil abandoned its stockpiling strategy. The two countries agreed to coordinate export policies in an effort to stabilize the world price at the lower level.

"There is among the coffee producers an almost total lack of the cohesion, and willingness to collaborate, even if this is to short-term national disadvantage, essential to establish and operate an effective cartel," Anthony Edwards pointed out in *The Potential for New Commodity Cartels*. Are there to be new efforts to cartelize or to reach improved international agreements on commodities? Edwards concludes that a suitable international agreement would better serve the long-term interests of producing countries. The key word is "suitable," meaning that the attitudes of producers, users and industrial interests are compatible. Without satisfactory agreements, there is danger that commodity producers would keep trying to cartelize trade.

International commodity agreements seek to stabilize price and supply, establishing a floor below which prices may not fall, a ceiling to their upward movement, and a stockpiled reserve to ensure availability.

Commodity markets are subject to violent fluctuations. Tea, for instance. Tea prices, after a long decline, rose sharply in 1974. They began to fall again in 1975. This downward trend of prices continued for the first few months of 1976. In April 1976 there was a reversal, and prices increased until around July-August, when they eased to some extent. Prices began to rise again at the end of the year and increased to record levels at the end of the first quarter of 1977. After reaching these record levels, prices declined sharply.

Such fluctuations impose grave difficulties and cause serious disruptions in the economies of the producer countries, emphasize UNCTAD officials. Especially developing countries. (India and Sri Lanka are leading producers of tea.) There are few planners in developing countries whose plans have not gone awry because of the frequent aberrations that occur in the commodity markets. But these fluctuations and disturbances also hurt consumer countries by causing supply uncertainties and increasing inflationary pressures. They might be moderated, or even eliminated, by concerted international action.

Only five international commodity agreements of one kind or another have been negotiated in the post-war era. "The negotiation of even the successful agreements took many years of tortuous and frustrated effort," one secretary-general of UNCTAD commented. "The International Cocoa Agreement took 17 years to materialize. For the other commodities no lasting results have emerged so far, despite periodic confabulations between producers and consumers."

Agreements for tin and sugar were renegotiated in 1977. The tin pact was a near-miss, illustrative of the conflict between producer and consumer nations. In early 1977, tin prices rose as Bolivia, the world's second largest producer of the metal, refused to ratify the fifth International Tin Agreement. Prices broke through an established ceiling of $3.92 a pound. Bolivian mining representatives said they would like the price to reach $5 a pound. They claimed their production costs were about $3.60 a pound, significantly higher than in Southeast Asian countries, where tin was dredged from riverbed sediment. Bolivian tin was mined from hard rock. Prices hit $4.92 a pound in March.

At this point, it appears, international pressure was applied. In a single day's trading, tin prices dropped 8 per cent on rumors that the Bank of England was investigating trading activity and on news that President Jimmy Carter had been urged to release 30,000 tons of tin from the U.S. stockpile. Bolivia announced that it would sign the tin agreement.

A renegotiated sugar agreement was signed by 72 sugar-producing nations. The pact called for quotas to reduce world-wide exports from 16.8 million tons to 13.1 million tons. The quotas would remain in effect until the world price reached 15¢ a pound. The U.S. is the world's largest importer of sugar. (Americans consumed 94 pounds per person in 1976.) The biggest producers are Cuba, which accounts for 25 per cent of total world exports, and Brazil and Australia, each holding about an 8 per cent share of the world market.

In an economically interdependent world, it seems that market anarchy is not always allowed to govern prices and supply of important commodities. At times some form of international control—cartelization, international agreement—prevails.

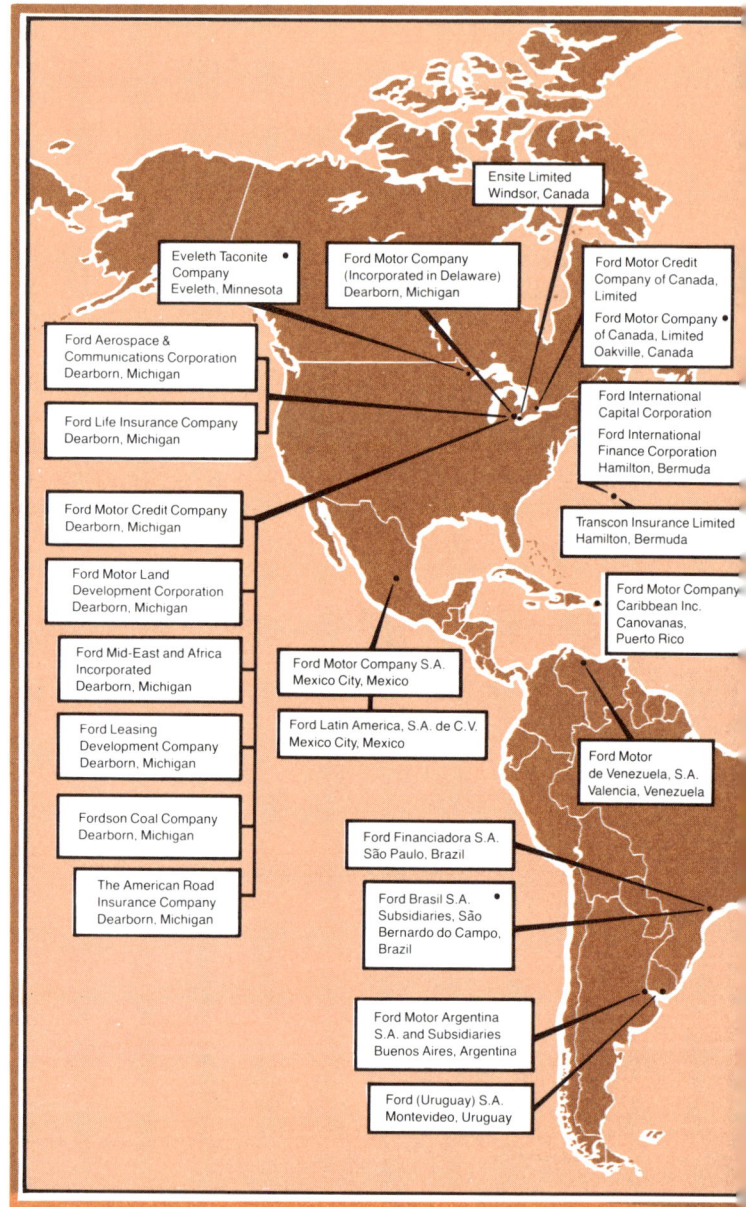

The global activities of the world's fourth largest multinational corporation, the Ford Motor Co., are indicated on the map. In 1977, Ford's sales reached a record $37.8 billion, 31 per cent above the previous high of $28.8 billion in 1976. A total of 6.5 million cars, trucks and tractors were sold. Ford's share of the U.S. car market was 23.4 per cent; its overseas operations generated 29 per cent of its worldwide sales. The year 1967 was the first in which the automotive industry sold more vehicles outside the U.S. and Canada than in North America. In that year, Ford established Ford of Europe, a regional organization; Ford Asia-Pacific was set up in 1970, Ford Latin America in 1974 and Ford Mid-East and Africa in 1975. Its sales of cars and trucks during 1977 totaled 891,390 in Germany, 563,384 in Britain, 129,466 in Brazil, 112,376 in Australia, 34,156 in South Africa. Ford employs 479,300 persons, about 220,000 outside the U.S. and Canada.

CHAPTER 3

Multinationals & Economic Power

Most views of multinational corporations are partisan. A trade official takes up the myth of the big, bad multinational, and refutes it. A labor leader focuses on the adverse worldwide consequences of the multinational's economic power. Others contend that the multinational is on the defensive today, or that its day is past, or offer their own rules for international investment.

It is a treacherous subject that is obscured by political and economic interests. For one thing, a precise definition of a multinational is still

Ford of Europe Incorporated

Ford Motor Company Limited and Subsidiaries

Ford Motor Credit Company Limited
Brentwood, Essex, England

Ford Motor Company (Belgium) N.V.
Antwerp, Belgium

Genk, Belgium Branch

Ford Tractor (Belgium) Limited
Antwerp, Belgium

Ford Motor Norge A/S
Kolbotn, Norway

Ford Motor Company Aktiebolag
Stockholm, Sweden

O/Y Ford A/B
Helsinki

Ford Motor Company A/S
Copenhagen, Denmark

Ford Nederland N.V.
Amsterdam, Netherlands

Ford Motor Company (Austria) KG
Salzburg, Austria

Henry Ford & Son Limited
Cork, Ireland

Ford-Werke AG and Subsidiaries

Ford Credit AG
Cologne, Germany

Cologne, Germany Branch

Ford France S.A.
Rueil-Malmaison, France

Richier S.A.
Credit Ford S.A.
Paris, France

Ford Lusitana S.A.R.L.
Lisbon, Portugal

Ford España S.A.
Ford Credit S.A.
Madrid, Spain

Ford Motor Company (Switzerland) S.A.
Zurich, Switzerland

Ford Italiana S.p.A.
Rome, Italy

Ford Motor Company (Egypt) S.A.E.,
Alexandria, Egypt

Japan Automatic Transmission Company, Ltd.
Fuji City, Japan

Ford Motor Company (Japan) Ltd.
Tokyo, Japan

Ford Lio Ho Motor Company Ltd.
Taipei, Taiwan

Ford Philippines Inc.
Makati, Rizal
Philippines

Mariveles Stamping Plant Branch
Mariveles, Philippines

Ford Motor Company of Malaysia, Sdn. Bhd.
Kuala Lumpur, Malaysia

Ford Motor Company Private Limited
Singapore

Ford Motor Company of South Africa (Proprietary) Limited
Port Elizabeth, South Africa

Note: Dealerships and less significant or inactive subsidiaries are not shown.

LEGEND
● Indicates subsidiaries in which there is an outstanding minority interest. All other subsidiaries are wholly or substantially wholly owned by Ford Motor Company or by its subsidiaries.

■ 50% owned company

Ford Motor Company of Australia Limited
Campbellfield, Australia

Ford Asia-Pacific, Inc.
Ford Credit Australia Limited
Melbourne, Australia

Ford Motor Company of New Zealand, Limited
Lower Hutt, New Zealand

GEOGRAPHY OF A MULTINATIONAL—FORD MOTOR COMPANY

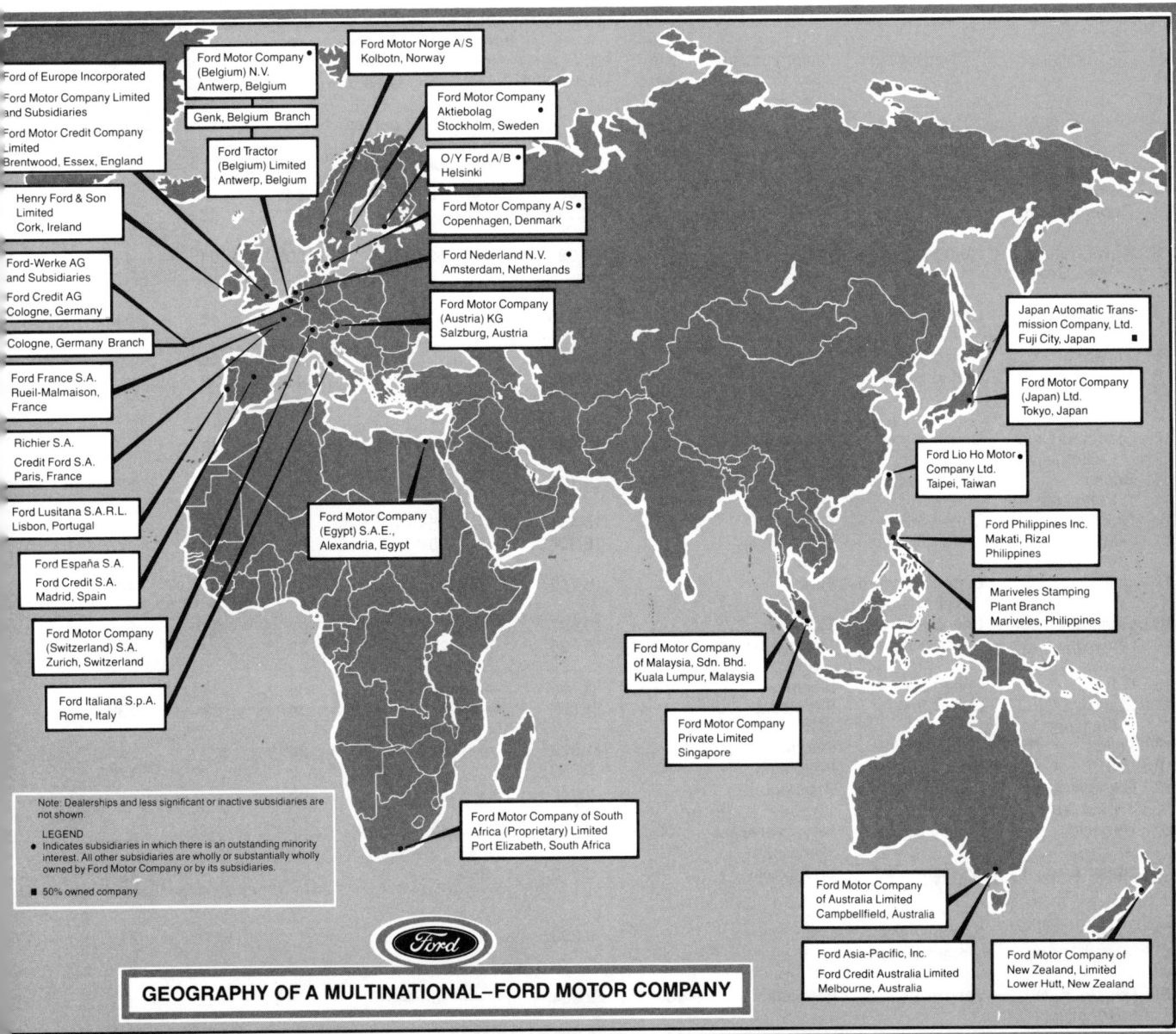

lacking. One may describe it simply as a company that operates in a number of countries.

Some basic statistics are "conspicuously murky," as Gurney Breckenfeld noted in *Saturday Review*. "Odd though it may seem in a world overflowing with numerical data of every kind, no one can say for sure just how many multinational companies exist—even how many are U.S.-based. . . . Nor do we know how big the sales and profits of multinationals are, in the aggregate. . . ."

(In a recent *Fortune* ranking of the world's largest industrial companies, the top 15 are all multinationals. Eleven are based in the U.S. Investment abroad by U.S. companies increased 10.5 per cent to $137.24 billion in 1976, accord-ing to the Department of Commerce. On the other hand, foreign investments in the U.S. increased by $1.7 billion to more than $30 billion.)

Both the past and contemporary history of the multinationals are damaging witnesses. The reputation of multinationals for corruption and violence goes back to the 19th century when Cecil Rhodes obtained concessions and mining rights in Matabeleland (Rhodesia). The Matabele wars followed. It goes back to the opening up of the Congo (Zaire) by the Belgians. "Some 2,000 white agents were sent to organize the rubber trade," Louis Turner recalls in *Multinationals and the Third World*. "Under their leadership, an armed headman was installed in each village. Reputable estimates suggest that

FOREIGN OPERATIONS OF WORLD'S LEADING INDUSTRIAL CORPORATIONS
As of end 1976

Rank[a]	Company	Nationality	Major industry	Government ownership (per cent)	Total consolidated sales (U.S. $ million)	Foreign sales Exports from home country	Foreign sales Sales of overseas affiliates to third parties	Foreign assets (per cent of total assets)	Foreign earnings (per cent of total earnings)	Foreign employment (per cent of total employment)
						As per cent of total consolidated sales				
1	Exxon	United States	Petroleum	-	48,631	--------72--------		54	. . .	. . .
2	General Motors	United States	Motor vehicles and parts	-	47,181	--------24--------		12	18	. . .
3	Royal Dutch/ Shell Group	Netherlands-United Kingdom	Petroleum	-	36,087	--------62[b]--------		50[b]	64[b]	49[b]
4	Ford Motor	United States	Motor vehicles and parts	-	28,840	--------31--------		40	45	51
5	Texaco	United States	Petroleum	-	26,452	. . .	. . .	54	45	. . .
6	Mobil	United States	Petroleum	-	26,063	. . .	. . .	49	38	. . .
7	National Iranian Oil	Iran	Petroleum	100	19,671	. . .	. . .	. . .	. . .	. . .
8	Standard Oil of California	United States	Petroleum	-	19,434	--------59--------		43	48	. . .
9	British Petroleum	United Kingdom	Petroleum	68	19,103	5	78	. . .	. . .	52
10	Gulf Oil	United States	Petroleum	-	16,451	--------55--------		43	46	. . .
11	IBM	United States	Office equipment	-	16,304	--------50--------		36	55	. . .
12	Unilever	United Kingdom-Netherlands	Food	-	15,762	8[c]	40[c]	36[c]	51[c]	44[c]
13	General Electric	United States	Electrical	-	15,697	12	26	27	37	30
14	Chrysler	United States	Motor vehicles and parts	-	15,538	--------28--------		33	22	47
15	ITT	United States	Electrical	-	11,764	--------49--------		36	39	. . .
16	Standard Oil (Indiana)	United States	Petroleum	-	11,532	--------25--------		34	22	13[d]
17	Philips	Netherlands	Electrical	-	11,522	--------37[b]--------		26[b]	. . .	78
18	ENI	Italy	Petroleum	100	9,983	. . .	. . .	. . .	. . .	17[e]
19	Française des Pétroles	France	Petroleum	35	9,928	--------54--------		65[f]	. . .	. . .
20	Renault	France	Motor vehicles and parts	100	9,353	--------45--------		. . .	. . .	. . .
21	Hoechst	Germany, Federal Republic of	Chemicals	-	9,333	35	32	. . .	. . .	43
22	BASF	Germany, Federal Republic of	Chemicals	-	9,203	25[f]	20[f]	. . .	41[f]	21
23	Petróleos de Venezuela	Venezuela	Petroleum	100	9,084	--------96--------		. . .		. . .
24	Daimler-Benz	Germany, Federal Republic of	Motor vehicles and parts	14[g]	8,938	39	21	. . .	. . .	17[f]
25	United States Steel	United States	Metal refining	-	8,604	3	*	*	. . .	. . .
26	Volkswagenwerk	Germany, Federal Republic of	Motor vehicles and parts	40	8,513	--------62--------		. . .	. . .	32
27	Atlantic Richfield	United States	Petroleum	-	8,463	--------17--------		6	7	. . .
28	E.I. Du Pont	United States	Chemicals	-	8,361	11	16	17	21	. . .
29	Bayer	Germany, Federal Republic of	Chemicals	-	8,298	27	48	44[f]	28[f]	62
30	Nippon Steel	Japan	Metal refining	-	8,090	31	1	4	. . .	1[f]

Most earnings figures refer to after-tax net income. If the domestic earnings are at loss, but the over-all group shows a profit, the foreign earnings percentage is considered to be 100. Many figures are estimates. They are not strictly comparable between companies.

An asterisk (*) indicates that the amount is less than 5 per cent.
A plus sign (+) indicates that foreign activities are profitable, but the over-all group is at loss.
a Ranked in descending order of total consolidated sales.
b Foreign excludes Europe.
c Foreign excludes European Economic Community.
d Foreign excludes North America.
e 1975 data.
f Estimated.
g Kuwaiti interest.

Source: Transnational Corporations in World Development: A Re-Examination (United Nations, 1978).

between five and eight million Congolese were killed in the course of 23 years. Roger Casement's investigations in 1904 showed that the Congolese were expected to produce 20 baskets of rubber from the jungle four times a month for no pay." The struggle for domination, land and resources continues in Rhodesia and Zaire today.

In 1973, the International Telephone & Telegraph Corporation was linked to the military overthrow of the Allende government in Chile. A U.N. commission and a center later were established to examine the activities of what the U.N. preferred to call the transnationals (so designated because not all multinationals are corporations but may be government entities, cooperatives or partnerships). The center undertook the task of collecting and analyzing information about the transnational, of setting international standards of accounting and reporting and of investigating ways of dealing with corrupt practices.

In 1975–76, the large-scale use of bribery by American corporations in their operations overseas was revealed. A total of 233 U.S. corporations were found to have made $412 million in questionable payments since 1970. Boeing Co., which admitted making $70 million in questionable payments, topped the list. Others making large payments were Exxon Corp., $46 million; Northrop Corp., nearly $32 million, and Armco Steel Corp., $17.5 million. Legislation prohibiting U.S. corporations from bribing foreign officials was enacted.

Multinational corporations operate in basic industries—oil, chemicals, aerospace, automobiles, shipping, pharmaceuticals. They are criticized for exporting jobs, exploiting the economies of developing countries, rigging prices. Many countries are concerned about the ownership and control of key economic sectors by foreign enterprises, the extent to which they may encroach upon political sovereignty. The transfer of technology to developing countries is acknowledged as being beneficial, but it is pointed out that the goods produced often are geared to the needs of the advanced countries. A distinctive characteristic of multinationals is their flexibility in choosing where to establish production units. The "runaway" industry leaves a country in which labor costs are high for one in which they are low. Labor unions also may be weakened or neutralized and strikes circumvented by the shift of production to other countries.

On the whole, multinational corporations are continuing to expand, the U.N. reports. One indication is the rise in the value of foreign investment stock held by the leading seven home countries as well as other nations from $158.4 billion in 1971 to $287.2 billion in 1976. The leading home countries were the U.S., Great Britain, Japan, West Germany, Switzerland, France and Canada.

Current levels of oil production and consumption are displayed on this world map. Leading countries are shown, with production and consumption by 1,000 barrels daily, exports and imports by 1,000 metric tons per year. Worldwide reserves in the millions of barrels are indicated by region and country.

CHAPTER 4

Energy

Where the big oil reserves are as of Jan. 1, 1978

Total World Reserves 645.997 million bbls.

MIDDLE EAST

COMMUNIST

WESTERN HEMISPHERE

AFRICA

EUROPE

ASIA-PACIFIC

| 366.166 | 98.000 | 75.870 | 59.450 | 26.662 | 19.749 |

Oil reserves. million bbls

CANADA
1.360.0
24.321
6.000

UNITED STATES
16.980
254.307

UNITED STATES
8.240.0
29,500

MEXICO
990.0
14.000

MEXICO
675

VENEZUELA
2.280.0
36.697
18.200

COLOMBIA
140.0
960

13

2

ECUADOR
180.0
8.403
1.640

BRAZIL
795
41.867

BRA
16
8

PERU
90.0
730

ARGENTINA
440.0
2.503

ARGENTINA
495
6.232

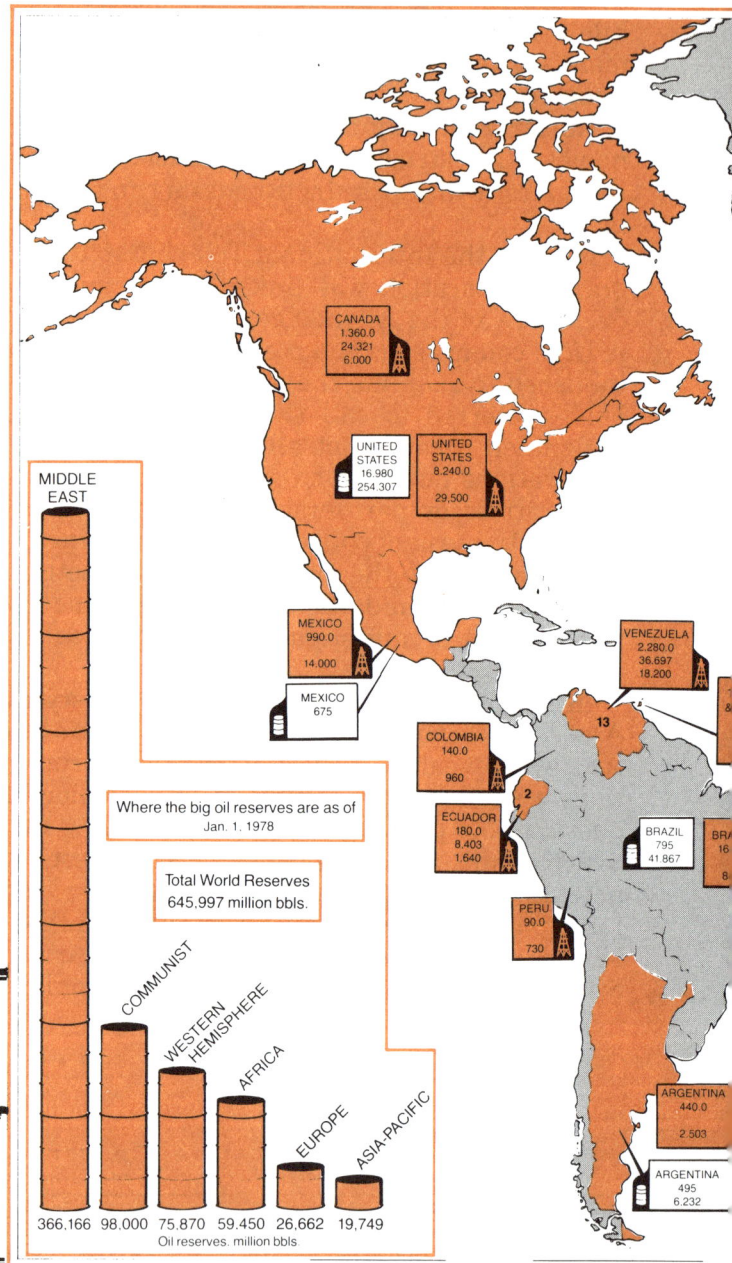

What is the nature of the energy crisis? Are we running out of oil? How long will coal reserves last? Is nuclear energy safe? Will alternative sources of energy—solar, wind, "biomass" (vegetation, crop-waste) conversion—be developed?

These are difficult questions. There are almost as many interpretations and sometimes almost as many answers as there are experts and authorities. The experts, themselves, differ about efficacy, cost, safety. Sometimes it is not easy to conclude whether government or business spokesmen are being honestly informative or misleadingly alarming.

The alarmist position is fairly well-known. In 1974, for example, following the Arab oil embargo and price rise, U.S. officials declared that exorbitant prices imperiled the world's economy and could lead to "confrontation" and "a breakdown of world order and safety." Oil prices remained high, the public paid the tariff.

Three years later, President Carter presented a comprehensive energy policy to Congress. He said that it would only work "if the people understand the seriousness of the challenge and are willing to make sacrifices." He warned that delay in its adoption might mean "national catastrophe." Nevertheless, Congress deadlocked on the proposed measures—new taxes, conservation of petroleum products, an increase in the

NORWAY 175 93.180

NORWAY 270.0 14.625 6.000

SWEDEN 585 5.703

WEST GERMANY 2.885 107.819

NETHERLANDS 800 93.180

UNITED KINGDOM 775.0 3.836 19.000

UNITED KINGDOM 1.870 110.630

U.S.S.R. 7.500 6.353

U.S.S.R. 10.920.0 15.920 75.000

BELGIUM-LUX 560 12.863

FRANCE 2.385 109.693

AUSTRIA 230 1.616

SWITZERLAND 270 6.232

TURKEY 65.0 370

SYRIA 200.0 2.150

IRAQ 2,150.0 47.480 34.500

(Before the revolution)

IRAN* 5,650.0 141.483 62.000

CHINA 1.800.0 20.000

JAPAN 5.195 167.498

SPAIN 955 53.075

ITALY 1.970 110.951

ALGERIA 990.0 25.950 6.600

LIBYA 2.050.0 106.996 25.000

EGYPT 450.0 5.806 2.450

SAUDI ARABIA 8,950.0 426,512 150.000

KUWAIT 1,700.0 95.587 67.000

INDIA 200.0 3.000

INDIA 535 16.713

UAE 2.000 80.666 32.400

PHILIPPINES 192 6.370

BRUNEI 207.0 1.550

MALAYSIA 190.0 2.500

QATAR 350.0 14.379 5.600

OMAN 350.0 5650

THAILAND 194

NIGERIA 2,020.0 122,831 18.700

GABON 225.0 2.050

ANGOLA-CABINDA 195.0 1.160

INDONESIA 1,690.0 66,711 10.000

INDONESIA 228

AUSTRALIA 641 8.449

AUSTRALIA 430.0 2.000

SOUTH AFRICA 312

Major Oil Producing Countries

Producing Country 1976
Oil production daily (bbls.) ——————→ 000
Exports (1,000 metric tons/annum) ——→ 000
Oil reserves (1,000 bbls.) Jan. 1, 1978 —→ 000

←— Consuming Country 1976
000 ←— Consumption daily (bbls.)
000 ←— Imports (1,000 metric tons/annum)

OIL PRODUCTION AND CONSUMPTION

Organization of Petroleum Exporting Countries (OPEC)

1 ALGERIA	8 LIBYA
2 ECUADOR	9 NIGERIA
3 GABON	10 SAUDI ARABIA
4 INDONESIA	11 QATAR
5 IRAN	12 UNITED ARAB
6 IRAQ	EMIRATES
7 KUWAIT	13 VENEZUELA

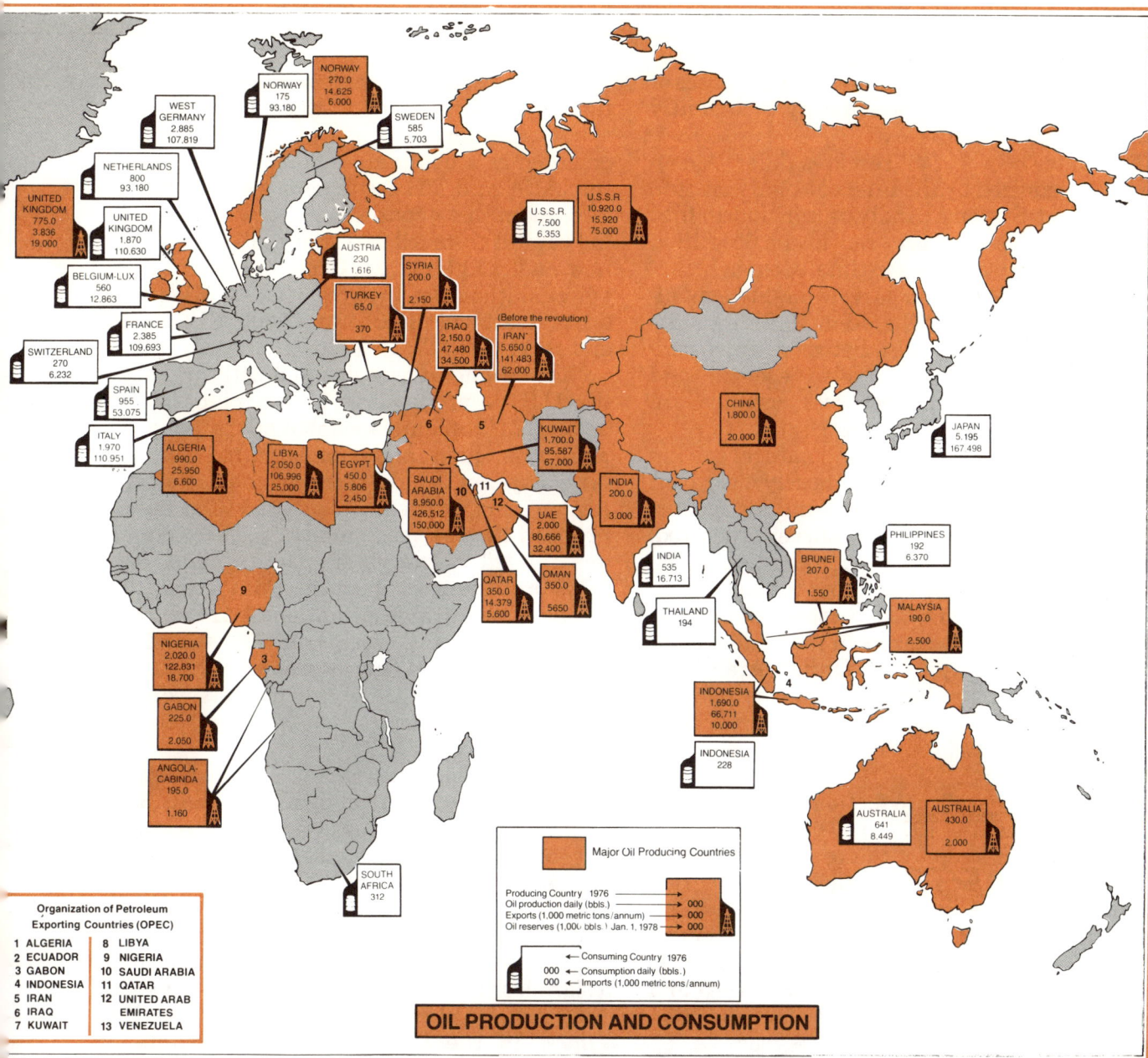

use of coal, insulation of homes and buildings— and then rejected, diluted or recast most of them. The public was not quite convinced of the need for them.

Carter generalized about catastrophe. The idea seemed to be that the U.S. would run out of fuel. His assertions were backed up by such Administration trouble-shooters as James R. Schlesinger, head of the newly created Department of Energy, and such extragovernmental institutions as the Organization for Economic Cooperation & Development (OECD). Schlesinger foresaw a possible oil shortage in the middle 1980s. The OECD said that if Western Europe, North America and Japan continued their current energy policies they wouldn't be able to meet their demand for oil by 1985.

Conflicting views were offered by many non-governmental energy experts. The Petroleum Industry Research Foundation—a non-profit group based in New York—predicted that there probably wouldn't be a global oil shortage before the end of the century. Peter Odell, director of the Economic Geography Institute at the Netherlands School of Economics, wrote in the *Manchester Guardian* that "the so-called 'generally accepted oil shortage' is the outcome of commercially-oriented interests rather than a statement of the essential reality of the oil resources of the world." Odell suggested that the production of oil could continue to increase for almost another 50 years—to about the year 2025 when the oil industry might be some three-and-a-half times its present size. For purposes of comparison, he noted, the industry is currently six times its 1950 size.

Estimates of world oil reserves differ. A conference organized by the International Institute for Applied Systems Analysis concluded that total oil resources are between 40 and 60 trillion barrels. Soviet scientists estimate, though cautiously, that 119 trillion barrels might be available. In *The Control of Oil,* John M. Blair points out the need to distinguish between "ultra conservative numbers" and "proven reserves" and "true reserves." True reserves usually are higher than proven reserves.

World output of crude oil and natural gas liquids, meanwhile, had risen by nearly 4 per cent in 1977 over 1976 to about 61.7 million barrels per day, a U.N. economic survey reported. Nearly all of the increase had occurred in nations other than those belonging to the Organization of Petroleum Exporting Countries. (Among the OPEC countries in the Middle East, only Saudi Arabia and the United Arab Emirates increased production. Major producers such as Iran, Iraq and Kuwait lowered their output. Sizable reductions also took place in Qatar and Oman.)

OPEC's share of production had declined from 53.5 per cent in 1973 to 50 per cent in 1977. The production share of the centrally planned economies had increased during that period from 17.5 to 21.9 per cent. The growth of oil output was largely the result of expansion in the Soviet Union and China. In addition, two new producing regions, the North Sea and Alaska, were contributing more than 2 million barrels per day by the end of the year.

Disputes about nuclear energy were almost as intense as those about oil.

Uncertainty and divided opinion about the future of nuclear power were to be found in several industrial countries, according to the International Atomic Energy Agency (IAEA). The reprocessing of spent fuel and the disposal or storage of nuclear wastes were especially controversial. The fast-breeder reactor used plutonium, a basic ingredient of nuclear weapons; reprocessing equipment could be employed to produce weapons-grade fissionable material. The problem of storing nuclear wastes, which will remain dangerously radioactive for thousands of years, has yet to be solved. Possible low-level emission of radioactivity by nuclear plants and plant safety were other disputed questions.

". . . In certain countries concern about . . . further proliferation of nuclear weapons or about . . . terrorist use of nuclear material emerged as a dominant element of . . . policy," the IAEA said. "These factors, coupled with environmentalist opposition . . . as well as escalating capital costs led to a sharp fall in orders for new nuclear plants. . . . Orders for new nuclear power stations declined from 53,000 MW [megawatts (electric)] in 1974 to 32,000 MW in 1975 and to 11,000 MW in 1976."

Nuclear energy was debated with urgency in the U.S. A proposed $2-billion plant at Seabrook, N.H. became a symbol of the issue. The plant was fought and delayed in the courts for several years. The Environmental Protection Agency and Nuclear Regulatory Commission reversed themselves a number of times on matters related to the plant's construction. Some 2,000 protestors occupied the plant site in 1977, receiving worldwide attention; 1,414 were arrested, and many were held for almost two weeks in National Guard armories throughout the state. Other anti-nuclear protests were carried out at plants in Vernon, Vt.; Port San Luis, Calif., Barnwell, S.C.

Abroad, demonstrations occurred in France, West Germany, Austria, Switzerland. In Basel, Switzerland, voters approved a law requiring city officials to oppose nuclear power plants. The federal government had planned to build a nuclear complex in the vicinity.

While the debate went on, reactors sold during past years had "gradually begun to supply a significant share of the world's power needs," Anthony J. Parisi reported in *The New York Times.* In the U.S., 68 nuclear reactors accounted for 8.9 per cent of the nation's installed power generating capacity in 1977. Elsewhere in the world, 138 reactors were "on line"; 21 foreign countries had nuclear plants, and at least 20 more were committed to the technology. Sweden headed the world in the nuclear-power percentage of installed generating capacity—14.5 per cent. By this measure, Belgium, West Germany, France, Britain, South Korea, Taiwan and Switzerland were all ahead of the U.S. The Soviet Union is expected to have 6 per cent of its generating capacity nuclear-based by 1980.

Another source of energy—world coal supplies—would last about 800 years, the experts

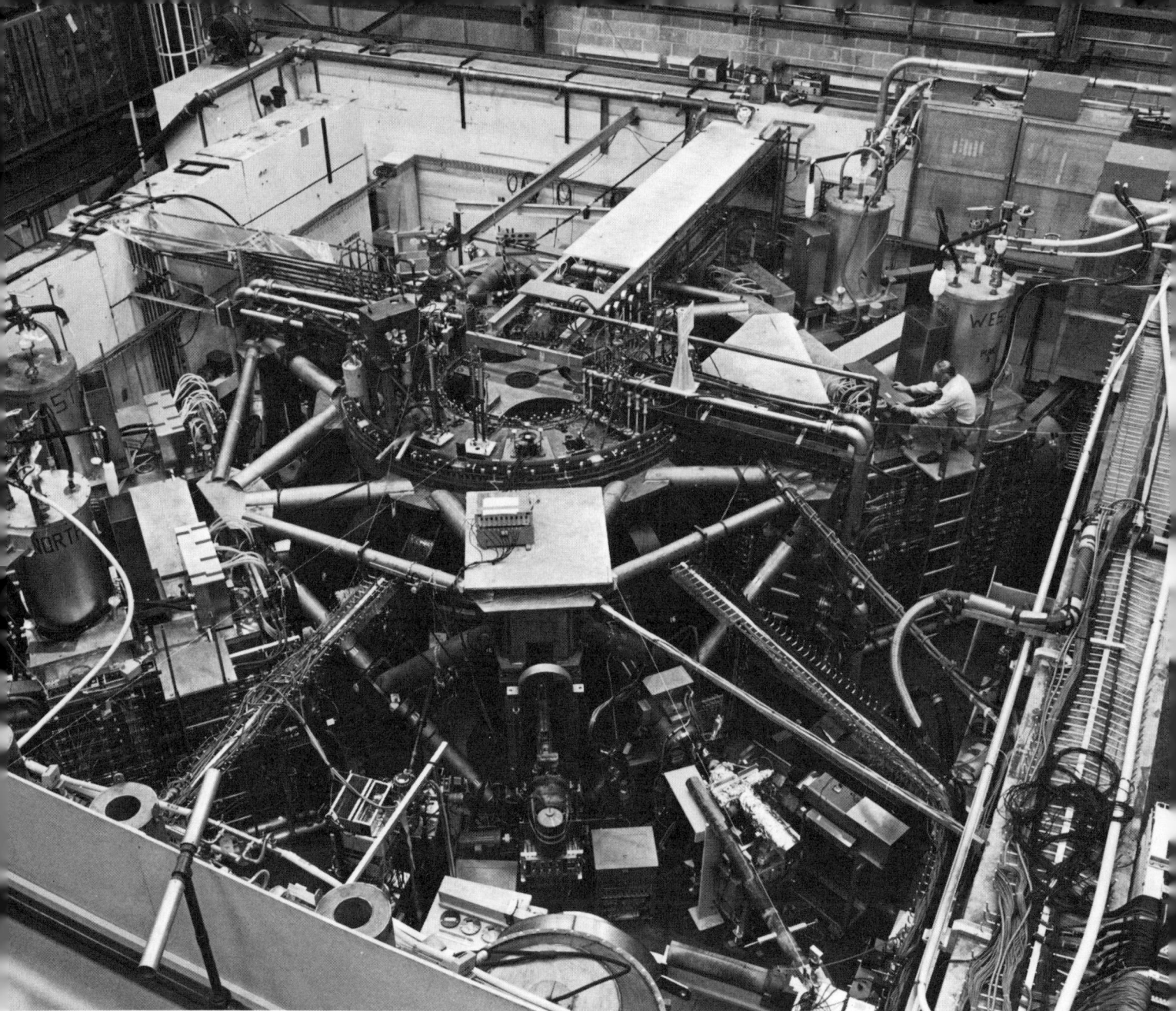

The achievement of energy through nuclear fusion is the objective of experiments at Princeton University with the Princeton Large Torus (PLT), above. The PLT set a new temperature record for a tokamak-type machine; a temperature of 60,000,000°C. was reached, well over the 44,000,000°C. minimum required for a sustained release of fusion energy. (Tokamak machines contain the fusion reaction within a toroidal, or doughnut-shaped, magnetic field. The hydrogen-based fuel converts to a plasma when heated to the high temperatures.) Temperature is one of three critical elements needed to achieve a self-sustained fusion reaction. The other two elements are confinement time (the number of seconds the hot plasma can be confined within the device) and density (the number of particles in a cubic centimeter of the plasma). A new device, the Tokamak Fusion Test Reactor (TFTR), is scheduled for operation at Princeton in 1981. It is twice the size of the PLT. A sustained release of fusion energy may be possible in the TFTR, according to scientists. With nuclear fusion, an inexhaustible supply of energy would become available.

say. U.S. reserves are extensive. Coal reserves are even greater in the Soviet Union and China. Asia as a whole is believed to have two-thirds of the world's coal reserves, wrote John Maddox. In Western Europe, the coal seams are thin and deep compared to those in the U.S. In Europe, the productivity of miners working in deep mines averages only a little more than two tons per day compared with 15 tons from the bituminous mines of the U.S. Miner safety and health are acute problems. Since 1970, 125,000 American miners have been injured and 216 killed in major mine disasters. The costs of black lung disease are high, adding at least $1.50 to every $20 ton of coal. Seventeen out of every 100 miners contract the disease.

That the energy crisis might be solved by reason, imagination, effort, conservation, balanced

French solar furnace, located near Odeillo in the Pyrenees Mountains, used by the U.S. Department of Energy to test the first prototype boiler for a solar electric generating plant. Its capacity is one megawatt (1,000 kilowatts) of thermal energy. In the foreground, an array of 63 mirrors (heliostats), each measuring 6 meters (11.4 yards) by 7½ meters (14.2 yards), reflects sunlight onto curved mirror surface of the office building in the background. This in turn focuses the sunlight on an aperture in the tower at center, where temperatures of 7,000° F. can be produced.

use, development of new sources is indicated by numerous authorities.

Nuclear fission produces power. An alternative source of energy is nuclear fusion, the fusing together of atoms of hydrogen. In the process, great heat is released. Success with fusion power would solve the energy problem for all time since hydrogen is readily extracted from water. Scientists are still years away from knowing the best path to practical fusion power. They are trying different approaches.

". . . There are many reasons why the large corporations may fail to exploit even the most promising new technologies," John M. Blair emphasized. ". . . But permitting promising fruits of such research to remain unutilized is intolerable. The single most effective step toward increasing the supply of energy would be the development of oil shale, using the *in situ* process, if possible, or the conventional mining-and-crushing process, if necessary. . . . Just as the private utility companies' long-standing reluctance toward developing the electric power potential of Muscle Shoals led to the formation of the Tennessee Valley Authority, so also should the oil companies' long-standing apathy on oil shale lead to the establishment of the Oil Shale Authority. . . . On the basis of the time schedule set forth in the Bureau of Mines 1969 blueprint, such an agency should be able in a few years to produce 1 million and eventually 6 million barrels of motor fuel a day."

A variety of new energy sources—geothermal energy, solar energy, wind power, tidal power, sea-thermal power, hydrogen, ocean energy, volcanoes—will be studied in the next 20 years, said Joseph Barnea.

Great Britain is further along than the U.S. in energy planning, Robert Kolbe commented. Already Britain is enacting stringent conservation rules. Kolbe quoted from an energy discussion report, *Energy R&D in the United Kingdom:* "Thermal insulation of existing buildings, better energy housekeeping and management, using less material or materials with a lower energy content, and switching modes of transport can reduce the need for energy."

The energy debate stems from different conceptions of the future, "the solar utopia and the electrical, i.e., nuclear, utopia," said Alvin M. Weinberg, former director of the Oak Ridge National Laboratory. Both are conceivable, and the most prudent planning would aim at some combination of the two.

"The essence of the energy problem is not exhaustion of energy resources as a whole, but rather the conflict between the apparent eco-nomic imperative for energy growth and the rising costs of such growth," the Pugwash Council found. Most future growth should take place in the developing countries. Further increases in the industrialized countries should depend more on efficiency of use than on how much energy capacity is added. Research should be expanded considerably on the economic use of energy.

GLOSSARY

Backup—Reserve generating capacity of a power system.

Barrel (bbl)—A liquid measure of oil, usually crude oil, equal to 42 American gallons. (A container of 1-barrel capacity does not now exist in the oil trade.)

Breeder Reactor—A nuclear reactor so designed that it converts more non-fissionable uranium-238 or thorium into useful nuclear fuel than the fissionable uranium-235 or plutonium that it uses.

Chain Reaction—A nuclear reaction that stimulates its own repetition. In a fission chain reaction, a fissionable nucleus absorbs a neutron and splits, releasing additional neutrons. These can be absorbed by other fissionable nuclei, releasing still more neutrons.

Coal Gasification—The conversion of coal to a gas suitable for use as a fuel.

Continental Shelf—The extension of the continental land mass into the oceans, under relatively shallow seas, as opposed to the deeper basins.

Cooling Pond—An artificial pond used to receive and dissipate waste heat, usually from a steam-electric power plant.

Crude—Oil in its natural state, before refining or processing.

Deep Mining—The exploitation of coal or mineral deposits at depths exceeding about 1,000 feet. Coal is usually deep mined at not more than 1,500 feet.

Energy—The capability of doing work. Most of the world's mechanical energy comes from non-renewable deposits of hydrocarbons, such as peat, coal, oil, or gas.

Fission—The splitting of an atom's heavy nucleus into two approximately equal parts (which are radioactive nuclei of lighter elements), accompanied by the release of a relatively large amount of energy and generally one or more neutrons.

Fusion—The creation of a heavier nucleus from lighter ones, such as those of hydrogen isotopes, with the attendant release of energy.

Geothermal Steam—Steam drawn from deep within the earth. There are about 90 known places in the continental U.S. where geothermal steam could be harnessed for power. These are in California, Idaho, Nevada and Oregon.

Liquefied Natural Gas (LNG)—A clear, flammable liquid both tasteless and odorless; almost pure methane.

Nuclear Reactor—A device in which a fission chain reaction can be initiated, maintained and controlled. Its essential component is a core with fissionable fuel. It usually has a moderator, reflector, shielding coolant and control mechanisms.

Refinery—A facility that separates crude oil into its usable chemical components.

Thermodynamics—The science and study of the relationships between heat and mechanical work. First Law: Energy can be neither created nor destroyed. Second Law: Heat cannot pass from a colder to a warmer body without the additional expenditure of energy.

Wheeling—Transmission of electricity by a utility over its lines for another utility.

FOOD PRIORITY COUNTRIES

Forty-three countries have been named as "Food Priority Countries" (FPCs) by the U.N. World Food Council. These countries have both severe food problems and the potential for increasing food production. Classified by degree of severity, they are listed below.

Degree of severity	No. of Countries	Countries
I (extremely severe)	8	Bangladesh, Mali, Upper Volta, Yemen A.R., Yemen D.R., Somalia, Tanzania, Niger
II (very severe)	23	Afghanistan, Benin, Cape Verde, Central African Empire, Chad, Egypt, Ethiopia, Gambia, Guinea, Guinea Bissau, Haiti, India, Indonesia, Democratic Kampuchea, Lesotho, Lao P.D.R., Malawi, Mauritania, Nepal, Pakistan, Rwanda, Sri Lanka, Uganda
III (severe)	12	Burma, Cameroon, El Salvador, Guyana, Honduras, Keyna, Madagascar, Mozambique, Phillipines, Senegal, Sierra Leone, Sudan

Their Conditions:

The FPCs account for more than half the population of developing countries (excluding China) and for over half their projected food deficits by 1985. While the criteria set the upper limit for per capita incomes at $500, only 11 have incomes of somewhat more than $300, and 26 have incomes of less than $200 per capita. Each FPC has a projected cereal deficit of 500,000 tons or more and/or a cereal deficit of 20 per cent or more of estimated requirements by 1985. The FPCs have all had very slow rates of growth of food production per capita from 1965 to 1975; 25 have had a per capita rate of growth of food production of 0 or negative. These statistics indicate the severity of food problems of the FPCs. In addition, all suffer from critical balance of payment constraints, which indicates that imports of food are not a viable solution to their food problems.

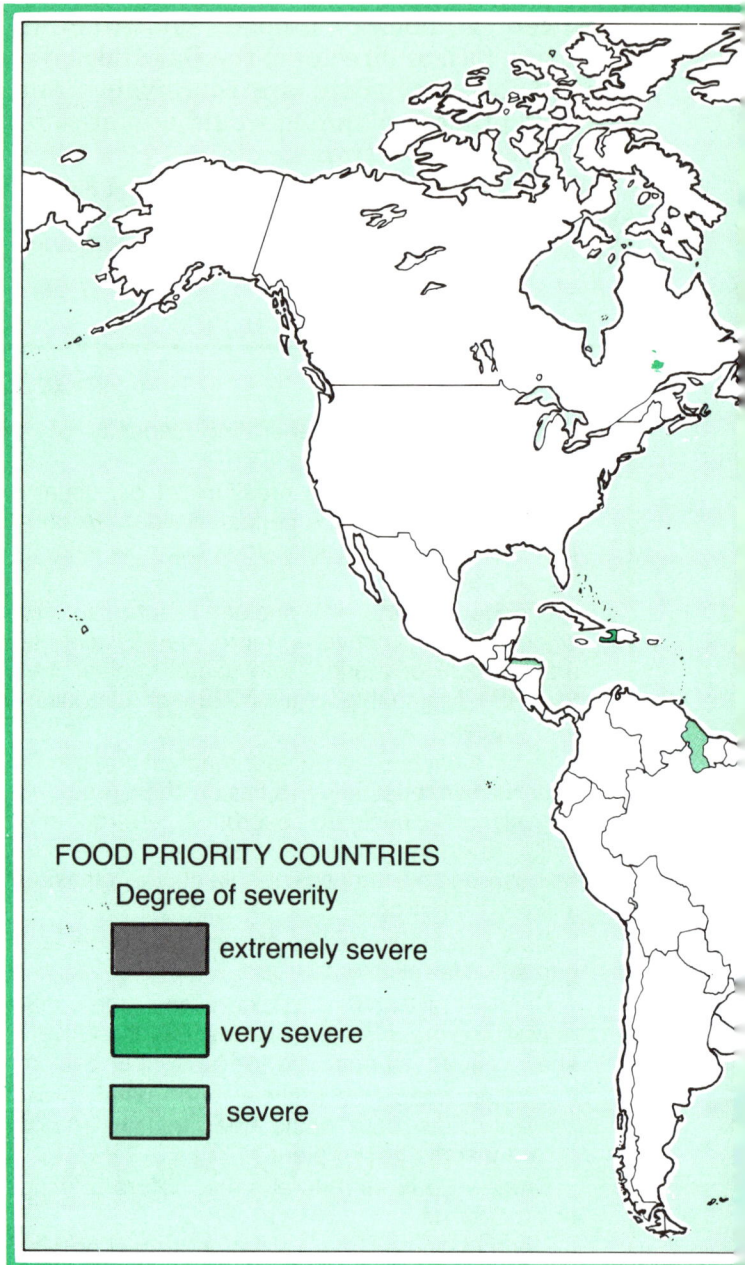

FOOD PRIORITY COUNTRIES
Degree of severity

extremely severe

very severe

severe

CHAPTER 5

No End to Hunger?

Hunger is a world problem requiring a world solution.
—John Laffin, *The Hunger to Come*, 1971

Famine is the specter—fears, memories, accounts, fantasies, predictions of famine.

Throughout recorded history, famines have occured periodically over widespread areas from the British Isles to China and Latin America. Bangladesh suffered famine in 1970-75, Afghanistan in 1971-72, the Sahel region of Africa in the early 1970s. During the Biafran secession

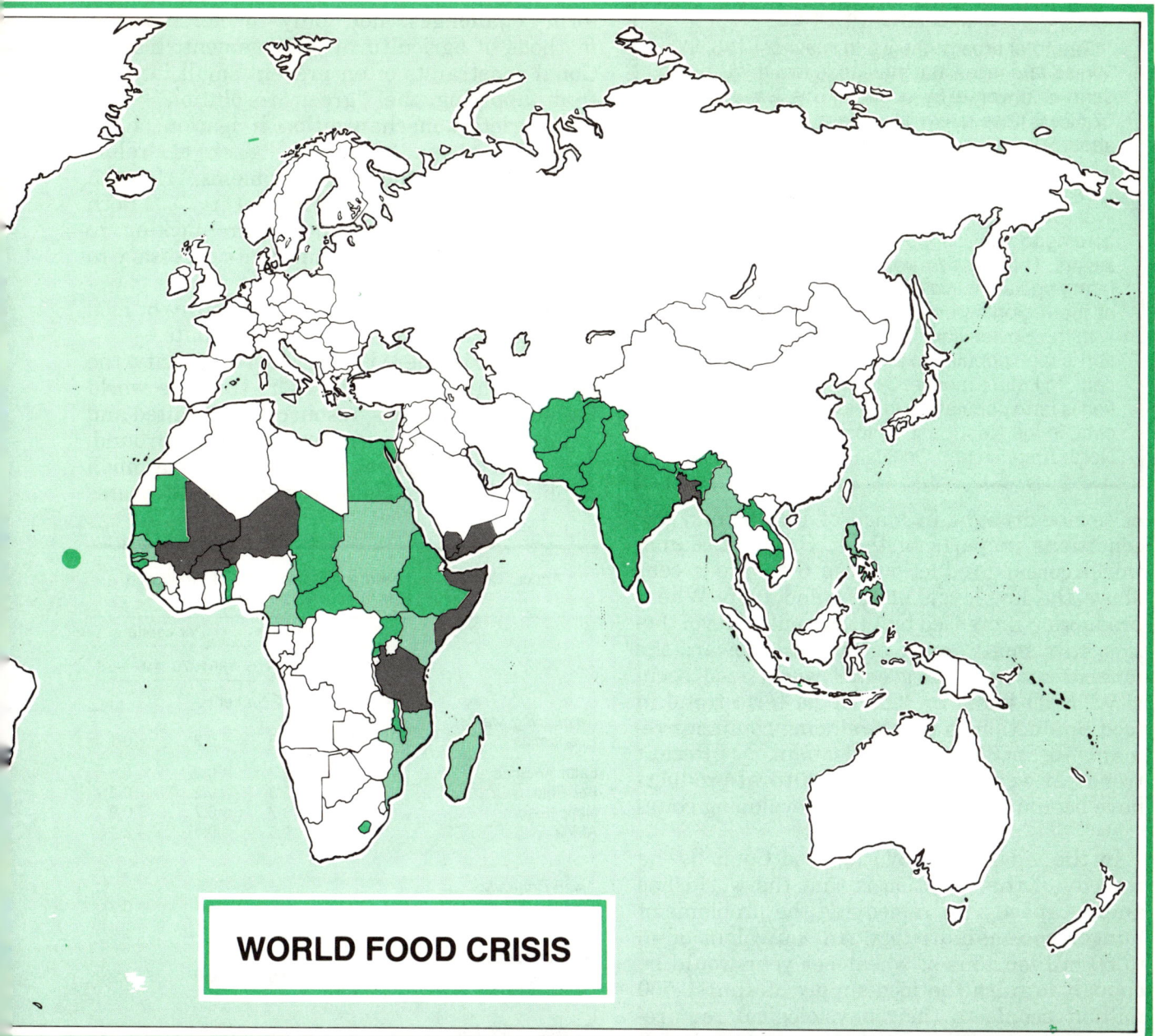

WORLD FOOD CRISIS

from Nigeria in 1967-70, an estimated two to three million people died of the effects of war and starvation. Starvation deaths were said to total sometimes as many as 10,000 a day.

Chronic malnutrition, however, is much more often the case in many parts of the world. Despite development efforts, hunger and malnutrition are increasing. Between 1969 and 1974, the U.N. Food and Agriculture Organization (FAO) estimates, the number of under-nourished people in developing countries increased from about 400 to 455 million. Less conservative estimates indicated that people suffering from malnutrition exceeded one billion in 1975. The effects of malnutrition are almost as serious as those of famine. Up to one-third of all children

born alive die from malnutrition and disease before they reach the age of five, the U.N. World Food Council reports. Of those who survive, between one-quarter and one-half suffer from severe or moderate protein-energy malnutrition in the poorest countries. Every year at least one hundred thousand children go blind due to severe vitamin A deficiency.

At the moment, global food and fertilizer supplies are relatively plentiful. World grain stocks have recovered from a decline earlier in the decade. Production of grains (including rice) in 1977 was an estimated 1,436 million tons, only 9 million tons below the record grain output of the previous year. World food production had increased by 2 to 3 per cent during 1976. In spite

LAND AND PEOPLE

The total area of the world is almost 196,900,-000 square miles, but more than two-thirds of the earth is covered by oceans. This leaves some 57,529,000 square miles of land surface. Of this, about 12 per cent, or some 5,792,000 square miles, is cultivated and regularly under crops.

Overall, just under half the world's population lives on farms—about 1.923 billion in 1975, according to the U.N. Food and Agriculture Organization. Thirty-seven per cent of the total world farm population lives in the Far East; 65 per cent of the region's population is farm population.

In the Soviet Union, 21 per cent of the population is farm population and in Europe about 17 per cent. In Latin America, 38 per cent of the population is farm population, in Africa, more than 70 per cent, in the Near East, almost 60 per cent, and in North America and Oceania, about four per cent.

of severe drought in much of Europe and dry conditions in parts of the U.S. and Oceania, world cereal production rose 6 to 7 per cent above the low levels of 1974 and 1975. Wheat production increased by 14 per cent. "Nevertheless, only small progress was made toward the longer-term goal of greater world food security," FAO said. ". . . The longer-term trend in food production in the developing countries remains disappointingly inadequate. . . . Recent trends in world trade in agricultural products have been unfavorable for the developing countries."

In the view of the World Food Council, the tragedy of the situation is that the world has ample capacity for remedying the problems of hunger and malnutrition. An equivalent of 40 to 60 million tons of wheat per year would be enough to raise the food supply of almost 500 million people to their physiological requirements, the council says. This is no more than 3 to 5 per cent of present world cereal consumption, or 10 to 15 per cent of the cereals that are being fed to livestock in developed countries. "Much more could be done with the available resources and more resources could be mobilized," Dr. John A. Hannah, executive director of the council, says. Among the measures recommended by the council are 1) a 4 per cent annual increase in agricultural production by developing nations; 2) agrarian and institutional reforms; 3) providing small farmers with the resources to produce food; 4) effective credit, marketing, and distribution systems; 5) increasing the capacity of the hungry to buy food. Con-

troversial, each and all. For example, land reform challenges not only ownership but methods of agricultural management. Institutional constraints often prevent small farmers from applying the "green revolution"—new seed varieties, mechanization, irrigation, chemical fertilizers and pesticides. "There is a reluctance to address these food problems," Hannah told a council meeting in Mexico City. ". . . Both conviction and better means are lacking to achieve the political commitments necessary to proceed. . . ."

The whole question of the possibility of food sufficiency remains a matter of dispute.

On one side, there is the school of scarcity, the new Malthusians. They assert that the world faces acute scarcities, resources are limited and irreplaceable, there isn't enough to go around. This outlook is expressed variously: in a much publicized Club of Rome report that advocates

Annual Changes in World and Regional Food Production, 1961-70 and 1971-75

	Total		Per capita	
	1961–70	1971–75	1961–70	1971–75
	. . . . Percent			
Developing Market Economics	2.9	2.5	0.3	−0.1
Latin America	3.0	2.7	0.3	−0.1
Far East	2.7	2.8	0.2	0.3
Near East	3.3	3.7	0.7	0.9
Africa	2.9	0.5	0.4	−2.1
Asian Centrally Planned Economies .	2.8	2.4	1.1	0.7
Total developing countries	2.9	2.5	0.6	0.2
Developed Market Economies	2.5	1.8	1.4	1.1
Western Europe . . .	2.3	1.9	1.5	1.3
North America . . .	2.4	1.9	1.1	1.1
Oceania	3.4	1.3	1.5	0.7
Eastern Europe and The U.S.S.R.	3.2	2.1	2.2	1.1
Total developed countries	2.7	2.0	1.6	1.2
World	2.8	2.2	0.9	0.3

Source: The State of Food and Agriculture (FAO 1977)

A man suffering from hunger is portrayed in a seventh century sculpture in India.

inaction," Lappe suggests. "It can then require thousands of words to *undo* the intuitive but false conclusion of hopelessness. . . ." She argues: "How could a photograph capture the global system of production and use that operates to create scarcity? No picture could convey a system that in the all-inclusiveness of its scope and the banality of its everyday operation appears so normal as to be almost God-given—while in fact it is condemning most of humanity to continuing hunger."

That new agricultural and economic policies might enable the world to solve the problem of hunger and malnutrition is a view shared by such authorities as Sterling Wortman, Georg Borgstrom, Jean Mayer, Dan Morgan. Raise yields, they emphasize. Transfer technology. Finance development efforts. Assist managerial development. Maintain grain stockpiles. Reduce consumption among the affluent. (The average American eats about twice the protein his body can use.) Stabilize world grain prices. Coordinate economic, industrial and agricultural development. Development has not "failed," they say. It has never been tried.

trade-offs; in a *New York Times* story that says flatly, "world population has long since outstripped food supplies"; in a statement by the president of the Rockefeller Foundation, John Knowles, that "Malthus has already been proved correct." Taking that view a step further, some experts support a policy of triage, a "life-boat" ethic, that would abandon countries whose agricultural prospects are judged to be nil.

On the other side are those who say the food needs of the world can be met. Americans usually perceive the controversy in a series of visual images, Frances Moore Lappe points out in *Harper's*. A cartoon depicts crowded bodies ready to burst off a tiny earth; a picture of a peasant trying to scratch one last meal from a parched and depleted plot. ". . . These photo-images may actually paralyze us into frustrated

Indices of World Production of Agricultural, Fishery and Forest Products, 1971 to 1975

	1971	1972	1973	1974	1975[1]	Change 1974 to 1975[2]
	.....1961-65 average — 100.....					Percent
Total Production	123	123	129	131	132	+1
Agriculture ...	123	123	129	131	133	+2
Fisheries[3]	140	148	157	160	159	−1
Forestry	116	117	120	120	114	−5
Population	116	118	121	123	125	+2
Per Caput Total Production ...	106	104	107	106	106	−1
Agriculture ...	106	104	107	106	106	0
Fisheries[3]	121	125	129	130	127	−2
Forestry	100	99	99	98	91	−7

[1]Preliminary. [2]Percent changes from one year to another have been calculated from unrounded figures. [3]Excluding China.

Source: *The State of Food and Agriculture 1976* (FAO 1977)

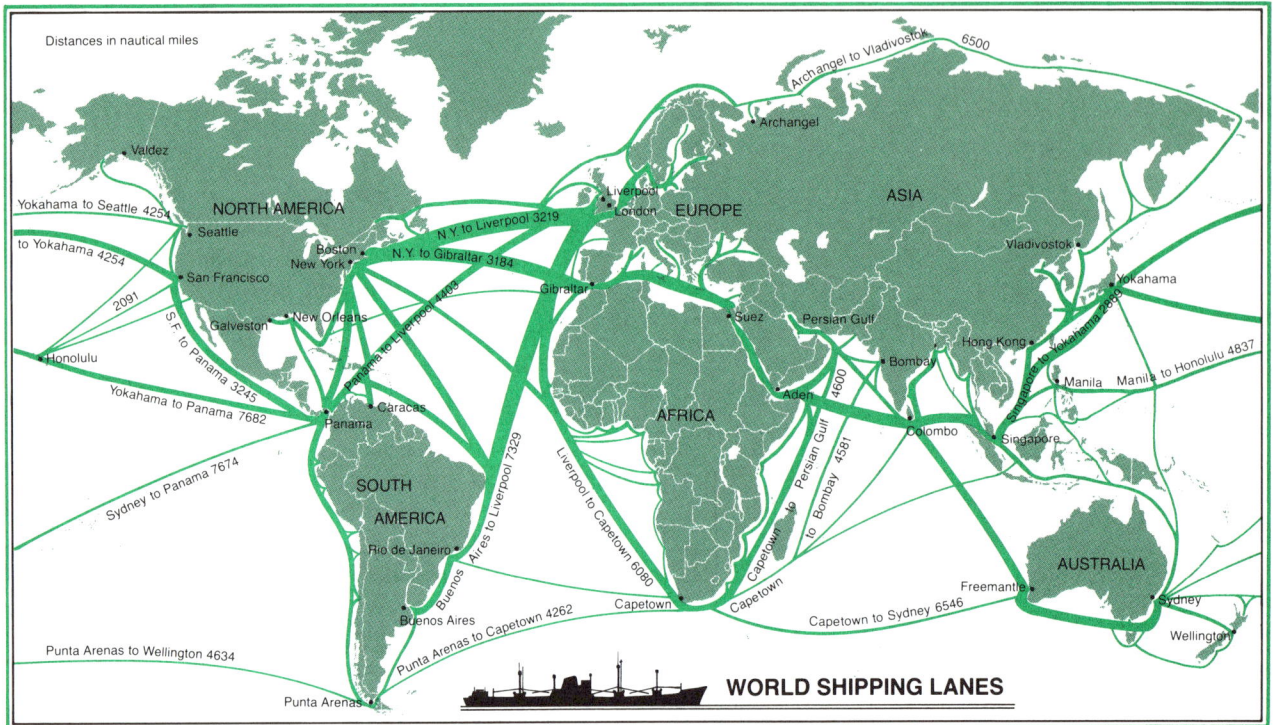

Distances in nautical miles

NORTH AMERICA
EUROPE
ASIA
AFRICA
SOUTH AMERICA
AUSTRALIA

Valdez
Yokahama to Seattle 4254
to Yokahama 4254
Seattle
San Francisco
2091
S.F. to Panama 3245
Galveston
Honolulu
Yokahama to Panama 7682
Boston
New York
New Orleans
N.Y. to Liverpool 3219
N.Y. to Gibraltar 3184
Panama to Liverpool
Caracas
Panama
Sydney to Panama 7674
Rio de Janeiro
Buenos Aires to Liverpool 7329
Buenos Aires
Liverpool to Capetown 6080
Punta Arenas to Capetown 4262
Punta Arenas to Wellington 4634
Punta Arenas
Liverpool
London
Gibraltar
Suez
Persian Gulf
Aden
Bombay
Capetown to Bombay 4581
Capetown to Persian Gulf 4600
Colombo
Capetown
Capetown to Sydney 6546
Archangel
Archangel to Vladivostok 6500
Vladivostok
Yokahama
Singapore to Yokahama
Hong Kong
Manila
Manila to Honolulu 4837
Singapore
Freemantle
Sydney
Wellington

WORLD SHIPPING LANES

Travel and trade are catalysts of civilization. Today, the ship remains the major carrier of the world's commerce. Important shipping routes and distances are charted above. The "great circle" routes, the shortest distances between points, connect the world's chief ports. At the same time, supersonic flight, 1,350 m.p.h. at 50,000-60,000 feet, has brought almost any two points in the world within a 12-hour travel radius; it has reduced by half the size of the world for travellers and traders.

CHAPTER 6

Transportation Routes

A ship sails from New York to Rio de Janeiro in 11 days.

A supersonic aircraft flies from London to Bahrain in four hours.

Oil flows through a 789-mile pipeline from Prudhoe Bay on Alaska's North Slope to the ice-free port of Valdez.

Brazil builds a 2,500-mile Trans-Amazon Highway, the Soviet Union a 2,000-mile railroad across Siberia to the Pacific, the Baikal-Amur Mainline.

Turkey spans the Bosporus with the longest suspension bridge in Europe.

Each of the foregoing is or provides a transportation route, integrating an economy. Each makes the world smaller than it would otherwise be and everyone more involved in concerns of people on other parts of the earth.

Major sea routes link the world's leading ports. The principal routes are "great circle" routes, the shortest distance between two points

(North Atlantic, Transpacific, Gulf-Caribbean). Some routes are shorter than others but weather-bound. For example, the Northern sea route from Europe to the Far East (Archangel-Vladivostok), 6,500 miles, is shorter than the Southern route through Suez, 15,000 miles. Ice-breakers are able to keep it open 150 days of the year.

Despite technological advances in other means of transport, ocean transport by ship remains the major means of carrying world trade. Technology applied to shipping has produced a very wide variety of types of ships—tankers, ore carriers, container ships, passenger-cargo ships, hydrofoil craft, roll-on/roll-off vessels. The latter carry loaded trucks, motor cars, and any form of wheeled equipment.

World shipping today faces a number of serious problems. ". . . Each of these problems affects a large number of countries, rich and poor, market-economy and socialist, although

THE 12 HOUR WORLD

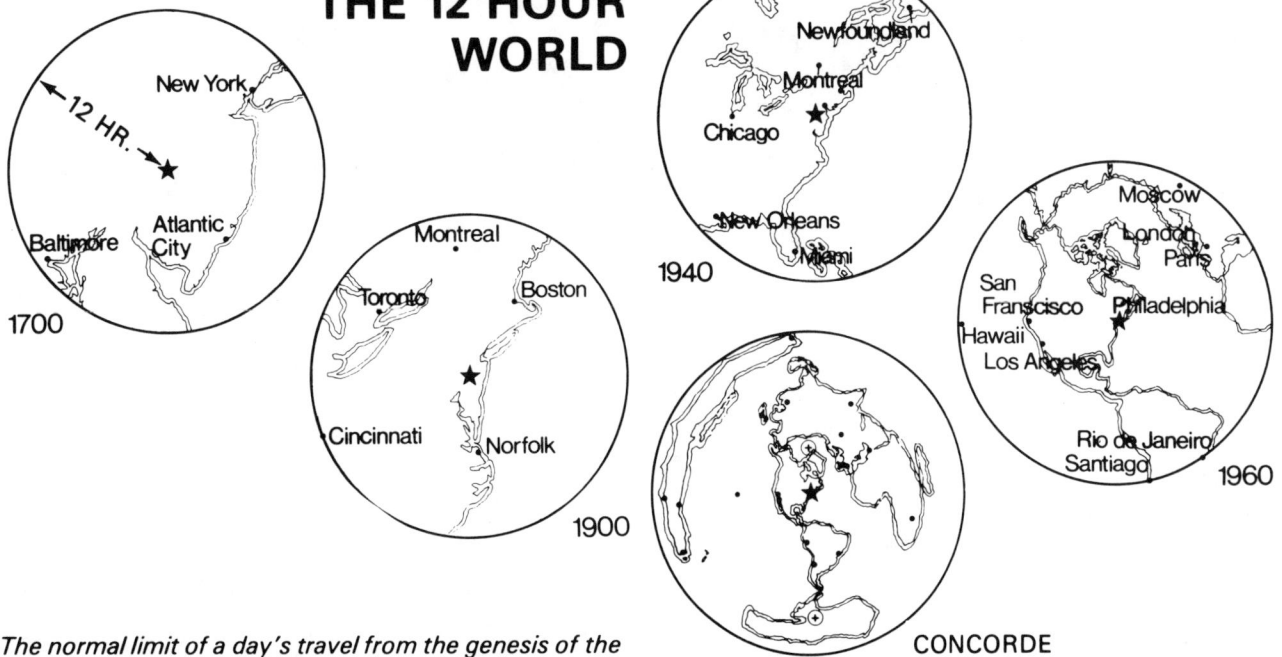

The normal limit of a day's travel from the genesis of the United States to the 12 hour world of supersonic travel.

not necessarily equally," according to the United Nations report "Shipping in the Seventies." Since the end of World War II, there has been a steady rise in the size of general cargo carriers in response to increasing world trade, and it appears that such ships have become too large. As a result, the ships have to call at numerous ports to obtain sufficient cargo, raising costs and transit time. The existing pattern of most liner services is irrational. It is quite common to find in a port four or five liners, all loading for the same destination, to depart within a day or so of each other, and each of them to call at a number of ports *en route*. Each of them will then be subject to delays due to congestion or unavailabilty of labor.

Such is the shortage of facilities at the Nigerian ports of Lagos, Port Harcourt, and Calabar that many freighters wait months to be unloaded. Sometimes, they are raided by pirates from motorized dugout canoes. On Nov. 21, 1977, in Lagos, pirates boarded a Danish ship, the *Lindinger Ivory*. They shot the captain and threw him overboard, wounded several crewmen and looted the ship. The goods later turned up ashore, selling at black-market prices. Nigeria expects to provide some 60 additional berths at the ports by 1980; other developing nations that are building facilities to handle both more traffic and new types of vessels include Venezuela, Brazil, Morocco, Libya, Saudi Arabia, Iran, India, and Pakistan.

A shipping slump currently afflicts the industrialized countries. There are too many ships and not enough cargo business to go around.

About 7 per cent of the world fleet was idled last year, the Scandinavians and Greeks suffering most. Shipowners' bank debts are up. The big international banks have granted moratoria to shipowners on between $150 million and $200 million in debts—and "worse is to come," *The Economist* warned. The prices of second-hand vessels are down. The bottom has dropped out of the supertanker market, and a tanker worth $50 million in 1973 might not have brought $10 million in 1978.

The world's largest merchant fleet, 74 million gross tons, sails under the Liberian flag, a so-called "flag of convenience," meaning that the owners register Liberian to escape taxes in their home countries. Greece operates a fleet totaling 23 million gross tons; Norway, 28 million; Great Britian, 33 million; Japan, 39 million. The Soviet Union's merchant fleet exceeds that of the U.S., 14 million gross tons to 12 million.

The U.S. Merchant Marine, being noncompetitive in costs of construction and operation, continues to decline. "American flag shipping, by total volume, is carrying less than 6 per cent of all U.S. foreign trade and commerce," Rep. Paul S. Trible, Jr. (R., Va.) pointed out in the House recently, calling for a revival. In 1975, U.S.-flag carriers transportred 5.1 per cent of all U.S. cargo, compared with 6.5 per cent in 1974 and a 10-year average of 5.6 per cent. American tankers took part in the movement of oil to the extent of 4.6 per cent. Carriage of bulk commodities by U.S.-flag ships amounted to 1.4 per cent.

Villagers in Rajasthan State, India, view an educational TV program transmitted by satellite; the community receiver has been placed in the village square.

CHAPTER 7

Communications

Human communication began with language. Its subsequent history ranges from the development of the pictograph and ideogram and alphabet to microelectronics and the international communications satellite. In the pictograph, symbols represented objects. To the sym-bolic representation of the object, the ideogram added the ideas and qualities associated with it. The alphabet, language's written characters, was transcended by modern technology—new ways of looking at the world.

Not so many years ago, homing pigeons were

still used to send important business and military messages relatively short distances—only a few miles. Then, instantaneous communications over long distances were made possible by the telegraph, telephone, radio and television. Today, the picture telephone, transmission of mail as facsimile over phone lines, computer-activated libraries have been introduced.

The communications satellite spans the globe today with radio and television signals, provides pathways for telephone, teletype, facsimile transmissions. Three synchronous satellites, properly placed at a distance of 22,300 miles above the equator, can connect any points in the world; at that height, their speed is synchronized with the rate of the earth's rotation, and they appear stationary. Two types of communications satellites have been orbited. Passive satellites reflect radio signals, bouncing them from ground transmitter to receiving station. Active satellites carry electronic equipment for receiving, amplifying and retransmitting signals, using power from solar energy cells on the satellite.

An integrated network of five satellites linking six continents is operated by the International Telecommunications Satellite Organization (INTELSAT), of which 95 nations are members. The INTELSAT satellites are positioned high over the Atlantic, Pacific and Indian Oceans. Three systems of commercial communications satellites offer domestic service in the U.S. The Soviet Union and Canada also operate domestic satellite networks.

Other worldwide changes in methods of communications are taking place. The radio spectrum is being stretched beyond the ionosphere to outer space. Developing nations demand that industrialized nations relinquish some of their radio frequency bands to them. (Radio frequencies are allocated and their use regulated by the International Telecommunications Union, which was founded in 1865 as the International Telegraph Union.) Interregional telecommunication networks—Asian and Oceanian, Latin American, European and Mediterranean, African—are being planned.

Development depends on telecommunications, John Rokeby writes. "Public services, the timely and efficient functioning of private business, commerce and industry, agricultural production and distribution, transport and public health and, not least, weather forecasting, all depend in one way or another on telecommunications, to say nothing of the increasing use of its services in education and in the personal lives of any population as living standards rise," Rokeby stresses.

Changes in communications have increased the flow of news, the variety of entertainment, the study of communication. Questions have arisen about the social effects of space communication, possible uses of satellites in education, potentialities of international communication networks, communications policies—the rights of individuals and the rights of sovereignty. A major world problem, John A. R. Lee points out, is that "we *know* more than we *use*." The great libraries of the world have been doubling in size about every 14 years. Despite this enormous outpouring, most research findings never achieve practical use or affect the world of the non-scholar.

Arthur C. Clarke, the science fiction writer who as a radio engineer in 1945 was the first to predict scientifically the development of communications satellites, has noted that no method of communication ever becomes obsolete, although it may become less important.

"What we are building now," Clarke says, "is the nervous system of mankind. . . . The communications network, of which the satellites will be nodal points, will enable the consciousness of our grandchildren to flicker like lightning back and forth across the face of this planet . . . without stirring from their homes. . . ." He forecasts that the satellite may help to enforce good behavior among reluctant parties. "The inexorable force of astronomical facts will destroy the political fantasies which have so long fragmented our planet." A basic world language will become necessary. It would be impossible to present educational broadcasts in each of the 6,000 languages now estimated to exist.

"A mere seven are spoken by half the human race, and if work could start with these, that would be an excellent beginning."

CANADA
13,785,647
60.4

CANADA

UNITED STATES

UNITED STATES
154,576,000
71.8

MONACO
23,740
96.5

BERMUDA
37,966
66.6

BERMUDA

MEXICO

ANGUILLA
272
4.2

MEXICO
3,308,832
5.2

JAMAICA

HAITI

PUERTO
RICO

GAMB
2,752
0.6

EL SALVADOR

BARBADOS

NICARAGUA

TRINIDAD
& TOBAGO

VENEZUELA
742,050
5.9

PANAMA

VENEZUELA

COLOMBIA

FR. GUIANA

ECUADOR

**Telephones by
Continental Area**

PERU

BRAZIL
3,987,072
3.5

FR. GU
8,88
17

Number of telephones

Telephones per 100 population

BOLIVIA

BRAZIL

PARAGUAY

HAWAII

CHILE

FRENCH
POLYNESIA

PARAGUAY
41,644
1.5

URUGUAY

ARGENTINA

ARGENTINA
2,539,535
9.8

	WORLD	NORTH AMERICA	EUROPE	ASIA	CENTRAL AMERICA	OCEANIA	SOUTH AMERICA	AFRICA
Telephones per 100	14.5	70.7	19.1	5.2	5.2	35.0	4.5	1.4
Number of telephones	398,182,000	168,362,000	143,871,000	59,426,000	4,880,000	7,897,000	9,856,000	3,890,000

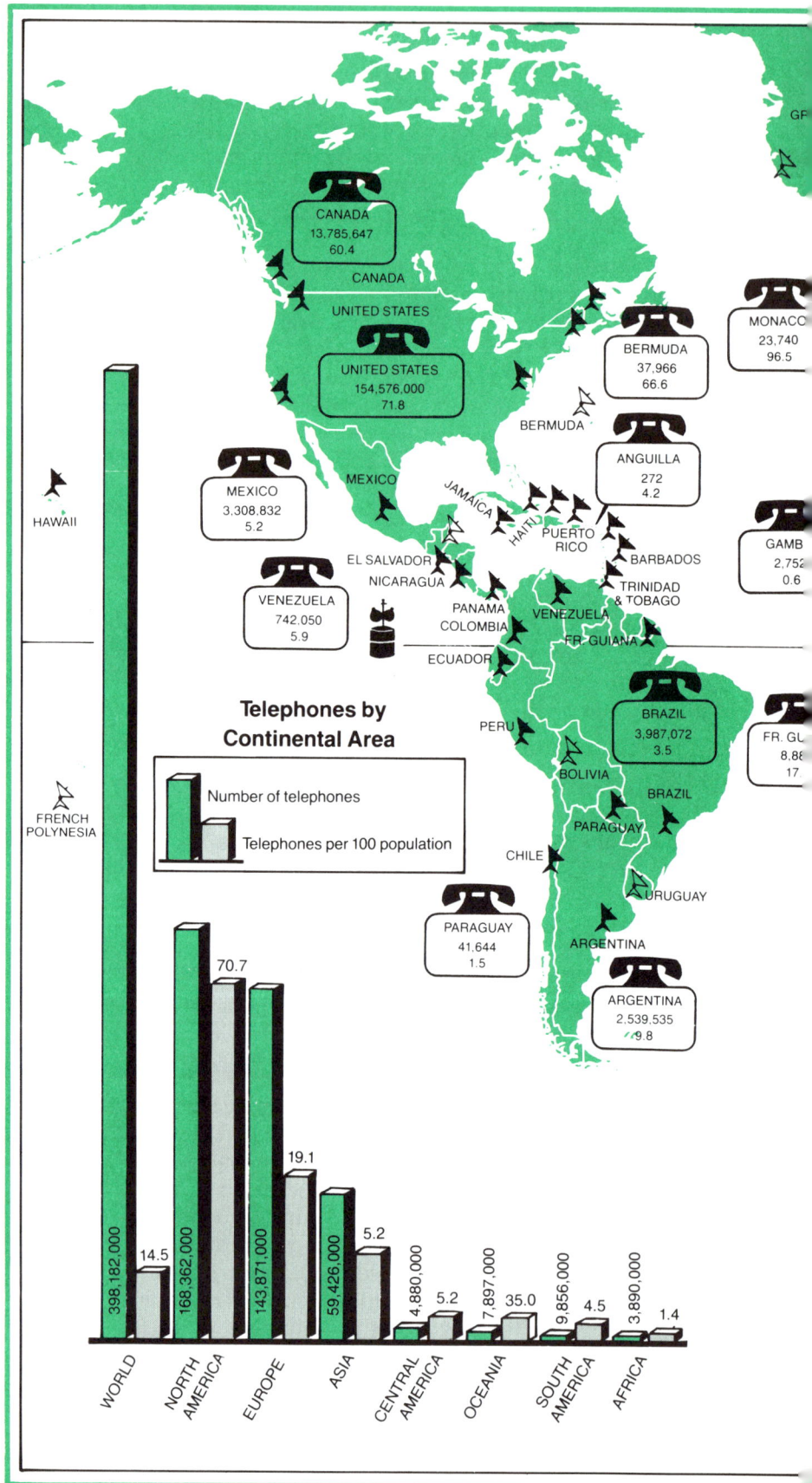

**Two worldwide systems of communications—telephone
and satellite—are represented on this map. Telephone
use is gradually increasing in developing countries. The**

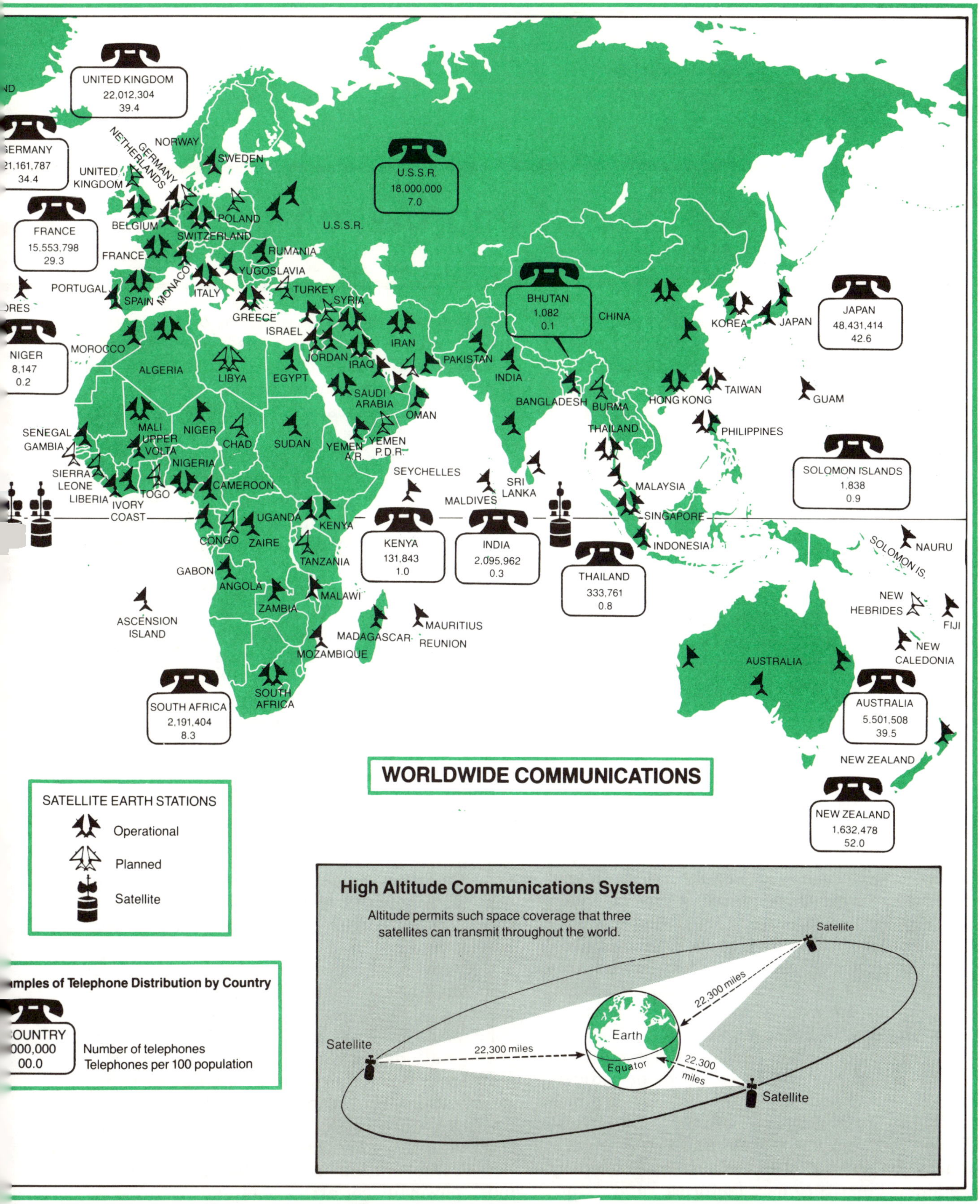

WORLDWIDE COMMUNICATIONS

UNITED KINGDOM
22,012,304
39.4

GERMANY
21,161,787
34.4

UNITED KINGDOM

FRANCE
15,553,798
29.3

NIGER
8,147
0.2

U.S.S.R.
18,000,000
7.0

BHUTAN
1,082
0.1

JAPAN
48,431,414
42.6

KENYA
131,843
1.0

INDIA
2,095,962
0.3

THAILAND
333,761
0.8

SOLOMON ISLANDS
1,838
0.9

SOUTH AFRICA
2,191,404
8.3

AUSTRALIA
5,501,508
39.5

NEW ZEALAND
1,632,478
52.0

SATELLITE EARTH STATIONS
- Operational
- Planned
- Satellite

Examples of Telephone Distribution by Country
COUNTRY
000,000
00.0
Number of telephones
Telephones per 100 population

High Altitude Communications System
Altitude permits such space coverage that three satellites can transmit throughout the world.

Satellite
22,300 miles
Earth
Equator
22,300 miles
22,300 miles
Satellite
Satellite

Country labels: NORWAY, SWEDEN, NETHERLANDS, GERMANY, BELGIUM, POLAND, SWITZERLAND, FRANCE, RUMANIA, YUGOSLAVIA, PORTUGAL, SPAIN, MONACO, ITALY, GREECE, ISRAEL, TURKEY, SYRIA, IRAN, JORDAN, IRAQ, PAKISTAN, INDIA, CHINA, KOREA, JAPAN, TAIWAN, GUAM, HONG KONG, BURMA, BANGLADESH, THAILAND, PHILIPPINES, MALAYSIA, SINGAPORE, INDONESIA, MOROCCO, ALGERIA, LIBYA, EGYPT, SAUDI ARABIA, OMAN, YEMEN, YEMEN P.D.R., SEYCHELLES, MALDIVES, SRI LANKA, SENEGAL, GAMBIA, MALI, UPPER VOLTA, NIGER, CHAD, SUDAN, SIERRA LEONE, LIBERIA, IVORY COAST, TOGO, NIGERIA, CAMEROON, UGANDA, KENYA, CONGO, ZAIRE, TANZANIA, GABON, ANGOLA, ZAMBIA, MALAWI, MOZAMBIQUE, MADAGASCAR, MAURITIUS, REUNION, ASCENSION ISLAND, AUSTRALIA, NEW ZEALAND, NEW HEBRIDES, NEW CALEDONIA, FIJI, NAURU, SOLOMON IS., U.S.S.R.

satellite network links six continents. "What we are building now," says Arthur C. Clarke, "is the nervous system of mankind....The communications network, of which the satellites will be nodal points, will enable the consciousness of our grandchildren to flicker like lightning back and forth across the face of this planet...."

Freedom of Information

What should ye doe then, should ye suppresse all this flowry crop of knowledge and new light sprung up and yet springing daily in this City, should ye set an *Oligarchy* of twenty ingrossers over it, to bring a famin upon our minds again, when we shall know nothing but what is measur'd to us by their bushel?
—John Milton, *Areopagitica* (In Defense of Freedom of Printed Matter), 1644

This presents a rampant danger: THE SUPPRESSION OF INFORMATION between the parts of the planet. Contemporary science knows that suppression of information leads to entropy and total destruction.
—A. Solzhenitsyn, Nobel Prize Lecture in Literature, 1970

There are two issues here. One is freedom of the press, the other, freedom of information.

Freedom of the press, implying freedom of all news media—the right to publish or broadcast the truth as one sees it—exists in Western Europe, North America, Japan, Hong Kong. However, even in these places, it may be weakened by self-censorship, threatened by subpoena use or limited by monopolistic practices.

Freedom of the press—at least, under this definition—does not exist in Communist countries, the military dictatorships of Latin America, many developing countries.

It is denied in Communist countries as a matter of socialist theory. "Newspapers, periodicals and other publications in the U.S.S.R. are produced by organizations of the Communist Party, trade unions, women and young people, and by artists' societies, collectives formed by academic institutions, factories and state farms," Yassen N. Zasursky and Yuri I. Kashlev, leading Soviet journalists, wrote recently.

"In this way, genuine freedom of the press—freedom for the working masses—is achieved, a situation quite different, of course, from that which existed in Tsarist Russia."

In Latin American dictatorships, opposition journalists disappear.

In developing countries, whose governments sometimes are unstable or capricious, newspapers may be closed, publishing licenses withdrawn, newsprint supplies withheld, foreign newsmen who provide the know-how expelled.

Freedom of information is a comparatively new concept, of which there is no generally accepted definition. Attempts to define it are "fraught with problems, especially of an ideological, political and legal order," says a U.N. Educational, Scientific, & Cultural Organization commission. But it would appear to embrace the authority to seek out information and ideas; the right to express opinions and to spread information by different means; and the freedom to receive information and ideas. Related concepts are the free flow of information, unimpeded across national frontiers, and a balanced flow of information. The transmission of information may be blocked by the jamming of radio broadcasts, withdrawal of accreditation from foreign correspondents, banning of periodicals and books.

Controversial aspects of freedom of information have been debated at a series of UNESCO meetings. The Soviet Union contended that the concept of the free flow of information disregards national sovereignty by implying that states are "obliged to open all their doors to any information from abroad, even that which is unfriendly or hostile." Many developing countries take the view that as a doctrine, the free flow of information "serves the interests of the most powerful countries, helping them to secure their cultural domination under cover of liberal, and not unattractive, ideas."

Western representatives contended that the "decolonization" of information should not be used as a pretext for certain regimes to bring information within the exclusive control of the state. The U.S. emphasized that the imbalance now characterizing the world distribution of information should be corrected, not by obstructing the right to communicate, but by enhancing the communication capacities of the developing countries.

For years, the controversy has focused on criticism by the developing countries of the major Western news agencies—Associated Press and United Press International (U.S.), Reuters (Great Britain) and Agence France Presse (France). The agencies are accused of inadequately covering or distorting news of the developing countries.

UNESCO has supported such projects as the establishment of an international pool for news distributed to the developing countries by Tanjug, the Yugoslav national news agency. In turn, UNESCO has been accused of attempting to convert news into a national concern that governments had the right to control. Amadou-Mahter M'Bow, UNESCO director-general, retorted that at present the dissemination of information was largely a one-way process, issuing from a few centers in the industrialized nations. Freedom of information, it seems, is just as subject to pressures and conflicts as is freedom of the press.

Weather satellites keep an eye on cloud cover, warn of storm development and movement. This photo by the U.S. satellite Geos 2 shows the position of 1978's Hurricane Ella.

CHAPTER 8

Climate

Climate varies, changes. It always has changed, meteorologists say, and will continue to change. On what scale is change likely? Global. In which direction is it likely to change? That is harder to say. Viewpoints differ. Theories conflict. And there are reservations. "Climatic change does not mean the subservience of all weather patterns everywhere to a simple cooling or warming trend: it means violent swings to extremes laid unpredictably on to the grand pattern that is seen historically as the Ice Ages" (Anthony Tucker, reporting in the *Manchester Guardian*).

Right now, the world may be getting colder. Astronomers have lately observed a 12-degree decline in the temperature of the sun's photosphere, or visible surface. The inference is that the sun is radiating less energy, and that might—or might not—mean colder weather is on the way.

Is the world entering a new ice age? Some computer models say it should be; some scientists think it is. "Some newspapers have scared the lay public with menaces about another ice age," notes *The Economist*. In fact, the scientists are talking about a "mini" ice age of the sort that occurred near the end of the middle ages and lasted until the mid-nineteenth century.

Conversely, it may be getting warmer. The level of carbon monoxide (CO_2) in the atmosphere is increasing along with emissions from the burning of oil, gas and coal. The CO_2 acts like the glass in a greenhouse. It is transparent to sunlight but holds in the heat from the earth that otherwise would escape into space. The effect may be to cause a rise in world temperature, shifts in growing seasons and rainfall patterns.

Other indicators of possible climatic change: Sunspot cycles have been associated with drought; high volcanic activity seems to be fol-

---

CLIMATE, WEATHER & METEOROLOGY

Climate is the average weather of a region over a period of years.

Weather is the general condition of the atmosphere at a particular time and place. It is universal news, unique in its affects, influencing all of man's activities and endeavors—agriculture and engineering projects, history and civilization. Man began studying weather in ancient times, the oldest comprehensive treatise being Aristotle's *Meteorologica*, about 400 B.C.

Meteorology is the scientific study of the atmosphere. It instructs, warns and advises people about the weather, provides forecasts. The weather map is an essential tool. Drawn several times a day, it is based on observations of pressure, temperature, wind, rain and other elements, on the ground and in the upper air.

The records of past weather observations enable meteorologists to offer information on climate and its evolution. This information is applied to agricultural production and the use and development of water resources, by different forms of transportation, efforts to reduce tropical storm damage and studies of weather modification.

lowed by a cooler climate; sea surface temperature influences wind directions, air temperature and rainfall.

Much is known about climate; a great deal more is unknown. The world's climate remains unpredictable. "We can't predict statistically whether a climate change is likely in the near future—next year, next decade, next century," says J. Murray Mitchell Jr. of the National Oceanic & Atmospheric Administration (quoted in *National Geographic*). "We must learn first why climate varies—what the major forces are and how they change, if indeed they change." The development of a coherent national climatic research program with international coordination has been recommended by the National Academy of Sciences (NAS). "Our knowledge of the mechanisms of climatic change is at least as fragmentary as our data," the NAS said. "Not only are the basic scientific questions largely unanswered, but in many cases we do not yet know enough to pose the key questions." In 1978, President Carter asked a substantial increase in funding for climate research.

Atmospheric research and the World Weather Watch (WWW) are among the activities conducted by the U.N. World Meteorological Organization. The main features of WWW are an observation system that includes surface stations, ships, aircraft and satellites; three world centers, at Melbourne, Moscow and Washington, plus a number of regional centers, for processing data; and a global telecommunications system for rapid transmission of data, analyses, forecasts, warnings. The Global Atmospheric Research Program (GARP) is a scientific effort combining both theoretical research and field experiments. GARP hopes to achieve a better understanding of climatic variations. Physical and mathematical bases for long-range predictions are being tested.

GARP, in collaboration with the International Council of Scientific Unions, is performing a global weather experiment this year. All available scientific and technical resources have been mobilized to observe the weather. The experiment is expected to increase scientific knowledge necessary to predict large-scale weather movements for periods of weeks, or even longer. It also will provide data for examining those physical factors of the atmosphere, land surfaces and oceans that are important for the study of climatic variability.

THE CLIMATIC RECORD

"The last postglacial thermal maximum [a warming up of the earth] was reached about 6,000 years ago, and climates since then have undergone a gradual cooling. This trend has been interrupted by three shorter periods of more marked cooling, similar to the so-called Little Ice Age of A.D. 1430–1850. . . . The well-documented warming trend of global climate beginning in the 1880s and continuing until the 1940s is a continuation of the warming trend that terminated the Little Ice Age. Since the 1940s, mean temperatures have declined and are now nearly halfway back to the 1880 levels.

"Climatic changes during the past 20,000 years are as severe as any that occurred during the past million years. At the last glacial maximum [the coldest period], extensive areas of the northern hemisphere were covered with continental ice sheets. . . . At northern midlatitude sites not far from the glacial margins (locations now occupied by major cities and extensive agricultural activity), air temperatures fell markedly, drastic changes occurred in the precipitation patterns, and wholesale migrations of animal and plant communities took place.

"The present interglacial interval—which has now lasted about 10,000 years—represents a climatic regime that is relatively rare during the past million years, most of which has been occupied by colder, glacial regimes. Only during about 8 per cent of the past 700,000 years has the earth experienced climates as warm as or warmer than the present.

"The penultimate interglacial age began about 125,000 years ago and lasted for approximately 10,000 years. Similar interglacial ages . . . have occurred on the average every 100,000 years during at least the past half million years. . . .

"About 65 million years ago global climates were substantially warmer than today, and subsequent changes may be viewed as part of a very long-period cooling trend. For even earlier times, the . . . climatic evidence becomes increasingly fragmentary. The best documented records suggest two previous extensive glaciations, occurring about 300 million and 600 million years ago."

—*Understanding Climatic Change,* National Academy of Sciences, 1975

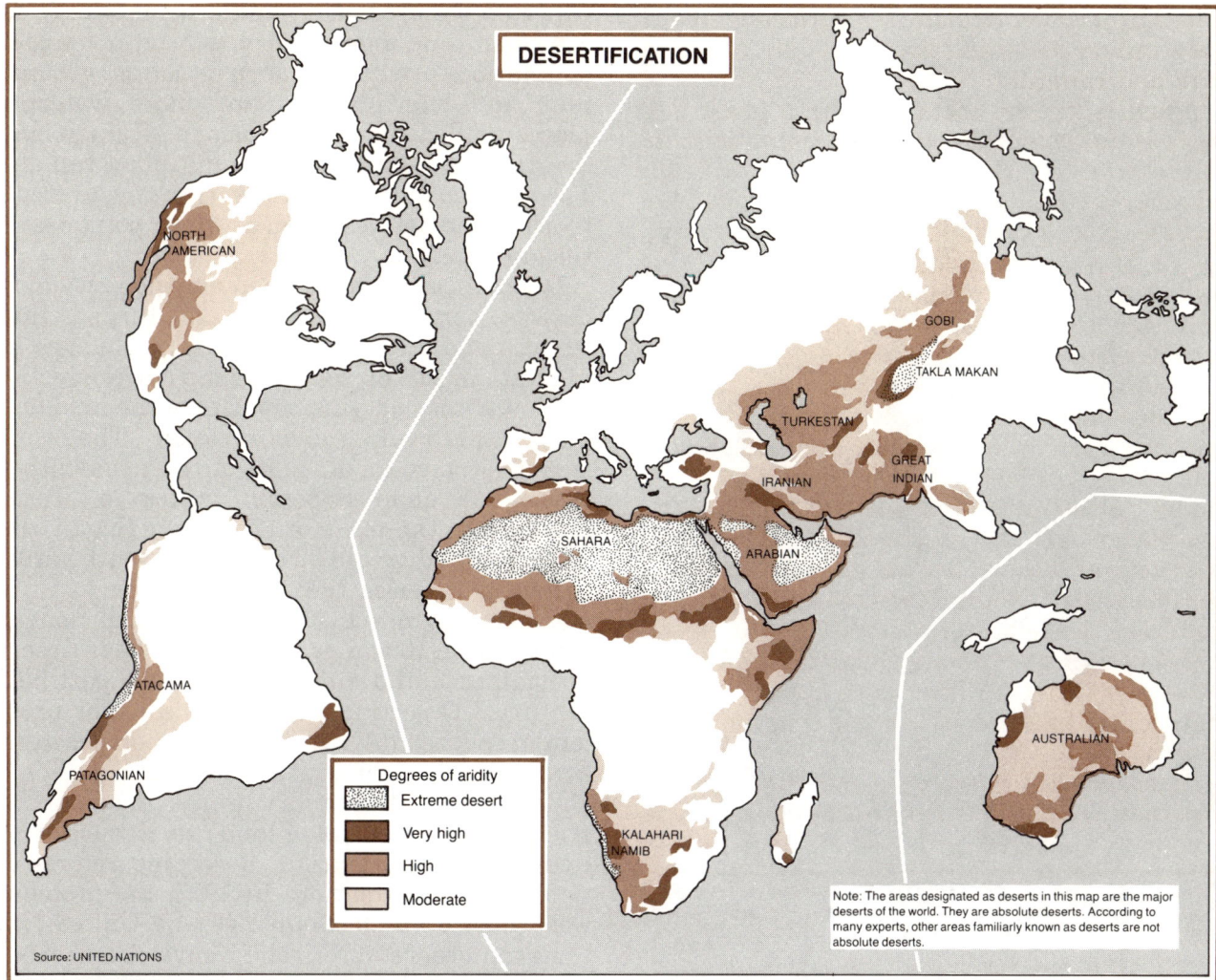

DESERTIFICATION

Degrees of aridity
- Extreme desert
- Very high
- High
- Moderate

Note: The areas designated as deserts in this map are the major deserts of the world. They are absolute deserts. According to many experts, other areas familiarly known as deserts are not absolute deserts.

Source: UNITED NATIONS

The spreading desert—"desertification," as it is called—is a worldwide phenomenon: savannas are transformed into steppes and steppes into desert. In the Sudan, for example, the Sahara has advanced 50 to 60 miles southwards during the past 17 years. The process is hastened by unwise economic and agricultural practices as well as growing human and livestock populations. The world's important deserts—and the possible deserts of the future—are charted above. Scientists say that the remedy to desertification resides in better land husbandry.

The Desert Advances: A World Problem

The Sahel ("shore" or "coast" in Arabic) is a region south of the Sahara Desert. It extends across Africa from Mauritania and Senegal in the west, through Mali, Niger, Upper Volta, and Chad, touching several other countries, to parts of Sudan and Ethiopia in the east. It is semi-arid, inhabited by nomad herdsmen and peasant farmers. In 1968-74, the Sahel was hit by drought, and several hundred thousand people and 20 million head of livestock perished. There were grain shortfalls of 30 per cent in Upper Volta, 50 per cent in Mali, Niger, and Senegal. Mauritania had practically no harvest

for two years. Farmers abandoned their villages and fields; starving nomads were sheltered in refugee camps. Hundreds of millions of dollars worth of grain were donated by foreign benefactors for famine relief.

But, the drought did not account for the scale of the catastrophe. A World Meterological Organization study concludes that "no serious analysis of available data is known to show a falling trend of rainfall." Annual rainfall in the borderlands south of the Sahara averaged 100 to 350 millimetres (mm.), further south 350 to 600 mm. The people of the Sahel lived within

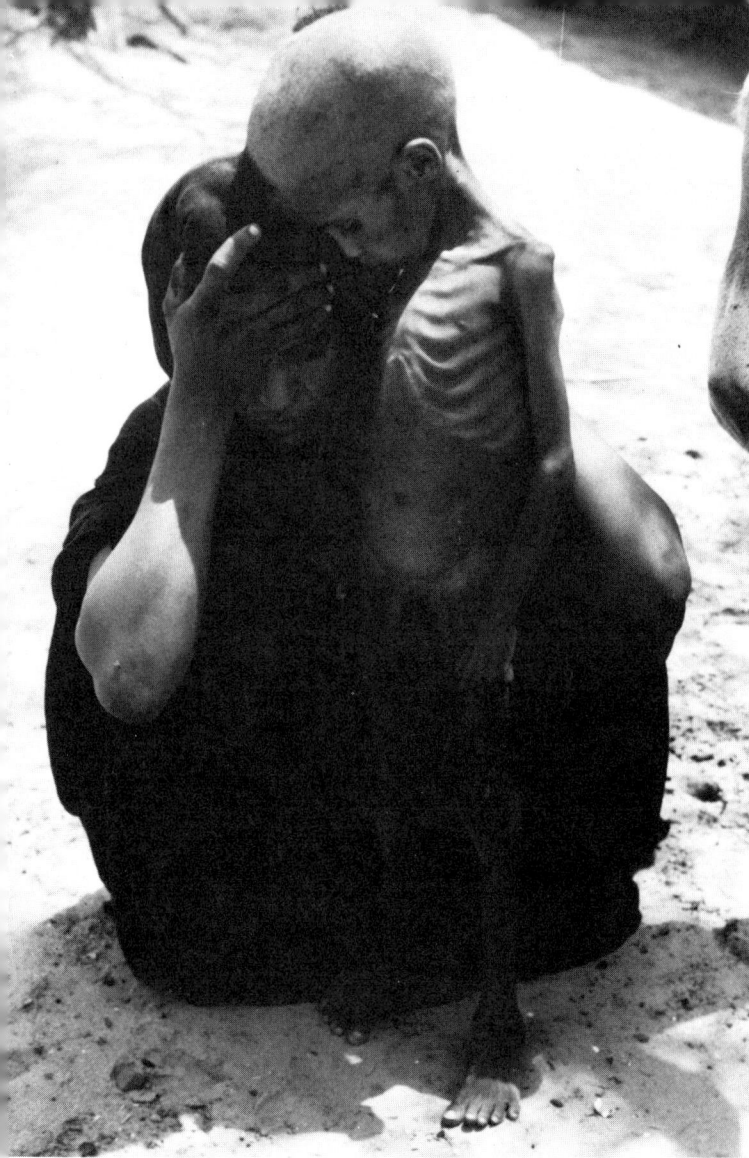

Mother and child are victims of Sahelian drought in Mauritania.

exported for processing and consumption." At the same time, more land has been put under cultivation—cash crops such as cotton, groundnuts and rice planted—and more watering places drilled for the herdsmen. Human and livestock populations have multiplied rapidly. The consequences include overgrazing, overcultivation and deforestation at which point desertification began.

Desertification is the phenonmenon by which deserts spread; savannas are turned into steppes and steppes to desert. The changes in vegetation, soil or water regime cut productivity, lower the carrying capacity of the land and make it more vulnerable to erosion. "The result is the spectacular advance of the neighboring desert," Yvonne Rebeyrol writes in *World Health*. "In the space of 17 years in Sudan, the Sahara has advanced 50 to 60 miles southwards. In South America the Atacama Desert . . . is advancing by one to two miles a year along a front of 50 to 100 miles. In Asia, the Thar Desert has gained half a mile a year for the past half century." Desertification also is a major problem in southern Africa, Autralia, northeastern Brazil, Mexico, the southwestern U.S.

Better land husbandry is the answer, the scientists say. Control of land use. Reduction of livestock. Careful grazing. Reseeding, reforestation. Land reclamation. In 1977, the problem was taken up by 94 countries at a United Nations conference in Nairobi, Kenya. An international plan to combat spreading deserts and a resolution urging more aid for the Sahelian countries were approved. The plan backs monitoring and mapping of desertification; the management of land as a ecological whole; soil and water conservation measures; the evaluation of factors that influence desertification.

If there is one central theme to the plan, the U.N. says, it is that action must not await complete knowledge about complex situations. The need is recognized for immediate action in applying existing knowledge, "not only to stop the physical processes of desertification, but to educate people in minimizing the harm done to the fragile ecosystems of drylands by existing economic and social activities."

Another theme is that all measures are to be directed primarily toward the well-being and development of the peoples vulnerable to desertification. Efforts to fight desertification "must thus be consistent with and part of wider development programs." The plan stresses the cultural and ecological variety in vulnerable areas and the overriding need for an approach that is both "sensitive and flexible."

the seasonal and cyclical patterns of rainfall deficiency, their ways of life specifically adapted to them. During a period of severe drought, farmers drew on reserves of millet. Among Peul nomads a family of four could subsist for a year with a single cow.

What happened in the Sahel had been building up for longer than the cyclical period between droughts. The region's precarious equilibrium apparently was upset by socio-economic circumstances left over from its colonial past, agricultural innovations introduced from the outside, and an ecological calamity that has come to be called "desertification." As a result of its colonial past, the region remained dependent and undeveloped. A "mono-economy" emerged, Alan Matt Warhaftig explains in *The Nation*. An economy that "produces little more than primary commodities: unprocessed mineral resources and agricultural goods which are

CHAPTER 9

Oil Spills

Oil spills in the seas are a worldwide, many-sided problem over which no jurisdiction fully extends; they are everybody's and nobody's problem. They aren't the average driver's problem, though they waste a commodity precious to him and will have a share in any future shortages of it.

They are scarcely a government problem. Nobody administers the oceans. Past the 200-mile limit, the waters are international.

Moreover, says Sen. Warren G. Magnuson (D., Wash.), chairman of the Senate Commerce Committee, "I don't see how you can have control when you have American-owned ships insured by the British, run by the Greeks, with Italian officers and a Chinese crew."

Nor are oil spills a media problem, although the press covers a tanker disaster in all its aspects, and now and then a journalist roars about the problem. In 1976, when the *Argo Merchant* leaked 7.7 million gallons of oil into the Atlantic near the Georges Bank, one of the world's richest fishing grounds, Richard Starnes wrote angrily (in *Outdoor Life*): "The tanker fleets are systematically murdering our oceans—and getting away with it."

They are the problem of the fisherman and the scientist and the environmentalist.

An estimated 400 million gallons of oil are dumped into the ocean each year. Four-fifths is emptied routinely by tankers pumping ballast or cleaning tanks. Tankers take on sea water ballast after unloading their cargoes; they dump the ballast when taking on new cargo. The ballast carries with it the residue of oil left after unloading. The residue is called "clingage." The remainder is spewed into the sea by tankers that are in collision, or run aground and break up, or explode, burn, and go down,

and by the operations of other ships, refineries, petrochemical plants and offshore oil wells. Tanker accidents are not uncommon. The biggest supertankers carry no more lights than a coastwise vessel, one writer notes, and there have been cases of other ships attempting to sail between their aft and fore lights. Nineteen tankers went to the bottom in 1976, in tonnage almost double the toll of the previous year.

Oil spills foul the seas. They pollute the water with poisonous, noxious substances. They kill bird, fish, and plant life in large numbers. They disrupt entire ecosystems, which depend on a diversity of organisms for stability and survival. They invade the marine food chain. Long-term effects are unknown, but (as Colin Moorcraft notes in *Must the Seas Die?*) "so far no marine biologist has contradicted the assertion that the seas are in decline. . . ." (Oil spills are a leading but not the only cause of water pollution. Other pollutants are chlorinated hydrocarbons, heavy metals, and industrial and radioactive wastes.) "This decline is not seen as a vague distant threat . . . but as a process which is already well under way. . . ."

Warnings of decline, however, evoke little response. Oil has a big market, and tanker owners say they operate the way they have to. In the U.S., action had been hesitant. The Coast Guard had failed to draft and enforce new regulations that might prevent oil spills in U.S. waters, Starnes charged. Then, in 1977, the Carter Administration introduced proposals in Congress that would have raised the standards for tanker safety.

The Administration proposed, for example, that tankers entering U.S. ports be required to have segregated ballast tanks and double bottoms. These modifications in tanker design

47

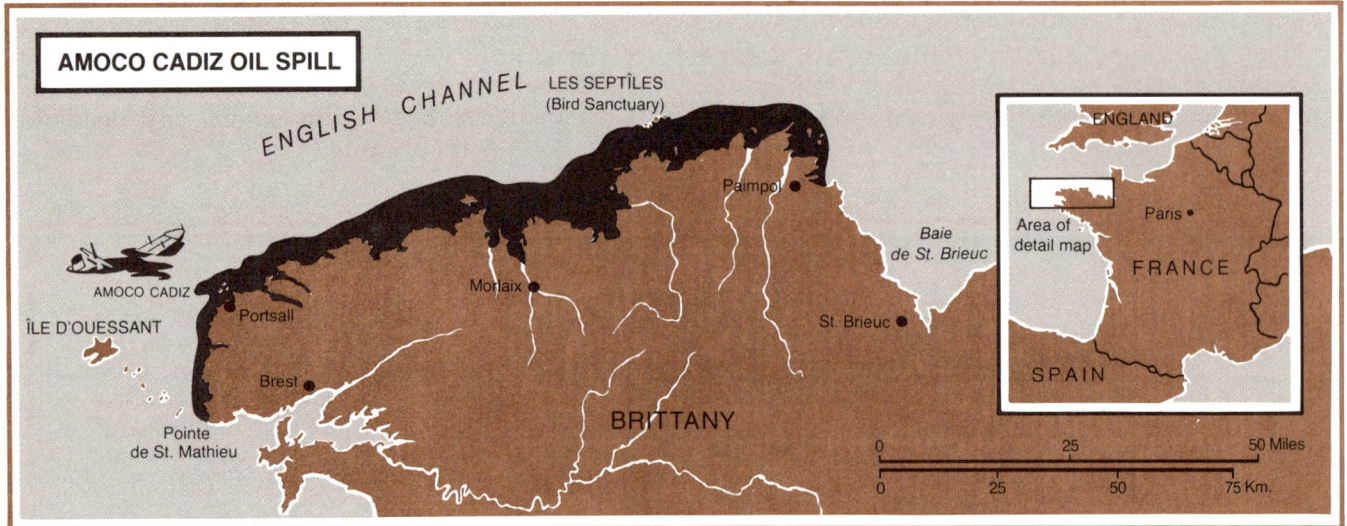

AMOCO CADIZ OIL SPILL

would help to control the spill problem, according to the U.S. Office of Technology Assessment. Segregated ballast tanks would allow tankers to empty ballast without washing clingage into the ocean. Double bottoms would offer protection against leakage in the event of an accident. A controversy arose about how much they would actually add to the cost of construction. Opponents said the added cost would be enormous, supporters estimated it would amount to a penny increase in the cost of oil per barrel.

In 1978, Congress approved and President Carter signed legislation requiring tankers of 20,000 tons or more to install segregated ballasts on a varying schedule to 1986. New tankers—those contracted for after Jan. 1, 1978—would be required to have double bottoms. Each tanker also would have to have up-to-date

The supertanker *Amoco Cadiz* broke in two on the Portsall rocks, spilling a record 46.2 million gallons of oil into the sea. The map locates the spill along the Brittany coast and (*see inset*) in the English Channel region. The channel is one of the most heavily travelled tanker routes in the world as well as one of the narrowest and consequently one of the most difficult in which to navigate. Oil spills are a major worldwide problem, involving regulation of tanker construction and operation. Disastrous spills will continue to occur, say the experts, until regulation is universally accepted and enforced.

charts and at least one English-speaking deck officer.

International regulation remains uncertain.

There is always the escape hatch—"freedom of the seas." The passage of ships on the high seas cannot be readily controlled. Interference with them is an act of war or piracy. "... A ship

THE SUPERSHIP

Supertankers are modern monsters of the deep. They are as long as or longer than the Empire State Building is tall, and their displacements are spectacular. The French supertanker *Bellamya* weighs in at 553,622 tons, the *Globtik Tokyo* (British) 483,664 tons, the *Porthos* (Liberian) 412,000 tons. In the trade, they are known as VLCCs, very large crude carriers, also as "mammoth tankers" and "oilbergs"; 80 per cent of a supertanker lies beneath the water.

Tankers grew in size from about 3,000 tons in 1874 to 12,000 by 1938, 16,000 four years later and 45,000 in 1956. The first supertankers, exceeding 100,000 tons, were built in the early 1960s. They couldn't go through the Suez Canal, but owners calculated that it would be equally

economical to send them around the Cape of Good Hope.

They display a look of "uncompromising functionalism," writes Noel Mostert in his book *Supership,* but are complicated and difficult to handle. They need plenty of sea-room, he points out, because they cannot respond to split-second timing. It takes at least three miles and 21 to 22 minutes to stop a 250,000 tonner proceeding at 16 knots.

Supertankers are highly vulnerable vessels, Mostert emphasizes. Hydrocarbon gas, which is given off by oil, has a very low flashpoint. The length of their hulls subjects them to severe stresses. Their plates corrode at a rate that has contributed to their sudden breakup at sea.

is subject only to the authority of her flag state," A. Nelson-Smith points out in *Oil Pollution and Marine Ecology;* "if that country fails to prescribe effective penalties against it, the vessel can discharge oil within a prohibited zone and avoid punishment . . ."

For the present, international efforts are being focused on the development of clean-up methods and the compensation of those who suffer damage from oil spills. In the absence of worldwide regulation, the experts say, destructive spills will continue.

THE OIL SPILL RECORD

On March 17, 1978, the supertanker *Amoco Cadiz* broke in two on rocks in heavy seas, spilling a record 46.2 million gallons of oil into the English Channel off the coast of Brittany. The vessel was en route with Arabian crude oil from the Persian Gulf to Lyme, England, when its steering mechanism failed. A tug was summoned, but its tow line to the tanker parted in strong gales.

Attempts to seal the oil leak or transfer the remaining cargo to other carriers was frustrated by continued heavy seas and treacherous reefs. By March 22, the spilled oil had blackened more than 70 miles of the Breton coast and had caused severe damage to the area's tourist, fishing and oyster industries.

The slick in the English Channel was estimated to cover 550 to 600 square miles. It was 60 miles long and, at its broadest point, 12 miles wide. In spots, it was a foot thick. The *Amoco Cadiz,* a 223,000-ton vessel flying the Liberian flag, was owned by a unit of Standard Oil Co. (Indiana) and on charter to an affiliate of the Royal Dutch/Shell Group.

The previous record spill was 30 million gallons by the *Hawaiian Patriot,* which exploded and burned some 360 miles west of Honolulu Feb. 24, 1977. Other big spills: Ekofisk North Sea oil well blowout, 8.2 million gallons, April 22, 1977; supertanker *Urquiola,* 21.9 million gallons, La Coruna, Spain, May 12, 1976; *World Glory,* 13.5 million gallons, off South Africa, June 13, 1968; *Torrey Canyon,* 29.4 million gallons, off England, March 18, 1967.

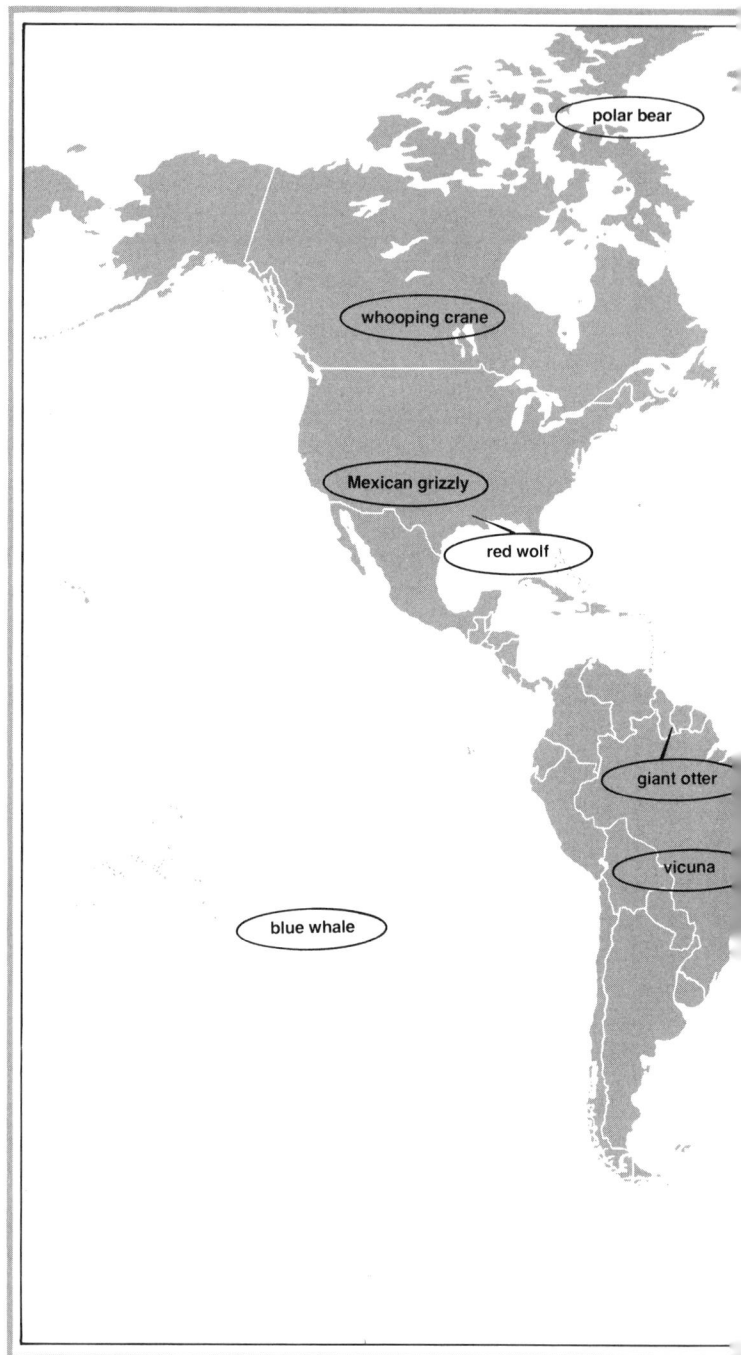

What of the world's wildlife? Much of it is vanishing. The tiger is an endangered species. The polar bear and gorilla, too. Some 170 species are listed as endangered in the U.S. and 427 elsewhere. Life is balanced in nature, scientists explain. Species develop evolutionarily—and the effects are beneficial. The chief enemy of disappearing species is man and the spread of his civilization. Efforts to protect wildlife are fragmentary. Some of the principal endangered species are depicted on the map.

CHAPTER 10

Endangered Habitats, Vanishing Wildlife

It is hard to imagine the world without the tiger, isn't it? Or the polar bear? Or the grizzly? Or the gorilla? Yet these and hundreds of other species are threatened, endangered, vanishing, well on their way to extinction; in the U.S., 170 species, in foreign countries, 427 species are listed as endangered. (Some 20,000 plant species also are on the endangered list.) Man is the

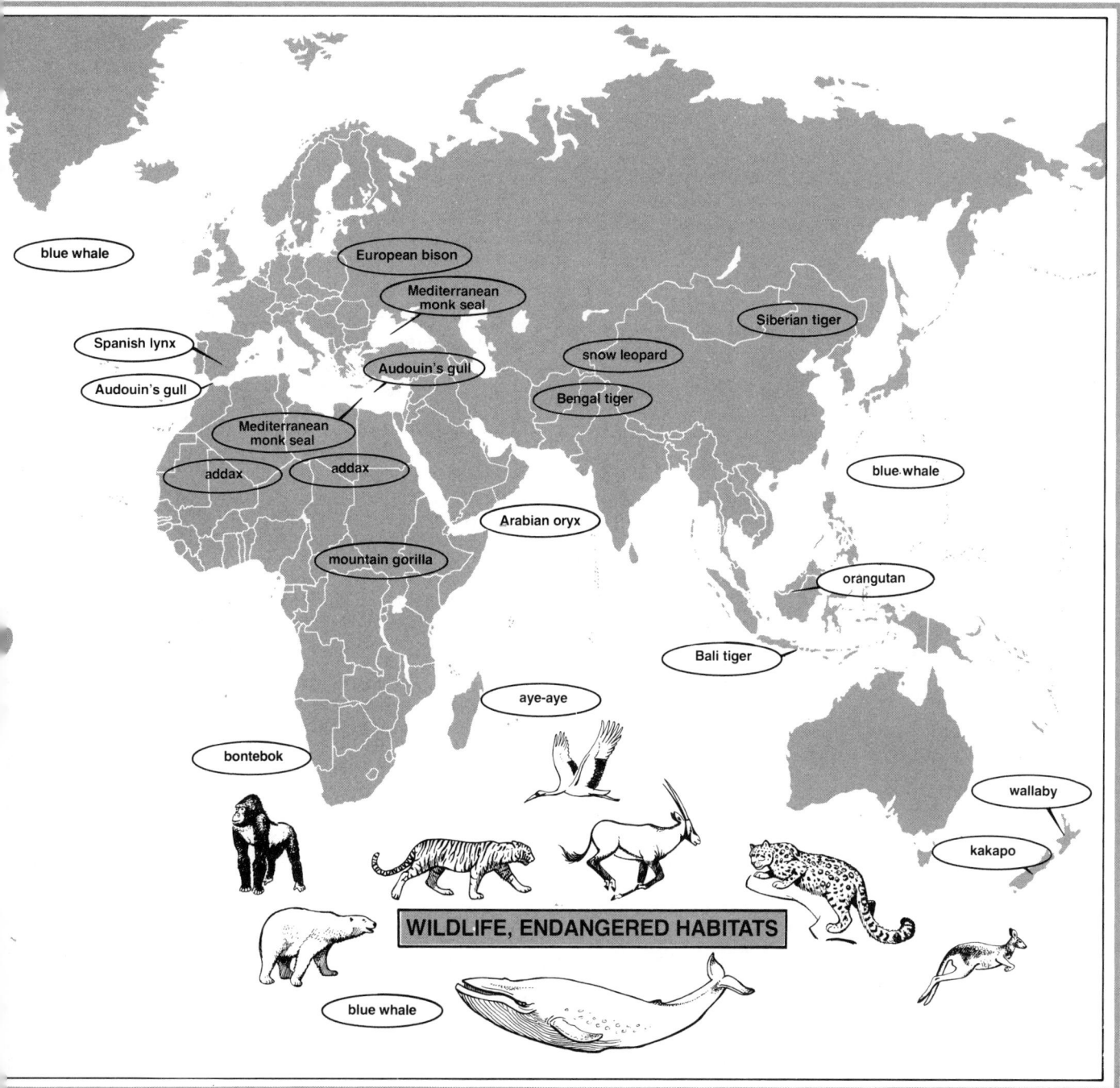

WILDLIFE, ENDANGERED HABITATS

Map labels: blue whale, European bison, Mediterranean monk seal, Siberian tiger, Spanish lynx, Audouin's gull, snow leopard, Bengal tiger, Mediterranean monk seal, blue whale, addax, addax, Arabian oryx, orangutan, mountain gorilla, Bali tiger, aye-aye, bontebok, wallaby, kakapo, blue whale

predator, rapacious and indiscriminate in his slaughter of wildlife, an omnivore. Man increases, spreads out and adapts technologically. Entire ecosystems are destroyed.

The plight of the animal or bird or fish on the brink of extinction is significant in itself. The image of the tiger is moving. A great beast. The miserable condition of a seabird with oil-soaked feathers is disturbing. It can't fly. It must reach land or sink. Ashore it often poisons itself by trying to clean its feathers with its bill.

But, aside from the creature's suffering, does its survival or extinction matter? Numerous species have perished in the past. The case of the Dodo bird rates only a guffaw today. The loss of the passenger pigeon is regretted. The demise of the Labrador duck, great auk, European lion not so well-known. Perhaps man has a destiny to fulfill. Perhaps he is doomed to become the sole inhabitant of the planet, except for domestic animals. The prospect is unhealthy.

Life is balanced in nature. The parts contribute to the well-being of the whole. ". . . The diverse but mutually interrelated living components of the biosphere—which include not only fauna and flora but soil, water, and air—are indispensable to human existence . . . ," write Noel M. Simon and Paul Geroudet in *Last Survivors*. These components form a living community and maintain a biological equilibrium of which man is a part.

And then there is another point, a corollary. Man and nature are subject to evolution over long periods of geologic time. The effects of evolution are beneficial. ". . . The whole essence of evolution is its creativeness: inadequate animals or plants may be ruthlessly discarded . . . but they are replaced by more successful life forms. . . . Species extinction by man . . . is the very antithesis of evolutionary progress. . . . [I]t is characterized by biological impoverishment," say Simon and Geroudet.

Wildlife protection efforts have a brief history, not much more than a century. The U.S. has established refuges for bison, bighorn sheep, elk, small game, waterfowl, pelicans. With protection, the sea otter and Alaskan fur seal have survived and multiplied. The insecticide DDT causes birds to lay eggs with extremely thin shells or no shells, and the embryos do not live to hatch; DDT has been banned in the U.S. and elsewhere. The number of whales that may be taken annually is being limited by international agreement, but the continued existence of the blue whale and the sperm whale and the bowhead whale remains uncertain. Trade in endangered species was prohibited by Congress in 1973, and in the same year by an international convention, signed by 30 nations, later increased to 55. In 1975, the U.S. Air Force abandoned a bombing range on a Texas island where the whooping crane wintered. In 1977, as the animal population of Africa dwindled, Kenya banned game hunting and sales of skins and trophies.

By and large, protection efforts are spotty and scattered; meanwhile, the rate of extinction is increasing. Scientists warn that in the absence of more vigorous protection 20 per cent of today's known species will become extinct by the end of the century. Thomas Lovejoy, program director of the World Wildlife Fund, remarks in the *Smithsonian,* "Limited resources . . . are . . . forcing us into employing on a planetary scale an environmental form of triage. . . ." He asks: "Should we be deciding on which species and which ecosystems to use our meager conservation resources? And which species and ecosystems should we decide to write off? . . . Should triage be based on the ease or difficulty with which a species might be saved? . . . Should we try to save the leopard rather than the cheetah, because the space needs of the latter are so demanding? . . . Why couldn't there be room for all?"

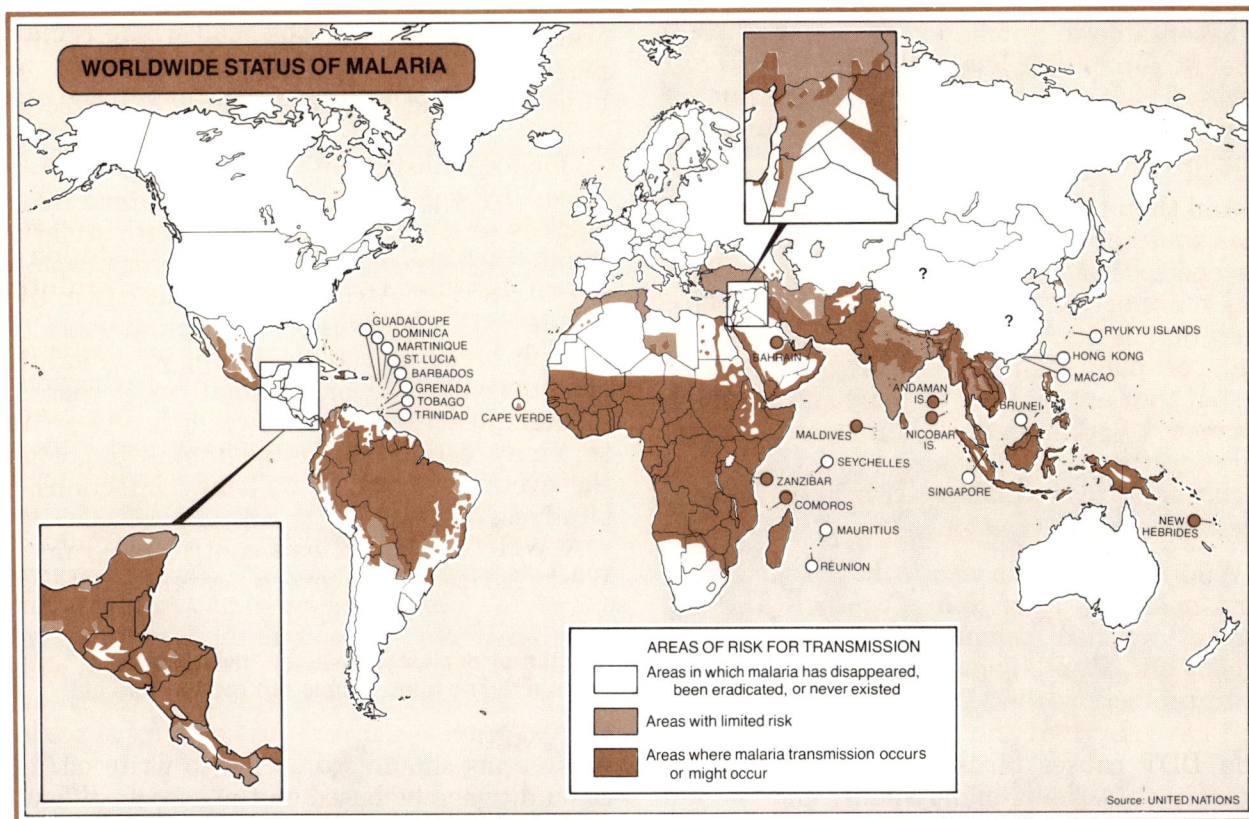

WORLDWIDE STATUS OF MALARIA

AREAS OF RISK FOR TRANSMISSION

- Areas in which malaria has disappeared, been eradicated, or never existed
- Areas with limited risk
- Areas where malaria transmission occurs or might occur

Source: UNITED NATIONS

Malaria remains a major public health problem in Africa, Latin America, the eastern Mediterranean, Southeast Asia, as the map indicates. Malaria has returned in recent years to wide areas that had been largely freed from the disease. The World Health Organization reports that the number of microscopically diagnosed malaria cases had increased from 3.2 million in 1972 to 7.5 million in 1976. The malaria situation is practically unchanged in tropical Africa; high rates prevail in most countries south of the Sahara. Malaria has reestablished itself at former endemic levels in Bangladesh, India and Sri Lanka. Reported cases increased in Southeast Asia.

CHAPTER 11

Man & Disease

Communicable diseases—malaria, other devastating parasitic diseases, cholera—and malnutrition (the "man-made disease") are the major health hazards of people in developing countries, and will be for years to come.

Malaria, the disease of the swamplands—the name derives from the Italian *mala aria,* bad air—has been a constant companion of man since earliest times. Hippocrates described it some 400 years before Christ. It is produced by a parasite, Plasmodium, which develops inside the red blood corpuscles. An English physician, Sir Ronald Ross, demonstrated in 1898 that it is transmitted from an infected person to a healthy person through the bite of a female Anopheles mosquito.

It is a progressive wasting disease that affects the lives of more than one hundred million people. In the epicenter of the disease—African countries south of the Sahara—malaria kills one million children every year. The resurgence of malaria in large areas that had been substantially freed from the disease was reported recently by the World Health Organization. As the mosquito became resistant to insecticides, the number of new cases of microscopically confirmed malaria rose from 3.2 million in 1972 to 7.5 million in 1976. The increase was particularly severe in India and Central America.

WHO's anti-malaria campaign aims to cut mortality and ease the impact of the disease on economic and social development. Eradication

The high plateau of Tabuk in the Philippines, once known as the "Valley of Death," had always been fertile but had been deserted by farmers because of high mortality from malaria. A national malaria team aided by the World Health Organization helped eradicate malaria in much of the area during past ten years by such operations as spraying (above). Many farmers have moved back. Tabuk is now described as northern Luzon's "rice granary."

is the ultimate goal. The strategy of eradication is based on reducing the density and life expectancy of the mosquitos rather than on wiping out the total mosquito population, Dr. Augusto Noguer, chief of the WHO malaria unit, explained in *World Health*. The advantage of this approach is that the battle against the transmitting insects can be carried into the interior of houses instead of being undertaken in the swamps where the insect larvae develop.

The idea is to reduce the contacts between people and mosquito, leading to an interruption in the transmission of the disease. If this interruption can be sustained long enough to ensure the removal of the parasite from its human host —in most cases this takes three to four years— the cessation of control measures and the return of the Anopheles to its former numbers will not mean the recurrence of malaria transmission. However, Noguer emphasized, the application of this strategy requires "... very elab-

orate planning, considerable funds, trained personnel, and operations carried out very punctually and to a high degree of perfection. . . ."

Onchocerciasis, or "river blindness," is caused by a parasitic worm and spread by the blackfly in tropical Africa and South America. It infests between 20 to 40 million people in Africa. In West Africa alone, about one million people are the victims of "river blindness." The blackfly breeds in rapidly flowing water as large as the river Nile or as small as a seasonal stream. Reactions to the worm larvae in the skin may lead to intolerable itching and, where the eyes are involved in heavy infections, to blindness.

A WHO onchocerciasis control program for West Africa now covers seven countries—

A victim of onchocerciasis, or "river blindness," is led by a child. The blind man is not yet 40 years old.

Benin, Ghana, Ivory Coast, Mali, Niger, Togo and Upper Volta. In the rainy season, rivers are surveyed and treated weekly. The biodegradable insecticide ABATE is applied by aircraft.

Another parasitic disease, schistosomiasis, is caused by worms and carried by snails. It is a disease of irrigated lands. Countries such as Egypt that depend on irrigated agriculture consider schistosomiasis to be their major public health problem. There are three types of the disease—two, intestinal, found in Africa and Latin America, and in Asia and the Philippines, respectively: the other, urinary, widespread in Africa and the Middle East. In all, several hundred million people are afflicted, their health undermined by damage to many organs of the body, sometimes fatally.

Cholera is a much-feared and acutely infectious disease of the intestines. It is caused by bacterial contamination of food and water supplies. Death follows overwhelming dehydration by diarrhea and vomiting. In 1976, a total of 66,804 cases of cholera were reported, the lowest number in five years. During the next two years, however, an upsurge of the disease in the Eastern Mediterranean, its appearance in Kenya, and an outbreak in the Gilbert Islands aroused international concern.

WHO focused on oral rehydration in treatment of cholera victims. Oral rehydration was found to reduce the need for the use of expensive intravenous fluid. Field studies in the Lao People's Democratic Republic, Philippines and Turkey confirmed its effectiveness.

COMMUNICABLE DISEASE CONTROL: THE NEAR-ERADICATION OF SMALLPOX

Efforts to alleviate or eliminate communicable diseases may be measured, health authorities suggest, by the near-eradication of the scourge of smallpox, which has occurred in epidemics since prehistoric times. Smallpox once killed, blinded or scarred thousands of people in India every year. The country has now been certified free of the disease.

During 1976 and 1977, smallpox was limited to the nomadic population of the Ogaden, which includes part of northern Kenya, southern Ethiopia and Somalia. Two cases of smallpox were reported Aug. 2, 1978 in Etitrea. WHO would certify global eradication of the disease only after no case had occurred for two years.

Protection against smallpox is provided by vaccination of children before they reach their first birthday.

BLUEPRINT FOR WORLD HEALTH

Essentials of global health were outlined recently by Dr. Halfdan Mahler, director-general of the World Health Organization. They include:
■ Adequate food and housing, with protection of houses against insects and rodents. Water to permit cleanliness and safe drinking. Basic sanitation; suitable waste disposal.
■ Caring for the poorest one billion people "who are just managing to survive on this earth."
■ A new type of health education—active health learning, which is neither oversophisticated or condescending and explains health technology in a language that can be understood.
■ Action against communicable diseases.
■ The provision of ante-natal, natal, and postnatal care.
■ Immunization of all children against the common diseases of childhood by 1990.
■ Learning to live with fewer drugs. Some 150 drugs could meet "the vast majority of health care needs."
■ Research—for new knowledge and for applying existing knowledge.

In the tropics and subtropics, a large majority of the people suffer from malnutrition, a leading cause of ill health. Not only does malnutrition give rise to specific deficiency diseases, but it increases susceptibility to communicable diseases. The principal deficiency diseases in the world today are anemia (iron deficiency); endemic goiter (iodine deficiency); kwashiorkor (severe protein deficiency); marasmus (calorie deficiency); and xerophthalmia (Vitamin A deficiency). Anemia is probably the most common form of malnutrition, though kwashiorkor is very widespread.

What are the reasons for malnutrition? "The causes . . . are built into the very nature of society as it functions today; in the socio-economic and political structures, both nationally and internationally," Dr. Moises Behar contended in *World Health*. "It has been repeatedly said that scarcity of foods is the main factor responsible. This may be true at the family level for those populations affected, but it is not true on a global basis, nor is it true for most of the countries where malnutrition is still a serious problem. It is rather a problem of uneven distribution between countries and within countries. . . ."

That is the humanitarian viewpoint; in the background, the Malthusian controversy persists.

CHAPTER 12

Cancer & the Environment

Three major causes of death in the U.S. have increased significantly in the recent past—homicide, cirrhosis of the liver, cancer.

Cancer is the second highest cause of death. (Heart disease is first.) Eighty to 90 per cent of the cancer cases may be traced to environmental or occupational causes, scientists report. Occasionally, this circumstance breaks into the news, as in a study of the health dangers of an industrial substance or the unusual geographical grouping of a series of cancer cases. But for the most part it is not widely recognized; upon becoming known it seems to produce more controversy than alarm, more rebuttals than remedies.

Cancer frequently is associated with the victim's or society's "way of life," the existence of disease calling into doubt a consumer product or industrial process. Many people respond as if neither is to be questioned, as if a way of life cannot be modified. Consequently, difficulties are established for investigators, legislators, enforcement agencies; scientific findings are refuted or compromised, half-measures adopted or inquiries redirected.

Cigarette smoking is the clearest example of the relationship between a personal habit and ill-health. Lung cancer. Yet just as many Americans, particularly young Americans, as ever are smoking.

Excess drinking has been shown to be related to oesphageal cancer, excess exposure to sunlight to skin cancer. These are habits that might be changed, but often addiction proves to be more powerful than the threat of future ill-health.

Saccharin, hair dyes, coloring dyes, a sleep-wear flame-retardant (Tris), bacon and other meats cured with nitrites are other suspected cancer agents.

Numerous occupations convey an increased risk of developing cancer. Rubber workers die of cancer at rates ranging from 50 to 300 per cent greater than in the general population, asbestos workers experience a lung cancer rate seven times higher than in control groups. Polyvinyl chloride workers succumb to angiosarcoma, organic chemists to cancer of the pancreas and lymphomas, workers producing dyestuffs to bladder cancer.

In 1970, Congress set up the Occupational Safety & Health Administration (OSHA) to fix standards against job-caused cancer. The ineffectiveness of OSHA recently was assailed by the General Accounting Office (GAO), Congressional watchdog. Protective measures for only 15 substances had been imposed in the previous five years, the GAO said. At that rate it would "take more than a century to establish needed standards for substances already identified as hazards."

Geographic clustering of cancer cases indicates a community causal factor, according to epidemiologists. Communities with copper-smelting facilities have been found to have a higher than average rate of lung cancer. Counties where chemical plants are concentrated have an increased incidence of bladder cancer. In Salem County, N.J., bladder cancer mortality among white males is the highest in the nation; 25 per cent of the employed persons in the county work in the chemical industry. Last year, an excess of cases of leukemia and Hodgkin's disease was discovered among children in

AGE-ADJUSTED RATE

Signif. High, in Highest Decile

Signif. High, not in Highest Decile

Cancer Mortality, 1950-69, By County
Trachea, Bronchus & Lung—White Males

Air Pollution?

Asbestos?

**Cancer Mortality,
1950-69, By County**
Bladder—White Males

Chemicals?

**Cancer Mortality, 1950-69,
By State Economic Area**
Mouth & Throat—White Females

Textiles?

CANCER AND THE ENVIRONMENT

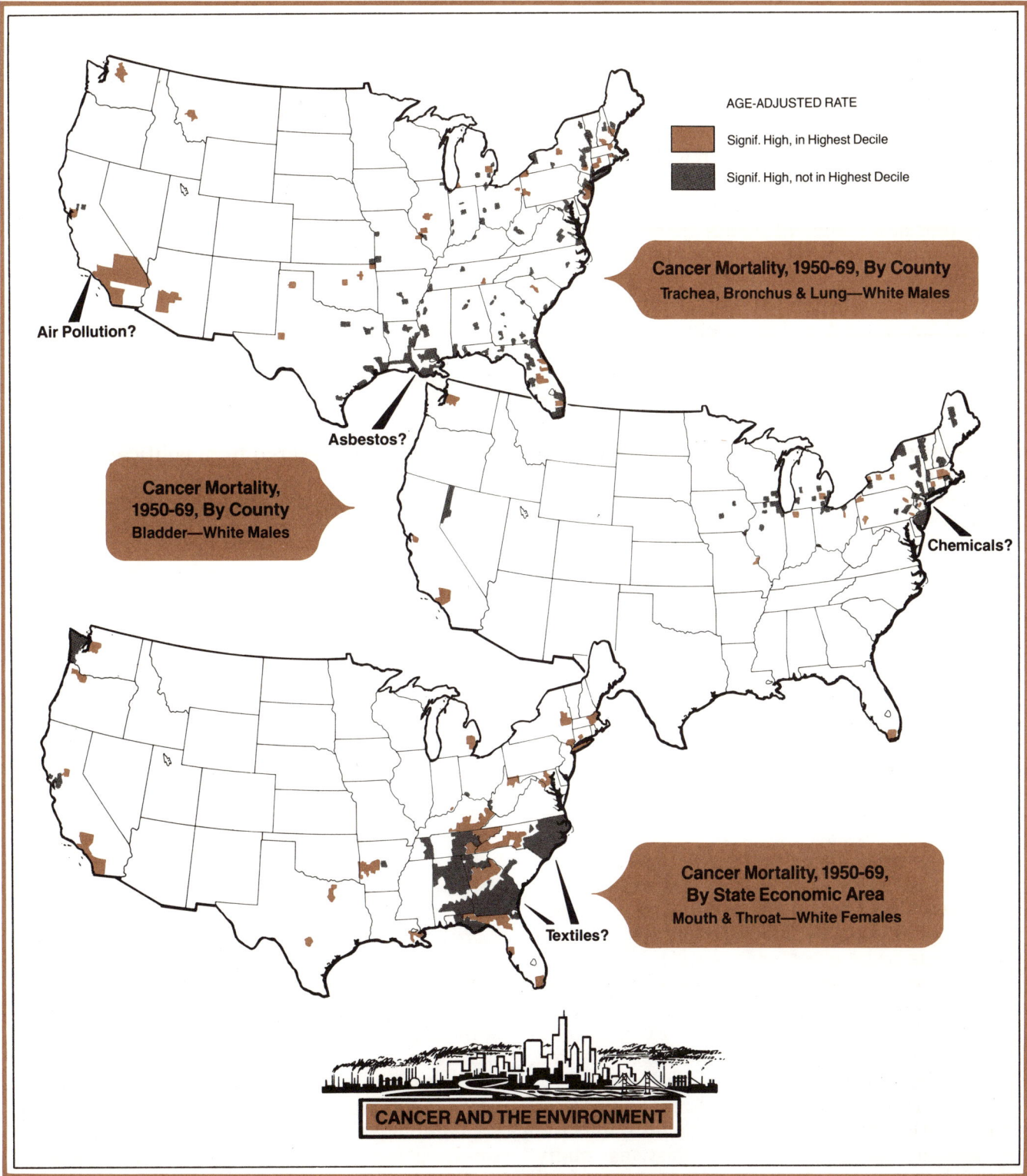

Statistics pinpoint localities in which cancer rates are high. Counties with significantly high rates were charted by the National Cancer Institute in its 1975 _Atlas of Cancer Mortality for U.S. Counties 1950-69._ Examples are provided here. In addition, certain industries and environmental factors give rise to increase rates of cancer, say scientists. Various places in which these circumstances exist are indicated on the above maps.

Rutherford, N.J., which is ringed by chemical facilities.

New Jersey has the third highest rate of cancer deaths in the U.S., 142.8 per 100,000 persons. The District of Columbia is first, with a rate of 168.2, and Maryland second, with a rate of 143.7. Rhode Island is fourth with 142.4, New York fifth with 141.6. Utah has the lowest cancer death rate, 94.6 per 100,000 persons.

Potent new chemical agents are being synthesized and introduced into commerce and the workplace, "generally without prior, adequate testing for carcinogenicity or for other adverse public health and ecological effects," warns Dr. Samuel S. Epstein, a leading expert on occupational and environmental medicine, writing in the *Bulletin of the Atomic Scientists.* Dr. Epstein urged a program of action to reduce the incidence of cancer. Some of the priorities, he said, were:
- Toxic substances legislation, vigorously enforced.

WHO STUDIES CANCER FACTORS

A worldwide cancer surveillance network relating environmental factors to the incidence of cancer in various populations is being organized by the U.N. World Health Organization.

The program will attempt to identify and evaluate the chemical, occupational and lifestyle factors that influence cancer. The surveillance network will collate data gathered by national cancer registries and fund limited surveys in poorer countries.

- Increased research on environmental cancer by the National Cancer Institute and other federal agencies.
- Insulation of research from political and economic pressures.
- Economic analyses that do not distort the costs of compliance with regulatory standards.

CHAPTER 13

Danger Spots

This moment in world affairs is relatively peaceful; an uncertain stability has been achieved.

"We've come through a long period of turmoil and doubt," President Carter said in his 1978 State of the Union message. "For the first time in a generation, we are not haunted by a major international crisis or by domestic turmoil."

Early this year, however, a regional dispute with worldwide implications developed: Chinese actions against the Vietnamese, which many observers warned might cause a Soviet counterpunch.

Problems and danger spots are numerous, but not clear-cut. The number of factors that must be considered in any attempt to assess the world's situation is extraordinary. An overview such as Neville Brown's *The Future Global Challenge* offers an historical perspective. Brown chooses the time frame 1977–90 and considers the possibilities of prediction. He surveys the age of "total war": mass mobilization, ideological commitment and global strategy. And he tries to integrate his observations into an appreciation of menacing trends and their interaction.

Nuclear weapons. Superpowers. Thousands of megatons. Balance of terror. These are elements of the equation.

The nuclear stand-off was as evident in 1969 as it is today. At that time, the Stockholm International Peace Research Institute (SIPRI) reported that spending on arms was rising faster than production of goods and services. Three years ago, SIPRI warned that the risk of nuclear war was being increased by government campaigns to reduce fear of the consequences. The potential for violence had assumed gro-

tesque dimensions beyond an individual's comprehension. If nuclear war came to Europe, the societies there would cease to exist.

Thirty years ago, nuclear weapons could be delivered only by bombers, SIPRI noted. Now they are deployed in a bewildering variety of forms: intercontinental ballistic missiles (ICBMs), submarine-launched ballistic missiles (SLBMs), medium-range ballistic missiles, intermediate-range ballistic missiles (IRBMs), short-range ballistic missiles, depressed trajectory ballistic missiles (DTs), fractional orbital bombardment systems, free-fall tactical bombs, free-fall strategic bombs, air-to-surface missiles, air-to-surface stand-off missiles, air-to-air missiles, army artillery shells, navy artillery shells, howitzer projectiles, torpedoes, rocket torpedoes, depth charges, demolition devices, land mines, sea mines, anti-ballistic missiles and so on.

The development of nuclear-weapons systems is continuing unabated. Efforts to control the arms race have produced no significant results, SIPRI commented; the proposed SALT II treaty would be insufficient, certainly would not limit the arms race qualitatively. Yet bilateral force reductions in Europe are not likely to occur until SALT II has been negotiated; political leaders emphasize that political detente could not survive without a military detente.

Detente, which signified the end of the Cold War, developed in the late 1960s. It was formalized in 1972 when former President Richard M. Nixon journeyed to Moscow as the first U.S. chief executive to visit the Russian capital. Nixon and national security adviser Henry A. Kissinger met with Communist Party General Secretary Leonid I. Brezhnev and other Soviet

A fragile detente holds the superpowers in check. Though nuclear war is the greatest danger, each of the world's trouble spots casts its own shadow over a locality or region. A number of these conflicts are pinpointed on the accompanying map.

officials. The U.S. and Soviet Union reached agreement on SALT I, which was ratified by the Senate later that year. Health, environmental, technological and space pacts also were signed.

The two nations said they would work for "peaceful coexistence" on the basis of respect for "sovereignty, equality, noninterference in internal affairs and mutual advantage." They reaffirmed support for a peaceful settlement of the conflict in the Middle East, where the "Yom Kippur" war broke out the next year; they set forth their standard positions on Vietnam, where war was to continue for another three years; and they agreed that a European security conference should be held "without undue delay." The conference, attended by 35 nations, met in Helsinki three years later, following Watergate and Nixon's resignation.

Nixon's successor, Gerald R. Ford, signed the Helsinki accords, the major provisions of which endorsed the permanence of European borders and promised to respect "fundamental freedoms, including the freedom of thought, conscience, religion or belief." Since 1977, detente has been troubled by President Carter's human rights campaign, the Soviet crackdown on dissidents, Brezhnev's refusal to meet with Carter and aggressive Soviet policy in Africa. Widespread hostilities are a threat in Africa and the Middle East. There are active belligerencies in a score or more of world danger spots. The outlook for peace is as speculative as the future of detente.

What are the danger spots? What are the dangers?

In the Middle East, war between Arabs and Israel is always a possibility. Lebanon remains a potential battleground for such antagonists as Moslem and Christian Lebanese, Palestinian Arabs and Israelis, and Syrians and other Arabs. The Persian Gulf is as volatile an area as the oil that helps give it significance.

Berlin, whose Western enclave has from the beginning been a deeply embedded capitalist thorn in a communist-ruled country, attracts trouble like a magnet attracts iron. Neither North nor South in Korea has ever been content with the uneasy truce that halted the fighting there 26 years ago.

The ideological contest between the Soviet Union and China has provided repeated minor

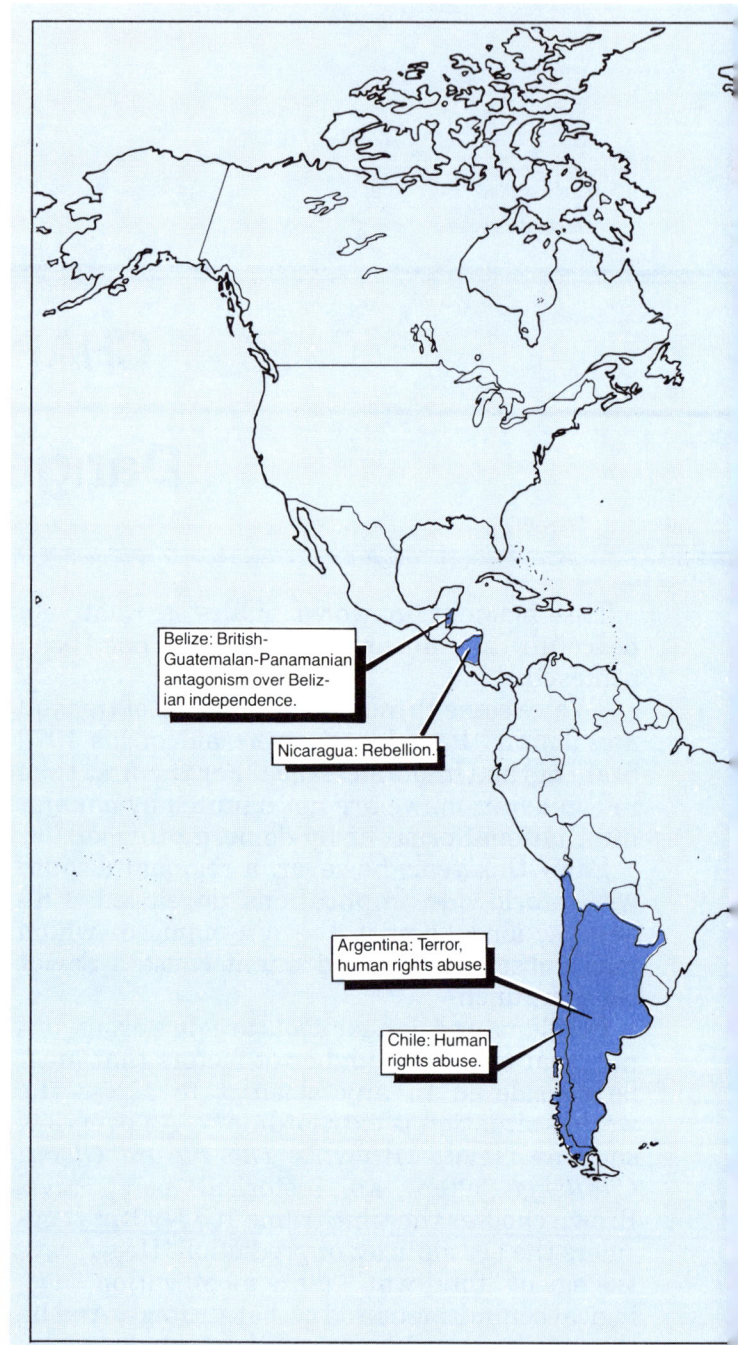

Belize: British-Guatemalan-Panamanian antagonism over Belizian independence.

Nicaragua: Rebellion.

Argentina: Terror, human rights abuse.

Chile: Human rights abuse.

border clashes and threatens the future peace of the world. In the Indian Ocean, strong U.S. and Soviet naval forces confront each other in what could become a struggle for control of strategic sea-lanes.

Similarly, East-West rivalries are evident at many points in Africa, including the "Horn," Zaire, and, potentially, South-West Africa (Namibia). Rhodesia and South Africa are centers of conflicts between whites and blacks, conflicts that have advanced in the former country to guerrilla war. The Marxist regime in Angola, meanwhile, continues to be challenged by re-

Berlin: City a focus of East-West German antagonism.

Northern Ireland: Communal strife, terrorism.

Italy: Widespread terrorism, growing Communist power.

Cyprus: Greek-Turkish communal strife.

Persian Gulf: Iran's new Islamic Republic under pressure.

Soviet-Chinese Border: Ideological rivalry aggravates tensions.

Afghanistan: Rebellion against Soviet-supported regime.

Korea: Danger of war in divided country.

Horn of Africa: Soviet-Cuban role in Ethiopian-Somali struggle.

Pakistan: Political violence.

Indochina after Vietnam War: Horror in Cambodia. Vietnamese invasion of Cambodia. Chinese thrust into Vietnam. New refugee problems.

Chad: French involved in civil war.

Middle East: Arab opposition inflamed by Israeli-Egypt treaty. Warring factions in Lebanon.

Indian Ocean: Superpower rivalry, race for bases.

Zaire: Rebellion in Shaba.

Angola: Rebellion, border tensions.

Rhodesia: Racial struggle, guerrilla campaign, surrounding states involved.

South Africa: International concern over apartheid, independence for Namibia.

DANGER SPOTS

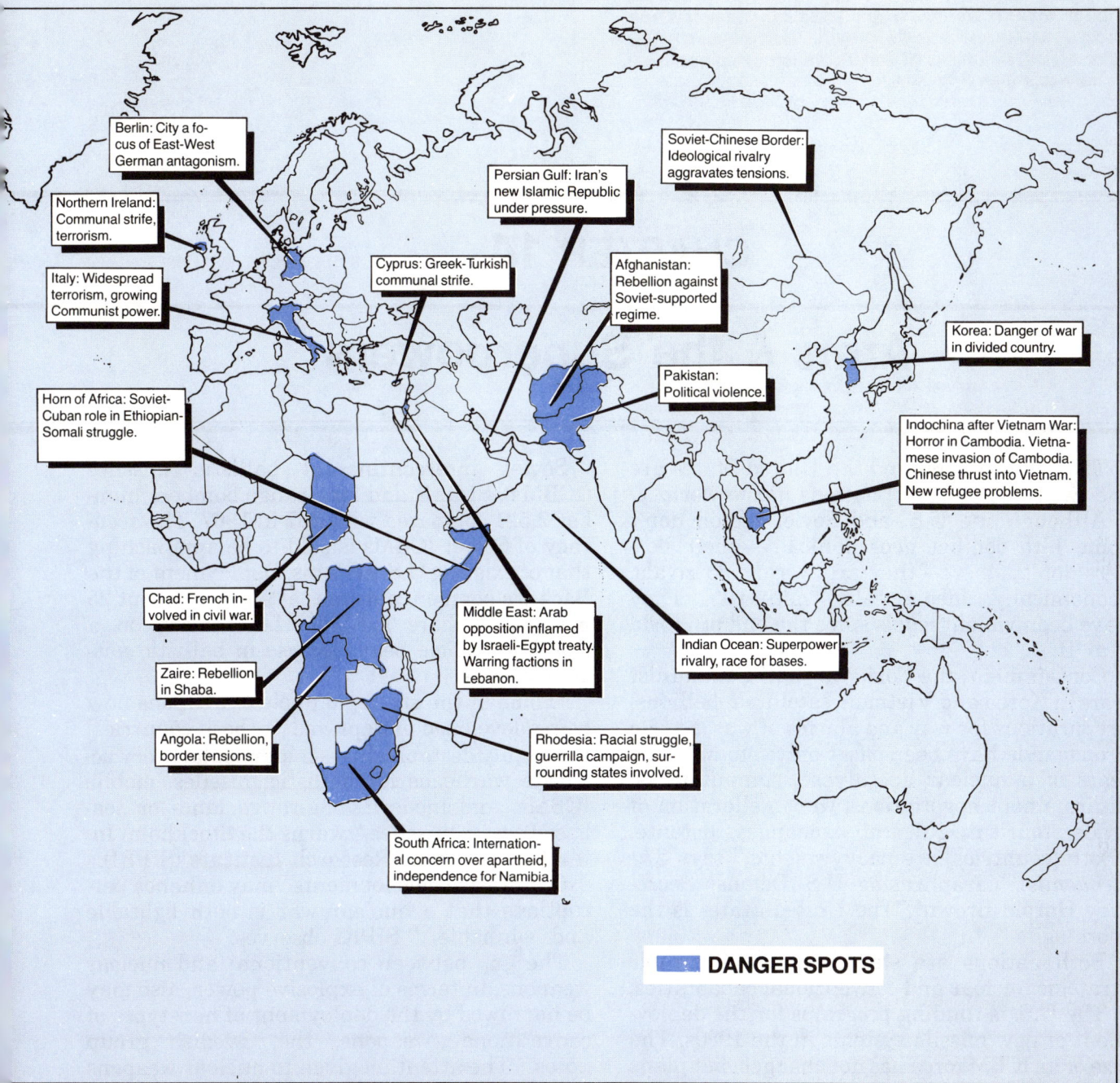

bels; government and Cuban troops oppose them. Two invasions in the past two years have shaken copper-rich Zaire, which received substantial Western military assistance on both occasions. An on-again, off-again civil war was in progress in Chad with French troops chasing guerrillas.

No settlement had been reached between the Greek and Turkish communities on Cyprus where Turkish forces had brought about a *de facto* partition of the island. Separatist bombs and sentiments rocked Corsica, garrisoned by French troops. Terrorist campaigns in Italy at

times seemed to threaten the survival of that country's democratic government. Communal violence between Protestants and Roman Catholics in Northern Ireland did not appear susceptible to a political solution.

In Latin America, Belize was the subject of heated words between neighboring Guatemala and Great Britain. Nicaragua was awaiting the next episode in the fight between the ruling Somoza family and its middleclass and left-wing opposition. Argentina and Chile were ready, it was said, to go to war to determine the ownership of three islands south of Tierra del Fuego.

CHAPTER 14

Arms & the Superpowers

The Soviet Union and the United States are the two most powerful nations in the world.

Although the U.S. and Soviet Union don't come into conflict geographically—their borders don't adhere—they are worldwide rivals, economically, ideologically, militarily. They have been violent rivals since the end of World War II.

Containment, the Cold War, anti-Communist wars in Korea and Vietnam, satellite rebellions, preparations for war and alarms of war, hostile propaganda have been offset only somewhat by fears of a nuclear apocalypse, summit talks, disarmament negotiations, the amelioration of trade, tourism, cultural exchanges, detente. "Both [countries] are heavyweights," says *The Economist,* paraphrasing U.S. Defense Secretary Harold Brown. "The United States is the more agile."

Both nations are steadily improving their strategic nuclear and conventional capabilities.

The U.S. is funding programs for the deployment of new missile systems in the 1980s. The size of its ICBM force has not changed, but plans are going ahead to improve the accuracy of Minuteman III. Improvements of Minuteman software, reported the International Institute for Strategic Studies (IISS), would increase accuracy from about 0.25 nautical miles (nm) to 700 feet by the end of the decade—"and significantly enhance the ability to destroy hardened targets." Construction of the first ten 24-tube Trident submarines continues and testing has started on the 4,000nm-range Trident I missile. The Trident missile would almost double the effective range of American submarine-launched ballistic missiles (SLBMs). Flight testing continues on the air-launched cruise missile.

Soviet intercontinental ballistic missiles (ICBMs), SLBMs and long-range bombers number 2,521 compared with 837 in 1967. The accuracy of Soviet ICBMs is said to be approaching that of existing U.S. systems. Deployment of the Backfire bomber continues at a rate of about 25 per year. There are reports of work on a charged-particle beam for use in ballistic missile defense.

"Some of the strategic nuclear weapons now being developed or deployed [by both countries] are highly destabilizing—in particular, very accurate warheads for ballistic missiles, mobile ICBMs, and modern long-range land- or sea-based cruise missiles," warns the Stockholm International Peace Research Institute (SIPRI).

Qualitative developments "may enhance perceptions that a nuclear war is both fightable and 'winnable,'" SIPRI observes.

The gap between conventional and nuclear weapons, in terms of explosive power, also may be narrowed by the deployment of new types of conventional weapons, the Swedish group notes. "The attention given to nuclear weapons tends to obscure the considerable advances being made in conventional weapons. One such weapon is the fuel air explosive (FAE). The blast-wave effect of an FAE [such as] ethylene oxide is equivalent, weight for weight, to the explosive effect of several times as much TNT. Current efforts aim at substantially increasing the TNT equivalent of FAEs. . . ."

Meanwhile, by reducing support personnel, the U.S. added an army division and proceeded with plans to add two more, and the Soviet Union deployed new aircraft with improved range, payload and avionics and increased the size and quality of its navy.

World military expenditures amounted to

about $325 billion in 1976, that is, as much as was spent on health and more than was spent on education. Military spending continued to rise annually. U.S. defense appropriations, for example, increased from $91 billion in fiscal 1976 to $104 billion in fiscal 1977 and to $110 billion in fiscal 1978. Soviet defense spending is as controversial as it is difficult to assess. SIPRI estimates that the Soviets spent $61 billion on defense in 1976; the U.S. intelligence estimate is $126 billion. "No single figure for Soviet defense expenditure can be given," says IISS, "since precision is not possible on the basis of present knowledge. The declared Soviet defense budget is thought to exclude a number of elements such as military R&D [research and development], stockpiling and civil defense—indeed some contend that it covers only the operating and military construction costs of the armed forces. . . . Furthermore, Soviet pricing practices are quite different from those in the West. . . ."

Soviet military spending in recent years has outrun U.S. spending by as much as 40 per cent, the Pentagon says. The Pentagon's estimates are based on Central Intelligence Agency (CIA) calculations of what the Soviet military effort would cost if duplicated by the U.S.

In an article in *Foreign Policy,* the Pentagon estimates are challenged by Rep. Les Aspin (D, Wis.). Aspin declares that this method is invalid for a major element of defense spending: pay to military personnel. The U.S. pay scale is far higher than the Soviet one, but Soviet spending was figured with the assumption of parity in pay, he said. Aspin also criticizes the Pentagon for omitting defense spending by U.S. and Soviet allies. He said that, based on Defense Intelligence Agency figures, members of the North Atlantic Treaty Organization are spending a total of $140 billion annually, while the Warsaw Pact countries spend $121 billion. The CIA concedes that the method "tends to overstate" Soviet military expenditures, but it maintains that the margin of error is "clearly not large enough to alter the basic conclusion that the Soviet military program overall is currently significantly larger than that of the United States."

In the U.S., the defense budget is a matter of annual legislative debate. While there are some —peace groups, Sen. George McGovern (D, S.D.) —who oppose increased spending, the debate essentially concerns its shape and emphasis, representing a tug of war between the Pentagon, the White House and Congress. Defense Secretary Brown told Congress in 1978 that the

A U.S. Polaris A-3 missile is fired by a submerged submarine.

U.S. would have to increase its military budget by more than $50 billion during the next five years to maintain parity with the Soviet Union. He said there was a "standoff or stalemate" between the U.S. and Soviet Union in strategic nuclear strength.

The global power balance is discussed. Could the West remain secure? Is Moscow tilting the balance against us?

Controversy was stoked by a CIA estimate of

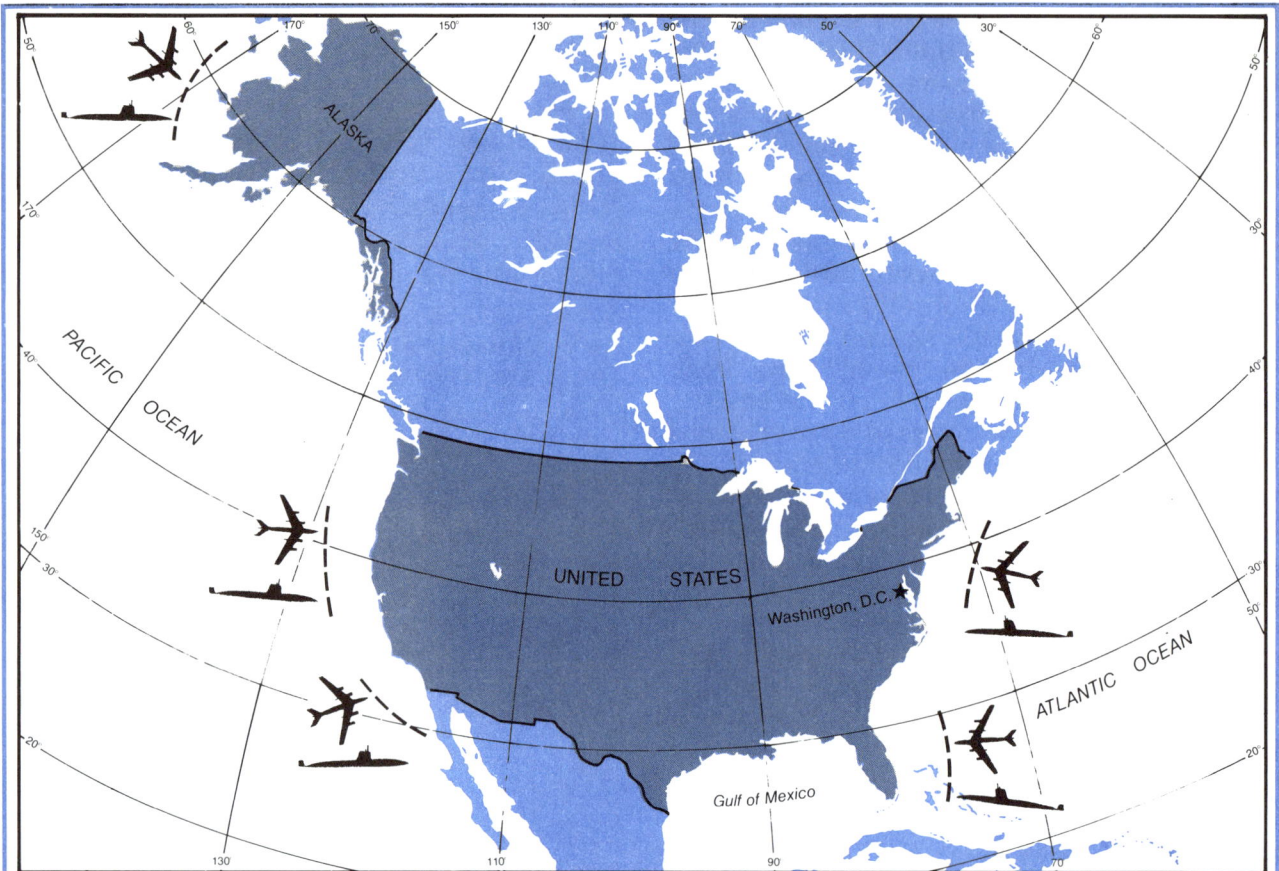

U.S.-SOVIET MUTUAL THREAT

U.S. and Soviet targets covered by cruise missiles with range of 1600 miles (2574 km).
Missiles could be launched by aircraft or submarine from at least 200 miles (322 km)
outside Warsaw Pact and U.S. territories.

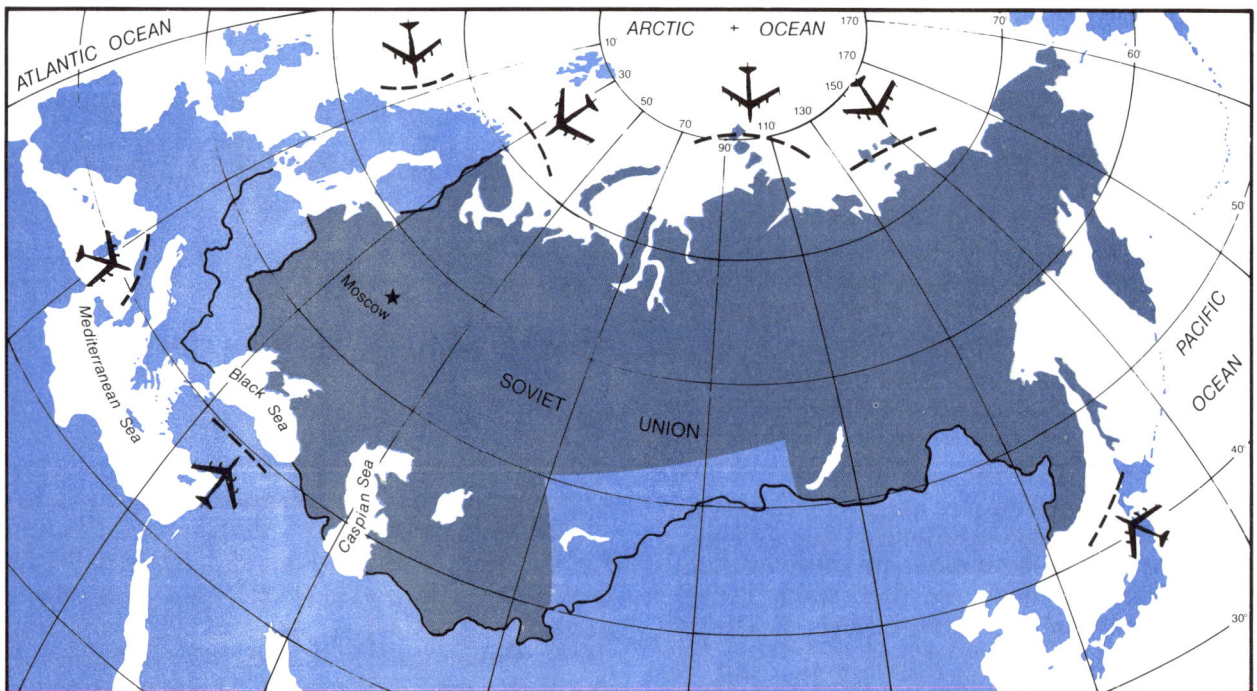

Soviet strategic aims. According to *The New York Times,* the CIA study advanced as its majority opinion the view that the Soviets were aiming at achieving superiority over, rather than rough parity with, U.S. military forces.

The issue was examined by the Senate Foreign Relations Committee in 1977. Following closed-door testimony, senators said that the "worst-case" view—that the Soviet Union sought military superiority—was just one of the two views presented in the national intelligence estimate, not a consensus. Sen. Jacob K. Javits (R, N.Y.) said that the worst-case view was countered by "the general intelligence estimate which would indicate that American policy is proceeding on the right assumption, that is, that the balance of terror still remains the policy of both countries."

The dispute intensified.

A Brookings Institution study says that the Soviet buildup requires an increase of U.S. capabilities in the Middle East and Europe. An IISS survey finds that despite the buildup, "the overall [East-West] balance still appears to make military aggression seem unattractive."

Senior officers at U.S. Tactical Air Command headquarters are reported to be disturbed about the qualitative improvement of the Soviet Air Force. Secretary Brown says that the U.S. was "the most powerful" country in the world, adding, "We don't necessarily care whether the Soviets have more tanks than we do."

Particular weapons, weapon systems and strategies also are debated. In 1977, President Carter decided against producing the B-1 bomber, a supersonic plane the Air Force had proposed as a replacement for its aging B-52s. Instead of a new manned bomber, Carter said, the U.S. should start deploying cruise missiles. It was estimated that a fleet of 244 B-1s would have cost about $25 billion, or about $100 million per plane. The cruise missiles were expected to cost less than $1 million apiece.

The concept of deterrence is illustrated in the maps left. Strategic nuclear weapons deployed by the U.S. and Soviet Union are in position to reach virtually every part of each target country; the threat of destruction is mutual. According to many planners and analysts, this would appear to rule out the use of strategic arms by either side. Qualitatively improved, more accurate missiles continue to be built, however, and the fear of an annihilating first strike persists.

Carter deferred production of the neutron bomb last year. The neutron bomb is as controversial as any weapon ever considered. It kills by emission of radiation but limits blast and heat damage to a radius of several hundred yards, rather than several miles as with the hydrogen bomb. Supporters claim it would redress the balance of forces in Central Europe. Opponents say that the very reasons that

The U.S. Strategic Air Command's heavyweight missile, Titan II, is launched directly from its underground storage silo.

CRUISE MISSILE: AN 'OLD' WEAPON

Cruise missiles are small, pilotless aircraft powered by air-breathing jet engines and capable of guidance in flight. They are not ballistic missiles; the latter are powered by rocket engines and follow a predetermined path. Cruise missiles are old weapons, notes the Stockholm International Peace Research Institute *Yearbook* 1978. They date back to the German V-1 or "buzz-bomb" of World War II. Shortly after the war, the U.S. and Soviet Union began developing these missiles, producing a variety of types.

A number of technological advances in recent years has favored further cruise missile development. ". . . The most important by far was the combination of the miniaturization of computers . . . with an accurate data base about the coordinates of potential targets," according to the SIPRI *Yearbook*. "Very small but accurate missile guidance systems could thus be developed. . . . From very accurate maps which have become available using satellite mapping techniques, the positions of targets and the contours of flight paths can be obtained with unprecedented accuracy. . . ."

The AGM-86A, for example, is an air-launched cruise missile (ALCM) developed by Boeing. The ACLM is designed to have a small radar image and to fly at low altitudes. Defense would be both difficult and costly. ". . . Effective detection of ALCMs would probably involve look-down radars carried in Airborne Warning & Control System (AWACS) aircraft. To patrol a long frontier would require a fleet of such aircraft. . . . A large number of long-range interceptor aircraft would also be required. . . . The deployment of cruise missiles would, therefore, most probably escalate the arms race. . . ."

In 1977, President Carter cancelled production plans for the B-1 bomber and opted for a cruise missile force. ". . . The idea apparently is that . . . carrier aircraft should stay, say, 500–1,000 km. away from the borders of the Soviet Union and Eastern Europe, thereby avoiding contact with air defense systems. . . . The Carter Administration is also anxious to accelerate the deployment of air-launched cruise missiles so that it can begin in early 1980."

Apart from their high accuracy and comparative invulnerability, the cruise missile is cheap, the SIPRI *Yearbook* added. The unit cost is likely to be about $750,000—much less than the cost of a "modern main battle tank."

---

make it a more credible deterrent make it more likely to be used. Debate also focuses on technical issues: just how effective the bomb—compared to other weapons—would be against tank forces; what dangers the radiation would pose to civilians, and whether certain military tactics (for example, dispersal of forces) might largely neutralize the effectiveness of the bomb. Carter says the "ultimate decision" on the weapon would be "influenced by the degree to which the Soviet Union shows restraint in its conventional and nuclear arms programs."

With each generation of weapons, the issues multiplies. Go slow on the M-X missile? Has the Minuteman in its silo become vulnerable to destruction? Is counter-force a first-strike strategy? Is the SLBM a first-strike weapon? Do killer satellites foreshadow space war? "It is difficult to 'make a fix' on the nuclear arms race because it is a moving target," writes Sidney Lens in *The Day Before Doomsday*. "The technology, the strategy, even the level of hostility between the two superpowers keep changing. . . . There is, in addition, the feeling that it is a drama on another planet. . . . In the distance, scientists and engineers work on· . . . , strategists in Pentagon-sponsored research institutions—'think-tanks'—debate. . . . But apart from the enduring conflict between the United States and the Soviet Union, there seem to be no threads that bind the nuclear arms race to the everyday world. . . ."

What is real, after all? One's own daily life, or grand strategy? Surely, the former. Nonetheless, the effects of the latter might be cataclysmic. The Prussian military philosopher Karl von Clausewitz sounded like a simple warrior compared to today's military leaders. Von Clausewitz said, "War is an act of force, and to the application of that force there is no limit." His dicta have been displaced by modern weaponry. As a contemporary observer, Phil Stanford of the Center for Defense Information, points out, "Just one nuclear submarine can destroy any country on earth."

"The unleashed power of the atom," said Albert Einstein, "has changed everything except our way of thinking. Thus, we are drifting towards a catastrophe beyond conception."

GLOSSARY

Anti-ballistic missile (ABM) system—An anti-missile missile defensive system.

Basic load—That quantity of nonnuclear ammunition authorized and required to be on hand within a military unit or formation at all times.

Capability—The ability of a country or coalition of countries to execute specific courses of action. Capabilities are conditioned by many variables, including the balance of military forces, time, space, terrain and weather.

Conflict spectrum—A continuum of hostilities that ranges from subcrisis maneuvering to cold war situations to the most violent form of general war.

Critical terrain—A single geographic feature, natural or manmade, the seizure, retention, destruction or control of which would afford a marked advantage to one or more countries or coalitions.

D-Day—The day a specific military operation begins. D+1 is the following day, and so on.

Feasibility study—An analysis to ascertain strengths and weaknesses of a possible course of action, with special consideration for risks, costs and the adequacy of available resources.

Intention—The determination of a country or coalition to use capabilities in specific ways at specific times and places. Intentions are conditioned by such variables as interests, objectives, policies, principles, commitments and national will.

Intercontinental ballistic missile (ICBM) —A rocket-propelled vehicle capable of delivering a nuclear warhead more than 3,000 miles.

Kiloton—The nuclear equivalent of 1,000 tons of TNT. The weapon dropped at Hiroshima had a yield of about 14 kilotons.

Maneuverable reentry vehicle (MARV)— A missile stage capable of adjusting its trajectory while reentering the earth's atmosphere. *See also* Reentry Vehicle.

Megaton—One million tons of TNT equivalent.

Multiple independently targetable reentry vehicle (MIRV)—Two or more reentry stages carried by a single missile and capable of being targeted independently.

National security interests—Abstract wants and needs concerned primarily with preserving a state from harm. Self-preservation, independence, territorial integrity, physical security, freedom of action, national credibility, internal stability and economic well-being are prominent examples.

Reentry vehicle—The portion of a missile designed to carry a warhead back into the atmosphere.

Submarine-launched ballistic missile (SLBM)—A ballistic missile carried and launched by submarine.

Sortie—One operational flight by one aircraft.

Strategic nuclear operations—The use by one major power of nuclear weapons against the homeland of another major power.

Tactical nuclear operations—The use by a major power of nuclear weapons against regional targets so as to influence the outcome of local conflicts.

Turnaround time—Time required to load an aerial or sea transport, proceed from port of embarkation to port of debarkation, unload, reload (if desired), return to original point, and unload.

Members of North Atlantic Treaty
Organization (NATO) and European
Economic Community (EEC)

NATO but not EEC

EEC but not NATO

⊙   NATO Military Headquarters

•   Subordinate NATO Military Headquarters

Members of Warsaw Pact and Council
for Mutual Economic Assistance

★   Warsaw Pact Headquarters

★   Subordinate Warsaw Pact Headquarters

Reykjavik   ICELAND

Dublin

IRELAND

UNITE
KINGDO
London

Paris

FRANC

Prospective European
Economic Community
member

SPAIN
• Madrid

PORTUGAL

Lisbon

Prospective European
Economic Community
member

A geographic perspective of opposing North Atlantic Treaty Organization (NATO) and Warsaw Pact countries is vividly offered in this map. Principal and subsidiary NATO and Warsaw Pact military headquarters are marked. The members of Western and Eastern European economic blocs—the European Economic Community and Council for Mutual Economic Assistance—are also indicated. NATO and the Warsaw Pact alliances were formed in the early years of the Cold War. Uncertainty and controversy continue to beset the alliances. Are NATO forces strong enough to throw back a Warsaw Pact attack? The Warsaw Pact nations, for example, are reported to have a better than two-to-one edge in tanks over NATO. How great are the strains within the alliances themselves? Last year, Rumania refused to accept Soviet demands for an increase in Warsaw Pact spending. Rumanian President Nicolae Ceausescu called the proposed defense increase "a particularly heavy burden on our countries."

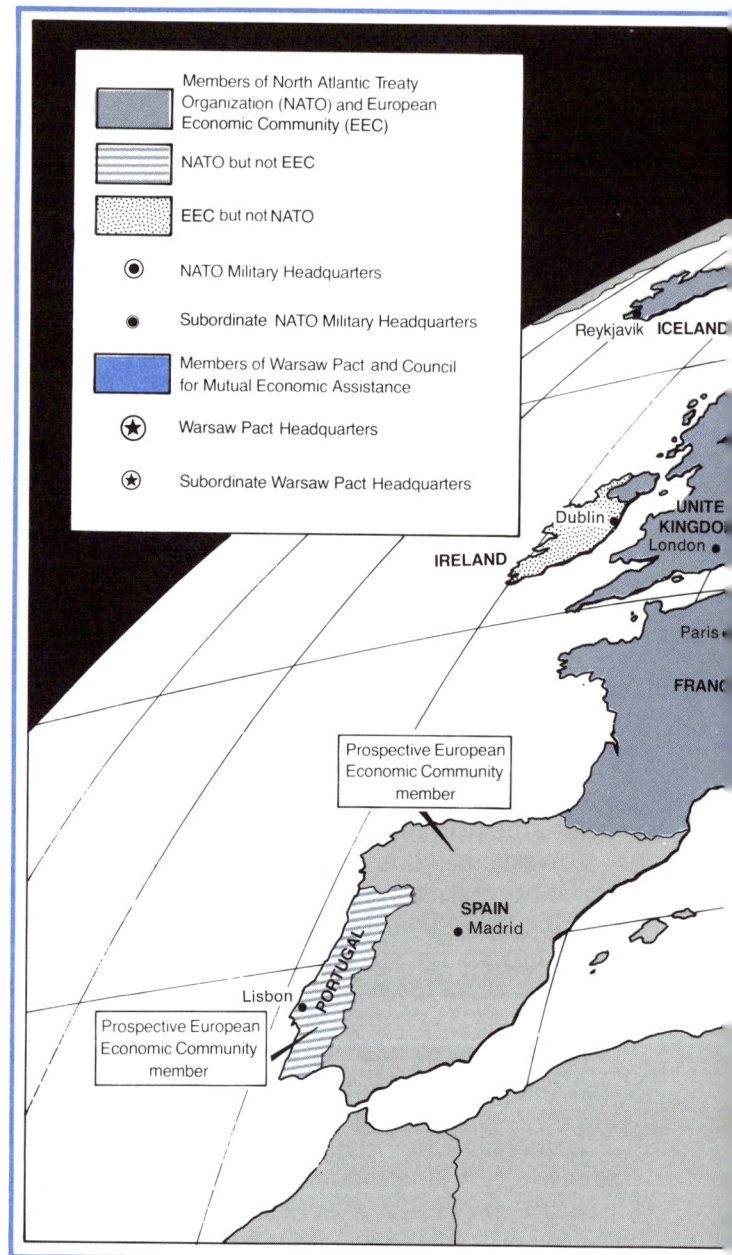

CHAPTER 15

NATO & the Warsaw Pact

The world's two major power groupings are the 15-member North Atlantic Treaty Organization (NATO) and the seven-member Warsaw Pact. Western or capitalist nations gather under the NATO umbrella. Eastern or communist countries seek shelter within the Warsaw Pact. Each of the antagonists declares that its organization is a defense alliance. Fearful of the

FINLAND
Helsinki

NORWAY
Kolsaas
Oslo
Stockholm
SWEDEN

Moscow

SOVIET UNION

DENMARK

NETHERLANDS
Amsterdam

E. GERMANY
Berlin
Zossen-
Wundsdorf
Warsaw
POLAND
Legnica

BELGIUM
Brunssum
Bonn
Seckenheim
Prague
Milovice CZECHOSLOVAKIA

LUX.
WEST
GERMANY
Bern
Vienna
AUSTRIA
Tokol Budapest
HUNGARY

RUMANIA
Bucharest

SWITZ.
YUGOSLAVIA
Belgrade

Associate member
COMECON

BULGARIA
Sofia

ITALY
Rome

Tirana
ALBANIA

GREECE

Ankara
TURKEY

Naples

Athens

Prospective European
Economic Community
member

NATO AND WARSAW PACT COUNTRIES

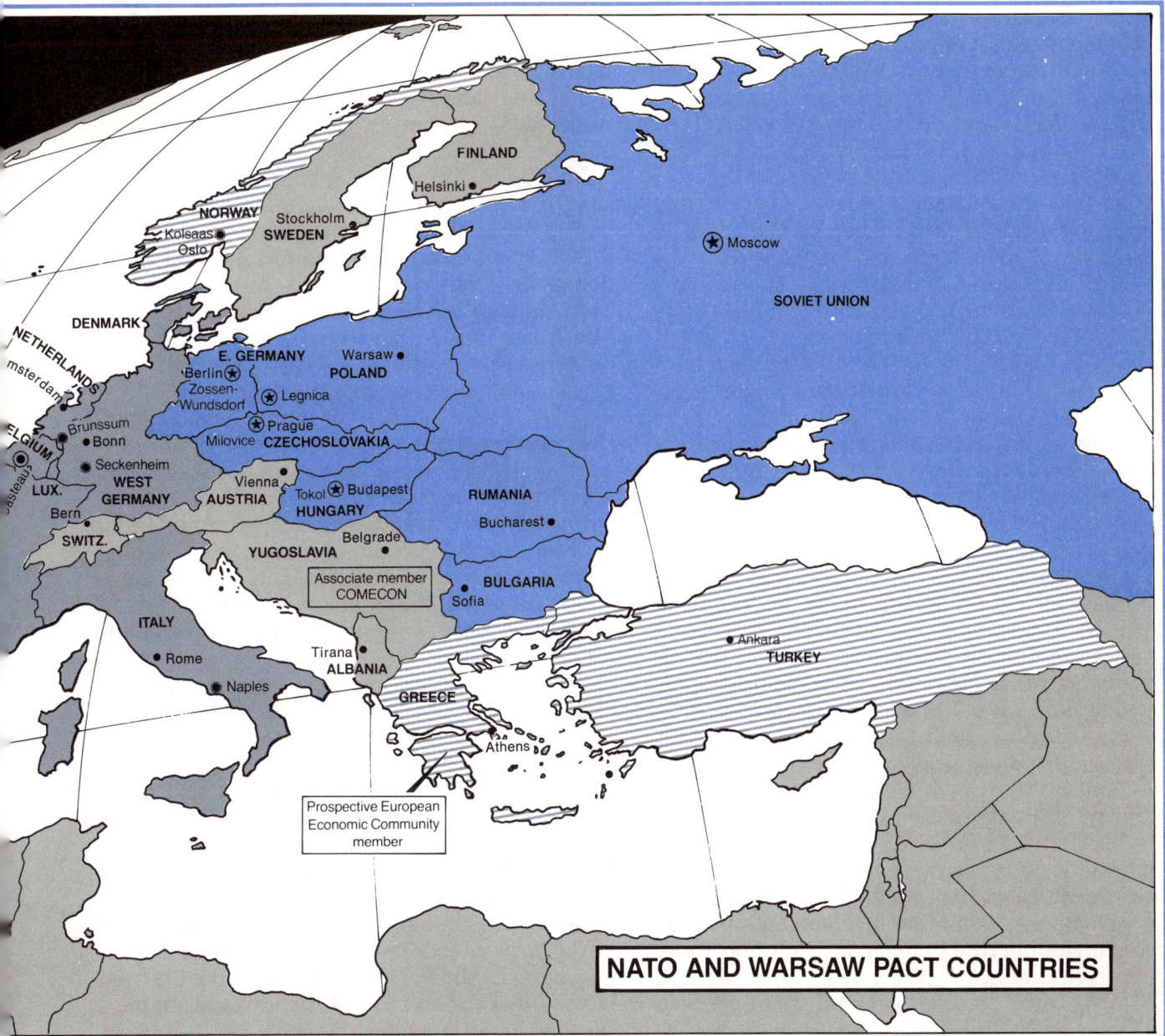

other, they have built strong forces that divide Europe and threaten mutual nuclear destruction.

Both alliances originated with the Cold War, NATO in 1949, the Warsaw Pact in 1955. Though the Cold War receded with detente, the fundamental issues in the conflict, which concerns opposing views of society, man and freedom, remain unresolved.

The principal military commands of NATO are Allied Command Europe (ACE), Allied Command Atlantic (ACLANT) and Allied Command Channel (ACCHAN). ACE headquarters is located at Casteau, near Mons, Belgium.

Commands subordinate to ACE include Allied Forces Central Europe (AFCENT), with headquarters at Brunssum, the Netherlands; Allied Forces Northern Europe (AFNORTH), Kolsaas, Norway; Allied Forces Southern Europe (AFSOUTH), Naples, and ACE Mobile Forces (AMF), Seckenheim, West Germany.

The headquarters of the Warsaw Pact's command is in Moscow. Among the Soviet military headquarters in the Warsaw Pact area are Legnica, Poland (Northern Group); Milovice, Czechoslovakia (Central); Tokol, Hungary (Southern), and Zossen-Wunsdorf, near East Berlin (Group of Soviet Forces in [East] Germany).

THE MILITARY BALANCE

NATO combat troops in northern and central Europe number about 630,000, Warsaw Pact troops about 945,000. In southern Europe NATO forces total approximately 560,000, Warsaw Pact forces about 390,000. NATO warplanes total 2,350 in northern and central Europe, 950 in southern Europe; Warsaw Pact aircraft add up to 4,075 in northern and central Europe and 1,575 in southern Europe.

The Warsaw Pact nations have a better than two-to-one edge in tanks over NATO. In 1978, the Soviet Union increased its tank force by 7,000 to a total of 50,000. Overall, the Warsaw Pact has 65,525 tanks, compared to NATO's 25,-373, of which 10,500 are American.

NATO is said to have some 7,000 nuclear warheads, deliverable by a variety of vehicles—aircraft, short-range missiles and artillery. The figure for Soviet warheads is probably about 3,-500, delivered similarly. Summing up: on the crucial central front, Warsaw Pact forces are larger than NATO's in every category except nuclear warheads.

". . . The numerical pattern over the years so far has been a gradual shift in favor of the East, with NATO relying on offsetting this by a qualitative superiority in its weapons that is now being eroded as new Soviet equipment is introduced," says *The Military Balance 1977–78,* published by the International Institute for Strategic Studies. However, the annual study concludes, "the overall balance is such as to make military aggression appear unattractive." It adds that "NATO defenses are of such a size and quality that any attempt to breach them would require major attack. The consequences for an attacker would be incalculable, and the risks, including that of nuclear escalation, must impose caution. . . ."

A long-term defense program was approved last year by NATO. Under the program, NATO members would increase their defense budgets 3% annually during the next 10–15 years. The cost of the program in its first phase 1979–83 is estimated at $60 to $80 billion; the U.S. would pay a little more than half the total cost. The program sets goals for improvements in several military areas, including combat readiness, reinforcement capability, command control and communications and joint weapons design and production.

Some Pentagon and State Department officials question whether NATO members actually would follow through, reports *The New York Times.* A major problem is that despite so many new goals, there is no clear set of priori-

ties. Moreover, the program is said to represent American priorities by and large. One official quoted by *The Times* says: "Governments have paid lip service to the idea of upgrading NATO defenses for over 20 years. It remains to be seen whether this time it will be different."

The tensions within the NATO alliance are numerous, both military and political, and a subject of continuous debate and reevaluation.

Militarily, for example, NATO members are said to fear the recent deployment by the Soviet Union of the SS-20 missile. "Somewhere in the forests of the western Ukraine, a Soviet SS-20 pokes its long nose toward the sky," writes Takashi Oka in the *Christian Science Monitor.* "Its three independent warheads are targeted on Antwerp? Hamburg? a NATO airfield?" The SS-20 is a mobile, intermediate-range missile. It is a "gray area" system of ambiguous capabilities, neither a battlefield weapon nor of intercontinental range and therefore not considered at strategic arms limitation talks. NATO has no equivalent within its arsenal. How may NATO counter the SS-20? Should the U.S. Pershing missile, designed for battlefield use with a range of 400 miles (650 kilometers), be developed into a weapon with a range of 1,125 miles (1,800 kilometers)?

NATO's southern flank is viewed as vulnerable to the hostility between two of its members—Greece and Turkey. Greece withdrew its armed forces from NATO, following the Turkish invasion of Cyprus in 1974, but still takes part in NATO military planning. Eight years earlier, under President Charles de Gaulle, France had pulled out its forces, while maintaining its political ties with NATO. For three decades, the voting strength of the Communist Party in western Europe has troubled NATO planners. In the event of a Communist election victory in France or Italy, how would its position in the alliance be affected?

The difficulties and uncertainties of the Warsaw Pact nations are somewhat less apparent. Col. Marc E. Geneste points out in *U.S. Naval Institute Proceedings,* however, the "all-directions" defense problems of the Soviet Union—its adversaries to the east and west, the U.S. strategic threat, the divisions within its empire. (Rumania refused to increase its defense expenditures. How reliable an ally would occupied Czechoslovakia be?) Furthermore, the NATO countries are far stronger economically than the Soviet bloc. In fact, says Geneste, "if, some day in the future, historians had to explain why the western allies had lost World War III, they could charge only the western strategic and tac-

Aircraft with airborne warning and control system (AWACS) radome mounted on top. Plane's sophisticated radar can penetrate about 240 miles into Warsaw Pact territory.

tical doctrines." Namely, U.S. adherence to retaliation in kind, mutual assured destruction (MAD) strategy. Geneste emphasizes the necessity of common defense, the U.S. helping Western Europe to defend itself by supplying it with the weapons it needs, particularly the neutron bomb, "smart" kilotons or megatons to nullify armor.

THE SCENARIO

Reality and fantasy are inevitably mixed in the study of a possible future war in Europe. Force levels and capabilities, political and economic factors are part of the realistic assessments of military planners. So are the intelligence reports provided by reconnaissance satellites, spy planes, and airborne warning and control systems (AWACS). AWACS aircraft, for example, are modified Boeing 707s. They carry sophisticated radar that can penetrate some 240 miles into Warsaw Pact territory and give NATO members 15 minutes warning of an attack by low-flying planes. Ground radar would give only three minutes warning.

Scenarios, war games, abstract models, historical examples, and even novels are aids to study. All may be used "to increase the analyst's comprehension of the dangerous and unfamiliar terrain which he is trying to map," Herman Kahn wrote in *Thinking about the Unthinkable*. A scenario results from an attempt to describe in some detail a hypothetical sequence of events. It can emphasize different aspects of "future history."

The basic scenario for war in Europe relates a sweep by Warsaw Pact armies through West Germany toward the Rhine, the Ruhr industrial area and the English Channel. How long would it take Soviet units to reach the Rhine? Some scenarists say 48 hours, others say up to

six days. The North German plain is a traditional invasion route, but urban sprawl is said to be causing NATO to reconsider its strategy. "We have to review our concept of a Soviet invasion . . . across the North German plain," an American armored cavalry commander told Drew Middleton of *The New York Times*. "There just isn't room anymore and we have to think about new tactics in the light of presumed Soviet objectives."

Last year, Sir John Hackett got together a team of English experts to publish an apocalyptic scenario, *The Third World War, a Future History*. Sir John is a former commander of the British Army of the Rhine. In this scenario, war breaks out Aug. 4, 1985. It develops from incidents the previous December in the Gulf of Aden and leads to a full-scale conventional Soviet attack on NATO. The war escalates rapidly. Cities in England and the Soviet Union are destroyed by nuclear weapons. "Because of the authors' professional qualifications and experience and their knowledge of force dispositions and battle tactics, the book has a realism that might escape a nonmilitary author," comments Middleton.

Convincing descriptions of NATO "on standby for World War Three" are presented in a recent novel, *The Belgrade Drop*, by Gary Vaughan. An AWACS aircraft on patrol verifies that Warsaw Pact divisions are at action stations. ". . . In the snow on the long bridge across the Evros, Greek and Turkish soldiers shook hands for the first time since the Cyprus invasion. At Karup, twelve hundred miles to the northwest, Danish pilots blew on their fingers in the cockpits of their Saab Draken interceptors. . . ."

". . . The symbols of our present predicament," I. F. Clarke said in *Voices Prophesying War 1763–1984*, "are the flash in the sky, the mushroom cloud, the dead city. . . . These are the present signs of future disasters. They provide a code by which it is possible to picture the situation before mankind. . . ."

The major naval powers in the world are the U.S. and Soviet Union. Great Britain, which dominated the seas for centuries, ranks third. Naval planners deploy their forces for sea control, protection of shipping routes, and coastal defense. Strategic decisions of the superpowers can be deduced from the locations of U.S. and Soviet fleets and bases as shown on the map. U.S. fleets are designated by number and Soviet fleets by area. Geographically, say naval strategists, the Soviet navy may be at a disadvantage. Russian territory, for example, is accessible to the sea at only four points — and these are separated by great distances. Moreover, two of these points, at the entrances to the Baltic and Black Seas, are not under Soviet control.

CHAPTER 16

Control of the Seas: Naval Competition

Naval planners of necessity view the world as a whole. Their approach to the problems of sea power must be comprehensive. They must try to understand world economic patterns and world strategy, technology and different types of ships and aircraft.

The classic objectives of naval power are command of the sea, protection of shipping routes,

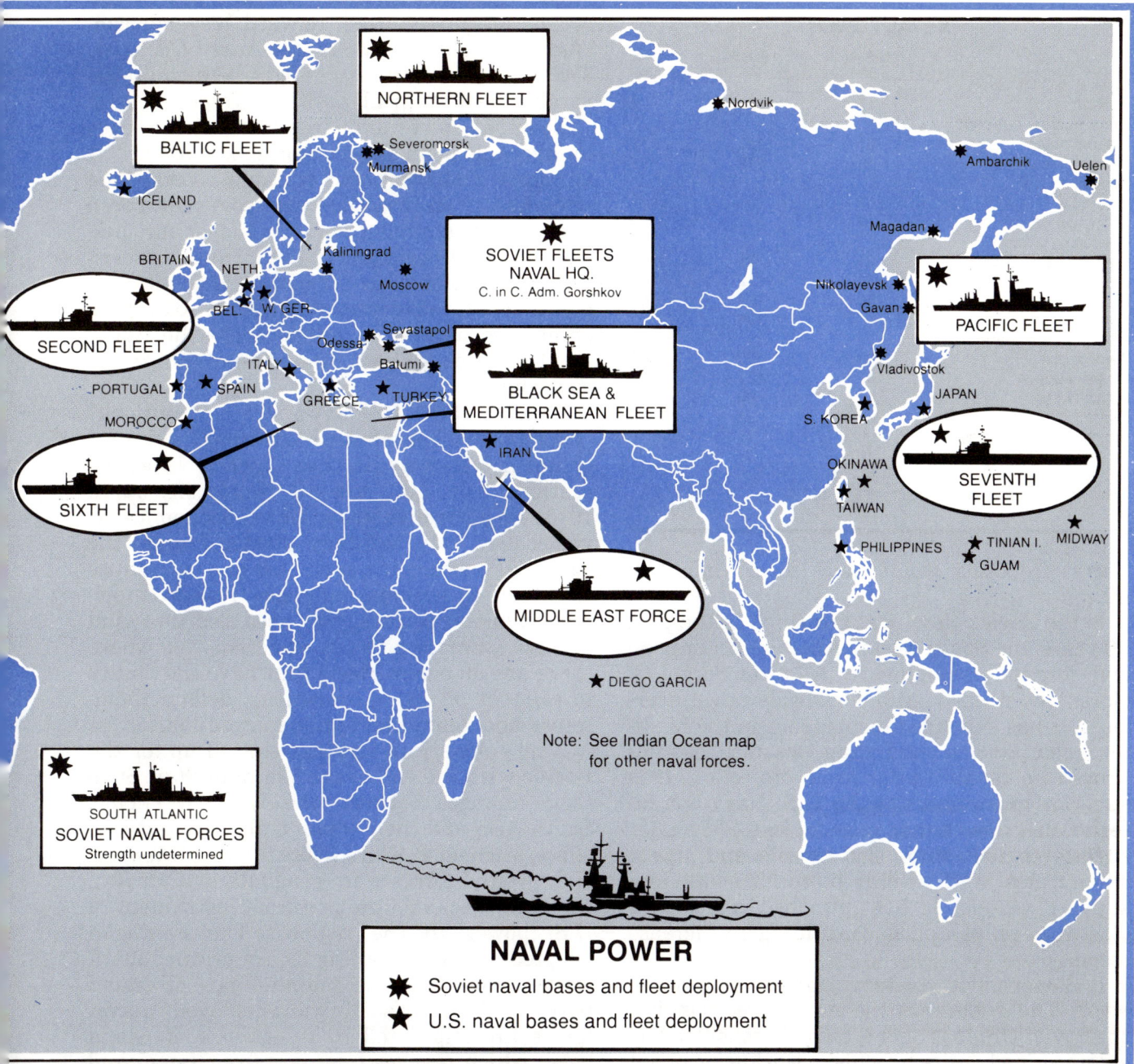

BALTIC FLEET

NORTHERN FLEET

Nordvik

Severomorsk
Murmansk

ICELAND

Ambarchik

Uelen

Kaliningrad

Magadan

BRITAIN

NETH

SOVIET FLEETS
NAVAL HQ.
C. in C. Adm. Gorshkov

Nikolayevsk

SECOND FLEET

BEL   W. GER

Moscow

PACIFIC FLEET

Gavan

PORTUGAL   SPAIN

ITALY

Odessa   Sevastapol

GREECE   TURKEY

Batumi

BLACK SEA &
MEDITERRANEAN FLEET

Vladivostok

JAPAN

MOROCCO

SIXTH FLEET

IRAN

S. KOREA

OKINAWA

SEVENTH
FLEET

TAIWAN

MIDDLE EAST FORCE

PHILIPPINES   TINIAN I.   MIDWAY
GUAM

DIEGO GARCIA

Note: See Indian Ocean map
for other naval forces.

SOUTH ATLANTIC
SOVIET NAVAL FORCES
Strength undetermined

NAVAL POWER

✴ Soviet naval bases and fleet deployment

★ U.S. naval bases and fleet deployment

and coastline defense. Today, the U.S. Navy's missions in support of these objectives include strategic deterrence, projection of power ashore and naval presence. These are represented respectively, for example, by the ballistic missile nuclear submarine (SSBN), amphibious forces and the Sixth Fleet in the Mediterranean Sea.

The navy's missions change from era to era—and as a result naval questions are perennially controversial.

Is the U.S. Navy big enough? The U.S. Navy has 470 ships, reduced from 951 in 1968. Major units: two groups of nuclear-powered subma-

rines—41 SSBNs and 61 attack—13 aircraft carriers (three are nuclear-powered, 94,000-ton giants costing $2.4 billion each), 26 cruisers, 39 missile and 15 gun destroyers, 65 frigates, 65 amphibious assault ships.

A five-year building program is under way, its final goals yet to be determined. The Carter Administration has submitted plans that would increase the Navy to 525 ships. The top admirals are seeking a 600-ship Navy. Soaring costs, cost-overruns and delays in construction already approved are serious problems; the Administra-

NAVAL POWER

	U.S.A.	U.S.S.R.	U.K.
Ballistic missile sub-marines	41	62	4
Other nuclear-powered submarines	61	120	12
Other submarines	10	273	18
Nuclear aircraft carriers	2		
Other aircraft carriers	11	1	2
Helicopter cruisers		2	2
Guided missile cruisers	26	35	8
Destroyers	54	112	3
Frigates	65	108	56
Corvettes		106	
Amphibious warfare vessels	65	290	70
Minesweepers	43	161	27
Patrol craft	13	60	16
Oilers	8	21	17
Submarine rescue ships	8	15	
Fleet ocean tugs	16	58	13

Principal source: *Jane's Fighting Ships 1977–78*

tion's proposals would save more than $20 billion.

Is the Soviet Navy still growing? In the past 20 years, the Soviet fleet has become an impressive force. Commanded by Admiral Sergei G. Gorshkov, it has staged worldwide naval exercises. It has expanded its presence in the Mediterranean and in the Indian Ocean. It has improved its capability for force projection. It is superior in numbers to the U.S. Navy but inferior in gross tonnage. It deploys 236 major surface combat ships, 265 missile and attack submarines, and several hundred small and support vessels. It has launched many new classes of ships and is continuing to increase steadily.

Is Soviet naval strategy aggressive or defensive? "The evidence of the last ten years is that the Soviet Union is not necessarily consumed by a determined desire to achieve worldwide naval superiority," Lieut. Comdr. J. T. Westwood, U.S. Navy, observed not long ago in *U.S. Naval Institute Proceedings.* The new *Kiev* class of antisubmarine warfare cruisers (ASWs) was of particular interest in judging Soviet naval strategy, Westwood said. The primary target of these ships "would appear to be Western SSBNs, including the forthcoming Trident class, with their great missile ranges." Another interpreter, Jurgen Rohwer, however, warned in *Problems of Communism* that Gorshkov might succeed in introducing the classical concepts of naval power through the backdoor of defensive weaponry.

The U.S.-Soviet rivalry for mastery of the oceans has just started, Edward Wegener concluded in his book *The Soviet Naval Offensive.* The West's "trump card" might be its more favorable geographical position, Wegener said. "The situation of Russia in relation to the sea is unfavorable in an almost grotesque manner." It is poorly endowed with suitable coasts; long stretches of its coastline are so encumbered with ice that shipping is impossible, or only possible for short periods of the year. Russian territory is accessible to seagoing traffic at four points separated by vast distances. Two of these points are located on inland seas—the Baltic and the Black—whose entrances are not in Soviet control.

What is the U.S. Navy's strategic outlook? "Our country has a forward strategy," Admiral James L. Holloway III, then Chief of Naval Operations, told *U.S. News & World Report* in 1975. "We are overseas-oriented economically, politically. Our military strategy uses the oceans as barriers in our defense and as avenues of extending national influence. And to implement a forward strategy we need a certain kind of navy." Carriers to provide air power where there are no bases. Fleets that have the ability to conduct offensive operations, defend themselves and defend forward-deployed forces.

A new American strategy shaped up for the Pacific with the end of the Vietnam War. Strategic linkages between the Western Pacific, South Asia and the Persian Gulf were put into effect, Michael T. Klare wrote in *The Nation.* As U.S. ground forces were gradually withdrawn, the Navy became "the principal instrument of U.S. power in the region." The Pentagon adopted a strategy calling for American superiority at sea and the maintenance of island bases. "America's forward-deployed naval forces are supported by a network of island bases which reaches in an arc from Japan and Okinawa in the northwest Pacific to Taiwan, the Philippines and Guam in the southwest Pacific, and then on to Singapore and Diego Garcia in the Indian Ocean," Klare said. Of these bases, the most important were in Japan, Okinawa, Micronesia and the Philippines.

On the other side of the world, Pentagon plans to limit the Navy's role in the North Atlantic Treaty Organization were disputed last year by Secretary of the Navy W. Graham Claytor. Differences of opinion about U.S. naval strategy became apparent as memoranda by Claytor and Secretary of Defense Harold Brown were disclosed. Claytor protested that Brown was contemplating the withdrawal of carrier battle groups from the Mediterranean and concession of the Norwegian Sea to the Soviet Union. "Such concepts . . . will lead inevitably to the conclusion that a smaller and less capable Navy is somehow logical," he said.

Is the surface fleet obsolete? Air power had displaced the battleship. The SSBN was the most important agent of naval power today. Opposing naval squadrons no longer fought concentrated actions. The surface fleet was vulnerable to the guided missile. "The Navy leadership's attempts to put new emphasis on the procurement of cruisers, destroyers, and frigates, while blocking the development of promising alternatives, are neither justifiable nor prudent," William S. Lind contended in *U.S. Naval Institute Proceedings.* "It is unlikely that the Congress will stand idly by if its initiatives, moving toward new concepts and ship types, are thwarted. . . . The future of the surface navy lies in new types of ships: small, fast combatants such as hydrofoils—and small aircraft carriers." Warships of the 21st century, says designer Reuven Leopold, will feature greater aviation capability, the high-energy-laser gun, hybrid ship forms that combine different hull-supporting systems.

At present, ships such as the recently commissioned 11,000-ton cruiser *Virginia* are among the most advanced. The *Virginia* is equipped with a highly integrated combat system built around seven centrally located digital computers. It carries two helicopters, missiles, guns, torpedoes and an outstanding platform for additional equipment. In the crew's quarters, there are 17 living complexes, each with modular bunks for maximum privacy. Each complex has access to a lounge and recreation room. The ship has a library, gymnasium and barber shop. Like everything else, the Navy is changing.

U.S. naval task force in Western Pacific: The amphibious assault ship *Okinawa,* center, is surrounded by (clockwise from left foreground) the escort ship *Meyerkord,* the amphibious transport dock *Vancouver,* the tank landing ship *Peoria,* the dock landing ship *Thomaston* and the guided missile escort ship *Ramsey.*

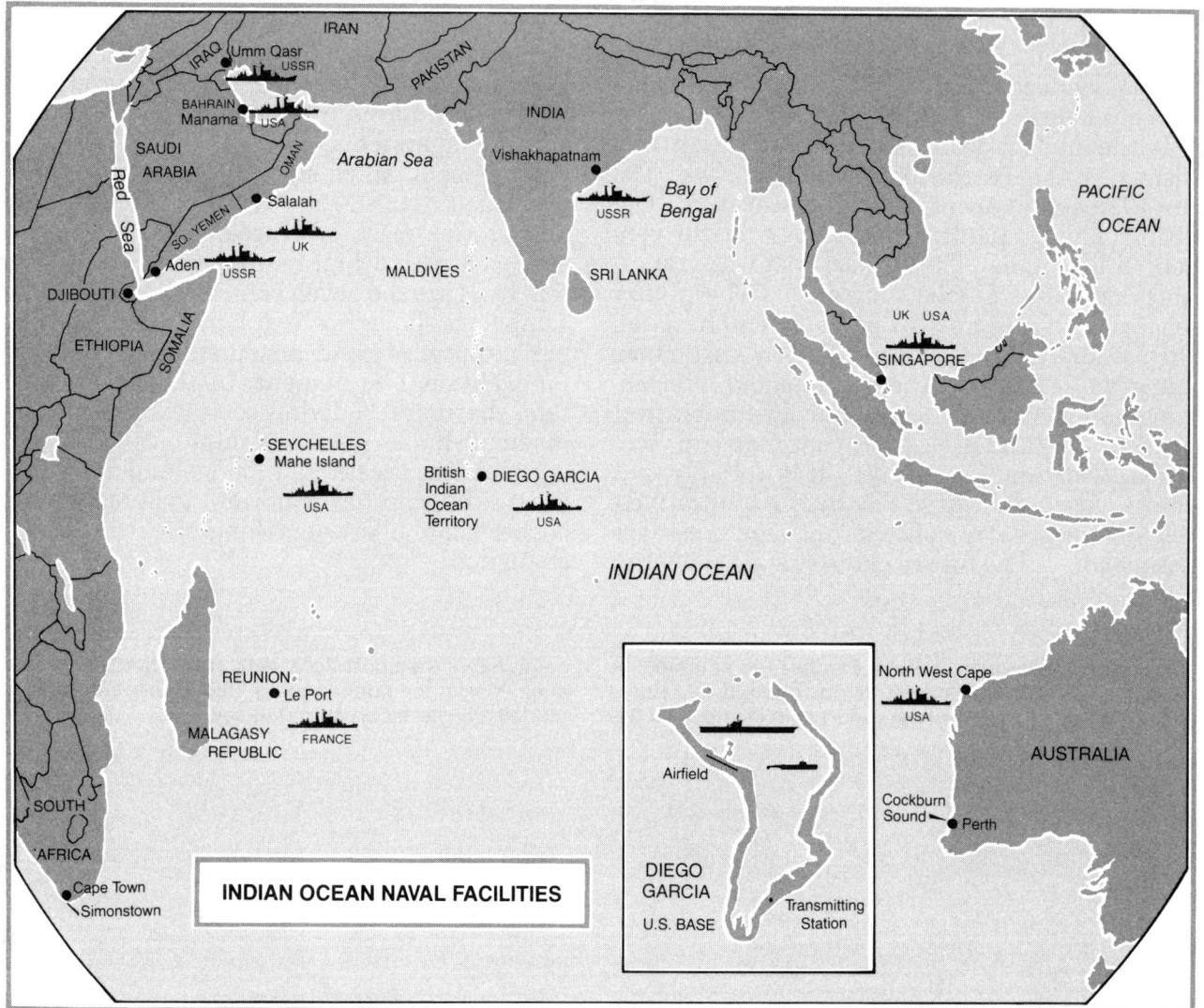

IRAN
IRAQ Umm Qasr
USSR
BAHRAIN
Manama
USA
SAUDI ARABIA
PAKISTAN
INDIA
Arabian Sea
Vishakhapatnam
Bay of Bengal
USSR
PACIFIC OCEAN
Red Sea
OMAN
SO. YEMEN
Salalah
UK
Aden
USSR
DJIBOUTI
ETHIOPIA
SOMALIA
MALDIVES
SRI LANKA
UK USA
SINGAPORE
SEYCHELLES
Mahe Island
USA
British Indian Ocean Territory
DIEGO GARCIA
USA
INDIAN OCEAN
REUNION
Le Port
MALAGASY REPUBLIC
FRANCE
North West Cape
USA
AUSTRALIA
Cockburn Sound
Perth
SOUTH AFRICA
Cape Town
Simonstown

INDIAN OCEAN NAVAL FACILITIES

Airfield
DIEGO GARCIA
U.S. BASE
Transmitting Station

CHAPTER 17

Bases of Rivalry in the Indian Ocean

The Injian Ocean sets an' smiles
  So sof', so bright, so bloomin' blue,
There weren't a wave for miles an' miles
  Excep' the jiggle from the screw.
The ship is swep', the day is done,
  The bugle's gone for smoke and play;
An' black ag'in the settin' sun
  The Lascar sings. *"Hum deckty hai!"**
—Kipling

---

*I'm looking out!

For two hundred years, Great Britain maintained a dominant presence east of Suez. Then, as British influence in the region declined following World War II, the U.S. based warships at Bahrain. A decade ago, the Soviet Union moved fleet units into the Indian Ocean.

Today, the Indian Ocean is a cockpit of superpower rivalry that focuses on shipping lanes, oil supplies, regional conflicts, and naval bases. A vital international body of water, it is the third largest ocean in the world (the Pacific is the

The great arc of the Indian Ocean links Africa, Middle and Far East, and Oceania. Its shipping lanes, regional conflicts, and naval bases are the focus of superpower rivalries. It is patrolled by strong naval forces of the U.S. and Soviet Union and the navies of the littoral powers. Negotiations to demilitarize the Indian Ocean, proposals to declare it a "zone of peace," have not been successful.

largest, the Atlantic, second largest), extending along a broad arc for nearly 10,000 miles from Cape Town to Perth. It provides U.S. shipping with trade routes to Iran and the Persian Gulf sheikdoms, India and Pakistan, Saudi Arabia and the African littoral states. Oil resources in the area are substantial. The U.S. oil industry has capital investments valued at about $3.5 billion in the Persian Gulf region, Seymour Weiss writes in the *Department of State Bulletin,* and in the event of war, naval forces would be required to protect the tanker route around the Cape to the U.S. and Europe.

The conflicts in the Middle East, Horn of Africa, and Southern Africa touch the Indian Ocean as the superpowers bid for the allegiance of local states and regional powers. ". . . If we look coldly at the region what we see are two chains of states, one chain leaning toward the Soviet Union and the other leaning toward the U.S. or China, or both," Martin Woollacott asserts in the *Manchester Guardian Weekly*.

South Africa and the U.S. agree on a need to safeguard the Cape sea route. Countries friendly to the Soviet union offer its navy bases and port facilities and both direct and indirect access to the ocean. China has gained leverage in East Africa.

Regional instability is constantly changing the terms of the competition. The Somali Republic, for example, ordered the Soviet Union out of its naval base at Berbera because of Moscow's support for Ethiopia in the Ogaden conflict. About the same time, Bahrain ended its base-leasing agreement with the U.S., although

American ships are still allowed to resupply there. To increase "operational flexibility," the U.S. is completing a major base at Diego Garcia, a British-administered atoll in the Chagos Archipelago 1,000 miles southwest of India. Fifteen miles long and a few hundred yards wide in most places, the horseshoe-shaped coral reef is no more than four feet above sea level; its lagoon is being deepened, its airfield lengthened, its fuel storage capacity enlarged.

Estimates of fleet strength in the Indian Ocean vary. Soviet task forces have been reported to range from six to twenty warships including nuclear-missile cruisers and submarines. American squadrons are said to have strategic (nuclear) and conventional capabilities. Naval vessels of other nations that sail the Indian Ocean are British, French, and Australian, Iranian and Indian. The Indian navy is the largest, but the Iranian navy was expected to quadruple in size by 1980, reported Lt. Cmdr. Thomas F. Green (USN) in "Building a Navy in a Hurry" (U.S. Naval Institute *Proceedings*, January 1978). Naval exercises called "Midlink" were carried out annually by members of the Central Treaty Organization (CENTO)— Britain, Iran, Pakistan, Turkey and the U.S.

For some time now, proposals have been put forward to demilitarize the ·Indian Ocean. In 1964, Sri Lanka urged that the region be declared a "zone of peace" from which the superpowers and nuclear weapons would be banned. The United Nations considered such a resolution on several occasions. In 1970, the Lusaka Conference of Nonaligned States recommended neutralization of the region. And in 1977, President Carter said he hoped to establish "mutual military restraint in the Indian Ocean" with the Soviet Union. A U.S.-Soviet working group was established; it met in Moscow, Washington and Berne, but it became apparent in 1978 that the idea was going nowhere.

Tensions remain high in one of the world's great ocean basins.

CHAPTER 18

The Arms Trade

World trade in arms is booming. The U.S. is the largest exporter of arms; the Soviet Union is second, France third, Great Britain fourth. The worldwide export of arms totaled $8.7 billion in 1973, compared to $4.4 billion ten years earlier and more than $20 billion in 1977.

In 1973, the U.S. led the world in arms sales with $4.7 billion, and the Soviet Union followed with $2.4 billion, France with $540 million, and Great Britain with $315 million. Four years later, the U.S. sold $11.3 billion worth of arms abroad, the Soviet Union an estimated $4 billion, France $2.9 billion, Britain $1.5 billion. West Germany exported $1 billion worth of arms, Italy $690 million, Israel $400 million. Other suppliers were Australia, Canada, China, the Netherlands, Sweden and Switzerland.

The arms trade has grown rapidly and consistently since World War II, the Stockholm International Peace Research Institute (SIPRI) has remarked. "But after the 1973 Arab-Israeli War the growth in this trade can only be described as explosive. The arms trade is now virtually out of control."

The most sophisticated conventional weapons systems are being demanded and received. Supplying countries are generally no longer reluctant to export even newly developed conventional weapons. Arms for export include British Chieftain tanks, Soviet SAM-2 and SAM-3 air defense systems, Belgian machine guns, Swedish laser-guided antiaircraft missiles, U.S. *Spruance*-class antisubmarine destroyers, French Mirage fighters, Israeli Uzi submachine guns.

Moreover, many recent arms contracts go far beyond the transfer of weapons—they include training, technical support, the establishment of maintenance and repair facilities in the pur-

chasing country, and construction projects, SIPRI said.

The chief clients were developing, or Third World, countries in the Middle East, Far East and Latin America. About 75 per cent of the trade in major weapons was with the developing countries. During the 1970s, this trade increased at an annual rate of 15 per cent. The Middle East was the most militarized region in

DELIVERIES OF U.S. MILITARY SALES
(in U.S. thousands)

	Fiscal Year 1978	Fiscal Years 1950-78
Australia	151,791	1,213,393
Belgium	28,039	183,548
China (Taiwan)	131,109	823,992
Egypt	50,794	61,684
Germany, West	238,544	5,779,056
Greece	128,050	1,072,784
Iran*	1,792,892	8,715,810
Israel	951,383	5,348,530
Italy	28,856	689,393
Japan	42,421	443,113
Jordan	110,842	490,156
Kenya	50,399	51,438
Korea, South	414,336	846,268
Kuwait	190,755	373,085
Morocco	89,097	175,042
Norway	28,750	318,338
Pakistan	48,336	215,475
Saudi Arabia	2.317,878	6,175,742
Spain	69,127	599,218
Sudan	47,376	47,376
Switzerland	48,806	244,334
Thailand	95,137	185,783
Turkey	159,875	422,530
United Kingdom	91,730	1,944,673
Yemen, North (Sana)	27,751	54,708

*Deliveries halted by 1979 after overthrow of shah's regime

Source: Security Assistance Agency, U.S. Defense Department

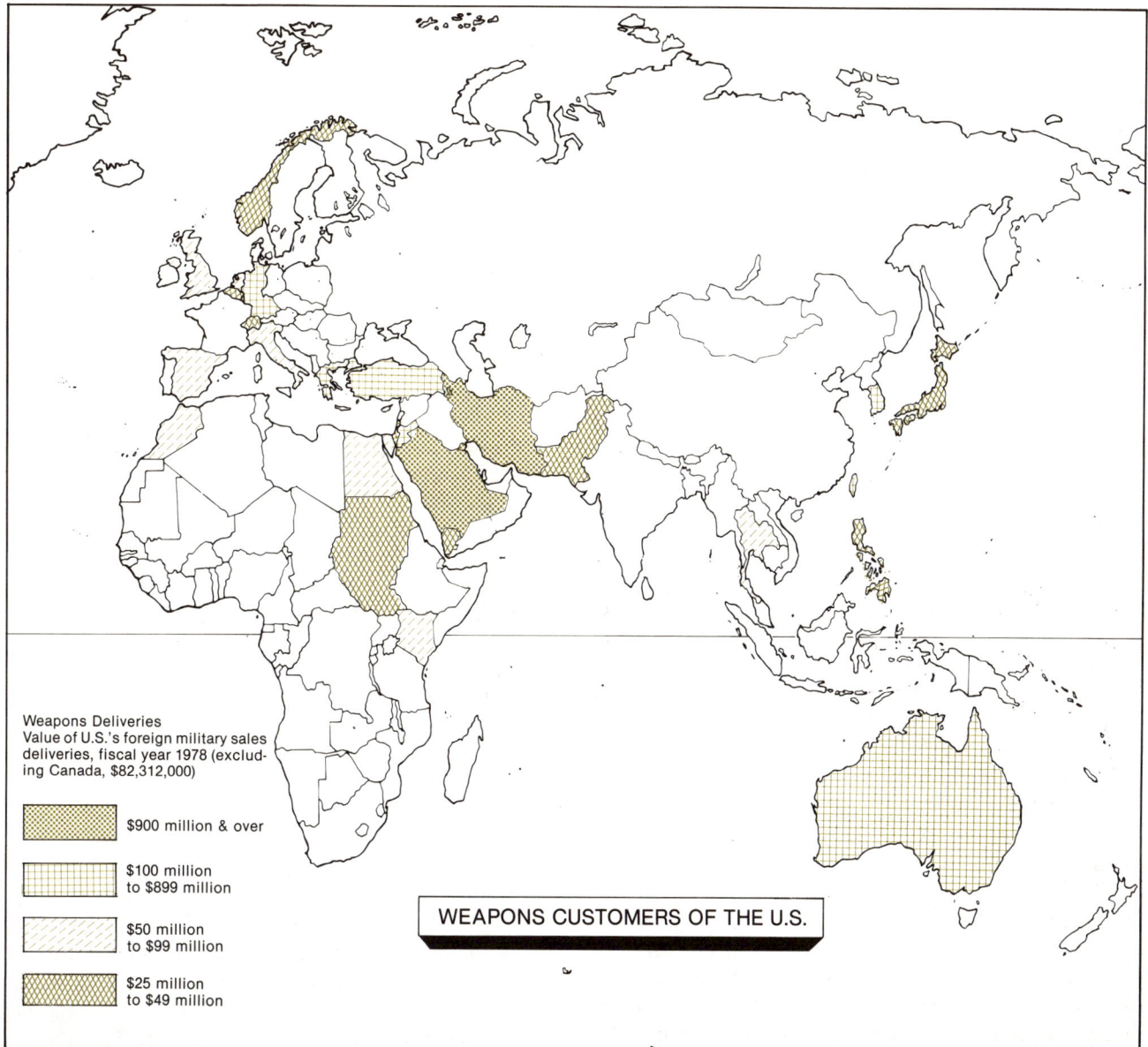

Weapons Deliveries
Value of U.S.'s foreign military sales
deliveries, fiscal year 1978 (excluding Canada, $82,312,000)

$900 million & over

$100 million
to $899 million

$50 million
to $99 million

$25 million
to $49 million

WEAPONS CUSTOMERS OF THE U.S.

The U.S., Soviet Union, France, Great Britain and West Germany provide about four-fifths of the world's arms exports. The U.S. is the largest arms exporter. In fiscal 1978, as the map indicates, its leading customers were Iran and Saudi Arabia. Other top arms recipients included Australia, South Korea, Taiwan, Turkey, West Germany. "In general," says the U.S. Arms Control & Disarmament Agency, "military expenditures increased in almost all regions of the world throughout the 1967-1976 period, even after adjustment for inflation. Overall, in real terms, the nations of the world spent nearly 20 per cent more for military purposes in 1976 than they had 10 years earlier."

the world and accounted for a total of 51 per cent of all major arms imports. Iran was the single country with the largest arms imports in the region, reaching 30 per cent of the total value for the Middle East during 1970–76.

The Far East was the second largest arms importing region. In South Asia, India was the biggest importer, depending heavily on the Soviet Union; Bangladesh and Afghanistan were other Soviet customers. Pakistan bought most of its heavy weapons from China. In Latin America, the U.S. position as the dominant arms supplier had declined in favor of France and Great Britain, while several large orders, particularly for submarines, had been placed with West Germany. Brazil and Argentina were the largest importers in the region.

Among industrialized nations, the trade in arms has been comparatively stable. It ranged

'MERCHANTS OF DEATH'

The great private arms manufacturers formerly were the subject of investigation and scorn as "merchants of death."

In 1921, the League of Nations' Temporary Mixed Commission on Armaments took a look at the international armament firms and suggested that they "have been active in fomenting war scares and in persuading their own countries to adopt warlike policies; have attempted to bribe government officials both at home and abroad; have organized international armament monopolies which have increased the price of armaments sold to governments."

In 1934, at the time of the U.S. Senate's munitions inquiry by the Nye Committee, the study *Merchants of Death,* by Helmuth C. Engelbrecht and Frank C. Hanighen, was a best-seller. The authors wrote: ". . . The arms industry has moved forward with growing momentum. . . . All these technical improvements, all the international mergers, the cooperation between governments and the industry bear an uncomfortable resemblance to the situation during the epoch preceding 1914. Is this present situation necessarily a preparation for another world struggle and what, if any, are the solutions to these problems?"

Governments conduct the arms trade today, and the products of arms manufacturers are an integral expression of a nation's economy and foreign policy.

in most years between 1963 and 1973 from $3 to $4 billion, twice dropping below $3 billion.

The U.S. has supported arms standardization in the forces of the North Atlantic Treaty Organization. But the export market had persuaded European countries to develop their own weapons systems. Consequently, *The Times* pointed out, NATO has "seven main battle tanks, 22 anti-tank weapons and two dozen models of combat aircraft. There is no longer a standard rifle bullet. Six tactical communications systems are being planned for the next five years, and no one can communicate directly with another. . . ."

The Americans "must be prepared to balance the trade by looking seriously at European products," according to a leading Dutch legislator. Last year, the U.S. took a step in that direction, announcing that its new XM-1 tank would be armed with a West German 120-millimeter gun. The German gun would be produced in the U.S. under license.

Many rationales for the arms trade have been offered. It promotes peace, enables nations to defend themselves, improves the balance of pay-

ments, offsets the increased cost of oil, permits the exerting of influence.

As a candidate for President in 1976, however, Jimmy Carter presented an opposing view. Carter deplored the U.S. role as "the world's leading arms salesman," mostly to developing countries. "Can we be both the world's leading champion of peace and the world's leading supplier of the weapons of war?" he asked. Soon after he took office, he announced a program aimed at reducing arms sales abroad. Sales would be made only in exceptional instances. The U.S. would not be the first supplier to introduce a new weapon into a region. Coproduction agreements for weapons, equipment and components would be prohibited. "From the outset, this policy was widely criticized as unrealistic and unworkable," *U.S. News & World Report* commented. "Some critics warned that if the Administration really attempted to implement the plan, the U.S. would be handcuffed in its conduct of foreign policy." It was said by many that the program had not survived last year's $4.8 billion sale of warplanes to Saudi Arabia, Egypt and Israel.

The control of the ever-increasing arms trade is "unquestionably an urgent necessity," SIPRI emphasized, adding that the distinction between conventional and nuclear weapons may be difficult to justify in the future.

"Already, some types of nuclear *delivery* systems have been transferred to Third World countries (for example, the U.S. Lance surface-to-surface missile to Israel and the Soviet Scud to Egypt, Iraq and Syria), and if the spread of production capacity for nuclear weapons in the wake of the spread of nuclear energy production is not safeguarded in time, the arms traffic may eventually come to include traffic also in nuclear weapons."

Top 10 U.S. Defense Contractors In Fiscal 1977

McDonnell Douglas Corp.	$2.57 billion
Lockheed Corp.	1.67 billion
United Technologies Corp.	1.58 billion
Boeing Co.	1.58 billion
General Electric Co.	1.52 billion
Rockwell International Corp.	1.48 billion
Grumman Corp.	1.43 billion
General Dynamics Corp.	1.37 billion
Hughes Aircraft Co.	1.09 billion
Northrop Corp.	1.05 billion

Source: U.S. Defense Department

The Arms Merchants
In order of Sales to the Third World 1970–76

Supplier	Value of arms supplied (In U.S. $ millions)	Per cent of world total	Largest recipient regions	Region's per cent of supplier's total	Largest recipient country in each region	Country's per cent of supplier's total
U.S.A.	12,303	38	Middle East	62	Iran	31
			Far East	27	S. Viet Nam	12
			South America	7	Brazil	2
U.S.S.R.	11,057	34	Middle East	57	Syria	23
			North Africa	13	Libya	13
			Far East	13	N. Viet Nam	7
U.K.	3,076	9	Middle East	49	Iran	26
			South America	22	Chile	8
			South Asia	14	India	12
France	2,963	9	North Africa	24	Libya	16
			Middle East	23	Egypt	5
			South America	18	Venezuela	6
Italy	562	2	Middle East	40	Iran	34
			South Africa	27	South Africa	27
			South America	18	Brazil	10
China	537	2	South Asia	46	Pakistan	46
			Far East	29	N. Viet Nam	11
			Sub-Saharan Africa	25	Tanzania	16
West Germany	451	1	South America	74	Argentina	22
			Far East	10	Singapore	6
			Sub-Saharan Africa	6	Nigeria	2
Netherlands	214	0.7	Middle East	40	Iran	28
			Sub-Saharan Africa	25	Nigeria	10
			South America	9	Argentina	6
Canada	178	0.6	South America	60	Peru	23
			Sub-Saharan Africa	28	Zambia	9
			Middle East	4	Lebanon	3
Czechoslovakia	87	0.3	South Asia	59	India	59
			Middle East	30	Egypt	11
			Sub-Saharan Africa	7	Sudan	7
Spain	70	0.2	South America	82	Uruguay	51
			Far East	11	Indonesia	11
			Middle East	7	Jordan	7
Australia	60	0.2	Far East	82	Indonesia	50
			South America	15	Brazil	14
			Middle East	2	Oman	2
Sweden	54	0.2	South Asia	87	Pakistan	87
			South America	9	Chile	9
			Sub-Saharan Africa	4	Sierra Leone	4
Poland	30	0.1	South Asia	99	India	99
			Far East	0.7	Indonesia	0.7
Yugoslavia	24	0.1	Middle East	78	Egypt	70
			Sub-Saharan Africa	22	Tanzania	13
Switzerland	17	0.1	South America	59	Argentina	41
			Far East	18	Thailand	18
			Middle East	12	Oman	12
New Zealand	12	0.04	South Asia	77	India	77
			Far East	23	Thailand	17
Japan	6	0.02	Far East	50	Philippines	50
			Sub-Saharan Africa	50	Zaire	50
Belgium	5	0.02	South Africa	50	South Africa	50
			Sub-Saharan Africa	50	Ethiopia	50
Ireland	2	0.01	Middle East	100	Oman	100
Third World countries	724	2	South Africa	24	South Africa	24
			Sub-Saharan Africa	19	Uganda	15
			South Asia	18	Pakistan	12
World total	32,427	100				

Table from Stockholm Peace Research Institute *Yearbook* 1978 (reprinted by permission)

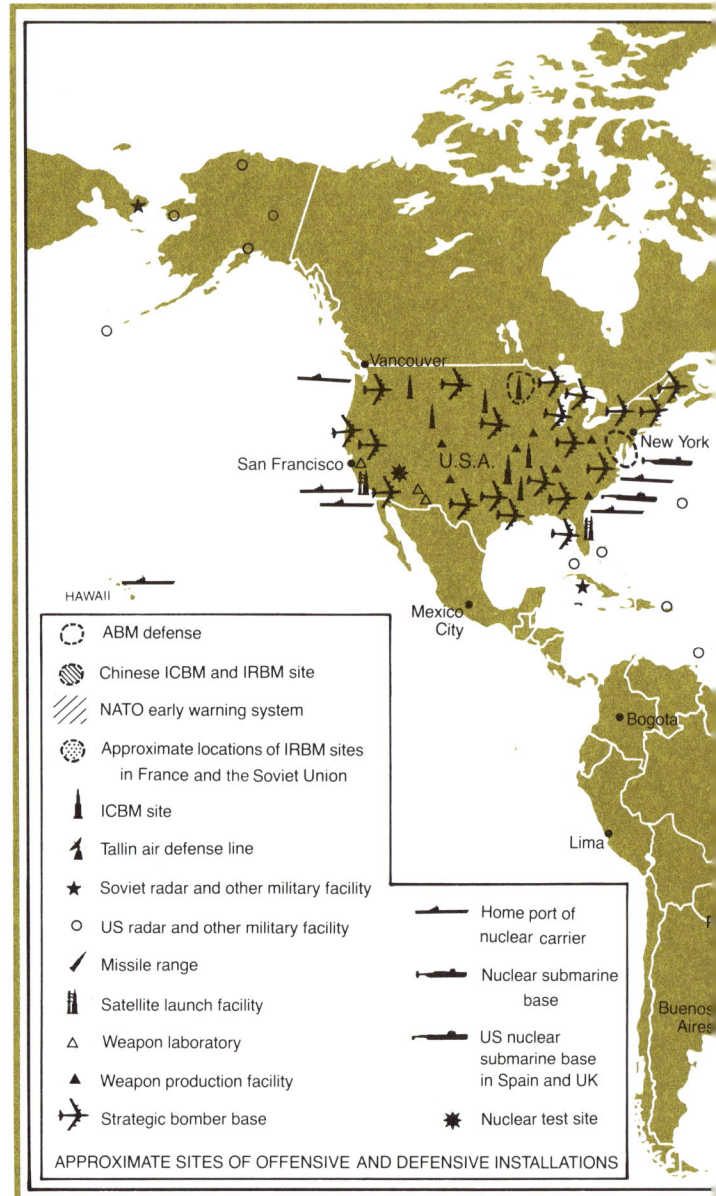

⊂⊃	ABM defense
◎	Chinese ICBM and IRBM site
⫽	NATO early warning system
⊛	Approximate locations of IRBM sites in France and the Soviet Union
▐	ICBM site
◢	Tallin air defense line
★	Soviet radar and other military facility
○	US radar and other military facility
◿	Missile range
▆	Satellite launch facility
△	Weapon laboratory
▲	Weapon production facility
✈	Strategic bomber base
▬▬	Home port of nuclear carrier
⬓▬	Nuclear submarine base
⬓▬	US nuclear submarine base in Spain and UK
✸	Nuclear test site

APPROXIMATE SITES OF OFFENSIVE AND DEFENSIVE INSTALLATIONS

These maps dramatically illustrate the general location and variety of nuclear weapons installations in the U.S., Western Europe and the Soviet Union. The inset map suggests the probable range of the effects of nuclear warfare in one area. A report by the U.N. Secretary General points out: "In certain quarters it is still military doctrine that any disparity in the conventional strength of opposing forces could be redressed by using nuclear weapons.... [W]ere nuclear weapons to be used ... they could lead to the devastation of the whole battle zone. Almost everything would be destroyed...." The possibility of nuclear war makes it essential that its effects be clearly and widely understood, the report adds. Six nations today have atomic warheads — the U.S., U.S.S.R., Britain, France, China and India. Israel is believed to have them. Further proliferation is a serious danger.

CHAPTER 19

Nuclear Arms Proliferation

Nuclear proliferation, an awesome issue, actually comprises three issues. The first question is the spread of nuclear arms. The second is the development of nuclear power. The third is nuclear disarmament. Each issue leads or gives rise to the other. Much of the time, they are obscured: the facts are not clear; events push past them.

There are moments, though, when the issues are plainly stated. "A multi-proliferated world would not be a stable world," declares Joseph S. Nye, deputy to the U.S. under secretary of state for security assistance, science and technology.

"But it is too late for nuclear power to be solely the toy of the industrialized democracies. Whether the nuclear opposition likes it or not,

BALANCE OF TERROR

Nuclear Offensive and Defensive Installations

Estimated fall-out contamination area after a 15-megaton nuclear explosion on London. Radiation dose is given for 36 hours after detonation.

Principal sources: Stockholm International Peace Research Institute and United Nations

the rest of the world is going nuclear," admonishes *The Economist* of London. "Total power is being wedded to total madness. The official delusion persists that we can buy security with superbombs. What we are buying instead is a colossal suicide pact," warns Norman Cousins.

Six countries are known to have atomic bombs—the U.S., the Soviet Union, Great Britain, France, China and India. Israel is believed to have them. In 1977, the U.S.S.R. asserted that South Africa was "nearing completion" of an atomic bomb; France warned South Africa of "serious consequences" if it staged a nuclear weapons test. John Vorster, then South African prime minister, denied that South Africa was developing nuclear weapons. Other countries

expected to have the capacity to build the bomb include Argentina, Brazil, Iran, Pakistan, South Korea, Spain. A number of countries— Canada, Sweden, Switzerland, West Germany and Japan—have the technical competence and resources to make atomic bombs but have produced none—yet. One observer predicted that if Korea got the bomb it would reverse Japanese anti-nuclear public opinion overnight.

The Non-Proliferation Treaty (NPT) of 1968 had been intended to prevent the spread of nuclear weapons. Nuclear powers had pledged not to transfer nuclear weapons to non-nuclear states, which in turn had agreed not to seek them. Safeguards for the operation of nuclear power plants were to be supervised by the U.N. International Atomic Energy Agency (IAEA).

Of late the treaty has been assailed as a failure. Several countries with the potentiality of producing atomic weapons have not signed the treaty.

Furthermore, the development of nuclear power and nuclear weapons are linked. A nonnuclear state can buy a reactor and use it as a springboard to nuclear explosives. Example: India set off a nuclear device in 1974 with material from a reactor furnished by Canada. Recently, West Germany contracted to sell Brazil eight reactors as well as fuel-reprocessing and uranium-enrichment plants. The price was $8 billion. The U.S. protested the sale, but West Germany insisted on going ahead with it. West Germany also contracted to build four nuclear plants in Iran. ". . . None of the nuclear exporting nations is willing to limit its nuclear exports to states agreeing to place all their nuclear activities under IAEA safeguards," Denis Hayes writes in his book *Rays of Hope: The Transition to a Post-Petroleum World.* "None wishes to lose a potential sale. . . ."

IAEA safeguards, themselves, are viewed by critics as insufficient to prevent the diversion of nuclear technology and materials to weapons' development. The agency's budget and staff are too small. And it has no authority to take action against violations other than to announce them. Since 1975, a group of nuclear exporting nations—the "London Club"—has been attempting to tighten up the rules. In 1977, they agreed on guidelines. Some adopted a more restrictive nuclear exporting policy than others. However, the guidelines require safeguards only on imported facilities and material. "This is a major weakness," says Frank Barnaby, director of the Stockholm International Peace Research Institute. "The fact that countries outside the NPT are subject to less stringent safeguards than those in it is an absurdity."

In the meantime, the superpowers discuss arms control measures that permit the existence of a very high level of arms. The possibility of disarmament is not taken seriously. Conscientious warnings about the consequences of nuclear war are delivered periodically. "The basic facts about the nuclear bomb and its use are harsh and terrifying for civilization; they have become lost in a mass of theoretical verbi-

MAJOR ARMS CONTROL
PACTS EVALUATED

(Evaluations of treaties, in quotation marks, by Stockholm International Peace Research Institute.)

1958 Antarctic Treaty provides that Antarctica shall be used exclusively for peaceful purposes; 19 signatories. "It is an important demilitarization measure. But it will be in constant jeopardy as long as the question of territorial sovereignty in Antarctica has not been definitely resolved."

1963 Partial Test Ban Treaty banned nuclear weapon tests in the atmosphere, outer space and under water; 108 signatories. "It has helped to curb radioactive pollution caused by nuclear explosions. But continued testing underground has made it possible for the nuclear weapon parties to the treaty to develop new generations of nuclear warheads."

1967 Outer Space Treaty prohibited the placing of nuclear or other weapons of mass destruction in orbit around earth; 77 signatories. "Weapons of mass destruction in outer space present apparently insurmountable problems of maintenance, command and control, making it easy for the nuclear-weapon powers to forgo them."

1967 Treaty of Tlatelolco bars nuclear weapons from Latin America; 22 signatories. "It will not achieve its principal goal until Argentina and Brazil, the only countries in the area with any nuclear potential and aspirations, are bound by its provisions."

1968 Non-Proliferation Treaty prohibits transfer of nuclear weapons by nuclear-weapon states and acquisition by non-nuclear-weapon states; 103 signatories. "It is being gradually eroded because of the inconsistent policies of the nuclear-material suppliers, the non-fulfilment of the obligations undertaken by the nuclear-weapon powers, and the lack of guarantees that nuclear weapons will not be used against non-nuclear-weapon states."

1972 SALT Interim Agreement froze the total number of U.S. and Soviet ballistic missile launchers; entered into force Oct. 3, 1972. "But it has not restricted the qualitative improvement of nuclear weapons—their survivability, accuracy, penetrativity and range. Moreover, the number of nuclear charges carried by each missile has been allowed to proliferate."

1974 Threshold Test Ban Treaty limited the size of U.S. and Soviet nuclear-weapon test explosions to 150 kilotons; not in force by Dec. 31, 1977. "The threshold is so high (ten times higher than the yield of the Hiroshima bomb) that the parties cannot be experiencing onerous restraint in continuing their nuclear-weapon development programs."

The United Nations General Assembly in May-June 1978 met (above) for the first special session it had ever held on disarmament. The meeting had been called a year and a half earlier on the expressed conviction that "peace can be secured through the implementation of disarmament measures, particularly of nuclear disarmament...."

age," the U.N. says in one report of many. A twenty-megaton* explosion on the city of Boston would cause such a degree of fall-out over an area with a radius of nearly thirty miles that

*Equivalent to the destructive power of twenty million tons of TNT.

half of the unsheltered people on the fringe of this area would die within forty-eight hours. Even if shelters were provided, high doses of radiation might be received that, even if not fatal, could still produce extensive radiation sickness as well as long-term somatic and genetic damage. It also has been estimated that in the absence of special protection, blast-induced deaths alone resulting from 400 high-level ten-megaton bombs, aimed at U.S. metropolitan areas, would kill more than half of the American people. Even if they were all in substantial fall-out shelters, the same proportion would be killed if the weapons were burst at ground level.

'THE MOST ACUTE AND URGENT TASK'

"We did not, obviously, make a major breakthrough towards halting the arms race," Lazar Mojsov of Yugoslavia, president of the U.N. General Assembly, said at the conclusion of its special session on disarmament, attended by 149 countries in New York May 23–July 1, 1978. "We were not able to agree on new and meaningful disarmament measures. What we have not accomplished now, we will do later. What we have done is to chart a new course and open new channels for further negotiations."

The main achievement of the special session was the establishment of a new negotiating body to replace the Geneva Disarmament Conference, which had met on and off since 1962. Thirty-one nations had taken part in the conference, with the U.S. and U.S.S.R. as co-chairmen. The new group is designated as the Committee on Disar-

mament. In addition to the nuclear-weapon states, the committee will be open to 32 to 35 other states.

It is expected that France and eventually China will join the committee's talks. Neither participated in the Geneva conference.

The session adopted by consensus a "final document" on disarmament negotiations. It emphasized: ". . . Unfortunately . . . the arms race is not diminishing but increasing and outstrips by far the efforts to curb it. . . . There has not been . . . any real progress that might lead to the conclusion of a treaty on general and complete disarmament under effective international control. . . .

"Removing the threat of a world war—a nuclear war—is the most acute and urgent task of the present day. . . ."

Terrorism is a political instrument. Its occurrence as a global phenomenon is indicated by the locations of a representative sampling of major terrorist events of the past decade, as shown on the map. On July 31, 1970, for example, Dan A. Mitrione of the U.S. Agency for International Development, assigned to advise the Uruguayan police, was kidnapped in Montevideo by the Tupamaros; his body was found ten days later. A bomb explosion Feb. 22, 1972 at the Aldershot army base, 35 miles from London, killed five waitresses, a gardener and an army chaplain; the Official Irish Republican Army took credit for the blast as retaliation for the "Londonderry massacre." (In Londonderry, Northern Ireland, British paratroopers Jan. 30 had shot to death 13 persons who were taking part in a march in defiance of a government ban on demonstrations.) Patricia Hearst, 19, granddaughter of the late newspaper publisher William Randolph Hearst, was kidnapped Feb. 5, 1974 from her Berkeley, Calif. apartment by the Symbionese Liberation Army (SLA); six suspected members of the SLA died in a gun battle and ensuing fire after police surrounded their Los Angeles hideout May 17. Seven pro-Palestinian terrorists hijacked an Air France jetliner June 27, 1976 and forced it to Entebbe airport in Uganda; Israeli commandoes landed at the airport July 3, freed the airliner's remaining 91 passengers and 12 crew members, and flew them to Israel. In 1978, former Premier Aldo Moro of Italy was kidnapped by Red Brigades terrorists March 16, and his five bodyguards were killed; Moro's body was found May 9 in a parked car in the center of Rome.

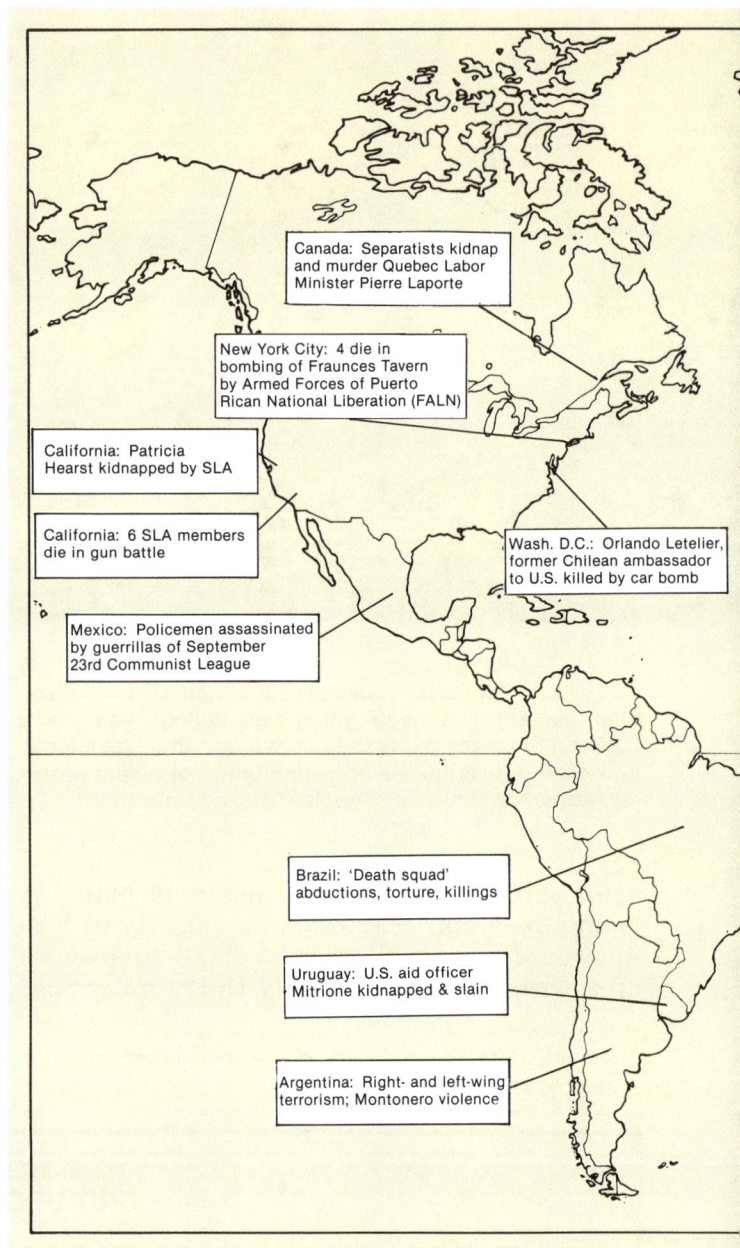

Canada: Separatists kidnap and murder Quebec Labor Minister Pierre Laporte

New York City: 4 die in bombing of Fraunces Tavern by Armed Forces of Puerto Rican National Liberation (FALN)

California: Patricia Hearst kidnapped by SLA

California: 6 SLA members die in gun battle

Wash. D.C.: Orlando Letelier, former Chilean ambassador to U.S. killed by car bomb

Mexico: Policemen assassinated by guerrillas of September 23rd Communist League

Brazil: 'Death squad' abductions, torture, killings

Uruguay: U.S. aid officer Mitrione kidnapped & slain

Argentina: Right- and left-wing terrorism; Montonero violence

CHAPTER 20

Terrorism

Terrorism is more than an international puzzle. At times it assumes the proportions of a tragic joke. It changes constantly, yet in the timeworn phrase, *"plus ça change, plus c'est la même chose."* Yesterday's terrorist may be today's prime minister—and tomorrow's dictator. Attitudes toward terrorism frequently are based on the answer to the question: whose ox is gored?

Fashions in terror change. Last year, diplomatic "bully-boys" were deployed for the first time, and their advent recorded by the press. In *Le Monde* (Paris), under the headline "Diplomacy not what it used to be," a cartoon por-

West Germany: Arab and Baader-Meinhof terrorist actions

Netherlands: South Moluccan extremists seize train and school

thern Ireland: Bombings shootings punctuate tarian violence

and: IRA bomb kills 7 dershot Army base

Italy: Red Brigades kidnap and murder ex-Premier Aldo Moro

Israel: Repeated terrorist attacks by PLO commandos

Spain: Terror campaign by Basque separatists

Japan: $6 million ransom paid to Red Army members who hijack airliner to Dacca, Bangladesh

Uganda: Israeli commandos rescue terrorist hostages at Entebbe

Congo: President Marien Ngouabi assassinated

Rhodesia: Incidents of terrorism accompany rebellion and guerrilla activity

TERRORISM AROUND THE WORLD
(Significant terrorist strikes and areas in which terrorists operate)

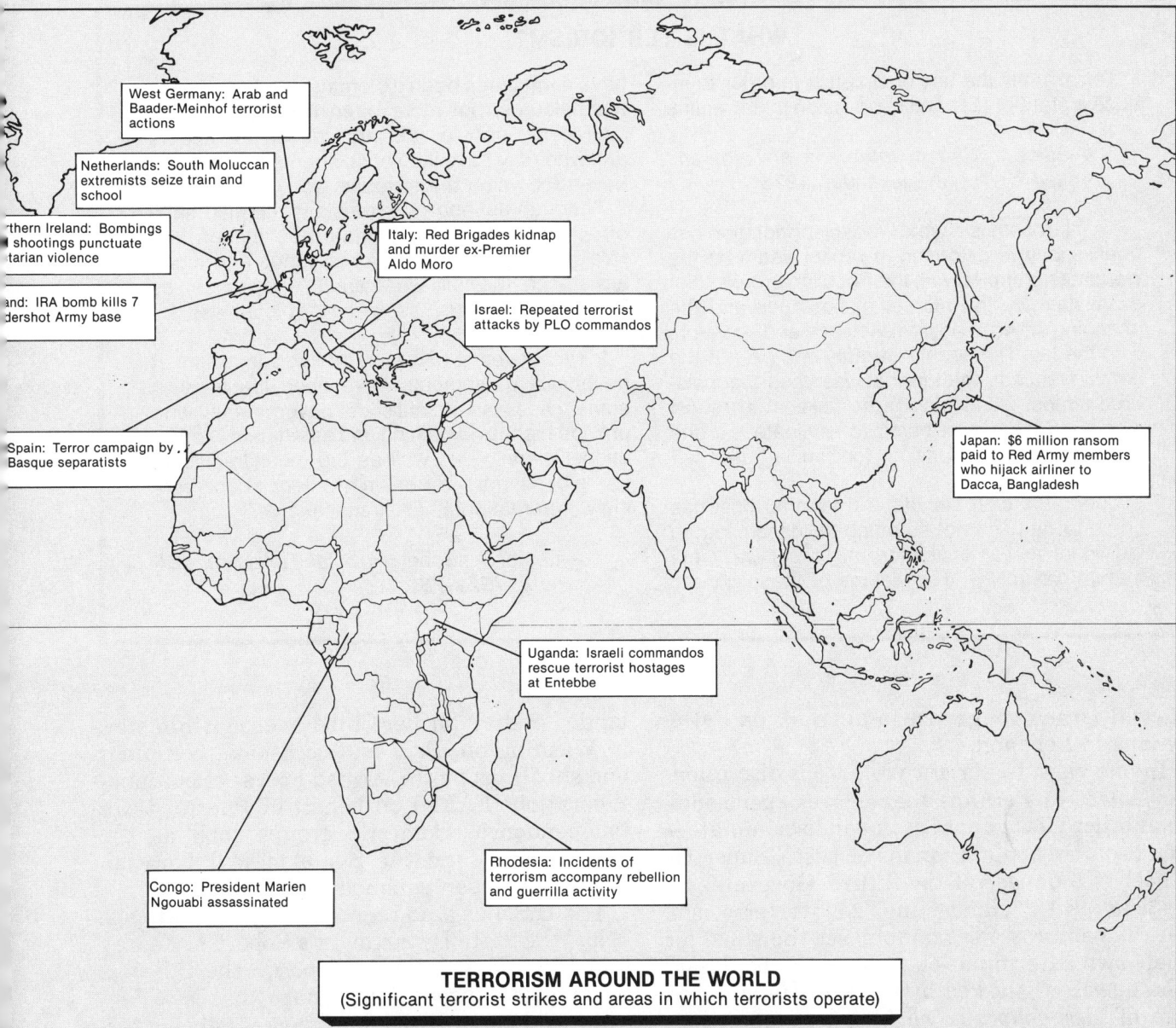

trayed a determined man firing an automatic pistol. "[D]iplomats . . . blazing away at policemen in the middle of the street . . ., that had never been seen until now," *Le Monde* observed. The cartoon and comment referred to an incident in which an Arab terrorist shot his way into the Iraqi embassy in Paris and held eight persons hostage until surrendering to police; as the captured terrorist was being taken away, embassy functionaries fired at him but missed, killing a French policeman.

Some experts contend that the incidence of terrorism is diminishing. Others assert that it is not on the wane. Writing in the *Christian Science Monitor* Sept. 7, 1978, Anthony Quainton, director of the Office for Combatting Terrorism in the U.S. Department of State, said bombings, kidnapping and assassinations were still taking place with unrelenting regularity. Terrorist attacks had taken a dramatic downturn, the *Monitor* reported the following week. The newspaper cited a Central Intelligence Agency (CIA) study that found terrorist incidents totaled 279 in 1977, 413 the previous year.

Meanwhile, the *Monitor* editorializes: "Humanity's capacity for fellow-feeling continues to be tested. . . . As the slaughter of the innocents goes on and on, the temptation is to give in to . . . callousness. . . . But the hundreds of men, women, and children killed in Iran's terrorist theater fire were real people. . . . So was the stewardess slain by Palestinian terrorists as she rode on a bus . . . in London. So were the victims

WHAT IS TERRORISM?

Terrorism is the use of violence in order to induce a state of fear and submission in the victim. . . .

—Saleem Qureshi, *International Terrorism,* edited by Yonah Alexander, 1976

. . . Terrorism is a word whose connotation has been subtly transformed in recent years as the world has grappled with the troubling problems of assassination, the murder of hostages and the changing styles of political violence and coercion.

In the late Nineteenth Century and on into the early Twentieth, the terrorist was usually considered almost identical with the political extremist who used his gun or bomb to eliminate the one individual who personified, for him, a hated tyranny. . . .

During the past decade, the term terrorist has come to be used not so much for describing an individual as for characterizing a politically extremist group. . . . The victims of these groups have sometimes been diplomats or other government figures, but more often they seem to be "innocent" people who are chosen at random and who may have little or no connection with the cause for which the terrorists act.

Although nationalist terrorists in the past have often depended on expatriate countrymen and foreign sympathizers for arms, funds and moral assistance, they still were almost always seen as being autonomous, as being "in business for themselves." . . .

In recent years, however, foreign supporters of nationalist movements have been identified in some cases as established governments who provide high-level training and assistance in operational planning as well as the more traditional forms of support. Terrorism has become increasingly "international" or "transnational." . . .

—Lester A. Sobel, *Political Terrorism, Volume 2, 1974–78*

of swift Israeli vengeance in air raids on Palestinians in Lebanon. . . ."

In one view, terroristic violence is discretionary, selective. Perhaps, the reverse of genocidal. In another view, it has become indiscriminate—and far more brutal than in the past. "Superviolence" is a danger of the future. Governments respond with clandestine counterterrorism. The Tupamaros, for example, set the stage for their own extermination. Who is the big loser? The question is asked by Bernard-Henri Levy, one of *"les nouveaux philosophes"* of France and the author of *La barbarie a visage humain.* The authentic dissident, he replies. Levy, in an article in *The New Republic,* then offers an extended metaphor. He writes: ". . . To the menace of genocide that states carry within themselves, terrorists answer with more, always more atom bombs; that is to say, with P.38 pistols. Children of Hiroshima, the guerrillas never cease to harp upon that primitive scene." And he concludes, "It is not a justification of them to say that . . . they are the toys of a terror that in fact does not belong to them. . . ." He considers terrorism as the "double" of war and preparations for war.

Unlike the countries of the Middle East and Western Europe, the U.S. has not been greatly troubled by international terrorism, although incidents of it have occurred—the killing of Orlando Letelier, former Chilean foreign minister, in Washington, D.C., and occasional bombings and shootings by the Armed Forces of National Liberation (FALN) on behalf of Puerto Rican independence. Domestic groups such as the Weathermen and the Symbionese Liberation Army have been subdued.

The U.S. has a no-ransom policy on hostages. "No," the State Department's Robert A. Fearey told *U.S. News & World Report,* "the U.S. has never paid ransom—and I hope that is widely known." Fearey listed four ways of fighting terrorism. Intelligence gathering. Physical security. Arresting perpetrators. Eliminating underlying causes, inequities and frustrations.

Major organization changes have been made within the executive branch to combat terrorism, Secretary of State Cyrus R. Vance testified last year before the Senate Committee on Governmental Affairs. President Carter had reorganized the National Security Council (NSC). A Special Coordination Committee (SCC) had been set up to handle, among other matters, crisis management. The SCC is headed by Zbigniew Brzezinski, national security affairs adviser; its members are the statutory members of the NSC and other senior officials. The SCC supervises a senior-level interagency group that coordinates agencies dealing with terrorism. The executive committee of the interagency group consists of representatives from the Departments of State, Defense, Justice, Treasury, Transportation and Energy, and the CIA and NSC. "... Specialized units in the U.S. intelligence community, as well as other agencies of the federal government," Vance said, "place high priority on the collection and evaluation of necessary intelligence. . . ."

International control efforts have been hesitant, many countries divided on the issue. The U.N. has yet to take action on a 1954 draft code that defines terrorist activities as an offense against peace. The Tokyo (1963), Hague (1970) and Montreal (1971) conventions provide for the apprehension, prosecution and extradition of those who hijack or sabotage commercial aircraft. Sixty-two countries have ratified the three conventions; 55 ratified none. In 1977, the U.N. General Assembly passed a resolution condemning hijacking and asking all nations to improve airport security. The resolution was adopted by consensus, without a formal vote, and was not binding on U.N. members. An *ad hoc* U.N. committee has been established to draft a convention against the taking of hostages. The committee divided itself into two working groups. The first working group will examine the more difficult questions and try to find some common ground by means of consultations; the second working group will concern itself with draft articles that are non-controversial.

On many votes, Arab and African members of the U.N. oppose anti-terrorist action. The issue is not clear-cut. Critical references to violence are balanced by affirmations of the right to self-determination, to condemn repressive acts by "colonial, racist and alien" regimes. Differing perspectives and clashing interests of different states make it difficult to secure an international consensus about which specific acts constitute terrorism as well as about which acts are political and which are simply crimes, Saleem Qureshi observes in the volume *International Terrorism*.

"Until the world settles in a new pattern of relationships," wrote David Watt in the *Financial Times* (London), "we must rely upon our expensively purchased knowledge of terrorist psychology and the skill and nerves of individual governments and individual air pilots. Caution and cunning, rather than bravado, are the most valuable commodities here, and we must foster them as best we can."

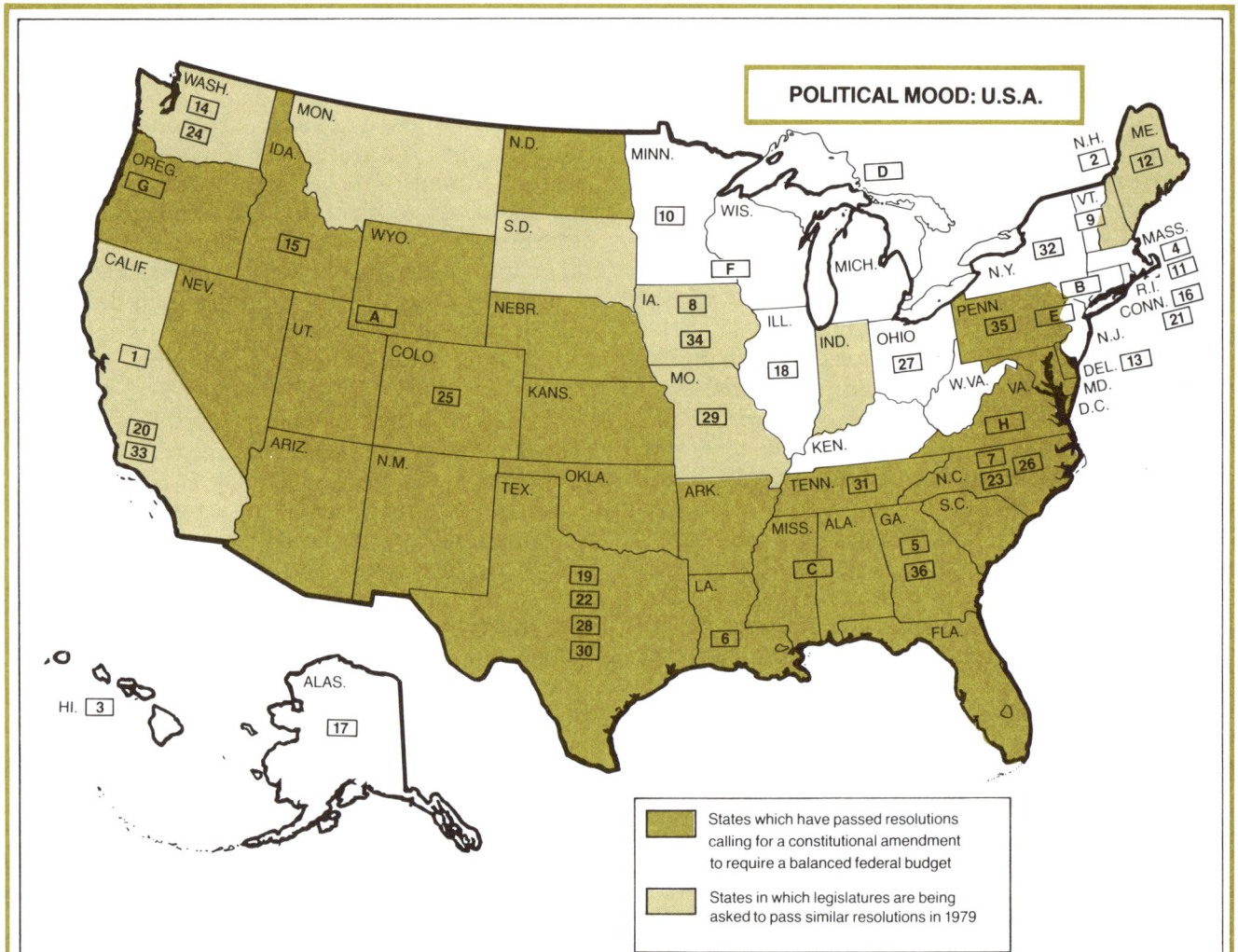

POLITICAL MOOD: U.S.A.

States which have passed resolutions calling for a constitutional amendment to require a balanced federal budget

States in which legislatures are being asked to pass similar resolutions in 1979

Major Anticipatory Democracy Projects in the United States

GROUP	DATE

The States
1. California Tomorrow — 1961
2. New Hampshire Tomorrow — 1969
3. Hawaii Commission on the Year 2000 — 1970
4. Massachusetts Tomorrow — 1971
5. Goals for Georgia — 1971
6. Goals for Louisiana — 1971
7. North Carolina Board Goals and Policy — 1971
8. Iowa 2000 — 1972
9. Vermont Tomorrow — 1973
10. Commission of Minnesota's Future
11. Massachusetts' Special Legislative Commission on the Effect of Patterns of Growth on the Quality of Life in the Commonwealth — 1973
12. Commission on Maine's Future — 1974
13. Delaware Tomorrow Commission — 1974
14. Alternatives for Washington — 1974
15. Idaho's Tomorrow — 1975
16. Commission on Connecticut's Future — 1976
17. Alaska Growth Policy Council — 1977
18. Illinois 2000 — 1977

Localities
19. Goals for Dallas — 1965
20. Los Angeles Goals Program — 1965
21. Greater Hartford Process — 1969
22. Fort Worth Sector Planning Program — 1969
23. Goals for Raleigh-Wake (North Carolina) — 1972
24. Seattle 2000 — 1972
25. Boulder Growth Study Commission (Colorado) — 1972
26. Dimensions for Charlotte-Mecklenburg (North Carolina) — 1973
27. Goals for the Greater Akron Area — 1973
28. Austin Tomorrow — 1973
29. Kansas City (Missouri) Alternative Futures — 1973
30. Goals for Corpus Christi — 1974
31. Nashville Citizen Goals 2000 Committee — 1974
32. Norwich, Citizens Unlimited (New York) — 1974
33. Santa Barbara, ACCESS (California) — 1974
34. Clarinda Citizens' Involvement (Iowa) — 1976
35. Greater Philadelphia Partnership — 1976
36. Atlanta 2000 — 1977

Multistate Regions
A. Federation of Rocky Mountain States — 1965
B. Choices for '76: Regional Plan Association (New York, New Jersey, Connecticut) — 1973
C. Commission on the Future of the South — 1974
D. Great Lakes Tomorrow — 1975
E. Delaware Valley Regional Planning Commission — 1975
F. Official Choices for the Upper Midwest — 1976

Substate Regions
G. Willamette Valley: Choices for the Future (Oregon) — 1972
H. Central Virginia Tomorrow (Lynchburg) — 1974

CHAPTER 21

The American Political Mood

The political mood in America is mercurial and fragmented. The electorate is vulnerable and uncertain, and a very large segment of it is passive. (In the 1976 presidential election, only 54.4 per cent of those eligible voted. According to the Gallup Poll, the number of eligibles who didn't even bother to register rose from 28 per cent in 1972 to 38 per cent in 1976. In the mid-term 1978 elections, only 34 per cent went to the polls, down from 36.1 per cent in 1974.)

Sen. Edward M. Kennedy (D, Mass.) is quoted as saying that "representative government is in the worst shape I have seen it. The Senate and the House are awash in a sea of special-interest contributions and lobbying."

Long-held or long-term views are unfashionable in America today; this makes assessments difficult. What is to be evaluated? What is to be taken seriously? Lives are not lived according to traditional or even enduring values but, it is said, according to "situational ethics," frantic opportunism, abrupt switches. Consequently, flip-flopping on political issues is understood. Candidates who address the issues least succeed the most, as Alan Wolfe puts it.

Is it helpful to view the issues as seen from left to right? Yes, for an appreciation of the atomized character of American life that isn't reflected in the two-party system. "Single-issue" politics is its latest expression. Issues abound—taxes and government spending, gambling, restrictions on homosexuals, abortion, smoking in public places, gun control, support of Israel, opposition to nuclear power.

In spite of apathy, there is a strong movement for citizens to initiate laws and pass them by referendum, to balance the federal budget by constitutional amendment, to recall officials who fall into disfavor.

The mood is wary. Is America a declining power? Recession in 1979? Guns or butter? What should a President do? What is the role of the Congress? Do the American people know what they want?

The latter question is the title of an article in *Commentary* by Paul H. Weaver, who writes:

". . . Representative institutions are being cut loose from their constituencies; the traditional, locally-based, interest-aggregating system of representation is giving way to a form of plebiscitarianism in which individual candidates appeal directly to mass audiences on the basis of images. . . .

"Under the influence of this kind of politics, government cannot govern. Issues and problems cannot be recognized . . . and thus policy cannot be shaped or administered in a way that

Voter dissatisfaction with American politics and national life is seeking new expressions. The map illustrates two of the most significant. More than 25 state legislatures have passed resolutions calling for a constitutional convention to draft an amendment that would require a balanced federal budget. If nine more states approve such a resolution, it would be necessary to call the convention. Congressional reaction has been cautious; the constitution has never been amended by convention, only through congressional action ratified by the states. Another response to political frustration is the growth of "anticipatory democracy," "a process — a way of reaching decisions that determine our future," writes Alvin Toffler (in a volume edited by Clement Bezold). Two crucial problems endanger the stability and survival of our political system today, says Toffler. First, lack of future-consciousness. Second, lack of participation. The forms that anticipatory democracy may take — state, regional and local experiments — are outlined on the map.

will allow it to become both effective and legitimate. . . . Hidden policy—those unintended or unacknowledged effects of programs fashioned in the unreal atmosphere of plebiscitarian public discussion—will come to dominate the society. . . ."

Other thoughtful analyses of the failures of American politics agree more or less on the symptoms of those failures. "It would be an exaggeration to say that America's two great political parties are dead," *The Economist* observes. "But that they are withering away is indisputable. . . ." *Time* comments, "the Vietnam War, Watergate and other scandals have left a deep residual cynicism. . . ."

A cartoon by Herblock in the *Washington Post* portrays an artist and his work, an intricate sculpture of arrows pointing in every direction at once, called "Elections '78 (with referendums)," the artist asking an appalled viewer, John Q. Public, "Well, how do you like it?"

During the early Johnson years, the American public was rallied by "consensus" in support of the Vietnam War and the "Great Society" programs. Mobilizing the "Silent Majority," Nixon twice won election to the presidency.

Now, both consensus and silent majority are shattered. The voter is having difficulty considering more than one issue or problem at a time. There are plenty of problems, mostly economic, but almost no agreement on how any of them might be solved or how they might be handled as a whole. For example, as President Carter announces each new phase of his anti-inflation program, the main response is skepticism. Many corporate leaders offer their backing to the President but say their pledges are conditional on union reaction. Several union leaders also qualify their compliance, saying it would depend on the action of prices.

The public's disillusionment with the two parties is seen as part of the explanation for the success of such non-party leaders as consumer advocate Ralph Nader, John Gardner and his Common Cause, Howard Jarvis and his Proposition 13. Even the tragedy of Jim Jones and his People's Temple in Guyana is cited as evidence that Americans long for leadership. Some observers warn that this mood of dissatisfaction—this willingness to follow a charismatic figure—might open America to the dangers that overtook Germany and Italy in the '30s, or to an extension of the disarray of the '70s.

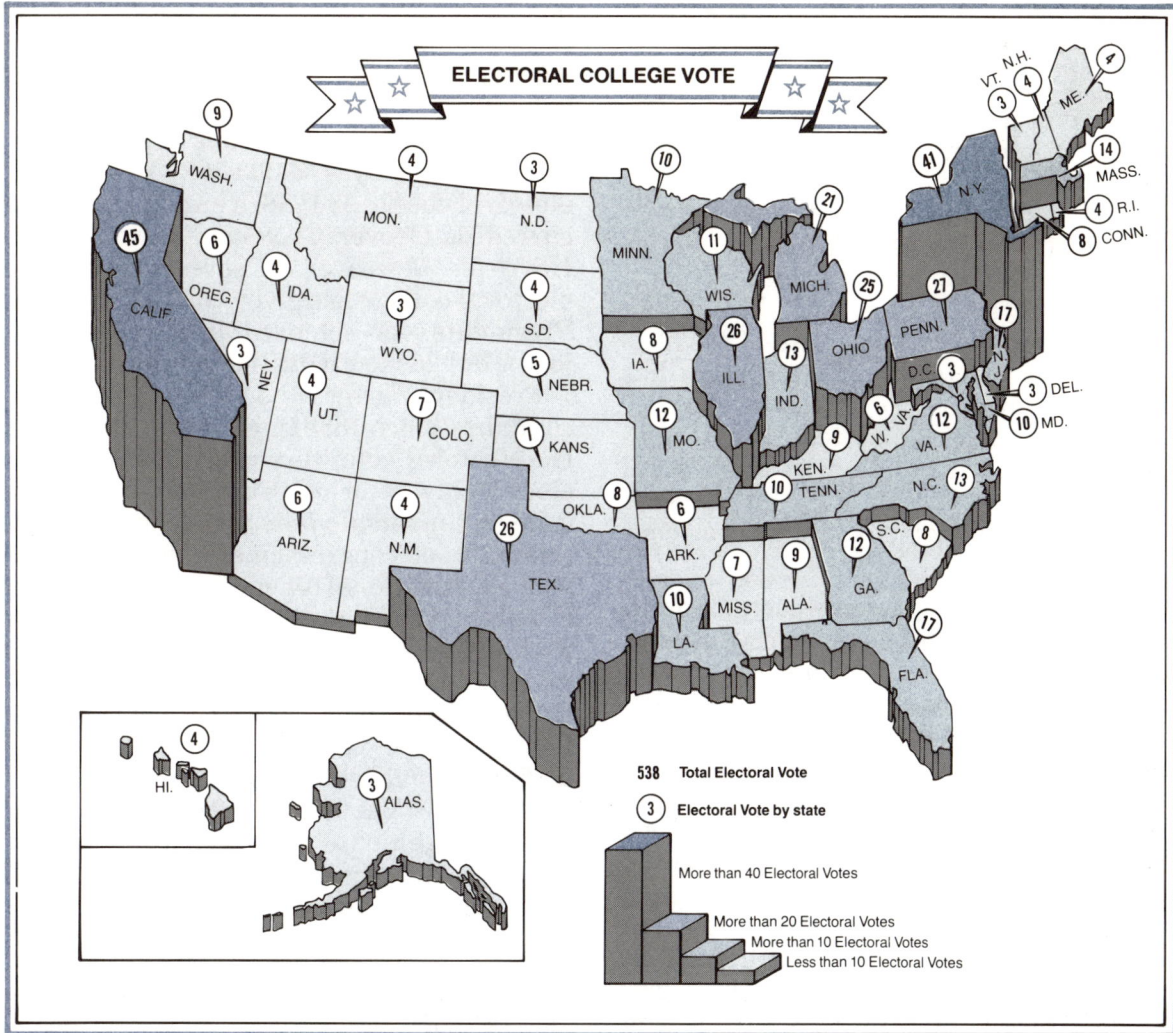

ELECTORAL COLLEGE VOTE

538 Total Electoral Vote

(3) Electoral Vote by state

More than 40 Electoral Votes
More than 20 Electoral Votes
More than 10 Electoral Votes
Less than 10 Electoral Votes

A constitutional amendment that would abolish the electoral college and provide for the direct popular election of the President and Vice President is being considered by Congress. The candidate receiving 40 per cent or more of the vote would be designated the winner. If no candidate won that plurality, a run-off election would be held. In Congress, the "real problem, as in the past," says *The New York Times,* "is defeating a filibuster by conservatives who are defenders of the electoral college." The current electoral college system makes it possible for a candidate to win a majority of electoral votes—and thereby election to the presidency— even if he receives only a minority of the popular vote. The distribution of the electoral vote—and with it the power of a minority of populous states to put a minority President into office— is portrayed above.

CHAPTER 22

Electoral College

The electoral college, which chooses the President and the Vice President, is in trouble. Although it is as venerable an institution as any in the republic, it represents something of uncertain value in American politics today. Many voters are unaware of its existence; some think it's a *college* one attends. "Every boy and girl should go to college and if they can't afford Yale or Harvard, why, Electoral is just as good, if you work."* Others seriously debate its pro's and

Presidential Lottery, by James A. Michener, p. 43

con's, while President Carter has proposed its abolition in favor of direct election of the President and Vice President.

Adopted at the constitutional convention of 1787, the electoral college system provides each state with a number of electors equal to its representation in Congress. Each party names its own slate of electors, for which the voters cast their ballots on election day. The electors later meet to translate popular votes into electoral votes. In each state, the Presidential candidate with the most popular votes gets all of the electoral votes. The electoral college system has thus become known as the "winner-take-all," general-ticket or unit-rule system. If no candidate for President wins a majority of electoral votes, the election is thrown into the House of Representatives. Election of the Vice President goes to the Senate.

Only two major changes have been made in the original system, both by constitutional amendment. To begin with, each elector voted "for two persons" without indicating which they preferred for chief executive and which for Vice President. In 1800, Thomas Jefferson and Aaron Burr, Democratic-Republican Party nominees for, respectively, President and Vice President, each received the same number of unspecific electoral votes, and it took 36 ballots of the House of Representatives for Jefferson to be chosen as President. The Twelfth Amendment, ratified in 1804, provided for separate balloting for President and Vice President. The Twenty-third Amendment, ratified in 1961, permitted District of Columbia residents to vote in Presidential elections and awarded the district three electors, or no more than states with the least population.

Critics of the electoral college's role emphasize the undemocratic nature of a system that prohibits a direct vote for President and that has resulted on three occasions in the election of a President with fewer popular votes than his opponent. In 1824, Andrew Jackson, who had received more popular votes than John Quincy Adams, failed to win a majority of electoral votes. The House elected Adams. In 1876, Samuel J. Tilden tallied 4,285,992 popular votes, Rutherford B. Hayes, 4,033,768. Hayes took the electoral count. In 1888, a similar distortion occurred as Grover Cleveland lost to Benjamin Harrison. Moreover, in several instances, the electoral college has given the country minority Presidents who achieved an electoral vote majority but lacked it in the popular vote.

President Carter, who almost became the first candidate since 1888 to win the popular but lose the electoral vote, very early in his term urged election law reforms—abolition of the electoral college, universal voter registration and public financing of congressional elections. A direct-vote constitutional amendment was proposed in Congress. One of the most controversial aspects of the amendment called for a runoff election if no candidate receives a 40-per cent plurality. Opponents of the amendment warn that establishing a 40-per cent plurality as a minimum for a winner would cause a proliferation of splinter parties, political factions, independent candidacies. "The genius of the Constitution is the effect it has on the *character* of majorities. The electoral college promotes unity and legitimacy by helping to generate majorities that are not narrow, geographically or ideologically, and by magnifying (as in 1960, 1968, 1976) narrow margins of victories in the popular vote" (George F. Will in *Newsweek*).

The debate has fundamentalist overtones. Advocates of reform point out the dangers of the House contingency election procedure, its potential for producing a constitutional crisis, a deadlock. Defenders of the electoral college contend that the dispute involves the future of the two-party system and possibly of federalism, itself.

CHAPTER 23

Dollar Crisis

A huge trade deficit and rising domestic inflation continue their severe pressure on the U.S. dollar.

American imports exceeded exports by a record $28.45 billion in 1978, surpassing the previous year's record of $26.72 billion. Imports in 1978 amounted to $172.02 billion, exports $143.57 billion. A very sharp increase in the cost of oil imports, rising 31 per cent to a record $42.1 billion, accounted for much of the 1977 trade deficit. In 1978, benefiting from stable prices, the cost of oil imports declined to $39.5 billion. However, the Organization of Petroleum Exporting Countries had set oil price increases of at least 14.5 per cent for 1979.

Growth in consumption helped to fuel near "double-digit" inflation. Retail sales, housing starts and personal income all climbed. Consumer prices in October 1978, for example, rose 0.8 per cent, the equivalent of a 9.6 per cent annual rate. The index for the month stood at 200.9 per cent of the 1967 (base) average, meaning that consumer prices were slightly more than double their average level in 1967. Analysts noted that inflation had been accelerating in recent years. Consumer prices had doubled in the 25 years between 1942 and 1967, but doubled again in only the next 11 years.

The federal budget deficit, personal and corporate debt are placing still further pressure on the dollar. The convergence of pressures in a new crisis is feared, and the question of how it might be headed off is debated among government officials, economists and public alike. Should mandatory wage-price controls be enacted? How about credit controls? Gas rationing? Balancing the budget is viewed by many as a big step to a solution. Austerity measures are preferable, they say, to more inflation and a possibly worse contraction.

Foreign inflation fighters have learned, *U.S. News & World Report* says, that the strength of a country's currency in the foreign exchange markets can mean "success or failure in whipping inflation." A strong currency means lower prices for imports and, ultimately, lower domestic prices.

DECLINE OF THE DOLLAR: 1977–78

The U.S. dollar started a fresh downward movement in mid-1977.

The value of the dollar declined July 21, 1977 to a record low of 2.256 West German marks before Bonn intervened to buy dollars and boost the exchange rate to 2.264. However, the dollar continued to depreciate against the Japanese yen, falling July 21 from a value of 264.73 yen to 264.28 yen. In contrast to past periods of pressure on the dollar, Carter Administration officials and many economists were unconcerned about the dollar's weakening position.

The value of the dollar fell to a postwar low in Tokyo Oct. 18 when it closed at 252.03 yen. The dramatic increase in the value of the yen (14 per cent since January) was "part of a widespread move against the dollar that is only now being temporarily curbed by massive central-bank intervention in the foreign exchange markets and by rising U.S. interest rates," *Business Week* said Oct. 24. Treasury Secretary W. Michael Blumenthal indicated that the Administration would not intervene to prevent a further decline in the dollar unless foreign exchange markets became "disorderly."

The value of the dollar plunged on the world's foreign exchange markets in 1978. Chief causes were the severe U.S. trade deficit, the volume of oil imports, domestic inflation. The accompanying map shows how the dollar fell in value as compared with the world's strongest currencies—the Swiss franc, West German mark and Japanese yen. However, foreign currencies that increased in value also included the Austrian schilling, British pound, French franc, Finnish markka, Spanish peseta. In fact, very few currencies did not rise in relation to the battered U.S. dollar; among those that fell, as will be seen on the map, were the Canadian dollar, Chilean peso, Hong Kong dollar and Iranian rial.

Consumer Price Changes in the U.S.

"The inflation that we are suffering today began many years ago and was aggravated in 1973 and 1974 by a quadrupling of OPEC oil prices, widespread crop shortages, excessive Soviet grain purchases, substantial devaluation of the dollar, and a worldwide industrial boom that led to double-digit inflation both here in the United States and around the world. Inflation has now become embedded in the very tissue of our economy. It has resisted the most severe recession in a generation. It persists because all of us—business, labor, farmers, consumers—are caught on a treadmill which none can stop alone. Each group tries to raise its income to keep up with present and anticipated rising costs, and eventually we all lose the inflationary battle together."

—President Jimmy Carter, April 11, 1978

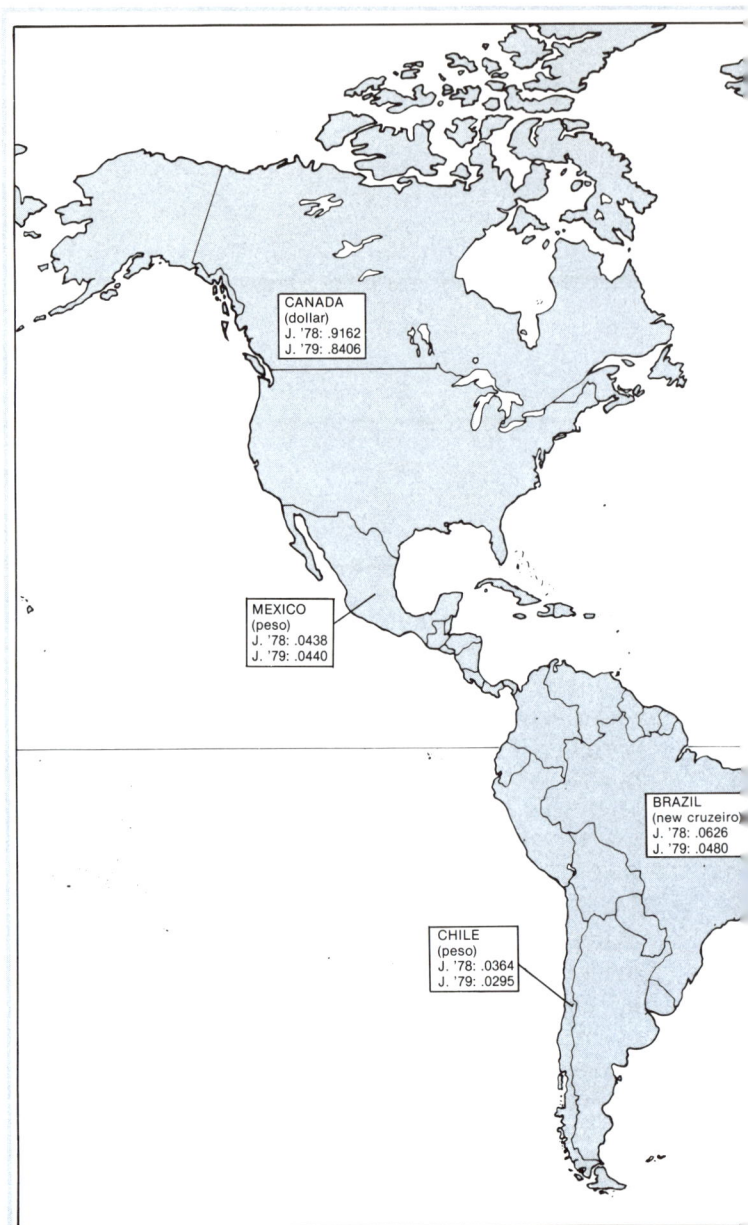

CANADA
(dollar)
J. '78: .9162
J. '79: .8406

MEXICO
(peso)
J. '78: .0438
J. '79: .0440

BRAZIL
(new cruzeiro)
J. '78: .0626
J. '79: .0480

CHILE
(peso)
J. '78: .0364
J. '79: .0295

By the end of November, the mark had risen 8.4 per cent against the dollar since 1976, the Swiss franc 13.3 per cent and the yen nearly 25 per cent. The dollar hit a record low against the yen Dec. 15, when one dollar was worth 238.03 yen.

In a major policy shift, the Carter Administration moved Jan. 4, 1978 to halt the decline of the dollar. The Treasury Department and the Federal Reserve Board announced that the U.S. would intervene "actively" to "check speculation and reestablish order in the foreign exchange markets." The immediate effect of the Administration's announcement was dramatic: the dollar soared in value. Its recovery, however, proved to be short-lived. Skepticism overtook the foreign exchange markets as traders tested the Administration's resolve to support the sagging currency.

The dollar resumed its slide in February. By Feb. 23, the dollar had plunged to new record lows against the West German mark ($1 bought 2.023 marks) and the Swiss franc ($1 was worth 1.80 francs). The dollar's steep drop grew worse from late February to April. In trading April 3 in Tokyo, one dollar was worth 218.18 yen, compared with 230 yen only a week before.

The dollar fell to new record lows during the summer. Its decline against the Japanese yen was particularly dramatic. It fell below the psychologically important barrier of 200 yen July 24, closing at 199.05. The Bank of Japan bought about $400 million to halt the slide but was forced to withdraw from trading after half an hour because of intense selling pressures. The dollar's losing streak continued. It hit new lows in each of nine consecutive trading days, falling 9 per cent to 184.65 yen by Aug. 6.

The dollar also weakened against European currencies. Market conditions were described as "chaotic," as traders sold dollars at a frantic

SWEDEN
(krona)
J. '78: .2150
J. '79: .2308

FINLAND
(markka)
J. '78: .2523
J. '79: .2533

HOLLAND
(guilder)
J. '78: .4484
J. '79: .5025

BELGIUM
(franc)
J. '78: .0308
J. '79: .0345

LEBANON
(pound)
J. '78: .3336
J. '79: .3350

BRITAIN
(pound)
J. '78: 1.9670
J. '79: 2.0245

ISRAEL
(pound)
J. '78: .0653
J. '79: .0525

WEST GERMANY
(mark)
J. '78: .4848
J. '79: .5422

JAPAN
(yen)
J. '78: .004206
J. '79: .005140

FRANCE
(franc)
J. '78: .2176
J. '79: .2395

SPAIN
(peseta)
J. '78: .0124
J. '79: .0143

HONG KONG
(dollar)
J. '78: .2169
J. '79: .2085

SWITZERLAND
(franc)
J. '78: .5197
J. '79: .6079

AUSTRIA
(schilling)
J. '78: .0628
J. '79: .0744

IRAN
(rial)
J. '78: .01420
J. '79: .01340

SINGAPORE
(dollar)
J. '78: .4308
J. '79: .4600

ITALY
(lire)
J. '78: .001154
J. '79: .001199

SAUDI ARABIA
(riyal)
J. '78: .2865
J. '79: .3032

AUSTRALIA
(dollar)
J. '78: 1.1470
J. '79: 1.1480

SOUTH AFRICA
(rand)
J. '78: 1.1505
J. '79: 1.1507

DECLINE OF THE DOLLAR 1978-79
Figures show numbers of U.S. dollars that a unit of foreign
currency could buy on Jan. 3, 1978 and Jan. 3, 1979.

NEW ZEALAND
(dollar)
J. '78: 1.0255
J. '79: 1.0590

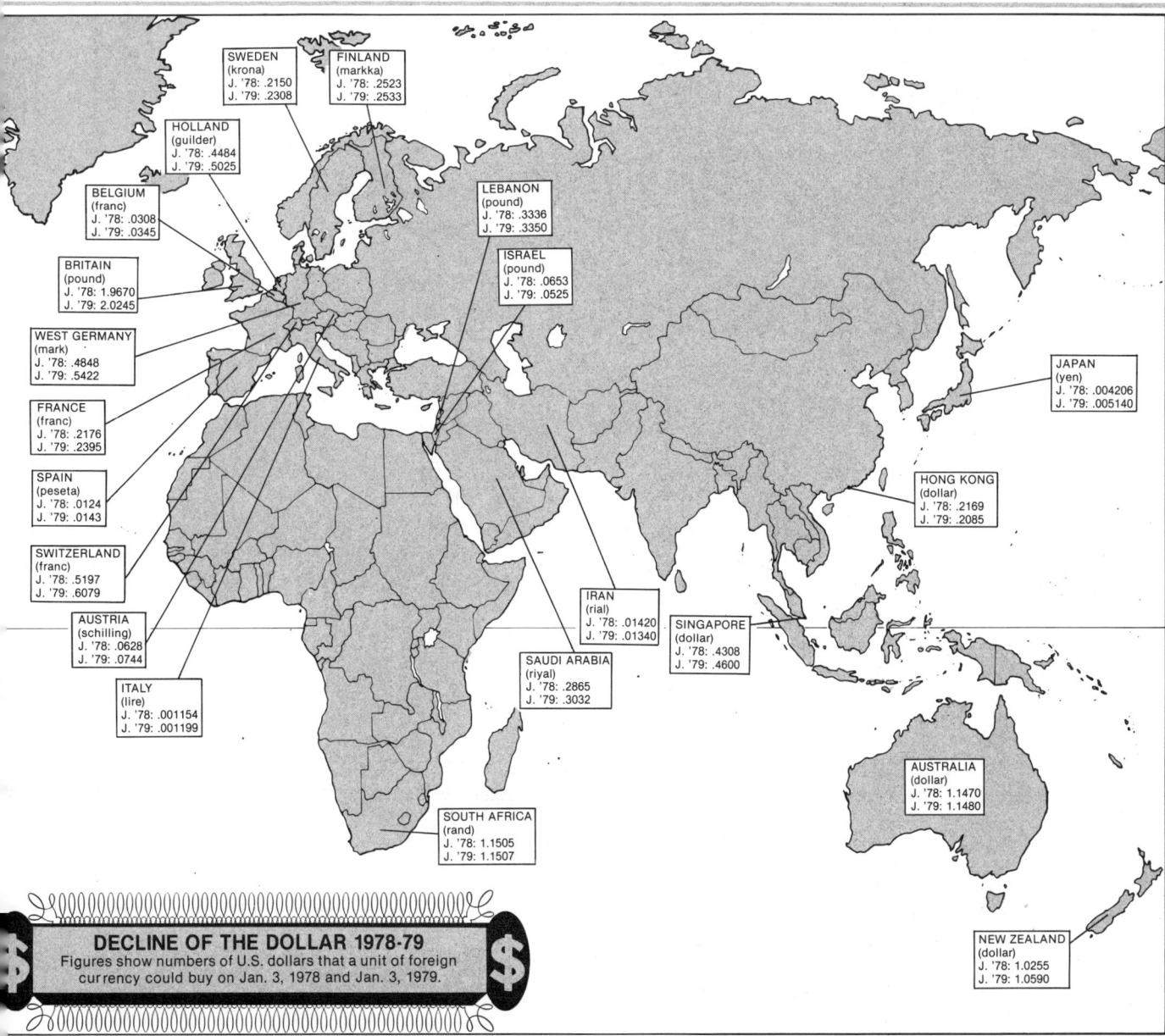

pace and the central banks of Japan, West Germany and Switzerland sharply cut back their intervention in support of the dollar. By Aug. 15, one dollar was worth 1.919 marks and 1.55 Swiss francs, both record lows. President Carter expressed "deep concern" Aug. 16 about the dollar's precipitous decline.

New lows followed. On the Frankfurt exchange market Oct. 30, the dollar traded at 1.-727 marks; in Zurich, the dollar was worth 1.48 Swiss francs. In Tokyo trading Oct. 31, the dollar fell to 176.08 yen.

Carter announced a series of emergency actions Nov. 1 to halt a heavy selloff of the dollar. The measures, which included a pledge of "massive intervention" to support the dollar, a quintupling of gold sales and a sharp increase in the discount rate, had an immediate effect abroad and in the U.S. The value of the dollar then rebounded. Reaction on the New York Stock Exchange was euphoric, despite the hike in interest rates. The Dow Jones industrial average climbed more than 35 points, a record-breaking single-day advance. As the dollar ended trading Dec. 29, it had risen to 1.823 West German marks, 1.63 Swiss francs and 195.05 yen.

But in 1979 the dollar is still in trouble. Observers can see no fundamental improvement in the dollar position as long as U.S. trade deficits continue, as long as the inflation rate remains high, as long as the country continues to consume ever greater amounts of increasingly expensive foreign oil . . . as long as there is no reversal of the conditions that cause this "flight from the dollar."

THE ORIGINAL PLAN OF HOUSTON

We the undersigned do hereby certify this to be a correct and literal copy of the "First Lithographed Map of Houston" as made for A.C. & J.K. Allen, by F. Snell & Thuret, Canal St. N.O.

Scale - Same as large Map

BUFFALO BAYOU

COMMERCE ST.

FRANKLIN ST.

CONGRESS ST.

PRESTON ST.

PRAIRIE ST.

Congress Sq. Square

Court House Square

Church Reserve

School House Square

BRAZOS SMITH LOUISIANA MILAM TRAVIS MAIN FANNIN SAN JACINTO CAROLINA AUSTIN LAMAR

CHAPTER 24

'Can America's Cities Survive?'

America built cities, places of work and exchange, of riches and opportunity and culture. "Here was a city," Theodore Dreiser wrote of Chicago, "which had no traditions but was making them. . . . Chicago would outstrip every other American city, New York included. . . ." Both cities were to grow bigger, but neither was to fulfill the dreams of its critics.

In New York in 1904, Henry Adams observed prophetically that the outline of the city had become "frantic in its effort to explain something that defied meaning. Power seemed to have outgrown its servitude and asserted its freedom. . . . The city had the air and movement of hysteria, and the citizens were crying, in every accent of anger and alarm, that the new forces must at any cost be brought under control. . . ."

Many years later, Lewis Mumford attempted to redefine the possibilities of urban life. He recalled Aristotle—"Men come together in cities in order to live; they remain together in order to live the good life"—and proposed new patterns of life and thought to remake the cities, reorient them.

A period of slum clearance and suburban construction followed the Second World War and produced many positive results but no solution to the dilemmas of value and development. In the 1960s and 1970s, a crisis of urban decline, a convergence of problems, numerous and chronic, overtook the older cities of the Northeast and North Central states.

CITIES IN TROUBLE, CUT SPENDING. MAYORS SEEK HELP IN D.C. CAN AMERICA'S CITIES SURVIVE? Those were the headlines. New York, Chicago, Philadelphia, Detroit, Cleveland and other major cities were in turmoil. Their financial distress was acute.

The Cleveland public school system ran out of money but was kept operating by federal court order; late last year Cleveland defaulted on its debts. Buffalo and Yonkers, N.Y. received emergency state assistance to avert financial collapse. Monroe, La., city of 56,400 persons, defaulted on its municipal payroll Sept. 17, 1976 and was rescued by the federal government. Cincinnati dismissed 500 city employes to reduce a $12.7-million deficit in fiscal 1977. State employes were laid off in Connecticut.

A survey by the Joint Economic Committee of Congress reports that state and local governments had been forced to cut services, raise taxes and defer capital spending. Among the causes are inflation coupled with recession, unemployment, a decline in the tax base, an increase in welfare costs.

New York's plight was particularly desperate and, for the nation's greatest city, humiliating. In 1975, the city approached default and bankruptcy several times. Its total publicly-held debt was reported to be a staggering $14 billion. City notes were sold at discounts so deep that their effective rate of interest rose to 16.5 per cent. A debate over federal aid developed, and at first President Ford refused assistance. As the number of persons on welfare in the city passed the one million mark, financial control measures were enacted. The Municipal Assistance Corp. was created by the state legislature to refinance the city's debt and act as its fiscal agent, and a state board was set up to carry out budgetary reforms, enforce austerity and direct the flow of city revenues, which would be deposited daily. Subsequently, the city was rescued by state, federal and union pension fund aid. Both assistance and control measures were renewed in the following years. New York is still a depressed city of much diminished quality.

Other urban difficulties are intensified by economic distress. Crime soared. Housing decayed. (Gov. Edmund G. Brown Jr. of California spoke of the "bombed out cities of the East.") Racial hostility mounted. Population fled. But the cities of the Southwest burgeoned during the 1970s. San Diego, Calif. and San Antonio, Tex. displaced Washington, D.C. and Cleveland from the top ten cities with the most population. Houston, Tex. was fifth, displacing Detroit.

Houston is on the way up, the nation's third largest port and home of the world's largest petrochemical complex, designated by *Newsweek* as supercity and "capital of the fast buck." It

now has twice as much office space as in 1970, and some of its new buildings are architecturally innovative. It has no zoning restrictions. Its philosophy is open-collar conservative: keep taxes and living costs down. It offers the typical adornments of metropolitan life (professional ball teams and professional opera, ballet and theater companies) and some of its typical problems—an increasing crime rate, police brutality cases, traffic congestion, air and water pollution. "Much of the city stinks of malodorous oil by-products, of toxic carbon monoxide clouds laid down by traffic, of sulphurs and pulpwood, and of those special greasy, funky odors indigenous to the ghetto poor," writes Larry L. King.

Houston expanded outwards by annexing unincorporated communities. That way it extended its tax base and avoided being strangled by suburbs. Charlotte, N.C. and Kansas City, Mo., are using the same device to maintain their growth.

Federal aid to cities remains a major issue. Between 1972 and 1976 federal aid flowed to cities through revenue sharing programs. Federal revenues amounting to $30.2 billion were shared with state and local governments. In 1977, legislation extending federal programs for cities through 1980 was signed by President Carter. The bill authorized $12.5 billion in urban aid over the period and $1.2 billion in fiscal 1978 for federal housing assistance. Last year, Carter proposed new legislation to aid the cities by combining job opportunities, fiscal relief, investment incentives, additional services and community participation.

Reaction to the program ranged from qualified praise to outright criticism. Vernon E. Jordan Jr., executive director of the National Urban League, termed the program "disheartening" and "a missed opportunity." Jordan renewed his call for an "urban Marshall Plan." Mayor Lee Alexander of Syracuse, N.Y., president of the U.S. Conference of Mayors, said the plan did not "give enough attention to the critical national problems of unemployment, housing, and transportation." But, he said, he was "very enthusiastic" about the new spending and tax incentive proposals. New York City Mayor Edward I. Koch described Carter's urban policy as "encouraging" but pointed out that "There's only $150 million for housing for the whole country." Veteran civil rights activist Bayard Rustin assailed the plan as "a mishmash with a little bit—too little—for everybody. . . . [T]he government won't face the problem squarely."

Many wonder whether a fresh infusion of funds would solve the cities' difficulties. It

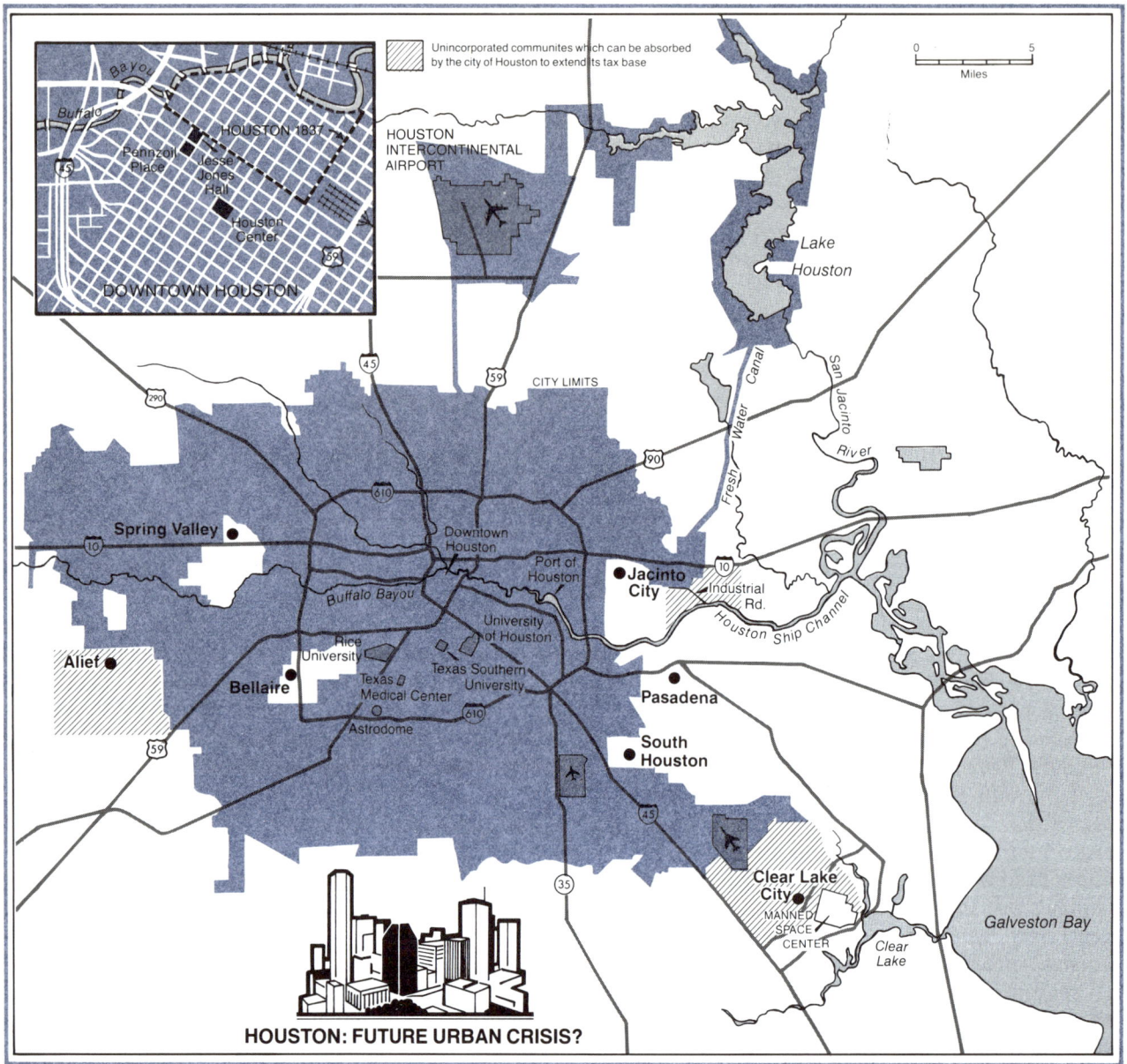

Unincorporated communies which can be absorbed by the city of Houston to extend its tax base

HOUSTON 1837

DOWNTOWN HOUSTON

Buffalo Bayou

Pennzoil Place

Jesse Jones Hall

Houston Center

HOUSTON INTERCONTINENTAL AIRPORT

CITY LIMITS

Lake Houston

Fresh Water Canal

San Jacinto River

Spring Valley

Downtown Houston

Port of Houston

Jacinto City

Industrial Rd.

Houston Ship Channel

Buffalo Bayou

University of Houston

Alief

Rice University

Texas Medical Center

Texas Southern University

Pasadena

Bellaire

Astrodome

South Houston

Clear Lake City

MANNED SPACE CENTER

Clear Lake

Galveston Bay

0 ... 5 Miles

HOUSTON: FUTURE URBAN CRISIS?

might just keep them going. What is the future of the American city? Cities have universally been viewed as centers of civilization. But Americans appear to remain skeptical. For them, civilization takes the shape of the cultural center, and often, of speculative growth. The latter has its own rationale, despite the New York experience. "First comes the image of what we want, then the machinery is adapted to turn out that image," comments Jane Jacobs in *The Death and Life of Great American Cities.* "The financial machinery has been adjusted to create anti-city images because, and only because, we as a society thought this would be good for us. If and when we think that lively,

In Dallas, Tex. the people say, "We're not as big as New York, but we're catching up." Houston has jumped into fifth place among the nation's largest metropolises, displacing Detroit. The older cities in the Northeast and Midwest are in trouble, losing population and jobs, afflicted by financial crisis. The American urban crisis is hydra-headed. Can the older cities be revitalized? Will the newer and newly rich cities survive their own headlong growth? The map of Houston details the development patterns of a city that may be growing rapidly in the direction of urban crisis.

diversified city, capable of continual, close-grained improvement and change, is desirable, then we will adjust the financial machinery to get that. . . . The decay of cities . . . goes right down to what we think we want."

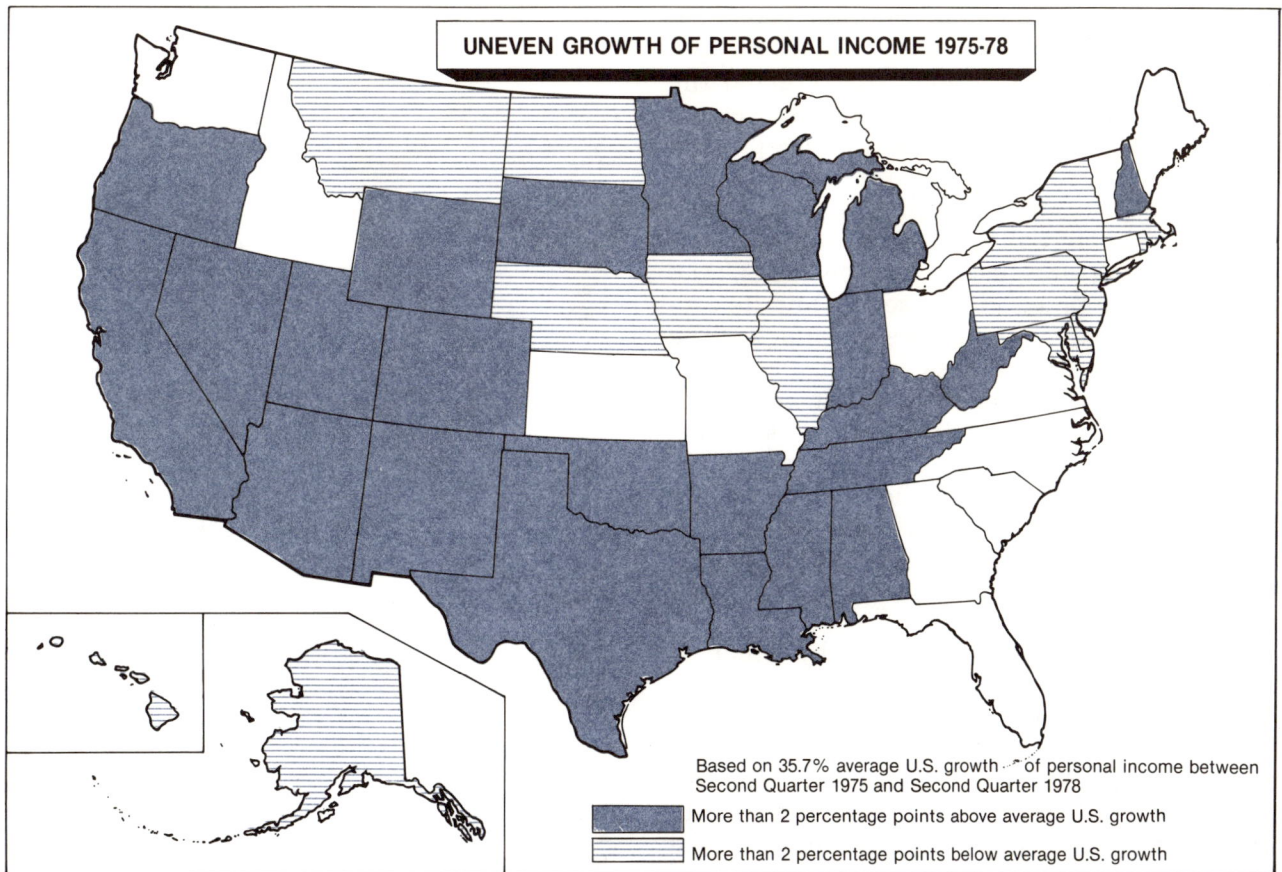

Based on 35.7% average U.S. growth of personal income between Second Quarter 1975 and Second Quarter 1978

More than 2 percentage points above average U.S. growth

More than 2 percentage points below average U.S. growth

Regional differences in the growth of personal income suggest the regional variations in national growth. During the past decade, the Southern U.S. has grown at twice the national rate. In addition, the distribution of military-related jobs is highest in the South and lowest in the Northeast. Correspondingly, recent growth of personal income is seen on the map to be above the average in the West, Southwest and a significant part of the South, while below the average in sections of the Northeast and Midwest.

CHAPTER 25

Patterns of U.S. Prosperity

Since 1970, the Southern part of the United States has grown at twice the national rate; 75 per cent of all new manufacturing jobs are in the South. The spread on military-related jobs is 48 per cent in the South, 29 per cent in the West, 12 per cent in the Midwest and 9 per cent in the Northeast.

The decision by American Airlines to move its headquarters—and 1,300 jobs—from New York to the Dallas-Fort Worth area (the "Southwest Metroplex") is interpreted by Texas boosters "as an especially vivid symbol of a long-term shift of money, business, industry and people from north to south and east to west," reports *The New York Times*.

Proclaimed for the past 90 years, the "New South" finally has arisen. The South has become "almost as wealthy as the rest of the country," asserts Jack Temple Kirby, and Jimmy Carter is the "ultimate regional synthesizer," an "eminently successful engineer-business-man-politician," a "Georgia Yankee."

The traditional leadership of the Northeastern Establishment is being challenged successfully by the "Southern Rim," Kirkpatrick Sale observes in *Power Shift*. The Southern Rim reaches across America from North Carolina through Tennessee and Oklahoma to Nevada, Arizona and California. Its power base, says Sale, is newly built on a massive expansion of population—from about 40 million people to nearly 80 million in just three decades; an "authentic economic revolution" that created the postwar industries of defense, aerospace, advanced technology, oil and natural-gas production and agribusiness; the enormous growth of the federal government and its "unprecedented accumulation of wealth, the great part of which went to develop and sustain the new areas"; the political development of the region and its control over the major committees and much of the inner workings of Congress.

At the same time, the large urban centers of the Northeast and North-Central states are declining, their industrial importance rapidly diminishing. The riches of the Northeast are flowing to other sections of the country, and the old money markets are no longer capable of supplying the capital needs of either the Northeast or the nation.

There are other measurements by which to appraise the regional differences in prosperity. One is metaphorical, the designation of the Northeast and Midwest as the "frostbelt" and of the South and West as the "Sunbelt," the former, unsympathetic, the latter, attractive. Another is spoken of as the "pork-barrel war," the yearly competition for federal dollars. In 1976, 204 members of the House of Representatives formed the Northeast-Midwest Economic Advancement Coalition. The coalition proposes changes in federal aid-distribution formulas, a moratorium on military-base closings and reductions, balancing of the high energy costs in the North and the lower prices in the energy-producing South. The North is forced "to import higher-priced foreign oil while the Sunbelt lives on cheaper domestic fuel," Richard S. Morris charged in the *Village Voice*. "Five hundred kilowatts in New York cost $3,733, but only $1,757 in Houston or $1,502 in Atlanta."

Taxes also are much higher in the Northeast than in the rest of America, says Morris. ". . . A New Yorker earning $17,000 pays 37 per cent more in total income taxes than does the average American earning a similar amount. . . . Much of this discrepancy is due to higher state and local tax levels in the Northeast. But more is due to the greater federal tax burden we must bear. . . . We pay more in taxes because we, in the Northeast, make more in income. Under the income tax law, of course, the more money you make the more taxes you are supposed to pay. But our tax laws take no account of the higher cost of living in the Northeast. . . ."

In New York City, many residents pay half of their salary for rent. Only Anchorage,

PERSONAL INCOME (Annual rate in $ millions)			
	2nd Quarter 1975	2nd Quarter 1978	% Growth
Ala.	16,374	22,993	40.4
Alaska	3,363	4,325	28.6
Ariz.	11,698	16,830	43.9
Ark.	9,305	13,282	42.7
Calif.	137,213	191,789	39.8
Colo.	14,987	20,810	38.9
Conn.	20,884	27,404	36.0
Del.	3,732	4,902	31.4
Fla.	46,232	62,556	35.3
Ga.	24,427	33,412	36.8
Hawaii	5,680	7,356	29.5
Ida.	4,137	5,640	36.3
Ill.	74,391	95,806	28.8
Ind.	29,205	40,472	38.6
Ia.	16,690	21,982	31.7
Kan.	13,376	17,916	33.9
Ky.	16,270	22,930	40.9
La.	18,008	25,588	42.9
Me.	4,947	6,764	36.8
Md.	25,971	34,035	31.9
Mass.	34,899	46,626	33.6
Mich.	53,565	75,760	41.4
Minn.	22,332	31,994	43.3
Miss.	9,302	13,218	42.1
Mo.	25,756	34,945	35.7
Mont.	3,934	5,035	28.0
Neb.	9,051	11,444	26.4
Nev.	3,854	5,761	49.5
N.H.	4,325	6,974	61.3
N.J.	49,227	63,587	29.2
N.M.	5,438	7,794	43.3
N.Y.	117,156	145,309	24.0
N.C.	26,460	35,897	36.7
N.D.	3,706	4,333	16.9
Ohio	61,090	82,937	35.8
Okla.	14,097	19,830	40.7
Ore.	12,940	18,716	44.6
Pa.	68,320	89,935	31.6
R.I.	5,263	6,974	32.5
S.C.	12,937	17,722	37.0
S.D.	3,372	4,775	41.6
Tenn.	19,716	27,336	38.6
Tex.	66,994	96,929	44.7
Utah	5,782	8,438	45.9
Vt.	2,284	3,086	35.1
Va.	28,314	38,892	37.4
Wash.	22,155	31,020	37.4
W. Va.	8,783	12,589	43.3
Wis.	25,348	35,939	41.8
Wyo.	2,253	3,545	57.3

HISTORIC SECTIONALISM

Regionalism, or sectionalism as it used to be called, is an old issue in American history. Nationwide parties have had their eastern and western wings. The free states clashed with the slave states. The financial interests of the East opposed the mining interests of the West.

In a nation as vast and varied as the U.S., the growth of sectionalism was almost inevitable, historian Frederick Jackson Turner wrote. Regional geography is a fundamental fact, Turner pointed out; moreover, there is a geography of opinion, racial stocks, social traits, literature, religious denominations. "We in America are in reality a federation of sections rather than of states," he said.

Honolulu and Boston are higher than the New York-New Jersey region for those families maintaining a moderate standard of living. Living costs in 1977 were highest in Anchorage and lowest in Austin, Tex., according to the Labor Department. Families in Anchorage had to spend $24,019 to enjoy a moderate life style. Families in Austin could maintain that same moderate standard of living for $14,776. In New York City, a family living on a moderate budget needed $19,972.

From 1929 to 1977, growth in personal income was below the national average in the New England, Mideast, Great Lakes and Plains states and above the national average in the Southeast, Southwest, Rocky Mountain and Far West, reports the Bureau of Economic Analysis of the Department of Commerce. Regional differences in wage rates, taxes, and land costs encourage manufacturing expansion in Southern-Western locations and discourage it in Northern-Central locations, writes Howard L. Friedenberg, discussing the findings in the department's *Survey of Current Business*.

Two other factors are significant. The continuing mechanization of agriculture released more low-paid workers for manufacturing jobs in the Southern-Western than in the Northern-Central regions. Moreover, because Southern-Western manufacturing consists mainly of nondurable goods, it is less sensitive to cyclical downturns than Northern-Central manufacturing, which consists mainly of durables.

A CITY, STATE & REGION IN DECLINE

In June 1978, Cleveland's credit rating was lowered by Moody's investment service from "A" to "Baa," which is defined as a category lacking "outstanding investment characteristics." In July, Moody's dropped the rating further to "Ba," below investment grade.

On July 10, Standard & Poor's, the other leading bond-rating service, suspended its ratings on Cleveland general-obligation bonds. There are "major unanswered" financial questions, and "the information doesn't exist," S&P's Robert Muller explained.

The exact status of Cleveland's financial condition, in fact, was unknown because the books were so jumbled. In early August, the city estimated that it had a $17 million deficit in funds. Officials attributed the cash shortage primarily to missing bond funds. These funds, they said, had been used for operating expenses instead of being reserved for the capital improvement projects tied to the bonds.

But an analysis by the Ernst & Ernst auditing firm Aug. 22 put the deficit in the treasury account at $52 million. Ernst & Ernst said it had found a balance of only $14 million as of June 30, when the city should have had $48 million of bond proceeds and $18 million of other funds, primarily federal grants, in its treasury account.

In this condition, with a substantial deficit caused by insufficient revenue for operating expenses, Cleveland was facing $17.8 million of notes coming due in September and October and another $15.5 million of notes coming due in December.

On Dec. 15, 1978, Cleveland defaulted.

Cleveland's financial woes are related to a declining population and tax base. Its population of 625,643 in 1976 represented a loss of 125,000 residents, or 17 per cent, since 1970. In that period, Cleveland dropped to 17th largest city in the country from 10th largest. Forty per cent of the city's population is black. About 20 per cent of all families receive some income from the Government-supported Aid to Families with Dependent Children program.

Along Euclid Avenue, one of Cleveland's main thoroughfares extending from its historic Terminal Tower, "there is an abundance of boarded-up houses and businesses, littered streets and desperate people," Reginald Stuart writes in *The New York Times*.

Other leading Ohio cities—Youngstown and Akron—also are in trouble. The steel plants in Youngstown are cutting back. The Youngstown Sheet & Tube Co. fired 5,000 workers in 1977, and U.S. Steel says it eventually will shut down its Mahoning River Valley facilities because of their "very serious competitive disadvantages." In Akron, major downtown stores and a truck tire plant are closing; other rubber industry employment is shrinking.

The state's economic condition is reflected in the financial difficulties of its schools. In 1976, public schools in eight Ohio school districts were closed for up to two months for lack of operating revenues. In 1977, the Cleveland school system ran out of money but was kept operating by order of the federal courts and an act of the state legislature; voters in Canton, Cincinnati, Dayton and Columbus rejected proposed tax increases for schools. In 1978, nearly 60 per cent of 198 school levy and bond issues on the ballot were defeated, including those for Cleveland and Columbus.

Belt-tightening is hitting the whole region. "It is not news that a big industrial city like this one [Cleveland] is on the decline," Stuart observes. "All the cities of the nation's great industrial crescent—Detroit, Pittsburgh, Akron, Buffalo, Milwaukee—have seen the sun set, so to speak, on eras of once-envied prosperity."

CHAPTER 26

Black Americans

"But I only want a job, sir," I said.
—*The Invisible Man*, Ralph Ellison, 1952

In 1968, the National Advisory Commission on Civil Disorders, named to study the riots of the previous summer, reported:

"Unemployment rates among Negroes have declined from a post-war high of 12.6 per cent in 1958 to 8.2 per cent in 1967. . . .

"Notwithstanding this decline, unemployment rates for Negroes are still double those for whites in every category . . . as they have been throughout the postwar period. . . .

"Unemployment rates are, of course, much higher among teenagers, both Negro and white, than among adults. . . . During the first nine months of 1967, the unemployment rate among nonwhite teenagers was 26.5 per cent; for whites, it was 10.6 per cent. . . ."

Unemployment among blacks remains an acute social problem. The rates are not only higher than a decade ago but still double or more than double those for whites. In July 1978, the jobless rate for blacks was 12.5 per cent, for whites, 5.3 per cent; for black teenagers, the rate was 37 per cent, for white teenagers, 16.3 per cent. A year earlier, black joblessness had reached 14 per cent compared to 7 per cent for whites; among black teenagers unemployment had soared to the highest level ever recorded, 40.7 per cent, among white teenagers, it registered 14.3 per cent. ". . . Such joblessness," wrote Benjamin Quarles, professor emeritus of history at Morgan State College, "brought despair and alienation to the black ghettos of New York City, which suffered widespread looting during the electrical failure on the night of July 13 [1977]." And Joel Dreyfuss observed in *The*

Progressive that ". . . While a number of social critics scoffed at 'root causes' as an apology for the looters, they were forced to concede that although the times have changed, the grievances remain the same."

Even more important perhaps than unemployment, the National Advisory Commission on Civil Disorders had pointed out, was the related problem of the undesirable nature of many jobs open to Negroes. ". . . Negro workers are concentrated in the lowest-skilled and lowest-paying occupations," the commission's report said. In 1977, a study by the U.S. Equal Employment Opportunity Commission found that between 1969 and 1974, the number of blacks listed as officials and managers in reports to the commission had risen from 1.4 to 2.9 per cent, while the number of black professionals and technicians had increased by one percentage point.

Black leaders called for full employment. Secretary of Labor F. Ray Marshall termed the black jobless figures "most disturbing" but said it a "serious misstatement" to say the Carter Administration "isn't doing anything" about the problem. The Administration added $4 billion to an existing program for funding public-service construction jobs and proposed welfare reforms that would help the poor to get jobs or job training.

The problem is debated from a number of perspectives.

Vernon E. Jordan Jr., president of the National Urban League, says in an appraisal, entitled "The New Negativism," in *Newsweek*, "A mood of antisocial negativism is creeping through the structure of American life, corroding our ideals and suffocating the hopes of poor

WHERE THE AMERICAN BLACKS LIVE
States with black population estimated at 25,000 or more

Wash. 2.3
Ore. 1.3
Nev. 6.0
Calif. 7.6
Ariz. 3.0
Colo. 3.4
Minn. 1.0
Wis. 3.1
Iowa 1.4
Nebr. 3.0
Kan. 4.7
Okla. 7.1
Tex. 12.5
Mich. 11.9
Ill. 13.7
Ind. 7.3
Ohio 9.6
Ky. 7.2
Mo. 10.6
Ark. 16.9
La. 29.8
Miss. 35.9
Ala. 25.4
Ga. 26.1
Tenn. 15.6
W.Va. 3.6
N.C. 21.9
S.C. 30.8
Va. 18.7
Fla. 14.2
N.Y. 13.2
Pa. 8.8
Mass. 3.6
R.I. 3.0
Conn. 6.1
N.J. 11.9
Del. 14.7
D.C. 71.9
Md. 20.1

Black Population
1,000,000 and over
25,000 to 499,000
500,000 to 999,999

Black percentage of state's population shown in circle. Where no circle appears, black population is less than 25,000.

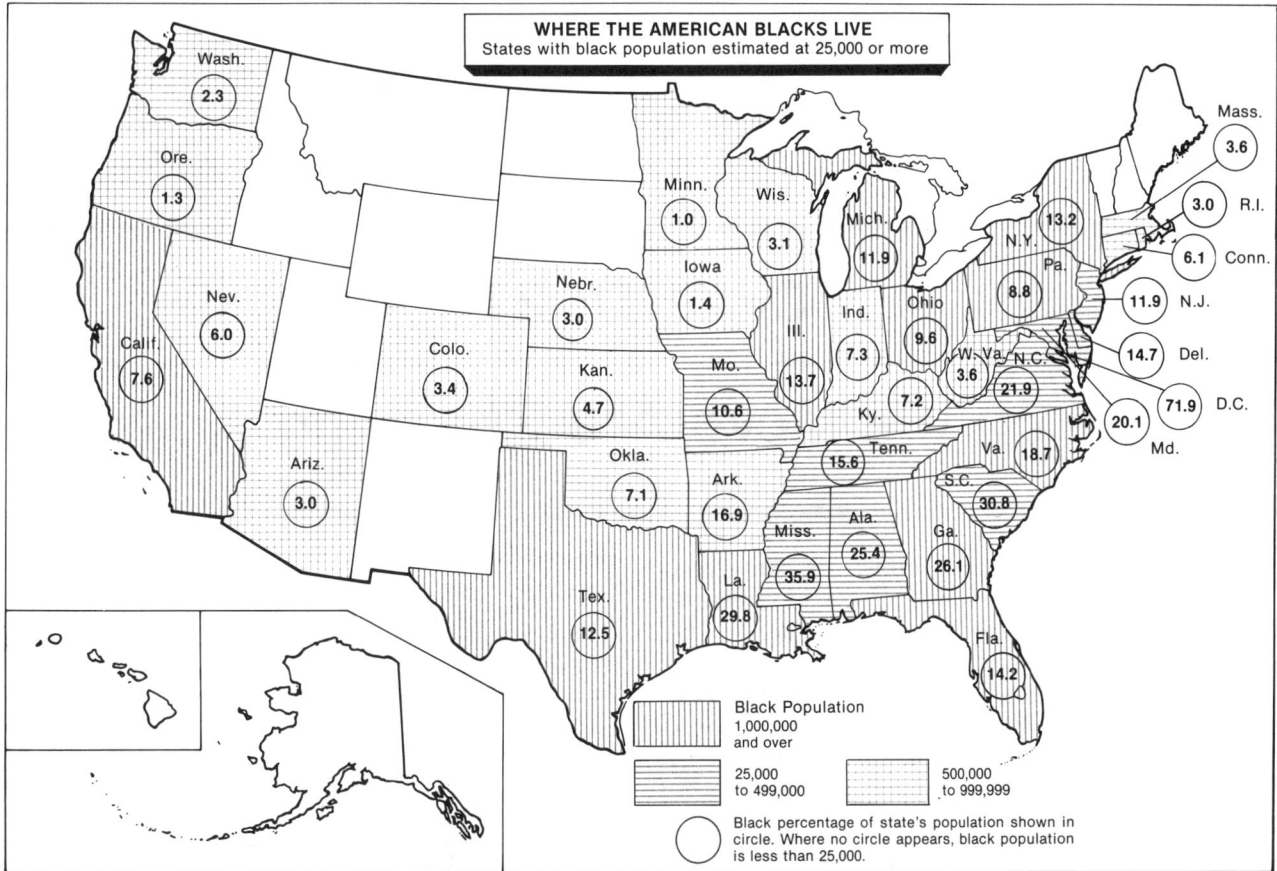

America's black population is concentrated, as the map shows, in such states as New York, Pennsylvania, Michigan, Illinois, Georgia, Florida, Texas and California. In many of these states, blacks live in urban ghettos, the central cities of the great metropolises; in each ghetto, the primary problem of the black is employment, job getting. Unemployment rates of blacks remain double or more than double those of whites.

people and minorities. . . . The New Negativism says we can't have high employment and low inflation. Its solution—tolerate unemployment in the name of fighting inflation—would trap black people and other minorities . . . , and it wouldn't solve the problem of inflation. . . ."

Senator Richard Lugar, a conservative Republican and former mayor of Indianapolis, interprets the problem thus: "Jimmy Carter, better than almost anyone else, knows what the people of this country are thinking. He knows that three-quarters of them aren't listening to Vernon Jordan. Most people in this country, sad to say, don't want to do *anything* about poor blacks or about these dying old cities." The *New Republic* offers this comment: "Mr. Lugar may be right. . . ."

(A recent Gallup Poll reported that most Americans, 81 per cent, opposed granting preferential treatment to minorities and women in entering college or getting jobs. They felt that ability as measured by test scores should be the main consideration in admitting people to schools and hiring.)

Fortune said, "The problem of black unemployment is simply too important to be left to those who are still bemused by the failed social doctrines of a bygone age. A wise policy today would be erected on two propositions. One is that much of the problem is simply beyond the reach of government. The other is that much of what government has been doing is only making the problem worse." The latter included, *Fortune* said, hikes in the minimum wage, the welfare laws that "have surely contributed something to the decline of the black family," and the shift away from vocational training in public-school curricula in many parts of the country.

CHAPTER 27

People on the Move Are Changing America

Shifts in population are changing America.

Growth itself is no longer a major issue in assessing U.S. demographic trends. At the time of the first national census in 1790, the U.S. population was 3,929,214. Ninety-five per cent of the population lived in rural places having fewer than 2,500 people. Only two cities, New York and Philadelphia, had populations of more than 25,000. By 1978 the U.S. population had reached 217.7 million, an increase of 1.7 million during the previous year. The growth rate was 0.79 per cent, or approaching zero, leveling off. Other factors—black migration, the problem of illegal aliens, regional changes, the concentration of population—have become more significant.

Blacks totaled 24.2 million in 1976, 11 per cent of the population. More than 50 per cent of the black population lives in the nation's central cities, in urban ghettoes. This concentration has been projected as increasing greatly by 1985. Warnings that this development is leading to a "society characterized by race stratification along social and economic lines as well as geographic separation" are still being pondered. However, the Census Bureau reported that between 1970 and 1976 the black population in the suburbs had increased faster than the white population; average annual rates of increase amounted to 5.2 per cent for blacks and 1.4 per cent for whites. Meanwhile, the black exodus from the South has ended, and a reverse movement is under way, with blacks leaving the Northeast and North Central states, going South and West, where the jobs are.

Legally, 390,000 immigrants—170,000 from the Eastern Hemisphere and 120,000 from the Western Hemisphere—are admitted annually

20 Most Poplous U.S. Cities
(1970 rank in parentheses)

		Estimated Population	Change Since 1970	Percentage Change
1	(1) New York	7,422,831	−472,732	− 6.0%
2	(2) Chicago	3,074084	−295,273	− 8.8%
3	(3) Los Angeles	2,743,994	− 65,819	− 2.0%
4	(4) Philadelphia	1,797,403	−199,395	− 6.6%
5	(7) Houston	1,455,046	+222,244	+18.0%
6	(5) Detroit	1,314,206	−199,395	− 6.6%
7	(8) Dallas	848,829	+ 4,428	+ 0.5%
8	(6) Baltimore	827,439	− 78,348	− 8.6%
9	(14) San Diego	789,059	+ 92,032	+13.0%
10	(15) San Antonio	783,765	+129,612	+20.0%
11	(11) Indianapolis	708,867	− 37,435	− 5.0%
12	(9) Washington	700,130	− 56,380	− 7.4%
13	(20) Phoenix	679,512	+ 97,950	+17.0%
14	(17) Memphis	667,880	+ 44,350	+ 7.0%
15	(13) San Francisco	663,478	− 52,196	− 7.0%
16	(12) Milwaukee	661,082	− 56,290	− 7.8%
17	(10) Cleveland	625,643	−125,236	−17.0%
18	(16) Boston	618,250	− 22,821	− 3.6%
19	(19) New Orleans	580,959	− 12,512	− 2.0%
20	(31) San Jose, Calif.	573,806	+112,594	+24.0%

lion. (The Mafia is described by *Time* as the only organized criminal group in the U.S. with a national structure.) GM's net profit in 1977 was $3.3 billion.

The Mafia dominates gambling, loan sharking, prostitution, labor racketeering, and might own as many as 10,000 legitimate firms (banks, hotels, restaurants, construction companies), the Justice Department says. Organized crime is expanding into new areas—the counterfeiting and theft of stocks and bonds, land development, pornography and arson. And it is migrating, particularly to the "sunbelt" states of the South and West; the mob goes where the money is.

"At the end of World War II, the strength of organized crime was in the big cities of the Northeast—Boston, New York, Cleveland, Detroit, Chicago . . . ," says Kirkpatrick Sale in *Power Shift*. "But as the population moved out, so did the mob. . . . Gambling centers . . . suddenly began blossoming across the [Southern] Rim in the 1950s: Miami Beach, Florida; Phoe-

nix City, Alabama; Biloxi, Mississippi; Gretna, Louisiana; Beaumont, Texas. . . . Today the extent of organized crime's operation in the Southern Rim is clearly vast. . . ."

Organized crime is "an extensive, successful and growing" enterprise in the southeastern states, the federal Task Force on Organized Crime reported in 1976. Legitimate businesses are not only infiltrated or manipulated, but taken over. The liquor industry, for example. Alcoholic beverage outlets are the underworld's retail market for all its goods and activities. Organized crime is "rapidly expanding" to include sophisticated white collar crimes. One city, subsequently identified as Fort Lauderdale, Fla., "seems to be the center for financial fraud for the entire nation." In addition to the large number of Mafia families and associates operating in this region, the Task Force found, there has been a significant growth in the number of "traveling criminals." These criminals, often referred to as the Dixie Mafia, cover approximately 17 states, and work together. As many as 10 to 12 gangs operate in one state at any given time, each under its own leader.

In the West, organized crime appears to be centered in metropolitan areas. It may take the form in one state of a variety of alliances resembling a loose-knit confederation. An unusual phenomenon is the apparent compatibility among crime figures; this contrasts with the feuding that often occurs in the East. Among the region's major underworld operations are:
- Fraud, particularly land and security fraud, crimes that frequently require specialization.
- The misuse of pension funds, which are often used to buy into a legitimate business.
- Fencing operations. Criminal ties in fencing operations extend outside the U.S.
- Drug smuggling and distribution. There are many independents in the areas bordering Mexico.

A directory listing 92 men as leaders of crime in California was published last year as part of the first report by the state's Organized Crime Control Commission. The directory includes photographs, addresses and descriptions. Several well-known business and labor leaders, not previously connected with organized crime by law-enforcement authorities, are on the list. During the past five years, the report says, about 50 organized crime figures "have either moved to or invested heavily in California." Many are from New York.

On the crime map, the Mafia extends across the nation—at least 24 "families" linked to each other and to other crime syndicates. Last

THE PRIVATE CITIZEN & THE CRIME SYNDICATE

The private citizen is the mob's biggest customer.

Organized crime provides such goods and services as illegal off-track betting, the numbers game, drugs, pornography, prostitutes, "black money" (racket money). That is the base of the mob's power, its corruption of law-enforcement officers and public officials—and of public apathy about its influence.

"There's no public outcry," says Thomas P. Puccio, head of the Organized Crime Strike Force for the Eastern District of New York.

The 1976 report of the federal Task Force on Organized Crime observed:

". . . Public demands for action against organized crime are infrequent and short-lived, usually sparked by cases of extreme violence or by revelations of widespread or high-level corruption. Sustained public awareness and concern are unusual in this country. . . .

"The public needs to be made aware that money lost on an illegal sports bet, paid to a loan shark or spent on a stolen television set or fur coat is likely to flow into a cash pool that will be used to bribe public officials, finance heroin traffic, and set in motion fraudulent bankruptcy schemes. People who are appalled by details of underworld violence may not realize how they contribute to the 'dirty money' that finances such violent acts. . . ."

year, the Mafia bosses in Boston, New York, Philadelphia, Baltimore, Chicago, Cleveland, Detroit, Milwaukee, St. Louis, Kansas City, Denver, San Francisco, Los Angeles, New Orleans and Miami, as well as in Buffalo and Rochester, N.Y.; Atlantic City, N.J.; Rockford, Ill. and Montreal were identified by the Federal Bureau of Investigation (FBI). In New York, the FBI and the police disagree about who is the Mafia "boss of bosses," the head of the city's five families. The FBI says he is Frank Tieri, while the police argue that Joseph Bonanno is the big guy. However, the FBI and the police agree, *The New York Times* reports, that "organized-crime membership is greater now than it has ever been."

Much of what is reported about the Mafia, the mob, is sensational and speculative. In 1975, for instance, Sam Giancana, a Chicago Mafia boss, was shot to death. Giancana had been tied in testimony before the Senate Select Committee on Intelligence to Central Intelligence Agency (CIA) assassination plots against Cuban Premier Fidel Castro.

Giancana's reputed West Coast lieutenant, John Roselli, appeared before the committee. Roselli was murdered in 1976. The committee's investigation uncovered a relationship between the late President John F. Kennedy and a woman then known as Judith Katherine Campbell. The woman was referred to in the committee's report as a "close friend" of Kennedy—and of Giancana and Roselli. She denied that she was "a go-between for the Mafia" in her relationship with Kennedy, or that she was aware Giancana and Roselli were helping the CIA. The investigation stopped short of making clear the significance of its disclosures.

In 1976, Don Bolles, a reporter for the Arizona *Republic*, was fatally injured when a bomb exploded in his car. Bolles had covered land fraud and organized crime in Arizona. He had informed fellow reporters before the bombing that he was working on a story about an alleged land deal involving three top Republican officials—Sen. Barry Goldwater, Rep. Sam Steiger and former state GOP chairman Harry Rosenzweig.

A team of 36 journalists was formed to inves-
tigate Bolles' murder. In a series of articles, the team identified more than 200 persons in Arizona as having Mafia connections. The controversial reports accused Goldwater, his businessman brother Robert Goldwater and Rosensweig of "condoning the presence of organized crime through friendships and alliances with mob figures." The three men were linked to "a web of relationships in Arizona, Nevada and California with important lieutenants of underworld financier Meyer Lansky." Sen. Goldwater denied the reporters' charges and threatened to sue for libel.

Silence is the key to the successful operation of the Mafia—the code of *omerta* (silence), vengeance carried out personally, and avoidance of all contact and cooperation with the legal authorities. It works so well that a counter-debate is still heard: is there a Mafia?

Thomas P. Puccio, head of the Organized Crime Strike Force for the Eastern District of New York, brushed aside the question in a recent interview with the *Times*. "There is a Mafia," he said, "based on testimony by its own members, on wiretaps, on surveillance and on the information we get from informers. Even the courts have taken judicial notice of the existence of the Mafia."

The bosses of the Mafia might go as far as denying their own existence, giving the nod to public relations campaigns that contend the existence of the Mafia has never been fully established. But, no alleged Mafioso has ever sued a newspaper for libel, ever ventured to test his claim to non-existence in court.

Attempts to obtain information about organized crime are limited by lack of intergovernmental cooperation, legal restrictions on investigative procedures, and "the difficulties of using statistical information . . . classified on a case-by-case basis only," the federal Task Force report emphasized.

No reliable research methodology has ever been developed. No national-level group has ever been appointed to undertake a systematic documentation of the extent of organized crime state-by-state and region-by-region. A thorough investigation of organized crime in the U.S. was recommended by the Task Force.

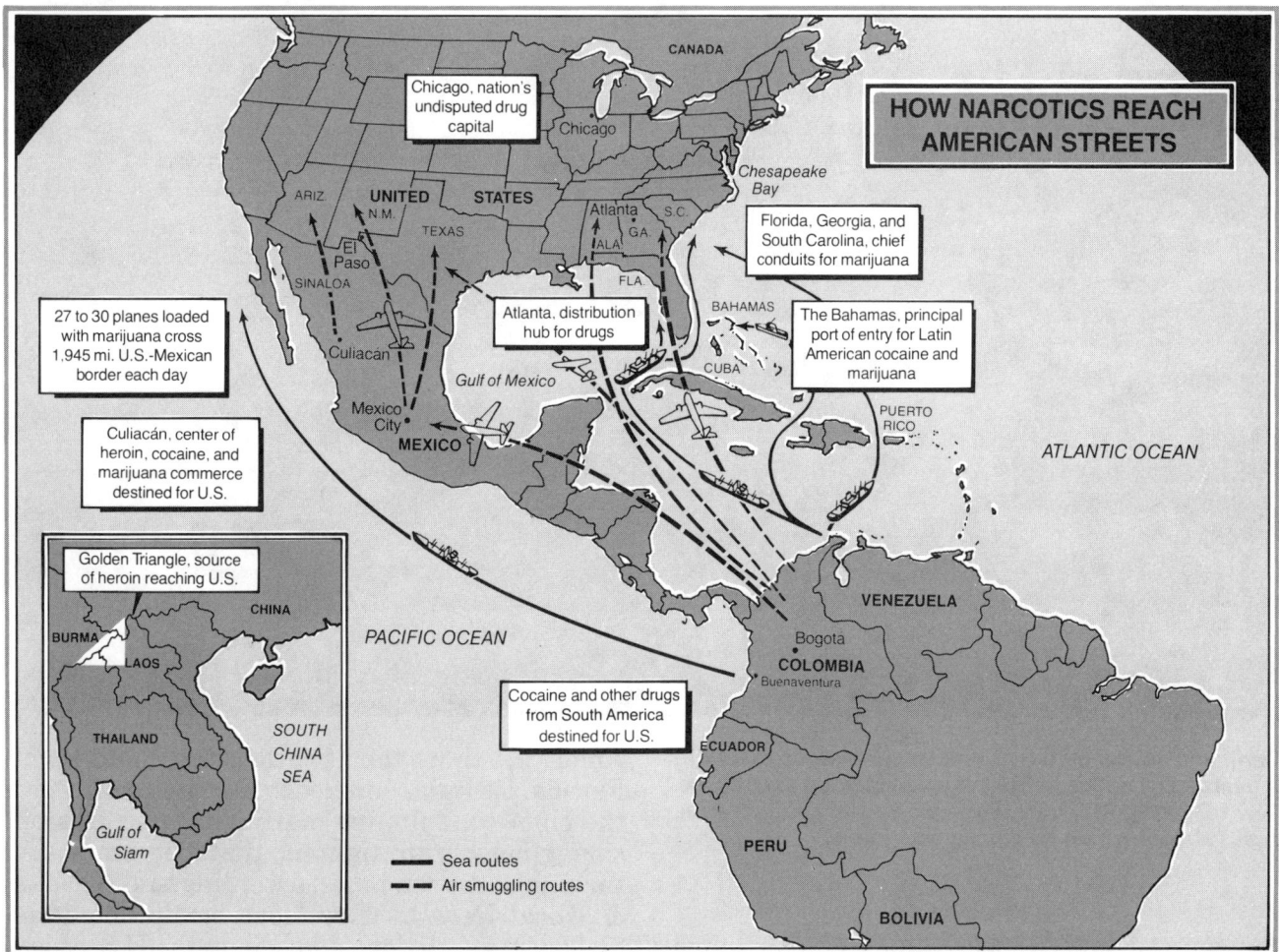

HOW NARCOTICS REACH AMERICAN STREETS

Chicago, nation's undisputed drug capital

Florida, Georgia, and South Carolina, chief conduits for marijuana

The Bahamas, principal port of entry for Latin American cocaine and marijuana

Atlanta, distribution hub for drugs

27 to 30 planes loaded with marijuana cross 1,945 mi. U.S.-Mexican border each day

Culiacán, center of heroin, cocaine, and marijuana commerce destined for U.S.

Golden Triangle, source of heroin reaching U.S.

Cocaine and other drugs from South America destined for U.S.

— Sea routes
-- - Air smuggling routes

CANADA · Chicago · Chesapeake Bay · ARIZ. · N.M. · UNITED STATES · TEXAS · El Paso · SINALOA · Atlanta · GA. · ALA. · S.C. · FLA. · Culiacan · Gulf of Mexico · BAHAMAS · CUBA · PUERTO RICO · Mexico City · MEXICO · ATLANTIC OCEAN · PACIFIC OCEAN · VENEZUELA · Bogota · COLOMBIA · Buenaventura · ECUADOR · PERU · BOLIVIA

CHINA · BURMA · LAOS · THAILAND · SOUTH CHINA SEA · Gulf of Siam

The routes by which narcotics enter the U.S. change frequently. For the moment, heroin, marijuana and cocaine are moving north from Latin America through the Southwest and South. Some of the air and sea routes are indicated on the map. Sources of narcotics also change rapidly. The "Golden Triangle," formed at the point where Thailand, Laos and Burma meet, is no longer a leading U.S. source of heroin as it once was.

CHAPTER 34

How Narcotics Reach American Streets

The routes by which narcotics reach the U.S. are changing rapidly; as some routes are shut down by law enforcement authorities, others open. Trafficking routes have become more flexible, says a report to the U.N. Commission on Narcotic Drugs, and more transit countries have become involved.

The Mexico-U.S. narcotics traffic is active. For example, Culiacan, capital of the Mexican state of Sinaloa, is a center of heroin, cocaine and marijuana commerce, much of it destined for the U.S. Ninety per cent of the heroin and 75 per cent of the marijuana reaching the U.S. comes from Mexico, the U.S. Drug Enforcement Administration (DEA) estimates. One-third of the cocaine entering the U.S. from Colombia is believed to pass through Mexico; other drug sources are Bolivia and Peru. (Americans now

Marijuana seized by U.S. Coast Guard in Boothbay, Me. is guarded by police in front of dock. Moored at dock are Coast Guard patrol boat (left) and 80-foot cabin cruiser (right) aboard which marijuana was found.

consume about 130,000 pounds of marijuana per day, reports *Time*. They spend $25 billion a year on the stuff. An estimated 66,000 pounds of cocaine are consumed annually in the U.S. at a cost of $20 billion.)

Between 27 and 30 planes loaded with marijuana cross the 1,945-mile U.S.-Mexican border each day, say U.S. Customs officials. The pilots land on isolated airstrips in the deserts of New Mexico, Arizona, Texas. Using advanced airfreight techniques, they are able to unload hundreds of pounds of marijuana in minutes.

Arizona is the major corridor for drug smuggling between Mexico and the U.S., an Investigative Reporters & Editors team found in 1977. There were 23 drug rings operating in the Mexico-Arizona corridor, five of which were wholly or partially controlled by organized crime.

However, the routes and methods of entry keep changing. In a series of articles, *The New York Times* reported during 1978 that narcotics smuggling is on the increase in Florida; that the Bahamas had become the main route for marijuana and cocaine entering the U.S. from South

America; that the Southeastern states of Florida, Georgia, and South Carolina now were the chief conduits for marijuana. As curbs on smuggling by air tighten, the drug czars are turning to the sea-lanes, according to *U.S. News & World Report*. They "load small freighters and yachts with dope and sail up the U.S. coastline, transferring cargoes to small boats. . . . Often the freighters, dirty and drab on the outside, are equipped with sophisticated radar and electronic eavesdropping devices to contact cohorts ashore and evade the police."

Distribution points are reported to include Atlanta and Chicago. Atlanta is the hub for "drugs from South America, and of course from Mexico," says Jack Salter, agent in charge of the Atlanta office of the DEA, according to the *Times*. Chicago has become the undisputed drug capital of the nation, reports *Newsweek*. The Mexico-Chicago connection supplies about 90 per cent of the heroin sold in the U.S. An estimated 10 or 11 tons of Mexican heroin with a retail value of more than $2 billion is smuggled into Chicago each year, nearly all of it coming across the Texas border by car.

Sources of narcotics changed as rapidly in recent years as the transit routes. The Turkish heroin trade was curtailed in 1972, and the "Golden Triangle," where the borders of Burma, Laos, and Thailand meet, is supplying

DRUG ABUSE: WORLD TRENDS

World trends in drug abuse and illicit demand, as summarized by reports to the U.N. Commission on Narcotic Drugs, indicate:

A continuing spread of heroin use . . . more deaths from drug overdose . . . increasing abuse of psychotropic substances . . . widespread misuse of marijuana . . . a general development towards multiple drug abuse . . . the persistence of traditional opium consumption in a number of countries.

less heroin to the U.S. Much of the latter's production now goes to Europe, reportedly through Amsterdam.

Law enforcement, in any case, remains difficult. "Our major problem is geography," Salter says. Georgia has 2,300 miles of shoreline, dotted with islands, coves, and inlets, a good deal of it deserted. It is easy for smugglers to elude coastal patrols.

Other problems are a scarcity of manpower and equipment. ". . . There is one patrol plane for the entire border from El Paso to the West Coast," the *Times* reports, "and a shortage of purchase money has made it nearly impossible for drug enforcement agencies to make big busts."

Finally, the high profits of drug peddling have generated a respectable, well-connected type of smuggler. In South Carolina, a former state legislator was charged with a smuggling operation that used an island partly owned by him and the governor; the governor is said not to be involved. In Florida, a circuit judge was convicted of conspiring to sell 1,500 pounds of marijuana.

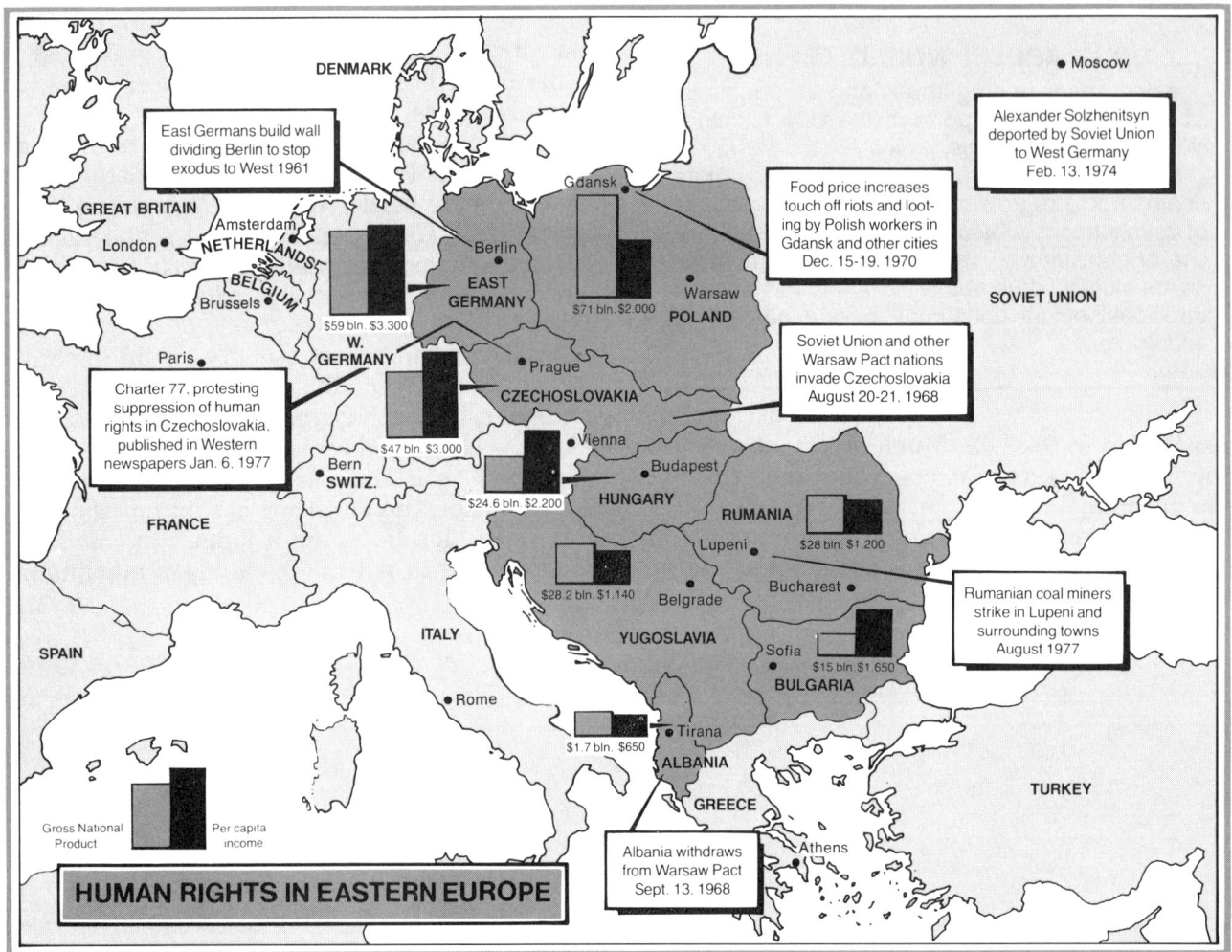

Moscow

Alexander Solzhenitsyn
deported by Soviet Union
to West Germany
Feb. 13, 1974

East Germans build wall
dividing Berlin to stop
exodus to West 1961

Food price increases
touch off riots and loot-
ing by Polish workers in
Gdansk and other cities
Dec. 15-19, 1970

Soviet Union and other
Warsaw Pact nations
invade Czechoslovakia
August 20-21, 1968

Charter 77, protesting
suppression of human
rights in Czechoslovakia,
published in Western
newspapers Jan. 6, 1977

Rumanian coal miners
strike in Lupeni and
surrounding towns
August 1977

Albania withdraws
from Warsaw Pact
Sept. 13, 1968

DENMARK
GREAT BRITAIN
Amsterdam
London
NETHERLANDS
BELGIUM
Brussels
Paris
FRANCE
SPAIN
Bern
SWITZ.
Berlin
EAST GERMANY
W. GERMANY
$59 bln. $3,300
Prague
CZECHOSLOVAKIA
$47 bln. $3,000
Vienna
Budapest
HUNGARY
$24.6 bln. $2,200
ITALY
Rome
Gdansk
Warsaw
POLAND
$71 bln. $2,000
RUMANIA
Lupeni
Bucharest
$28 bln. $1,200
Belgrade
YUGOSLAVIA
$28.2 bln. $1,140
Sofia
BULGARIA
$15 bln. $1,650
Tirana
$1.7 bln. $650
ALBANIA
GREECE
Athens
SOVIET UNION
TURKEY

Gross National Product
Per capita income

HUMAN RIGHTS IN EASTERN EUROPE

EASTERN EUROPE
A STATISTICAL SUMMARY

	BULGARIA	CZECHO-SLOVAKIA	EAST GERMANY	HUNGARY	POLAND	RUMANIA	YUGO-SLAVIA	ALBANIA
Population	8,848,000	15,136,000	16,790,000	10,600,000	34,360,000	21,450,000	21,560,000	2,550,000
Area (sq. mi.)	42,829	49,371	40,646	35,919	120,359	91,699	98,766	11,100
Capital	Sofia	Prague	East Berlin	Budapest	Warsaw	Bucharest	Belgrade	Tirana
Communist Party head	Todor Zhivkov	Gustav Husak	Erich Honecker	Janos Kadar	Edward Gierek	Nicolae Ceausescu	Josip Broz Tito	Enver Hoxha
Communist Party membership	817,000	1,380,000	1,900,000	754,000	2,758,000	2,747,000	1,629,082	101,500
Communist Party membership percentage	4%	7%	8%	8%	9%	9%	11%	13%
Gross National Product	$15 bln.	$47 bln.	$59 bln.	$24.6 bln.	$71 bln.	$28 bln.	$28.2 bln.	$1.7 bln.
Per capita income	$1,650	$3,000	$3,300	$2,200	$2,000	$1,200	$1,140	$650
Passenger cars in use	160,000	1,328,200	1,702,900	490,800	920,300	125,000	1,330,000	
Birth rate	0.63%	0.81%	0.30%	0.60%	1.02%	1.12%	0.95%	2.52%
Infant mortality (per 1,000 pop. under 1 yr.)	22.9	20.9	15.9	32.6	24.8	35.0	40.5	86.8
Life expectancy	68.58 (m) 73.86 (f)	66.53 73.49	68.5 74.9	66.7 72.9	66.83 73.76	66.83 71.29	65.42 70.22	64.9 67.0
Literacy	90%	98%	98%	98%	98%	90%	93%	75%

The issue of human rights divides Europe. On the one hand, there is the "wall"—the Berlin Wall—and on the other, conflict about political and individual liberty. In the West, freedom had a long and difficult development; in the East, the struggle for freedom has often been undertaken—and lost. That struggle is being continued today by Eastern European and Soviet dissidents.

CHAPTER 35

Human Rights in East Europe

In 1975, a 35-nation conference on European security and cooperation met in Helsinki. Europe's post-World War II boundaries were ratified. The "threat or use of force" as a means of settling disputes was renounced. In a development that was to become a major issue, the fundamental freedoms of thought, conscience, religion or belief were affirmed.

A year later, Robert A. Haeger cabled *U.S. News & World Report,* "You get the feeling of what people in Eastern Europe think of the Helsinki accords from a story that is being told in many capitals there. A woman in Khaskovo, Bulgaria applies for permission to journey to the West, citing 'Helsinki' as the justification. Response by the local bureaucrat: 'Comrade, this is not Helsinki. This is Khaskovo.'"

In 1977, Jimmy Carter became President of the U.S. and, in his inaugural address, expressed his concern for human rights. The existence, protection and violation of human rights emerged as a major issue in the first days of his Administration. Carter had proclaimed "what may be called 'moralpolitics,'" observes Arthur R. Rachwald in *Current History,* "a commitment to take the human rights provisions of Helsinki seriously and to end the lack of moral leadership that characterized the Nixon-Ford Administrations." (The "Carter doctrine" is the latest in six distinctly different policies the U.S. has followed toward the Communist countries of Eastern Europe since the end of World War II, Rachwald recalls. Its predecessors were "containment," "liberation," "peaceful engagement," "bridge-building" and Henry Kissinger's *realpolitik.*)

The issue of human rights touched off a widespread controversy. In Czechoslovakia, the members of Charter 77, a group that had signed a manifesto calling for the protection of human rights, were harassed by police. The U.S. accused Czechoslovakia of violating the Helsinki agreements. The leaders of the French, Italian and Spanish Communist parties urged "full application" of the accords. Rumanian dissidents, in an open letter, urged support for greater observance of human rights.

In Moscow, the chairman of a Soviet Helsinki monitoring group, Yuri Orlov, was arrested and charged with "anti-Soviet agitation." The Soviet Union protested "interference" in its internal affairs and warned that "ideological warfare" would hinder the progress of detente. Subsequently, Orlov was convicted at a trial that the U.S. State Department termed "a gross distortion of internationally accepted standards of human rights." He was sentenced to seven years in prison and five years' internal exile (banishment from the western Soviet Union). Other Soviet dissidents were tried and received similar sentences.

Debate at the first Helsinki review conference in 1977–78 was dominated by the question of human rights. The U.S. criticized violations in Eastern Europe, and the Soviet Union defended itself by reading a list of its constitutional guarantees. In its final document, the conference omitted mention of human rights, and most delegates agreed that very little had been accomplished. The U.S. representative, Arthur J. Goldberg, however, said that human rights had been put "prominently and legitimately into the framework of East-West multilateral diplomacy." A second review conference is scheduled for 1980.

Western analysts, meanwhile, note that a new Soviet constitution, adopted in 1977, does not differ in the area of human rights from the 1936 constitution. It guaranteed freedom of speech, press and assembly "in conformity with the interests of the working people and for the purpose of strengthening the Socialist system," as written in Article 50. But the addition of Article 59 more explicitly limited the rights. "Exercise of rights and freedoms shall be inseparable from the performance by citizens of their duties," it read. The new article was being used against Soviet dissidents who referred to the constitutional guarantees as a defense against charges that their activities were illegal.

To a degree, the observance of human rights varies from country to country in Eastern Europe. Yugoslavia, which broke with the Kremlin in 1948, is atypical. ". . . The country is a self-managed commonwealth," writes Dusko Doder in *The Wilson Quarterly,* "each citizen is a self-manager; together, citizens make decisions in a self-managed manner, suggesting a New England town meeting gone wild. . . ." In Poland, there is an "opposition tradition," "intellectual ferment" *(Le Monde),* while in Bulgaria "overt dissidence is practically nonexistent," according to Richard F. Staar. Czechoslovakia, occupied by 16 or more Soviet divisions since 1968, is gloomy, muffled. "Life has turned into a matter of sinking yourself in routine . . . think nothing, because it was your thoughts that betrayed you initially . . . ," says Joseph Hone in a BBC radio broadcast. ". . . Kafka . . . was the major prophet of its present state. . . ."

Map labels:

Bay of Biscay

Bilbao
VIZCAYA
GUIPUZCOA
ALAVA
Pamplona
NAVARRA
Rio Ebro

FRANCE
ANDORRA
P Y R E N E E S

GERONA
LERIDA
Gerona
BARCELONA
Barcelona
C A T A L O N I A
COSTA BRAVA

SPAIN
Rio Ebro
Lerida
TARRAGONA
Tarragon

Balearic Sea

Inset map:
ATLANTIC OCEAN
FRANCE
PORTUGAL
Basque Provinces
Madrid
SPAIN
Catalan Provinces
Lisbon
BALEARIC ISLANDS
MEDITERRANEAN SEA
Strait of Gibraltar

Scale: 0 25 50 75 Miles / 0 50 100 Km.

Spain's total population 36,448,481			
Basque People		**Catalans**	
Province	Population	Province	Population
VIZCAYA	1,178,055	BARCELONA	4,485,086
GUIPUZCOA	690,594	TARRAGONA	490,056
NAVARRA	490,531	GERONA	447,657
ALAVA	245,669	LERIDA	348,388
Total	2,605,849	Total	5,771,187

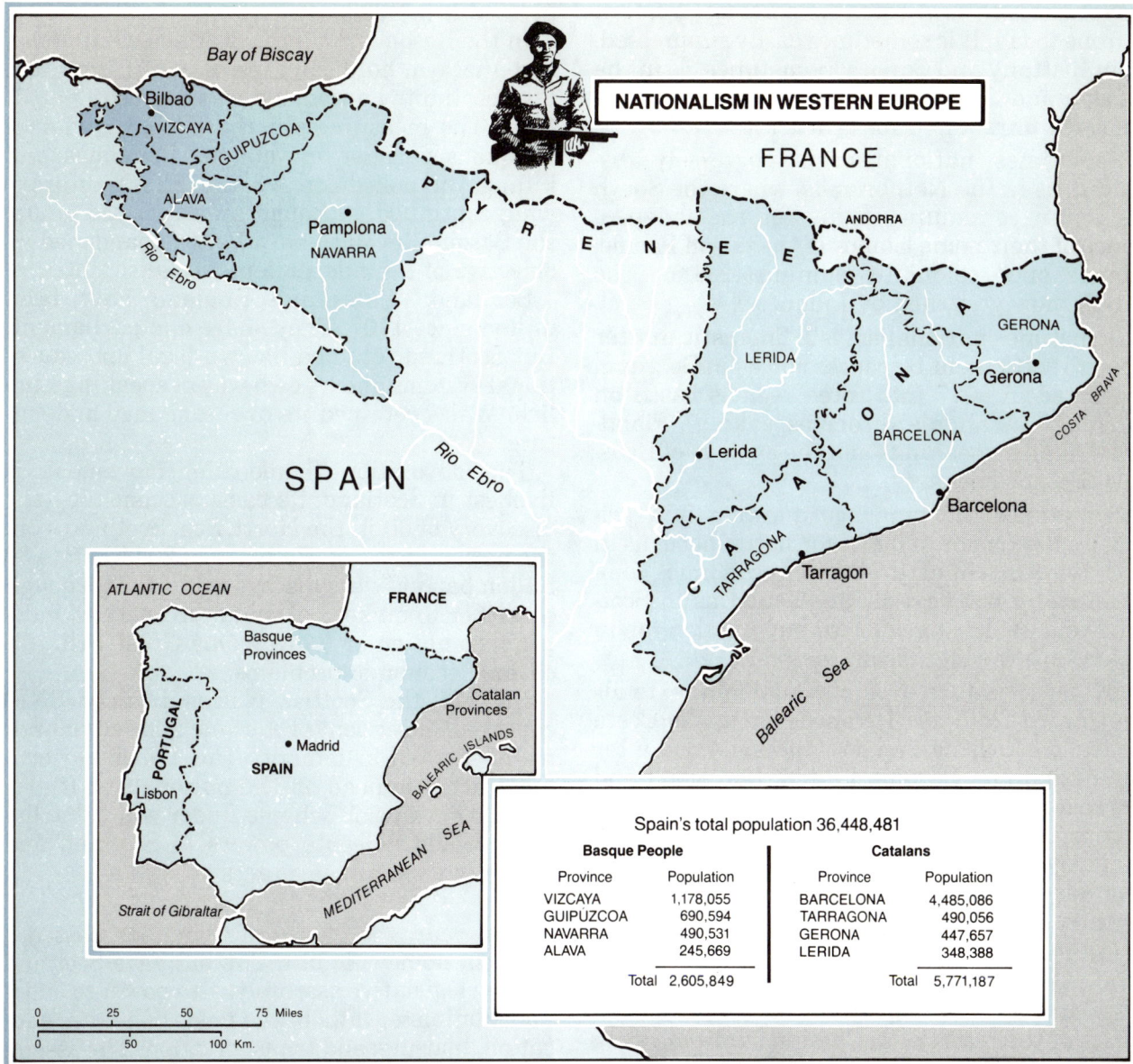

Centuries-old separatist movements remain strong among the Basque and Catalan peoples of Spain and are representative of nationalism as a force in Western Europe. Located on this map are the northern provinces in which the two peoples live. Within Spain's total population of almost 36.5 million, the Basques number 2.6 million and the Catalans 5.7 million. Culturally distinctive, the Basque and Catalan provinces also are among the most productive agricultural and industrial regions in Spain. The nationalist impulse in these and other areas frequently lead to terrorist bombings and assassinations, backing up demands for autonomy.

CHAPTER 36

Nationalism in Western Europe

The aspirations of a unique people may be expressed in the impulse to nationalism. To members of such a group, their desires are just: geographic unity, linguistic, cultural, political identity as a nation-state.

The impulse is troublesome to central authority, stimulating conflict, agitation, and violence.

Nationalism is a force in parts of Western Europe today. It is sometimes easily suppressed, as in Brittany and Corsica. Sometimes, as in the Basque and Catalan provinces of Spain, it has survived unrequited for centuries.

Sometimes nationalism is perversely displaced, as in the Netherlands, where the South Moluccan community fights for the independence of their home islands in the far-off Pacific, islands once colonially administered by the Dutch, now governed by Indonesia.

Sometimes nationalism is a linguistic matter open to settlement by concession as in Belgium, federated in 1977 into three regions based on language—Wallonia (French-speaking), Flanders (Flemish-speaking), and the enclave of Brussels (French-speaking).

Sometimes the language question is a primary cause of the demand for nationhood, as in the Basque country. Often, economic complaints and political dissatisfaction as in Scotland and Wales, or political suppression, as in Spain, are the significant factors.

In northeastern Spain, Catalonia extends southward from the Pyrenees along the Costa Brava, comprising four provinces, named after their capitals—Gerona, Lerida, Barcelona and Tarragona. It is an agriculturally and industrially productive region. It has preserved its own language (related to Provençal) and institutions and has struggled for autonomy since the 17th century.

Catalanism revived strongly following Franco's death. The outlawed red and yellow Catalan flag was displayed and the forbidden lyrics of the traditional Catalan *sardanas* sung once again. Demands for self-rule increased. Demonstrations were broken up and student protesters killed by the *Guardia Civil* in numerous cities.

On Sept. 11, 1977, a million Catalans observed their "national day" with a march through the streets of Barcelona. On Sept. 29, King Juan Carlos I issued decrees awarding limited autonomy to the Catalonian provinces. The decrees reestablished the Generalitat, Catalonia's ancient governing body, which dated back to the 14th century. It had been abolished in 1714 in the War of the Spanish Succession and not restored until the establishment of the

Second Spanish Republic in 1931. Franco suppressed it in 1939.

In the Basque provinces of Alava, Guipuzcoa, and Vizcaya, bordering the Bay of Biscay and France, limited autonomy was decreed Dec. 31, 1977. The measure split the ETA, the violent Basque separatist movement. Bombings and killings of policemen by the ETA's military wing continued, although an associated group, the Basque Revolutionary Party, abandoned its objective of an independent, socialist state.

Scotland, Wales and England have been united since 1707. They share one parliament. But Scotland retained its own legal and educational systems and its own way of speaking English. Wales retained its own language and culture.

The devolution (home-rule) movement is liveliest in Scotland; its basis is economic—the discovery of oil in the North Sea. Scotland's oil, the nationalists say. Reserves of 20 billion to 30 billion barrels were discovered in 1971, enough oil either to make Scotland a prosperous, independent nation or to overcome Great Britain's chronic economic problems.

In 1974, the Scottish National Party (SNP) captured 30 per cent of the vote and sent eleven members to Parliament. The Labor Government acted to head off the nationalists. It proposed a devolution scheme under which Parliament would delegate powers to Scotland and Wales but remain sovereign.

Last year, the House of Commons passed a Scottish home-rule bill. The bill gave Scotland its own legislative assembly with power to enact and administer laws in the fields of health, education, housing, and transportation. The assembly would not have power to collect taxes and would be able to administer only funds allotted to it. The bill provided for a referendum in which at least 40 per cent of the Scottish electorate would have to approve devolution for it to go into effect. Devolution, however, was defeated in March 1979 when only 32.9 per cent of the electorate voted for it. Aberdeen, Scotland's new oil capital, meanwhile, is booming. The North Sea oil field and drilling sites are 125 miles to the east, and Aberdeen has become a busy port. In 1980, it is expected, North Sea oil will bring Great Britain an estimated $7 billion in tax revenues and royalty payments.

CHAPTER 37

Northern Ireland

The facts are bitter and fearful. Communal strife between Protestants and Catholics in Northern Ireland (Ulster) is mirrored at the outset in language, as conflicts often are. Catholics prefer the term Northern Ireland, Protestants tend to favor the word Ulster. (Authors, as Ronald J. Terchek points out, use them interchangeably for the sake of linguistic variety.)

The facts are historical, national, religious, political, economic, cultural. They reflect an 800-year Anglo-Irish struggle.

The first English invasion of Ireland occurred in 1171. Subsequently, the English failed to subdue the Irish, while the Irish were unable to drive out the English.

Two further events are of particular historical importance. On July 12, 1690, the armies of King William III of England defeated the Catholic James II at the Battle of the Boyne; the victory is commemorated each year by Ulster Protestants. In 1922, Ireland was partitioned. The Irish Free State (now the Republic of Ireland) and Northern Ireland (six of the nine counties of the historic province of Ulster) were established.

The current "troubles" began in 1968. Catholics presented a list of grievances. They charged discrimination in housing, voting and employment, and conducted anti-government demonstrations.

In 1969, large-scale violence broke out; the worst religious rioting in more than thirty years took place in Belfast. British troops were called in to restore order. Violence grew— bombings, assassinations, reprisals, mass arrests, internment, torture.

In 1972, London suspended the Ulster government and reimposed direct rule.

Violence declined last year, but the political impasse remained; the Protestants refused to share power with the Catholics. ". . . There is among Unionists [Ulster Protestants] almost universal hatred and fear of Ireland's Roman Catholic majority and intense hatred of the Catholics who live within Ulster itself," wrote Andrew Boyd in *The Nation*. "That hatred is deep, apparently congenital and virtually ineradicable. . . . That is what Northern Ireland has been like for a very long time. . . ."

Many observers view the prospects for a settlement with pessimism. A conflict based on religious identity is one of the most intractable to solve, they say. Some consider—and reject—the reunification of Ireland as a possible outcome. ". . . What Ireland needs at this time is not 'unity' but a greater flexibility in division," Conor Cruise O'Brien suggests in *States of Ireland*. "The 'unity of Ireland' is a dangerous illusion but 'the unity of Northern Ireland' is also a dangerous illusion. There is no perfect way of sorting out the hostile and intertwined communities, but autonomy within direct rule offers the best hope. . . ."

Some put forward the "repartition" of Northern Ireland as the most workable solution. Of the six counties, Tyrone and Fermanagh, West Derry, South Armagh and South Down would be transferred to the Irish Republic. Most of the 500,000 people involved in such a transfer would be Catholics. Protestants unwilling to make the change could be resettled east of the Bann River. "In the end, what is the alternative to repartition and resettlement?" asks Joseph M. Curran, writing in *America*. "Not unity, not restoration of the pre-1969 order, not total integration in the United Kingdom or complete independence for Northern Ireland and not effective power sharing within the substate. . . ."

NORTHERN IRELAND COUNTIES

TOTAL POPULATION 1971

- Non-Catholic
- Catholic

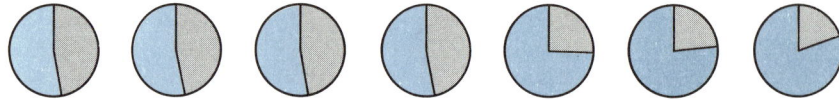

	FERMANAGH	TYRONE	LONDONDERRY	ARMAGH	BELFAST *	DOWN	ANTRIM
Total Population	49,935	138,158	174,530	132,678	356,830	308,910	352,599
Catholic	23,738	65,370	82,040	57,710	91,420	74,298	83,345
Presbyterian	1,742	24,426	39,821	18,585	93,376	103,269	124,498
Church of Ireland	15,658	26,564	31,443	32,000	87,579	67,329	73,745
Others and not stated denomination	8,797	21,798	27,226	24,383	84,455	64,014	71,011

TOTAL NORTHERN IRELAND POPULATION SIX COUNTIES	
Total Northern Ireland Population	1,519,640
Catholic	477,921
Presbyterian	405,717
Church of Ireland	334,318
Others and not stated denomination	301,684

*Belfast population is counted separately.

54% Non-Catholic   46% Catholic
NORTHERN IRELAND

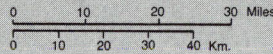

COUNTIES IN IRELAND

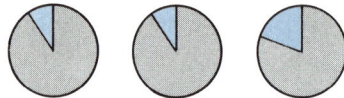

	DONEGAL	CAVAN	MONAGHAN
Total Population	108,344	52,618	46,242
Catholic	93,330	46,556	40,141
Presbyterian	6,030	905	2,971
Church of Ireland	6,818	4,513	2,402
Methodist	651	169	70
Jewish	9	1	1
No religion	118	23	24
Others and not stated denomination	1,388	451	633

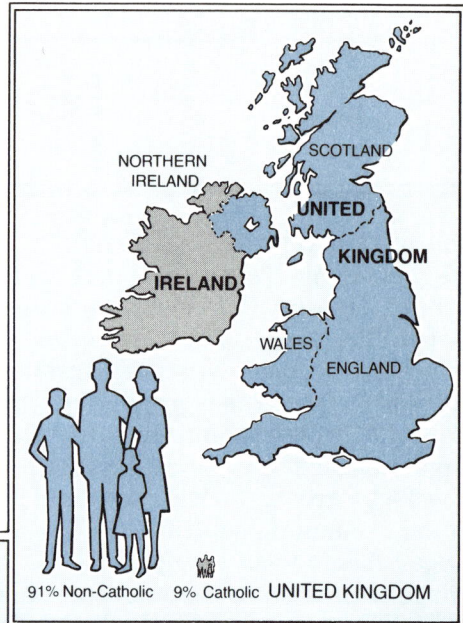

NORTHERN IRELAND
SCOTLAND
UNITED KINGDOM
IRELAND
WALES
ENGLAND

91% Non-Catholic   9% Catholic   UNITED KINGDOM

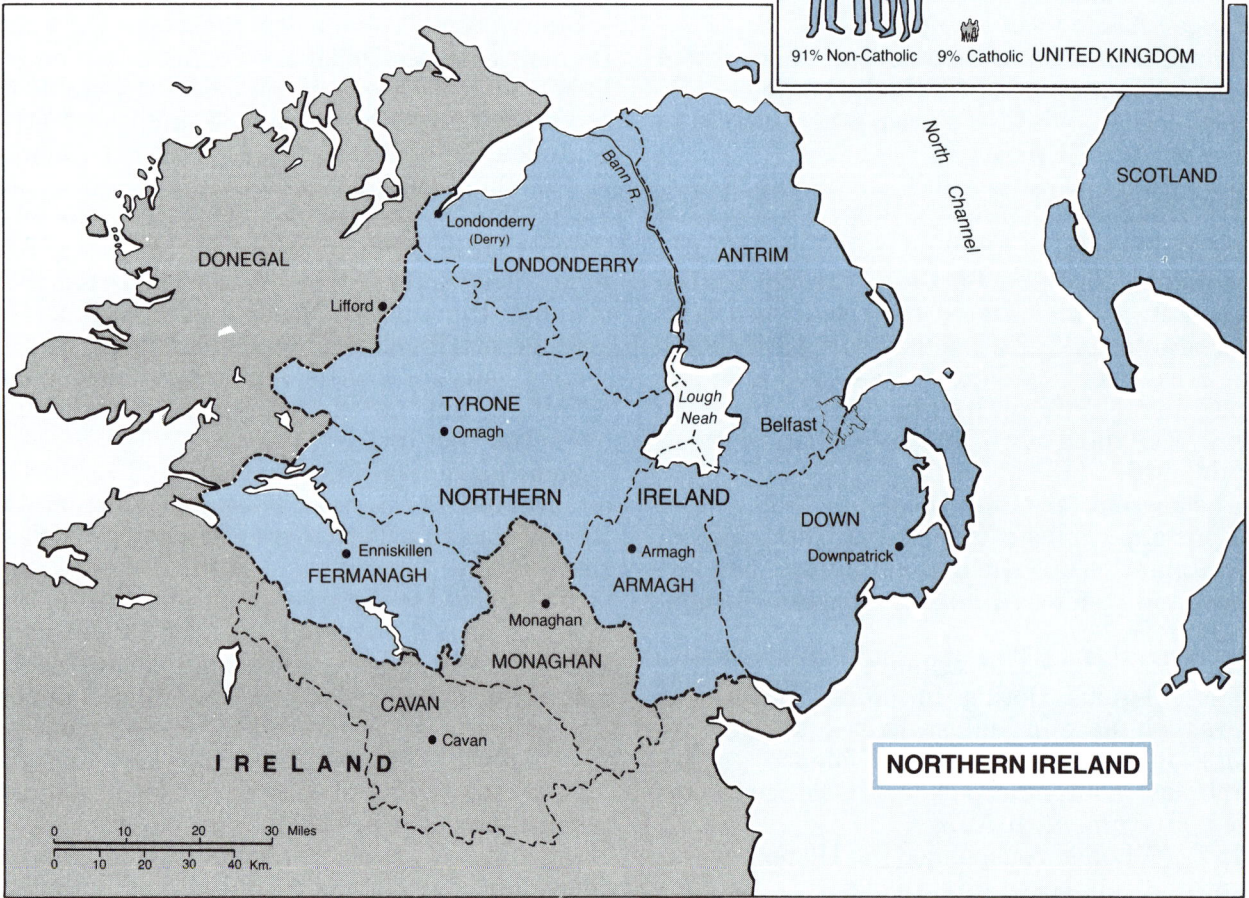

SCOTLAND

North Channel

Bann R.

DONEGAL

Londonderry (Derry)
LONDONDERRY
ANTRIM

Lifford

TYRONE
Omagh

Lough Neah

Belfast

NORTHERN   IRELAND

DOWN
Downpatrick

Enniskillen
FERMANAGH

Armagh
ARMAGH

Monaghan
MONAGHAN

CAVAN
Cavan

I R E L A N D

NORTHERN IRELAND

0 10 20 30 Miles
0 10 20 30 40 Km.

Others see glimmers of hope in government legislation that had made discrimination in housing and employment more difficult, in the successes of the movement led by Nobel Peace Prize winners Betty Williams and Mairead Corrigan and the dip in violence. If the terror ends, perhaps solutions would become clearer. "Before the factions can agree, the Catholic majority must be able, free of coercion, to elect its fair share of representatives in districts that have not been gerrymandered to their disadvantage: in a word, full civil rights," comments Carey McWilliams. ". . . But a basic condition to unraveling the tangle the British created must be

their willingness to begin a reassessment of the brutal consequences of the 'settlement' imposed in 1921. . . ." Almost all agree that the British army must not pull out precipitously, that an abrupt withdrawal might give way to an attack on the Catholic ghettos and to further violence.

In *Christian Century,* Vernon Schmid emphasizes movingly that ". . . whether one tends to see the war in political, economic, social or historical terms, what is undeniable is that people are caught up in it—people concerned about the future of a country whose children are growing up in a culture filled with overt violence. . . ." Some, at least, are saying: enough is enough.

The major factor generally blamed for the bloodshed in Northern Ireland—the division between Catholics and Protestants in the population—is depicted left. In Down and Antrim counties, the people are overwhelmingly Protestant. The counties of Fermanagh, Tyrone, Londonderry and Armagh are non-Catholic by small margins. The city of Belfast, whose population is counted separately, is mostly Protestant. The populations of the other three counties of the historic province of Ulster, which have been a part of Ireland since the 1922 partition, and of the United Kingdom as a whole also are charted. Communal warfare persists between Catholics and Protestants in Northern Ireland. Is a solution possible? Many view the prospects with pessimism, but some see hope in anti-discrimination laws recently passed and in an apparent decline in the incidence of violence.

CHAPTER 38

Latin American Military Regimes

Sixteen years ago, five Latin American countries were run by the military; today, military regimes govern two-thirds of the region, at least 13 countries, four people out of every five.

The generals overthrew civilian governments in Brazil in 1964, Panama and Peru in 1968, Bolivia in 1969, Ecuador in 1972, Uruguay and Chile in 1973, Argentina in 1976. El Salvador, Guatemala, Honduras, Nicaragua and Paraguay already were ruled by the military.

Two Latin American countries—Costa Rica and Venezuela—might still be called democracies. Colombia claims to be a democracy, but, says *Maclean's*, "banditry, rebellion and the fact that cocaine and marijuana are worth more than traditional exports make the boast a mockery." Mexico is governed by a one-party bureaucracy of technocrats, Cuba by Castro and the Communist Party.

Supposedly restorative votes were held last year in Bolivia, Ecuador, and the Dominican Republic, where Joaquin Balaguer had held power with U.S. support since 1965. The results of the balloting in Bolivia were challenged as fraudulent and then set aside as the military reasserted itself. In the other two countries, the actual significance of the balloting is uncertain. The victor in the Dominican Republic, for example, pledged that his administration would respect the "institutionality" of the armed forces.

Several patterns are discernible.

The generals speak the same language, with the exception for a time of reformist officers in Peru. They are no longer known as *caudillos* (strongmen); now, they rule through military-civil governments. They refer to themselves as "revolutionary" and represent themselves as "moralizing" forces. They justify their take-overs in white papers that refer to Marxist conspiracies and "economic, social, institutional, and moral ruin." They would carry out a "national reorganization" aimed at "control over the vital areas of security and development." They invoke a "state of siege" to cancel personal and political liberties. Political parties are placed "in recess." The state of siege would be

THE CIA & THE JUNTA

It was a South American military takeover like any other, according to the press reports.

Ecuadorian President Jose Maria Velasco Ibarra was overthrown Feb. 15, 1972, accused of "exploiting the people." He was flown to Panama by the air force. A three-man junta proclaimed a "revolutionary and nationalist" government. Ecuador was placed under a state of siege. Scheduled elections were suspended. A night curfew was imposed.

Three years later, in a book titled *Inside the Company: CIA Diary*, Philip Agee discussed the operations of the Central Intelligence Agency in Mexico, Uruguay, and Ecuador. A string of political figures, including a vice-president and several Cabinet members, had been on the CIA payroll in Ecuador, Agee wrote. CIA agents had influenced the activities of labor leaders, bishops and military officers. The public had been systematically misled by the dissemination of false information about Communist and left-wing groups, Agee charged.

Miles Copeland, a former high-ranking CIA official, said in a review of the book in the British publication *The Spectator*: "The book is . . . an authentic account of how an ordinary American or British 'case officer' operates. . . . All of it . . . is presented with deadly accuracy." Other CIA sources disputed Agee's account.

CHILE & HUMAN RIGHTS ABUSE

A resolution "deploring" the abuse of human rights in Chile and expressing "particular concern and indignation" about "the continuing disappearance" of Chileans was adopted Dec. 16, 1977 by the U.N. General Assembly. The vote was 96–14. Those voting against it were Chile, 12 other Latin American countries and Lebanon. The resolution was based on a report by the U.N. Human Rights Commission.

Excerpts from the report:

"... Chilean authorities systematically refuse to respect the right to liberty and security of person of those believed to be opposed to the present regime.... People continue to disappear in Chile after detention by security agencies and although the number of disappearances is currently not as high as in the past, no effective measures have been taken to stop this practice or to punish those responsible for it.... Torture continues to be inflicted on detainees.... The Constitutional Acts promulgated in September 1976 have proven to be a mere facade erected by a regime that wishes to appear as acting under constitutional authority and national and international legality."

made by the regime to show that missing persons have not actually vanished. "Nearly 50 families of missing detainees [in Chile] were visited by groups of two or three persons who tried to obtain declarations that the individuals were not missing," reports the U.N. Human Rights Commission. "In other cases the government responded with a simple denial or replied that no record of detention existed, that the person had been released, or that he had left the country." Sometimes, the bodies of victims turn up on the streets of city suburbs or secluded beaches. "The body of Marta Ugarte was found ... north of the city," Nicholas E. Roman wrote in a *Saturday Review* article on the Chilean junta. "The girl's ribs were broken—all of them —as were one of her arms and a leg. Barbed wire was wrapped around her neck."

Their economic policies often are similar. They refinance foreign debts; impose austerity measures; devalue the currency; administer wages and prices. In Argentina, the cost of living rose by 347.5% in 1976, up from 335% in 1975. The inflation rate was cut to 160% in 1977, as the government froze wages and curbed price increases; the purchasing power of real wages fell 56% during the year. The regime's economic policy assured "private enterprise, and national and foreign capital, all the necessary conditions to participate ... in the rational exploitation of our resources." Foreign investors would be encouraged through tax incentives and other measures to invest in Argentina.

Expressing its support for Argentina's financial policies, the International Monetary Fund in 1977 permitted the government to purchase

maintained until "we judge that the symptoms of normalization permit us to reduce or lift [it]."

Their regimes are brutal and violent. Left-wing movements, leaders, labor unions, publications are suppressed along with guerrillas and terrorists. "Death squads" operate under various names. The number of persons killed or imprisoned in Argentina, Chile, Uruguay is unknown. Victims disappear, and attempts are

VIDELA OF ARGENTINA

On Dec. 25, 1975, Lt. Gen. Jorge Rafael Videla, Argentina's army chief, demanded immediate "reforms in the country," punishment of "immorality and corruption," and an end to "political, economic and ideological speculation." Three months later, the Peronist government was overthrown by the commanders of the armed forces. Videla, described as tough-minded but ideologically moderate, was installed as president. He pledged to combat "subversive delinquency in all its forms" and called for "sacrifice, work and austerity" to resolve the nation's acute economic crisis.

A "dialogue" with political leaders on how Argentina would be returned to democracy was promised by the military junta several times in 1977.

Videla said the armed forces would offer concrete proposals. The suggested dialogue was ridiculed by the Buenos Aires newspaper *La Prensa*. It pointed out that Videla planned to consult political leaders without lifting the suspension of political activity. This was like trying "to make rabbit stew without the rabbit," the newspaper said.

Videla was born on Aug. 2 1925 in the provincial city of Mercedes. He was the son of an army colonel. In 1944, he was graduated from the national military academy, the Colegia Militar, and served in a series of army posts for the next 25 years. He was promoted to general in 1971. Two of his seven children are cadets at the Colegia Militar. In 1978, Videla's term of office was extended to 1981 by the military junta.

LATIN AMERICA MILITARY REGIMES

UNITED STATES

MEXICO

BAHAMAS

CUBA

HAITI

DOMINICAN REP.

JAMAICA

BELIZE

HONDURAS

GUATEMALA

EL SALVADOR

NICARAGUA

COSTA RICA

PANAMA

GRENADA

BARBADOS

TRINIDAD & TOBAGO

VENEZUELA

GUYANA

SURINAM

FRENCH GUIANA

COLOMBIA

ECUADOR

PERU

BRAZIL

BOLIVIA

PARAGUAY

CHILE

ARGENTINA

URUGUAY

Military regimes

Civilian regimes

OAS Members

Communist country

Democracy and good government are a rarity in Latin America. Rule is predominantly by military dictatorship or so-called military-civil regimes. There appear to be but two genuine democracies — Costa Rica and Venezuela — while Mexico is governed by a one-party bureaucracy, Colombia is riddled by banditry and rebellion, and the Dominican Republic is a toss-up. The situation is depicted on the map, which also identifies the one Communist country (Cuba) and the members of the Organization of American States (OAS).

159.5 million special drawing rights; the authorization was equivalent to a credit line of $137 million. In addition, the World Bank approved a $200-million loan to the Argentine national investment bank; the loan was cofinanced by the Bank of America, Lloyds Bank International and other international lenders.

The military chiefs emerge from social contexts that are alike. They are members of the

'I WILL DIE AND MY SUCCESSOR WILL DIE, BUT THERE WILL BE NO ELECTIONS'

The general is a karate fan. He compares himself to the late Generalissimo Francisco Franco of Spain. His wife says he is just a "tiny bit domineering." He runs Chile.

Gen. Augusto Pinochet Ugarte was named by President Salvador Allende Gossens as army commander Aug. 23, 1973. Pinochet succeeded Gen. Carlos Prats Gonzalez, Allende's staunchest military defender. Prats had resigned, reportedly as a result of pressure from army officials who charged that he had caused a left-right split in the army.

Less than a month later, on Sept. 11, Allende was ousted by a four-man military junta, which included Pinochet. Allende perished. Pinochet was sworn in as president two days later. Prats and his wife were assassinated in Buenos Aires in 1974.

Under Pinochet, Chile "institutionalized brutality and human torture," Salvatore Bizzarro writes in *Current History*. On the second anniversary of the coup, Pinochet said: "I will die and my successor will die but there will be no elections." Two years later, having consolidated control, he promised elections in 1984 or 1985. He revoked the regime's state of siege last year, saying the nation was in "a state of peace and there is support for the government." The right of *habeas corpus* was restored. The president would no longer be empowered to banish or exile persons. However, the state of emergency remained in effect—censorship, a nighttime curfew, restrictions on the right of assembly.

Pinochet was born in Valparaiso on Nov. 25, 1915. He was graduated from the national military school in 1936. He was named military attache at the Chilean embassy in Washington, D.C., in 1956. He visited U.S. Southern Command headquarters at the Panama Canal during the late 1960s and early 1970s. In 1968, he was promoted from colonel to general, and four years later he was appointed army chief of staff.

middle and upper classes in lands dominated by wealthy elites, industrialists, professional people and merchants. Three centuries of colonial rule by Spain had inhibited political development. Hispanic cultural traditions, such as Catholicism, an emphasis on "manliness" (the *macho* concept), the praising of aristocratic values, had helped to determine the level of material, intellectual, political and military growth.

Writing in *The United States and Militarism in Central America*, Don L. Etchison observes that except for Costa Rica, the armed forces have held a prominent position in politics from the time of the region's independence from Spain. "But since the middle of the 1950s a new international factor has been added to the sequence of causes that permit the armed forces in Central America to dominate the politics of

THE SOMOZA DYNASTY

U.S. intervention in Nicaragua ended in 1933. Anastasio Somoza, head of the Guardia Nacional, overturned the government in 1936 and became president the following year. He was shot to death in 1956 and succeeded by his son Luis.

A younger son, Anastasio, was elected president in 1967 and again in 1974. A graduate of the U.S. military academy at West Point, the younger Anastasio had served as commander of the Guardia Nacional; he has never relinquished the post. "It may be said that while the Guardia remains loyal, the president is safe," Meredith Nicholson, a member of the U.S. Legation in Managua, observed in 1939. The Guardia remains loyal.

"The country has been disastrously run by the Somoza dynasty," Penny Lernoux concludes in an article in *The Nation*. The Somozas own the largest companies, dominate the economy, and "terrorize the nation," she charges.

In 1978, the Guardia brutally repressed a nationwide rebellion that followed the murder of opposition newspaper editor Pedro Joaquin Chamorro. The rebels demanded Somoza's resignation, shouting such slogans as "Who killed Chamorro? Somoza!" and "We want democracy!" Many died as the Guardia fought demonstrators, students, guerrillas and Indians in the cities and countryside; hundreds were arrested. The chief of staff of the Guardia was assassinated.

Somoza offered reforms. He said he would grant legal recognition to "all" political parties; extend social security benefits to farm workers; grant an extra month's pay to all workers; name a committee of prominent citizens to investigate the murder of Chamorro. However, he vowed to serve out his term as president, which was scheduled to expire in 1981.

their countries," Etchison says. "Simply, substantial U.S. military aid to these armed forces to fight communism has helped them stay strong and influential." In 1961, the Central American Defense Council (CONDECA) had been established. CONDECA consisted of the defense ministers of five Central American states allied for joint military action. It was given the role of defending the Isthmus of Panama from Cuban invasion and subversive infiltration.

Subsequently, American policy in Latin America went through a number of phases— the Alliance for Progress, counterinsurgency, diplomatic recognition of military regimes, suspension or reduction to them of military aid, concern for human rights. The Alliance for Progress turned out to be disappointing. "Hardly a serious step was done towards the realization of basic reform," declared Boris Goldenberg in *The Cuban Revolution and Latin America*. Other writers described the Alliance for Progress as the economic arm of U.S. counterinsurgency policy. The U.S. Southern Command coordinated activities with Latin American military establishments. Some 30,000 Latin American military men and officers were trained at the School of the Americas in the Canal Zone. U.S. military groups (mobile training teams) operated in 16 countries, and military missions in U.S. embassies gave advice (and doubled as arms salesmen).

Latin American Arms Race

What we are doing is building up armies which weigh nothing in the international scale but which are Juggernauts for the internal life of each country. Each country is being occupied by its own army.
—Gabriel Gonzalez Videla, former president of Chile, 1955

The flow of arms continues, but its character has changed. Latin American nations are increasingly acquiring U.S. arms through commercial transactions (rather than through government aid) and turning to countries other than the U.S. for military supplies.

From the 1960s to 1975, the U.S. share of the Latin American arms market declined from 40% to 14%, reports the State Department's Arms Control & Disarmament Agency. The U.S. restricted the transfer of some advanced weapons to Latin America—smart bombs, laser-guided missiles, fighter aircraft. Peru, Brazil, Argentina, Colombia and Venezuela bought Mirage III fighters from France.

Latin America is looking to France, Great Britain and the Soviet Union for a large share of its arms; Israel is an important supplier to Central America. In addition, some countries— notably Argentina and Brazil—are developing their own arms industries with U.S., European and Canadian help. Argentina and Brazil, for example, are building destroyers under British license.

"With the increase in the number of countries capable of exporting arms, a noticeable competition for the Third World market broke out, resulting in what might be called a general commercialization of the arms trade," observes the Stockholm International Peace Research Institute (SIPRI). Average annual imports of major weapons by Latin American nations rose from $114 million in 1964–68 to $206 million in 1969–73 and $497 million in 1974–75, SIPRI found.

The trend toward direct commercial transactions could make ineffective the Carter Administration's announced policy of reducing or denying military aid to Latin American countries that violate human rights. Many of the direct purchases are financed by U.S. banks that do not consider the human rights issue in their transactions. Moreover, though Congress voted in 1976 to require advance notice of all commercial arms sales exceeding $7 million, police equipment sales rarely go that high. Smith & Wesson, the largest producer of firearms and law-enforcement equipment in the U.S., has been particularly successful in selling arms to Latin America, according to the *Latin America Political Report*.

U.S. SECURITY ASSISTANCE POLICY FOR LATIN AMERICA

Following are excerpts from a statement by Terence A. Todman, then Assistant Secretary of State for Inter-American Affairs, before the Inter-American Affairs Subcommittee of the House Committee on International Relations April 5, 1977:

The U.S. for many years has maintained close working ties with the Latin American military, both in purely military-to-military terms and in dealing with individual military leaders in their capacity as presidents and ministers of the various governments in the region.

This long association has developed an arms relationship with Latin American countries that has helped us maintain access to their military establishments, a matter of some importance since 15 Latin American and Caribbean nations today are governed by or under the aegis of the armed forces. Security assistance to these governments thus is a political tool that provides us an opportunity to exert some influence on their attitudes and actions. It is, in short, a means for protecting or advancing our interests, which are many and varied.

As we look at the wide scope of our interests and concerns in this region, we face an important question: How do we, working together with these governments, find ways of achieving improvements in the way the people of this hemisphere are treated?. . . .

We submit that wholesale elimination or even substantial reduction of our security assistance programs in Latin America would be inadvisable. . . .

We hope therefore that the executive branch will be allowed leeway to work with the military in Latin America, using the traditional tools of a relatively modest security assistance program to take advantage of whatever opportunities we might have to advance the cause of human rights and our other real interests in the hemisphere. . . .

In any event, U.S. policy towards arms aid and sales to Latin America is ambivalent. For the most part, it recognized military regimes as they took power and continues supplying military aid while calling for restoration of human rights. "A year and a half after Congress passed a comprehensive embargo on military sales to Chile, General Pinochet's armed forces are still receiving U.S. arms, ammunition and military equipment," Cynthia Arnson and Michael T. Klare protest in *The Nation*. Government officials reply that the supplies were in the "pipeline" before the cutoff.

To what uses would the arms deliveries to Latin America be put?

Chile is involved in border disputes with Peru and Bolivia. The Soviet naval presence in the Atlantic Ocean is growing, and each year, warships of Argentina, Brazil, Uruguay, Chile, Colombia,. Peru, Venezuela, and Trinidad and Tobago join American vessels in Operation UNITAS—Unity. "A frank answer is seldom given," John Gunther wrote some time ago. The countries south of the Rio Grande "want arms to help put down revolution. That is the simple gist of the matter."

ECONOMIC GROWTH & DECLINE IN LATIN AMERICA

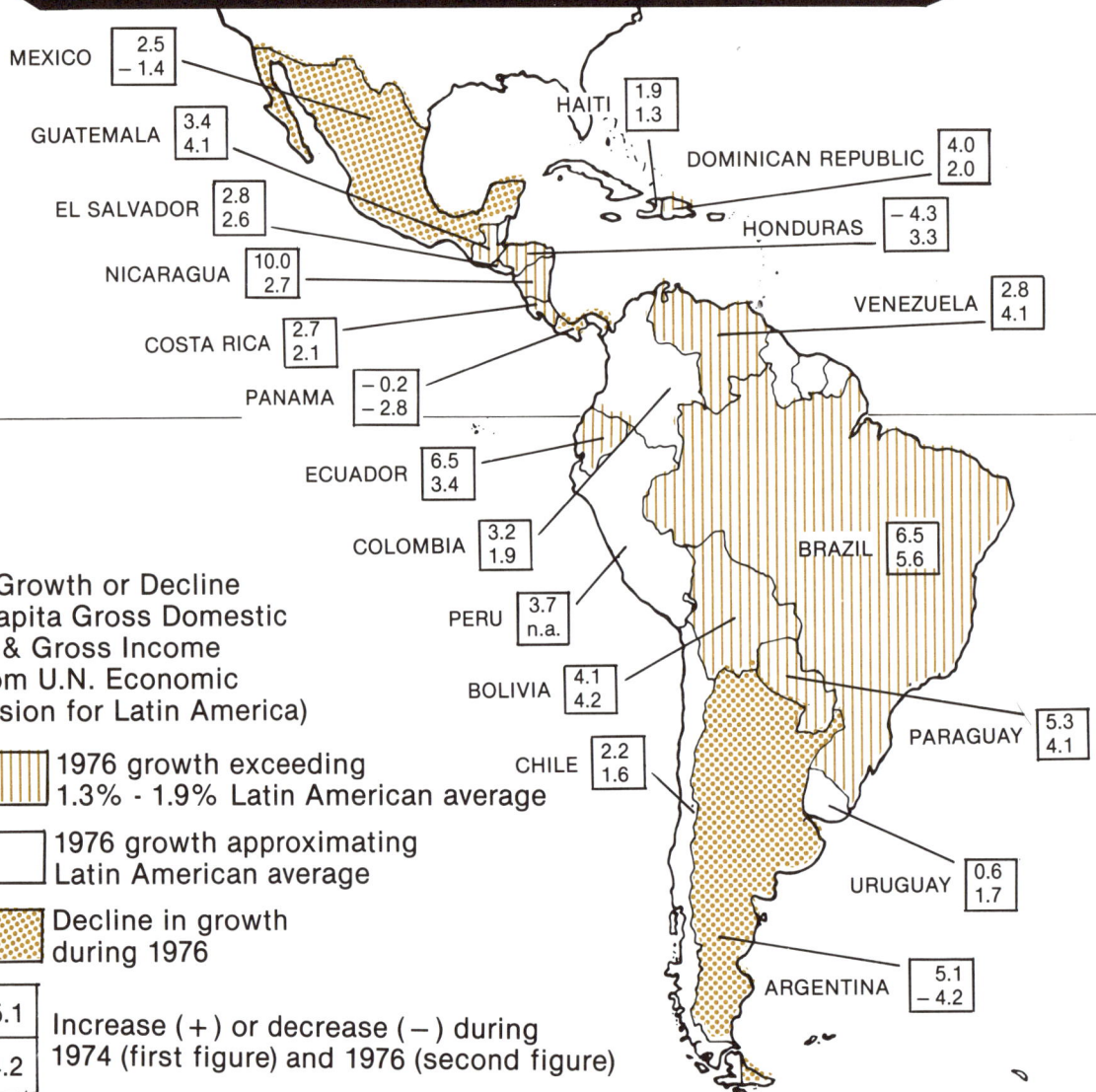

MEXICO
```
2.5
-1.4
```

HAITI
```
1.9
1.3
```

GUATEMALA
```
3.4
4.1
```

DOMINICAN REPUBLIC
```
4.0
2.0
```

EL SALVADOR
```
2.8
2.6
```

HONDURAS
```
-4.3
3.3
```

NICARAGUA
```
10.0
2.7
```

VENEZUELA
```
2.8
4.1
```

COSTA RICA
```
2.7
2.1
```

PANAMA
```
-0.2
-2.8
```

ECUADOR
```
6.5
3.4
```

BRAZIL
```
6.5
5.6
```

COLOMBIA
```
3.2
1.9
```

PERU
```
3.7
n.a.
```

BOLIVIA
```
4.1
4.2
```

PARAGUAY
```
5.3
4.1
```

CHILE
```
2.2
1.6
```

URUGUAY
```
0.6
1.7
```

ARGENTINA
```
5.1
-4.2
```

Rate of Growth or Decline
in Per Capita Gross Domestic
Product & Gross Income
(Data from U.N. Economic
Commission for Latin America)

1976 growth exceeding
1.3% - 1.9% Latin American average

1976 growth approximating
Latin American average

Decline in growth
during 1976

```
+5.1
-4.2
```
Increase (+) or decrease (-) during
1974 (first figure) and 1976 (second figure)

CHAPTER 39

Latin American Economic Development

The scale of economic development in Latin America is significant, but its effects are limited. Disparities in income distribution are deeply rooted. Unemployment and underemployment are widespread. Illiteracy rates are high.

"The struggle for power in Latin America in the coming years will affect the orientation of development policies and foreign economic relations," Colin I. Bradford Jr. predicts in his study *Forces for Change in Latin America: U.S. Policy Implications.* "At the center of this struggle are

Economic growth rates in Latin America have slowed. The causes are the "lagging effects" of the 1974-75 recession in the industrial countries and increasing oil prices, according to the Inter-American Development Bank. The map records the rate of growth or decline in per capita gross domestic product and gross income between 1974 and 1976 (data provided by the U.N. Economic Commission for Latin America). Most countries registered declines. For example, in Brazil the rate of growth dipped from 6.5 per cent to 5.6 per cent; in Chile, from 2.2 per cent to 1.6 per cent; in Nicaragua, from 10.0 per cent to 2.7 per cent; in Mexico, from 2.5 per cent to -1.4 per cent.

decidedly different views of future Latin American society."

Comparative underdevelopment of Latin America comes not from economic problems but from an inability to govern, Jean-Francois Revel asserts in *Commentary*. "The Latin American elites have carried to an extreme . . . the notion that everything bad that happens is never the fault of oneself, but always the fault of others."

In *Holocaust or Hemisphere Co-Op,* William O. Douglas recalls an "historic utterance" by the Archbishop of Lima 30 years ago, exalting the *status quo* as follows: "Poverty is the most certain road to eternal felicity." At a bishops' conference in Mexico City early this year, Pope John Paul II criticized Latin American priests who were moved by the "theology of liberation," political and social activism.

Raul Prebisch observes: "The acceleration of development demands sweeping changes in structures and in mental attitudes. . . . The economy's lack of the required dynamism cannot be made good by the mere passage of time. And the longer the time that is allowed to go by . . . the greater will be the social and political cost, or, in a word, the cost in human terms."

These viewpoints illustrate the conflicts that beset Latin American economic development today. Development is besieged by social, religious, hemispheric interests. To a great many people, it is as much a threat as a promise—and is resisted, or distorted. That is the basic contradiction in Latin American life today.

And it is reflected in the economies of the region. Latin American economies were characterized by slow growth and rising unemployment in 1977, reports the Inter-American Development Bank (IDB). The economic growth rate of Latin American countries slowed to an average of 4.5 per cent, mainly due to the "lagging effects" of the 1974–75 recession in the in-

dustrial countries and to the region's difficulties in adjusting to higher oil prices.

The regional unemployment rate reached alarming proportions because of the staggering expansion of the labor force from 67 million in 1960 to 97 million in 1975. "The projected increase to the year 2000 is equally awesome," says the IDB, foreseeing a Latin American labor force of 194 million at the turn of the century. Meanwhile, inflation becomes more pervasive; only Costa Rica was able to hold the inflation rate to five per cent or less.

Although its comments are not more specific since numerous statistics are not yet available, the IDB is emphatic in its judgment that Latin American economic performance is "not satisfactory."

Other sources provide somewhat more precise data. Argentina had the highest inflation rate in the world during the 12-month period ending June 1978, according to the International Labor Organization. The rate was 188.7 per cent. Inflation in Brazil was 38.8 per cent in 1977, the government reports. The Brazilian government keeps no unemployment figures. Unemployment in Santiago, Chile declined from a high of 19 per cent in 1975 to 13.3 per cent in 1977. The rate of unemployment (and underemployment) in Mexico is reported to be 53 per cent.

During the past 25 years, economic development in Latin America was rapid but very uneven. More than 60 per cent of Latin America's people continue to earn their livings in agriculture, often subsistence farming. The phenomenon of economic growth "is not equivalent to development itself," the 1977 report of the United Nations Economic Commission for Latin America (ECLA) emphasized.

Said ECLA: "Growth . . . has frequently failed to bring with it . . . well-being and social justice, since the system of production has continued to prove incapable of providing an answer . . . to urgent problems such as . . . mass poverty, growing unemployment, the inadequacy of basic social services. . . ."

The greater part of the rural population has not benefited from economic growth, ECLA points out. Their situation has given rise to mass migration to the cities, which has intensified the maldistribution of income, underemployment, and low productivity of much of the labor force. Unequal distribution of income in Latin America is a constant in both crisis and boom periods. Figures for the decade 1960–70 show that the poor half of the population ob-

The unevenness of Latin America's economic develop-ment is reflected in its great cities, near which the poor live in shanty towns. Here, the city is oil-rich Caracas, Venezuela. The primitive housing of the *barrio* (or dis-trict) of San Jose is in the foreground, while the modern city rises in the background.

ECONOMIC CHANGE IN LATIN AMERICA
Gross Domestic Product & Gross Income

	Total			Per Capita				
	1974	1975	1976[b]	1970	1975[b]	1974	1975	1976[b]
	Annual growth rates			Dollars at 1970 prices		Annual growth rates		
Argentina	6.5	−1.4	−2.9	1,208	1,304	5.1	−2.7	−4.2
Bolivia	6.7	6.8	6.9	260	318	4.1	4.1	4.2
Brazil	9.6	4.0	8.7	445	637	6.5	1.1	5.6
Colombia	6.5	4.9	5.2	508	606	3.2	1.6	1.9
Costa Rica	5.5	3.4	5.0	656	796	2.7	0.6	2.1
Chile	4.1	−12.9	3.5	850	742	2.2	−14.5	1.6
Ecuador	9.9	8.6	6.8	355	471	6.5	4.9	3.4
El Salvador	6.0	4.3	4.8	397	440	2.8	1.1	2.6
Guatamala	6.4	2.1	7.1	417	494	3.4	−0.7	4.1
Haiti	4.3	2.2	3.8	99	109	1.9	−0.3	1.3
Honduras	−0.8	1.4	6.9	289	286	−4.3	−2.1	3.3
Mexico	5.9	4.2	1.9	893	986	2.5	0.9	−1.4
Nicaragua	13.7	1.2	6.1	394	450	10.0	−2.1	2.7
Panama	2.6	0.6	—	868	916	−0.2	−2.2	−2.8
Paraguay	8.3	4.8	7.1	353	429	5.3	1.9	4.1
Peru	6.9	3.3	3.0	525	591	3.7	0.3	—
Dominican Republic	7.5	5.1	5.5	351	478	4.0	1.7	2.0
Uruguay	1.6	3.6	2.8	905	890	0.6	2.5	1.7
Venezuela	5.9	5.5	7.2	1,180	1,346	2.8	2.4	4.1
Latin America	*6.9*	*2.6*	*4.2*	*640*	*756*	*4.0*	*−0.1*	*1.3*
Gross income of Latin America[c]	*9.0*	*0.8*	*4.7*	*. . .*	*. . .*	*6.0*	*−2.0*	*1.8*

[a]At factor cost. [b]Preliminary figures. [c]Gross domestic product plus terms-of-trade effect.

Source: Economic Commission for Latin Commerce, United Nations

tained only 14 per cent of the total income, the next 20 per cent received a similar percentage and the 30 per cent with the highest income received the remaining 72 per cent.

The situation grew worse in the first half of the 1970s. In addition to the impact of inflation, the effects of some anti-inflationary measures fell on the lowest income sectors of the population. Concentration of wealth also increased, favoring foreign investment and the "so-called" middle and upper sectors. "In other words, poverty and extreme poverty remain at relatively high levels in both urban and rural areas in Latin America," says ECLA.

LAS GAVIOTAS: TECHNOLOGIES FOR RURAL DEVELOPMENT*

About nine years ago, Paolo Lugari Castrillon, a 32-year-old Colombian community organizer, set out to show that the *Llanos* (plains), the largely uninhabited last frontier of Colombia, could offer a more fruitful solution for that country's expanding population than further migration to crowded cities.

The Colombian government provided Lugari with land for a center in the middle of the *Llanos*. He named the center *Las Gaviotas* after the fresh-water seagulls, well-liked by the

---

*From a case study presented at the United Nations Conference on Technical Cooperation Among Developing Countries, Aug. 30–Sept. 12, 1978, in Buenos Aires.

people, which nest in the many webs of creeks and small rivers that cover the 300,000-square-mile plains.

Las Gaviotas, under Lugari's plan, was to be a center that analyzed the special needs of the tropical plains and the 100,000 residents. It would develop ways of settling the *Llanos* and of providing employment without disturbing the region's ecological balance. Social services were needed for settlers as well as simple machines that would help the isolated farmer work more efficiently.

As a result of six years of work, *Las Gaviotas* now takes care of the educational, medical, transportation and supply needs of the farmers in the *Llanos. Las Gaviotas* also has developed six inexpensive devices: a water ram, a solar heater, a bicycle-pedalled yucca grinder, a hydraulic turbine, a windmill and a manual pump, that save the farmers weeks of work and provide pure water and electric power.

"We are really trying to create communities of people who 'think tropically', who know how to live in these tropical plains without destroying them," says Lugari. "Latin America was settled by people from temperate climates, and no one developed a style of farming for the tropics."

Las Gaviotas exchanges information with other technology centers in Asia and Africa and neighboring Ecuador through the United Nations Development Program (UNDP).

CHAPTER 40

Brazil

Brazil, a mosaic of concepts.

A beautiful girl on Copacabana Beach. The Bossa nova. Pele. The world's chief exporter of coffee. Brasilia, the airplane-shaped city. The Amazon, river of legend. Rain forests. The Mato Grosso.

The world's fifth country in size, sixth in population; 115 million people, one-third of all in Latin America. A "new" people, descendants of Indians, slaves, Europeans. Language: progress.

". . . Some 20 years ago Fortaleza, in the economically depressed Northeast region, had a population of 250,000," Stefan H. Robock recalls in *Saturday Review.* Its streets were filled with donkeys used for transportation . . . its few sidewalks . . . cluttered with bedraggled beggars. By [1974], the city had become a metropolis of 1 million and its streets were jammed with automobiles produced in Brazil."

Brazil is the economic giant of Latin America. Between 1968 and 1974, its economy grew at an annual rate of 10 per cent. Brazil was hailed as the economic "miracle." Its per capita income climbed by 1975 to $1,025, or 38th place in the world, up from 65th a decade earlier. Its annual rate of expansion is now 3 to 5 per cent. Its gross national product in 1975 was $109 billion, one-seventeenth of the U.S.' Its shipbuilding industry ranks sixth in the world, auto production eighth, steel output fifteenth.

Brazil is building a 2,500-mile Trans-Amazon Highway from the northeast to the borders of Peru and Bolivia. With Paraguay, it is constructing a $6 billion hydroelectric project on the Parana River. It plans to have 63 nuclear power plants in operation by the year 2000.

Brazil's economic development is supported by a firm agricultural base and vast natural resources. Sixty per cent of the work force is employed in agriculture, and commercial crops account for 70 per cent of its exports. It is the world's second largest producer of cacao, corn and oranges; other major crops are sugar, cotton, rice, wheat, soybeans. Mineral resources include iron-ore (one-third of the world's reserves), beryllium, quartz crystals, industrial diamonds, manganese, gold, tin, bauxite, gem stones.

Unevenness of development and contrasts to development abound. Examples are: the *favelas* (slums) of Rio de Janeiro and other cities; malnutrition, which affects 40 per cent of the population; life expectancy at birth of 57 for males, 61 for females, a literacy rate of 66 per cent.

Among economic problems: Inflation is chronic in Brazil; in 1976, the rate was 46.3 per cent; it dropped to 38.8 per cent in 1977. Expenditures for oil leaped from $507 million in 1972 to $3.07 billion in 1975, seriously jolting the trade balance. In 1976, exports totaled $10.12 billion, imports $13.62 billion, the deficit swollen by the price of imported oil. Until the oil price hike, Brazil had been second only to Venezuela in its foreign exchange surplus. In 1977, after four years of trade deficits, Brazil posted a $138 million trade surplus. Much of its foreign exchange earnings go to service its foreign debt, which is $31.2 billion, the largest of any developing country. Meanwhile, oil is $1.60 a gallon, and the cruzeiro is devalued regularly, 28 per cent in 1977 and 22.5 per cent in 1978.

Foreign investment in Brazil is substantial. The U.S. stake is more than $2.4 billion. Japanese investments amount to over $1 billion. The automobile industry is owned entirely by foreigners. Multinational corporations control

Map: BRAZIL — Agriculture, industry, and resources

VENEZUELA
COLOMBIA
GUYANA
SURINAM
FRENCH GUIANA
ECUADOR
PERU
BOLIVIA
PARAGUAY
ARGENTINA
URUGUAY
CHILE

ANDES MOUNTAINS

Rivers and places: Japura, Negro, Amazon, Manaus, Javari, Juruá, Purus, Madeira, TRANS-AMAZON HIGHWAY, Tapajós, Xingu, Araguaia, Tocantins, São Francisco, Paraná, Uruguay, Pôrto Velho, MATO GROSSO, Brasilia, Belo Horizonte, São Paulo, Santos, Rio de Janeiro, Pôrto Alegre, Belém, Fortaleza, Natal, João Pessoa, Recife, Salvador, Lima, Porto Velho

Industry boxes:
- Processed foods, Textiles, Cement
- Processed foods, Tobacco products, Textiles
- Iron & Steel, Textiles, Cement, Metal products
- Processed foods, Iron & Steel, Cement, Glass products, Textiles, Chemicals, Oil refining
- Processed foods, Chemicals, Iron & steel, Motor vehicles, Textiles, Oil refining, Machinery
- Processed foods, Textiles, Cement

Legend:
cacao, coffee, corn, cotton, oranges, rice, soybeans, sugar cane, wheat, bauxite (Al), beryllium (Be), coal (C), diamonds (D), gemstones, gold (Au), iron ore (Fe), manganese (Mn), quartz crystals, silver (Ag)

BRAZIL
Agriculture, industry, and resources

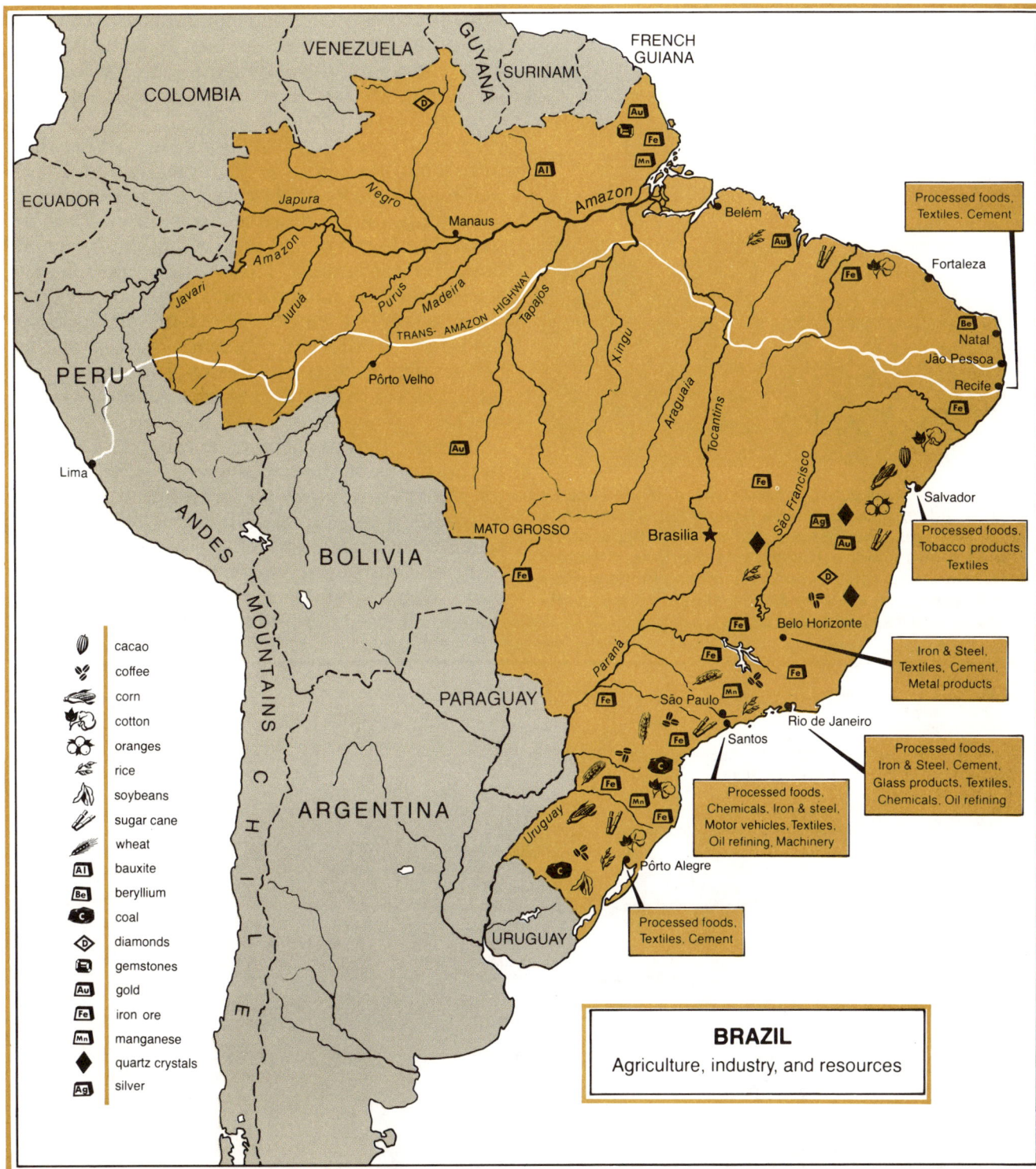

Brazil's record of economic growth in the past decade is considerable. It is based, as the map indicates, on a strong agricultural structure and great natural resources. In addition to being the world's leading exporter of coffee, Brazil is the second largest producer of cacao, corn and oranges; its shipbuilding industry ranks sixth, auto production eighth and steel output fifteenth in the world. Questions now asked about Brazil: Will it become a world power within the next 20 years? Will it become a nuclear power?

Steel factory near Belo Horizonte, Brazil. It is owned by Usinas Siderurgicas de Minas Gerais, S.A. (USIMINAS). With help from the International Bank for Reconstruction & Development, USIMINAS undertook a factory expansion program. Industrial production in the world's poorer countries, say economists, should grow at a rate twice as fast as agricultural output.

the production of synthetic fibers, chemicals and pharmaceuticals. The big oil companies are bidding to drill for oil.

A "nagging and unanswered question of the future . . . concerns the role and power of U.S. and other foreign businessmen to control Brazilian economic development," asserts Jordan M. Young in *Intellect* (in an article entitled "Brazil: World Power 2000?").

From all accounts Brazilians are viewing the future optimistically and pragmatically. They will make of it what they can. The government is building 11,000 miles of roads, linking them to navigable rivers and opening up the Amazon basin for settlement. Families are moving in, sometimes with no more than they can carry on their backs. To them, development "means jobs, land, food, health care; means 'progress' and a better life," reports Vic Cox in *The Nation* (in an article entitled "Brazil: the Amazon Gamble").

Development may coincidentally raise Brazil to the ranks of the superpowers. It is already the strongest military power in Latin America, has refused to sign the Nuclear Nonproliferation Treaty, is defying U.S. opposition by buying eight nuclear power plants and a reprocessing plant from West Germany; soon Brazil will have all it needs to build nuclear weapons.

15 YEARS OF GROWTH

	Units	1960	1975
Population	Millions	69.72	107.14
PRODUCTION—Index Numbers			
Total agricultural production	1961–5=100	96a	150
Industrial production	1970=100	52	164
PRODUCTION—Selected Items			
Iron Ore (Fe content)	000 MT	6,355	46,621
Crude steel	000 MT	1,843	8,306
Energy (coal equivalent)	Mill MT	9.36	25.41
CONSUMPTION—Selected Items			
Steel	000 MT	2,668	11,239
Fertilizer, phosphate	000 MT	86.0b	914.8
Energy (coal equivalent)	Mill MT	23.34	71.79
TRANSPORT & COMMUNICATION			
Passenger vehicles in use	000s	549.6	3,679.3c
Commercial vehicles in use	000s	667.0	1,001.9c
Telephones in use	000s	1,023	3,371
EXTERNAL TRADE			
Imports	Mill US$	1,462	13,658
Exports	Mill US$	1,269	8,670
PRICES—Index Numbers			
Consumer Prices	1970=100	10d	188
Wholesale prices	1970=100	11d	274
FINANCE			
Exchange rate—cruzeiro/US$		205.1	9.070

a) 1961; b) Average 1961/2 1965/6; c) 1974; d) 1963; 000 MT = Thousand metric tons; Mill MT = Million metric tons; 000s = Thousands

Source: *World Statistics in Brief* (United Nations 1977)

CHAPTER 41

Africa: Continent of Refugees

This continent has one of the worst, and least known, refugee problems in the entire world.
—John Worrall, *U.S. News & World Report,* Nov. 8, 1976

Racial discrimination. Underdevelopment. Illiteracy. Disease. Tribal rivalries. The legacies of colonialism. All are major issues in Africa. But one problem—that of refugees—possibly affects more Africans than any other.

Since 1977, more than 10,000 refugees from the war and civil war in Ethiopia have entered the Republic of Djibouti. They are accommodated for the most part in two camps—one sheltering 771 families near Ali Sabieh, 46 miles (74 kilometers) from the city of Djibouti on the Djibouti-Addis Ababa railway line, another sheltering 755 families near Kikhil, 75 miles (120 kilometers) southwest of the capital. Three-quarters of the refugees are women and children.

Repatriation of the refugees is not feasible, at least for the present. The Office of the United Nations High Commissioner for Refugees (UNHCR) is studying the possibility of settling them in Djibouti. This solution poses problems. Djibouti is poor in natural resources, and the country is arid. Agriculture is limited to a few irrigated market gardens. Almost all food must be imported. In addition, the young republic, which became independent two years ago, is experiencing an economic crisis. More than 50 per cent of the population is unemployed or underemployed, UNHCR reports.

What can refugees do? A survey among the heads of families in the two camps showed that: 39 per cent are small shopkeepers, 28 per cent are agricultural workers (of whom the majority are gardeners), 9 per cent are shepherds, 14 per cent are craftsmen (masons, carpenters, mechanics) and teachers. The remaining 10 per cent have no professional qualifications.

Refugees are a major problem throughout Africa. There are at least 1.5 million refugees in 12 African countries. They have fled war, *coups d'état,* guerrilla fighting, tribal massacres in Sudan, Uganda, Equatorial Guinea, Zaire, Angola, Burundi, Rwanda, Rhodesia (Zimbabwe), South Africa, South-West Africa (Namibia). According to UNHCR, there are 530,000 refugees in Zaire; 260,000 in Sudan; 250,000 in Angola; 167,000 in Tanzania; 70,000 in Mozambique; 64,000 in Zambia; 60,000 in Gabon; 20,000 in Botswana; 13,000 in Djibouti; 11,800 in Ethiopia; 6,000 in Kenya. The total number in Cameroon is not known.

In 1978, Poul Hartling began a five-year term as UNHCR chief, succeeding Prince Sadruddin Aga Khan, who had held the post for 12 years. Hartling had been prime minister of Denmark from 1973 to 1975 and foreign minister from 1968 to 1971.

A 40 per cent increase in UNHCR expenditures in 1978 was due to the growth in the number of new refugee situations and the number of refugees, particularly in Africa, Hartling says. Approximately two-thirds of UNHCR's general program expenditures would go to that continent. Thousands of refugees from South Africa, South-West Africa and Rhodesia are continuing to arrive in bordering countries and even beyond, he reports.

There are more than 8 million refugees throughout the world, adds F. J. Homann-Herimberg, acting UNHCR director of assistance. Following years of devastating war, a massive problem of displaced persons and refugees exists in Indochina. For example, more than 95,000 displaced persons from the Lao Peo-

Sudan
Total number of refugees:
260.000
Origin: Ethiopia
Number of refugees being settled
or to be settled: 31.500

Ethiopia
Total Number of refugees:
11.800
Origin: Sudan
Number of refugees being settled
or to be settled: 11.800

Djibouti
Total number of refugees:
13.000
Origin: Ethiopia
Number of refugees to be
settled: 2.000

Kenya
Total number of refugees:
6.000
Origin: Uganda
Number of refugees to be
settled: 4.000

Tanzania
Total number of refugees:
167.000
Origin: Burundi, Rwanda, Uganda
Number of refugees being settled
or to be settled: 152.000

Mozambique
Total number of refugees:
70.000
Origin: Zimbabwe
Number of refugees being
settled: 50.000

Cameroon
Total number of refugees:
Not known
Origin: Equatorial Guinea
Number of refugees to be
settled: 2.000

Gabon
Total number of refugees:
Approximately 60.000
Origin: Equatorial Guinea
Number of refugees to be
settled: 4.000

Zaire
Total number of refugees:
530.000
Origin: Angola, Burundi, Rwanda
Number of refugees being settled:
22.000

Angola
Total number of refugees:
250.000
Origin: Zaire, Namibia
Number of refugees being settled
or to be settled: 220.000

Zambia
Total number of refugees:
64.000
Origin: Zimbabwe, Angola, Namibia
Number of refugees being settled:
13.000

Botswana
Total number of refugees:
20.000
Origin: Zimbabwe
Number of refugees being
settled: 4.000

- Refugee camp sites
- Cuban presence
- French presence
- Soviet presence
- Areas of conflict

THE AFRICAN REFUGEE PROBLEM

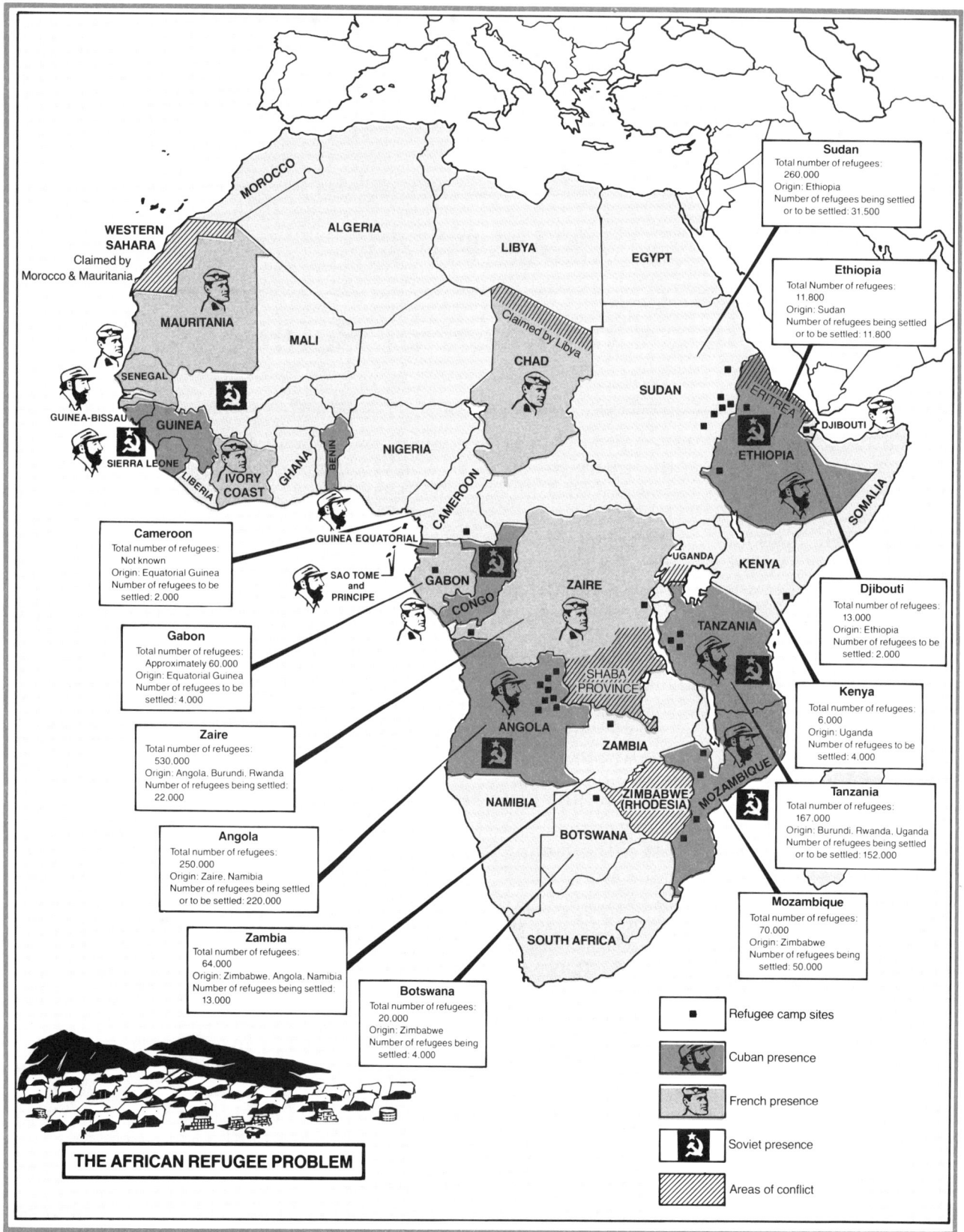

In Africa, there are at least 1.5 million refugees. They are to be found in 12 countries, says the U.N. High Commissioner for Refugees. Causes: war, coups d'etat, guerrilla fighting, tribal massacres. The map indicates the countries to which refugees have fled. It also shows another side of the problem in Africa—the presence of foreign (Cuban and French) troops as well as areas of Soviet influence.

Ethiopian refugee camp in Djibouti.

ple's Democratic Republic, Democratic Kampuchea and the Socialist Republic of Vietnam are now grouped at 15 reception centers in Thailand. In Latin America, the situation of many thousands of refugees continues to be tense and insecure. Says Homann-Herimberg: "You only have to take a quick look at the world map to see that UNHCR's main assistance activities correspond to the newspaper headlines—the troublespots, the areas of conflict."

AFRICA: CONFLICT & CONFUSION

What do we know about Africa? How much do our concepts evolve from confusing and fragmentary comments and reports? Such as:

A continent in conflict . . . Tribalism vs. nationalism . . . Oral tradition vs. literacy . . . Poverty and disease vs. great natural wealth . . . Headlines: "Thunder in Africa," "Millions of People on the Run". . .

Boundary disputes . . . Continuing civil war in Ethiopia . . . Coups in Ghana and Mauritania . . . Rebellion in Zaire's Shaba (formerly Katanga) Province . . . Desert conflicts in Western Sahara and Chad . . . Guerrilla warfare in Rhodesia/Zimbabwe and South-West Africa (Namibia) . . . *How Long Will South Africa Last?*

Superpower rivalries . . . Neo-colonialism . . . Is the Soviet Union trying to outflank Europe? . . . Marxist governments in Angola, Mozambique, Ethiopia, Congo, Benin, Guinea-

Bissau . . . 27,000 Cubans—troops, medical and other support teams, advisers—in 16 African countries . . . 14,000 French troops at bases from Reunion to Senegal . . .

An Organization of African Unity (OAU) resolution condemns "pacts with extra-African powers" and foreign military bases. . . . But the OAU agrees African nations have the right to request any measures, including foreign military aid, to preserve independence and territorial integrity. . . .

"Is there any chance of putting an end to these confrontations which are taking an increasing toll of innocent lives?" asks Andre Fontaine in *Le Monde.* . . . He notes the magnitude of the economic stakes in Africa. . . .

Africa . . . The second largest continent . . . More than 40 diverse, independent countries . . . Estimated total population 401 million, about three-quarters rural . . . Long, complex history . . . First civilization founded in Egypt in 3,400 B.C. . . .

Rich in copper, iron ore, manganese, bauxite, gold, gem and industrial diamonds, cobalt, uranium, oil . . . Enormous potential for hydroelectric power development . . . World's largest reserves of natural gas (in Algeria) . . . Nigeria's gross national product soon expected to surpass South Africa's . . .

The confusion seems as endless as the conflict.

CHAPTER 42

South Africa

Population and *apartheid* are the opposite poles of conflict in South Africa.

The country's estimated population is 26 million. Blacks outnumber whites nearly four to one. The 18.6 million blacks comprise 70 per cent of the population, the 4.3 million whites 17.8 per cent, the 2.4 million Coloreds (persons of mixed race) 9.3 per cent and the .7 million Asians 2.3 per cent. The blacks include 5 million Xhosas, 5 million Zulus and 3 million Sothos.

Of the whites, about 60 per cent are descendants of Dutch, German and French Huguenot settlers and are known as Afrikaners. The other 40 per cent are mostly of English ancestry. Population growth is rapid, annual rates are approximately Coloreds 2.7 per cent; blacks, 2.6 per cent; Asians, 2.5 per cent; and whites, 1.4 per cent.

Apartheid is a system of racial separation. It is a caste system, based on racial prejudice, white domination and police terror. Its effects are tragic. The black unemployment rate is estimated to be 20 per cent, the white less than 1 per cent. Pass laws disrupt and undermine black family life; one of these laws makes it a criminal offense for an African woman to live with her husband for more than 72 hours at a time unless she is entitled to reside in the same area as her husband. The overwhelming majority of African children stop schooling at the primary level; only 5.5 per cent are in secondary schools. The South African crime rate is one of the highest in the world, two and a half times that of the U.S.

The Afrikaners' view of *apartheid* is both defensive and defiant. The Nationalist Party, which upholds *apartheid* policies, is regularly returned to power. In the 1977 elections, it captured a total of 134 seats, a gain of 18 seats, and 65 per cent of the popular vote. Other parties took 30 seats. Rejecting U.S. proposals for an end to racial separation, John Vorster, then South African prime minister, said that such proposals would lead to "chaos and anarchy" and that "the end result . . . will be exactly the same as if [South Africa] were subverted by Marxists." Vorster added: "No other country has the right to interfere in our affairs or to prescribe to us."

Since the 1950s, a number of South African whites—politicians, schoolteachers, writers—have actively challenged *apartheid.* Some are now in exile or, like the poet Breyten Breytenbach, in prison.

Black leader Nelson Mandela has been jailed since 1962. At his trial, conducting his own defense, Mandela took notice that he had been accused of "inciting the people to commit an offense by way of protest against the law." He said, "Men are not capable of doing nothing, of saying nothing, of not reacting to injustice, of not protesting against oppression, of not striving for the good society and the good life in the ways they see it. Nor will they do so in this country. . . ."

Black opposition to *apartheid* has become more open—and violent. Among its manifestations: rioting, school boycotts, black consciousness. The white response remains police action, arrests, detention, bannings. Steve Biko, the black consciousness leader, died in police detention. Donald Woods, the outspoken anti-government editor of the East London *Daily Dispatch,* was banned—and fled into exile. Woods was asked to address the U.N. Security Council. He appealed for international pressure on the

BANTUSTANS

The development of bantustans, or "homelands" for Africans according to their tribal affiliations, is an integral part of South Africa's policy of *apartheid.*

Nine homelands have been designated specifically for African occupation: Transkei, Ciskei, KwaZulu, Bophuthatswana, Lebowa, Gazankulu, Venda, Swazi and Basotho Qua Qua. All Africans are to be citizens of their respective homelands, whether or not they reside in those areas.

Less than half of the African population now lives within the boundaries of the homelands. Far more live and work in urban areas and on white farms, although they are denied the right to be accompanied by their families.

Development of the homelands "has encountered major obstacles," says Julian R. Friedman, professor of political science at Syracuse University, in a paper prepared for the U.N. Center Against *Apartheid.* "Many of the areas are sharply deficient in water supply, as well as fertile land. No steps have been taken to incorporate significant income-producing mineral areas into the homelands. None has a very sound industrial base. . . ."

The South African government has granted varying degrees of self-rule to the homelands; two have attained "independence"—Transkei and Bophuthatswana. However, Friedman points out, the homelands are by law "subsidiary units of the Republic of South Africa. By no stretch of the imagination are they separate independent entities with an international identity of their own. . . ."

South African government, disengagement from diplomatic, cultural, sporting, military and economic ties.

U.N. resolutions condemn *apartheid* as a crime against humanity. The U.N. approved an embargo on arms shipments to South Africa—but without the specification of penalties for violators. Only in the case of South-West Africa (Namibia) has the U.N. been able to develop a strongly legal position. Historically, the League of Nations had placed South-West Africa under South African mandate following World War I. In 1966, the U.N. General Assembly voted to terminate the mandate. The basis for the Assembly's decision was its conclusion that South Africa had failed to fulfill its mandated obligations. Negotiations that were to have led to the independence of the territory under U.N. auspices approached collapse last year. A guerrilla force, the South-West Africa People's Organization (SWAPO), is fighting South African control. SWAPO has called on "socialist countries" for weapons.

Western and Communist stakes in South Africa, in southern Africa, are "quite different," writes Jennifer Seymour Whitaker in a Foreign Policy Association pamphlet.

The NATO allies and Japan have economic and strategic interests: investment and trade, mineral imports, a concern with the security of adjacent sea-lanes. Investment in South Africa is greatest by Britain, totaling $6 billion. American investment is estimated to be $1.7 billion. The U.S. is South Africa's largest trading partner; in 1976, total trade reached $2.1 billion. Britain was next with $2 billion. By the end of 1976, U.S. banks had $2.2 billion in outstanding loans to South Africa, while European institutions had lent $5.4 billion.

One of hundreds of rules by which *apartheid* is enforced in South Africa: A black man in Capetown displays his pass book.

SOUTHERN AFRICA: THE *APARTHEID* SCENE

The principal areas of racial conflict in Southern Africa are delineated above. They are South Africa, Rhodesia and South-West Africa (Namibia). In South Africa, *apartheid* (racial separation) is enforced legislatively; blacks are citizens of tribal homelands and must comply with rigid pass laws to travel or live elsewhere. Blacks are fighting a guerrilla war against a dominant white minority in Rhodesia; the Rhodesian army and air force carry the war into neighboring Mozambique and Zambia, where they raid guerrilla camps. The status of South-West Africa is confused. A former German colony, the territory had been administered by South Africa since the end of World War I. In 1966, the United Nations terminated South Africa's mandate, but South Africa continued to administer the territory in defiance of the U.N. As members of the South-West Africa People's Organization clash with South African forces, Western and U.N. representatives continue efforts to negotiate the territory's independence.

The Communist powers have no comparable interests, says Whitaker; "their investment—in military aid to the liberation movements—represents primarily a stake in the region's revolutionary future."

What are the prospects?

Blocking of the U.N. independence plan for South-West Africa suggests that "whites are moving further into their *laager,* or encampment, and intend to draw the military line, behind which they will fight, at the Angolan border," observes June Goodwin in the *Christian Science Monitor.*

Alan Paton is disquieted. "I write not to express my detestation of the policies of *apartheid,*" he says in *The New York Times,* "not because my government has cruelly and ruthlessly treated its more articulate opponents . . . but because I fear for the future of Afrikanerdom. I fear it is going to be destroyed. . . ."

"It is obvious that the continent's great and final confrontation will come in South Africa," the *Manchester Guardian* says in an editorial. "The West's position against that day has yet to be made fully clear. . . ."

IMPORTANT DATES

1488—Bartholomew Diaz of Portugal rounds Cape of Good Hope.

1652—Dutch settlers arrive.

1779—First of series of Kaffir Wars between whites and blacks.

1814—Congress of Vienna awards Cape territory to Great Britain.

1835–37—Great Trek. 10,000 Afrikaner farmers (Boers) migrate beyond Orange River.

1838—Boers defeat Zulus at battle of Blood River.

1840—Natal Republic established by Boers.

1843—British annex Natal.

1852—Independent Boer republic of Transvaal founded.

1854—Boer republic of Orange Free State.

1870—Diamonds discovered at what was to become Kimberley.

1877—Last (ninth) of Kaffir Wars.

1886—Gold discovered in southern Transvaal.

1899–1902—South African (Boer) War won by the British.

1910—British Parliament establishes Union of South Africa with dominion status.

1915—Boer uprising suppressed; German South-West Africa captured.

1919—League of Nations places South-West Africa under South African mandate; J. C. Smuts succeeds Louis Botha as prime minister; Asians prohibited from acquiring land.

1926—Africans barred from various skilled jobs.

1936—Land Act sets aside 13.7 per cent of South Africa for blacks.

1939—Smuts becomes prime minister again; South Africa declares war on Germany.

1948—Coalition of Nationalist and Afrikaner parties defeats Smuts' United Party.

1950—Suppression of Communism Act.

1953—Nationalist Party retains power with larger majority; subsequently, white control of country is strengthened and *apartheid* policies extended.

1960—About 70 black protesters against pass laws shot to death at Sharpeville; state of emergency declared.

1961—South Africa withdraws from British Commonwealth.

1964—*Apartheid* condemned by U.N. Security Council.

1966—U.N. General Assembly votes to end South African mandate over South-West Africa.

1971—International Court of Justice rules that South Africa's administration of South-West Africa is illegal and that South Africa should give up control of the territory.

1976—174 persons, all but two of them black, killed in week of protests in Soweto and other black townships surrounding Johannesburg against compulsory use of Afrikaans in black schools; death toll rises to more than 400 as violence spreads.

1978—South Africa sidetracks U.N. plan for independence of South-West Africa.

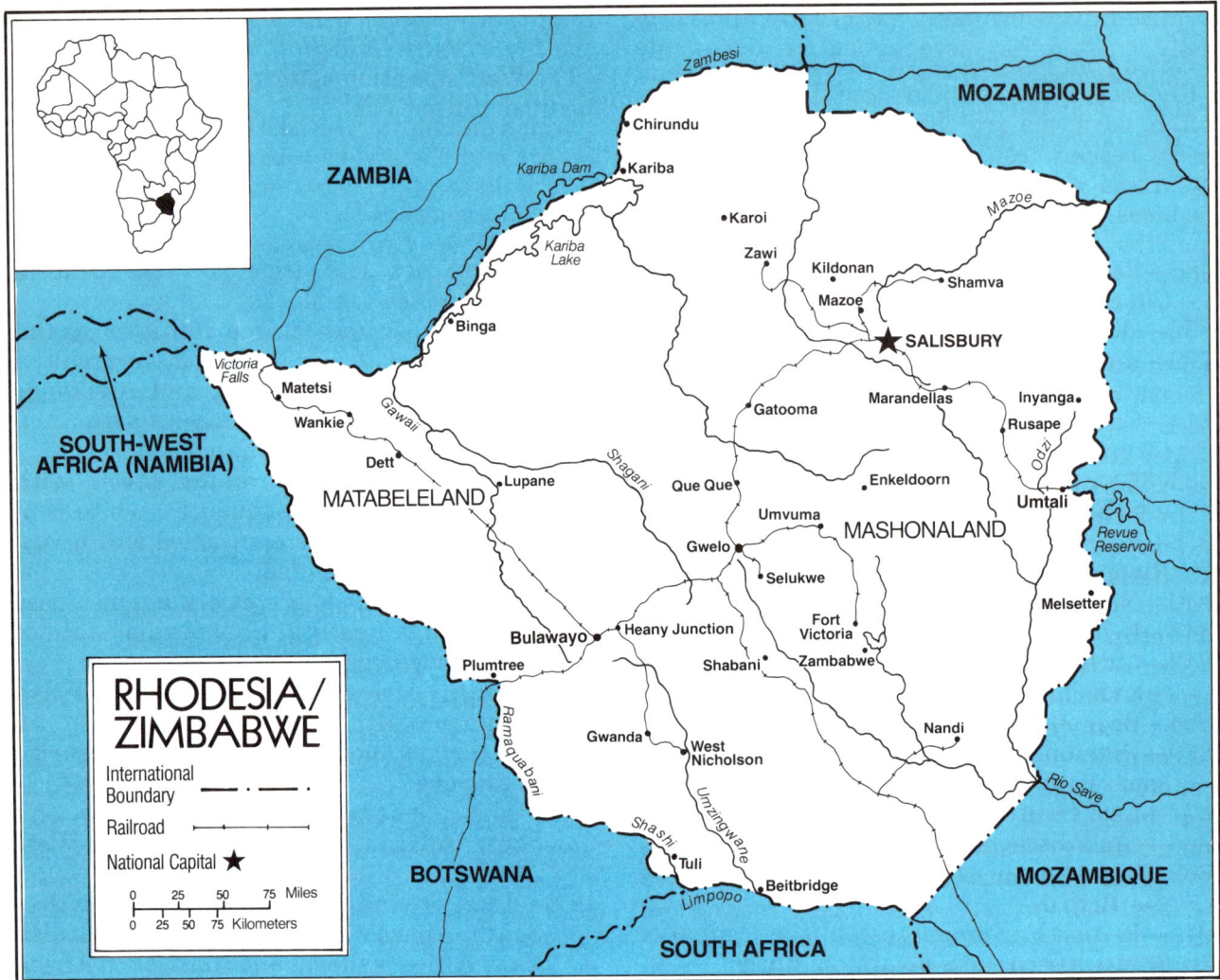

The guerrilla war in Rhodesia is seven years old. The Salisbury government has not succeeded in ending the fighting, Prime Minister Ian Smith concedes. Rhodesian forces periodically raid guerrilla camps in Mozambique and Zambia, two of the five "front line" states — countries that border or are near Rhodesia and oppose the Salisbury regime. (The others are Angola, Botswana and Tanzania.) Some 260,000 whites and 6.4 million blacks live in Rhodesia. Negotiations aimed at majority rule have brought no settlement.

CHAPTER 43

Rhodesia

Black nationalists of Rhodesia say they are taking back Zimbabwe (black nationalist name for Rhodesia) in the same way it had been taken —by conquest.

Guerrilla forces operated on four fronts. Three-quarters of the country was placed under martial law by the Salisbury government. There was speculation that the 260,000 whites of Rhodesia might soon be put to flight.

The majority—6.4 million blacks—would rule, or perhaps face each other in a civil war. A showdown was being foreseen between black tribal groups.

David B. Ottaway in the *Washington Post:* "Vietnam hands have begun calling Salisbury Africa's Saigon, a reference to the calm and false normality that prevailed in the Vietnamese capital until almost the day it was overrun by Vietcong and North Vietnamese soldiers."

It is a complex tragedy, hard to sort out.

Rhodesia is rich in farm land (tobacco, sugar, cotton, corn, tea are chief crops), minerals (asbestos, copper, iron, coal, chrome), and teak forests. Land was allocated according to race. On the basis of the ratio between land and population, the area allotted to the two population groups amounted to an average of 2.8 hectares for each black and 67.2 hectares for each white.

The disparity between the earnings of blacks and those of whites was enormous. "In 1964, the African agricultural wage was 4.6 per cent of the European wage; by 1974 it had dropped to 4.3 per cent," Marion O'Callaghan reported in the *UNESCO Courier*. "Child labor is often part of the farm school system, children being given half-day schooling and $1.50 [Rhodesian] to $3 [Rhodesian] for 30 days [of work]. . . . The mines present a similar picture. . . ." Unequal too was the setup in housing, voting rights and social welfare. African social welfare was maintained through the beer profits of halls frequently run by the municipalities.

Accurate information about the state of the economy is difficult to obtain. However, government budget deficits were up sharply, and revenue needs were being met by forced loans from individual and corporate taxpayers. Guerrilla warfare had virtually halted pest controls in the countryside, and capital equipment and irrigation systems were being destroyed. "A number of reports have speculated that the economy might collapse if the armed struggle continues at the current level of intensity," the U.N. General Assembly's special committee on Rhodesia said last year.

Rhodesian independence from Great Britain had been declared unilaterally by Prime Minister Ian Smith's government in 1965. Britain and the U.N. had termed the action illegal, and no country recognized the Smith regime or Rhodesian independence.

In 1966, economic sanctions were imposed by the U.N. Security Council; shipments to Rhodesia of arms, aircraft, motor vehicles, petroleum and petroleum products were embargoed. The sanctions were broadened two years later. They also were broadly violated.

Despite sanctions, the U.S. imported chrome, a strategic material, from Rhodesia between 1971 and 1977. Congress banned the imports in 1977 but conditionally removed the barrier last year.

In defiance of a government order, British oil companies supplied oil to Rhodesia from 1965 to 1977. Government officials had reached the conclusion that Rhodesia could not be prevented from obtaining oil without a confrontation with South Africa, asserted a report to the British Foreign Secretary. The British government, the report said, "was very conscious, simply on the economic level . . . [that such a confrontation] had to be avoided."

In 1972, the first clashes between black guerrillas and Rhodesian forces took place. By 1978, Smith conceded that his government had not succeeded in ending the fighting as "we had hoped"; on the contrary, insurgent activity and civilian and military casualties had increased. Periodically, the Rhodesian army raided guerrilla camps in Mozambique and Zambia. Cuban advisers were acknowledged by the rebels to be training their men in Zambia.

Negotiations paralleled the fighting but brought no settlement. In 1976, the British sponsored a conference in Geneva on the transition to majority rule; the talks ended in deadlock. In 1977, British and American diplomats toured southern Africa to seek support for new proposals to achieve majority rule; Smith scoffed at the proposals as "crazy" and "insane." In 1978, the prime minister and three black leaders signed an "internal" pact for majority rule. Power was to be transferred at the end of the year. The pact was rejected by guerrilla leaders, the U.S. and the U.N. The Smith government later got out a new timetable, delaying the handover until a referendum could be held.

The crisis divided people in many ways, as it

SOUTHERN RHODESIA? RHODESIA? ZIMBABWE?

Southern Rhodesia was named after Cecil Rhodes, South African business magnate, government official, administrator.

In 1965, after the former British protectorate of Northern Rhodesia became independent as Zambia, the white minority government in Southern Rhodesia undertook to change the name of the territory to "Rhodesia." Neither the British government nor the United Nations accepted the change, and the territory continues to be known officially as Southern Rhodesia.

African nationalists call the country Zimbabwe, the name of massive granite ruins dating back to the 11th century that rise on a hilltop to the south of Salisbury. Zimbabwe means "dwelling of a chief" in the Shona language.

moved from stage to stage. "What we have, we hold," the settlers used to say. Now, white departures were exceeding arrivals by more than 500 a month. Among the blacks, there are splits between the Shona, Ndebele, Karanga and Ndau ethnic groups. The Shona are Rhodesia's original inhabitants and the largest ethnic group; they "regard themselves as the logical and legitimate rulers of an independent Zimbabwe," writes Richard W. Hull in *Current History.*

Two nationalist groups—the Zimbabwe African National Union (ZANU) and the Zimbabwe African People's Union (ZAPU)—run the guerrilla war. Robert Mugabe heads ZANU. He reputedly is a Marxist, and was said to be receiving support from China as well as from the Soviet Union and Cuba. Joshua Nkomo heads ZAPU. He is viewed as more moderate and apparently had the backing of the Soviet Union and Cuba. The U.S. and Britain also were reportedly leaning to Nkomo as capable of keeping the country together with the whites having a role. Both ZANU and ZAPU were supported by the five so-called "front-line" states bordering Rhodesia—Angola, Botswana, Mozambique, Tanzania and Zambia.

Bishop Abel Muzorewa and the Rev. Ndabaningi Sithole had returned from exile to take part with Chief Jeremiah Chirau in Smith's "transitional" government. Having cooperated with Smith, their place in the Zimbabwe of the future was uncertain. Meanwhile, the contest for the riches of Rhodesia and for power in the new Zimbabwe seemed to be moving to a violent resolution.

PRINCIPAL FIGURES IN THE RHODESIAN DISPUTE

Ian Douglas Smith—Rhodesian prime minister since 1964, head of the ruling Rhodesian Front party. Unilaterally declared his country independent rather than negotiate a constitution that would have given power to the black majority. Known as "Good Old Smithie" to whites, he was a British fighter pilot during World War II.

Joshua Nkomo—leader of the Zimbabwe African People's Union (ZAPU), a black nationalist faction, and an exile from Rhodesia since 1962. Nkomo is a member of the Kalanga tribe, and most of his ZAPU recruits are members of the ethnically related Ndebeles, who formed about 20% of the Rhodesian black population. Nkomo received most of his outside support from Zambia, Botswana and the U.S.S.R. ZAPU was believed to have 700–1,000 guerrillas operating inside Rhodesia. In October 1976, Nkomo allied his faction with Robert Mugabe's faction to form the Patriotic Front.

Robert Mugabe—leader of the Zimbabwe African National Union (ZANU), jailed briefly in Rhodesia in 1964. Mugabe is a member of the Shona-speaking peoples, who made up at least 75% of the Rhodesian black population. ZANU is almost exclusively Shona and received most of its outside aid from Tanzania, Mozambique and China. ZANU was believed to have about 6,000–8,000 guerrillas operating in Rhodesia. Despite the formal Patriotic Front alliance, ideological and ethnic differences kept Nkomo and Mugabe apart.

Bishop Abel Muzorewa—considered the most widely known and the most influential black leader inside Rhodesia, a political moderate. A Shona, Muzorewa was leader of the United African National Council, which had replaced the African National Council formed to unite the various black nationalist factions. Muzorewa, who also headed Rhodesia's United Methodist congregations, attended American colleges.

Rev. Ndabaningi Sithole—former rival of Mugabe for control of ZANU. Sithole, a Shona, had quit the guerrilla struggle to participate in talks on a peaceful settlement for black majority rule. He was a Congregationalist, and like Muzorewa, American-educated.

Chief Jeremiah Chirau—a tribal leader, member of the Rhodesian Senate, considered a conservative. Chirau formed the Zimbabwe United People's Organization in December 1976 to represent Rhodesia's conservative blacks.

Leaders of the Front Line Black African States—so called because their countries border on Rhodesia or because they wielded influence with the guerrillas: President Agostinho Neto (Angola), President Seretse Khama (Botswana), President Samora Machel (Mozambique), President Julius Nyerere (Tanzania) and President Kenneth Kaunda (Zambia).

CHAPTER 44

Israel & the Occupied Territories

The six-day war of June 1967 made Israel an occupying power. Four parcels of real estate held by neighboring Arab states fell into Israeli hands.

The controversy over Israel and the occupied ("administered") territories is a tragic puzzle whose political, international, religious, ethnic, historic and ethical ramifications involve participants throughout the world and go back decades, centuries and, ultimately, millennia. The matter is entangled in great-power rivalries and Third-World alliances. It raises such questions as: Who actually has a right to the disputed lands? Will Israel ever really return the areas to Arab control?

The issue is enmeshed in arguments that have threatened world peace and may do so again. The occupied territories chafe under Israeli military control but do have a measure of local self-government. They enjoy other freedoms as well. They elect their own municipal officials, from mayors down. Those elected are frequently outspoken enemies of the Israeli regime. Public protests are frequent. Civilians, especially students, sometimes riot, clash with the Israeli military. There are many arrests.

The largest of the occupied territories is the Sinai Peninsula, on the southeast border of Israel. Taken from Egypt in 1967, the Sinai is a largely uninhabited expanse of rock and sand that is about twice the size of Israel itself. Following the Yom Kippur (or Ramadan) War of October 1973, Israel returned to Egypt a strip of Sinai territory along the Suez Canal.

In the 1967 war, Egypt had also lost control of the 27-mile (39-kilometer) sliver of Palestine known as the Gaza Strip. In this Israeli-occupied area are crowded about 458,000 Arabs, some of them Gazans but most of them refugees

(and their offspring) from other parts of the land that now is Israel.

The most significant of the four occupied areas is the West Bank, an irregular gob of land, some 85 miles (135 kilometers) long from north to south and ranging up to about 35 miles (55 kilometers) wide. This conquered area, on the West Bank of the Jordan River, appears on the map to be gouged out of east-central Israel. It had been annexed in 1950 by Transjordan (which thus acquired the rationale for changing its name to the Hashemite Kingdom of Jordan). Its approximately 760,000 Arab inhabitants, many of them originating in the area that is now Israel, are largely Jordanian citizens.

The truce line that had formed the West Bank's western border formerly separated Jordanian-held East Jerusalem (with the Old City of Jerusalem) from Israeli-held West Jerusalem. One of Israel's first acts after capturing East Jerusalem was to reunify the Holy City.

Looming to Israel's northeast for nearly 40 miles (62 kilometers), the occupied Golan Heights rise along the Syrian border between Jordan and Lebanon. Before it was seized by Israel, the Israelis charge, this escarpment had been used by the Syrian army as a safe and convenient platform from which to shoot at Israeli farmers working their fields in the *kibbutzim* below. Israeli leaders vow that they will never acquiesce in a territorial compromise that will allow the Syrians to resume this practice.

During a dozen years as an occupying power, Israel has not hesitated to take actions that it considers necessary for its security but that have been denounced by Palestinian Arabs and their supporters as violations of human rights. Occupied-area homes that allegedly shelter ter-

ISRAEL AND THE OCCUPIED TERRITORIES

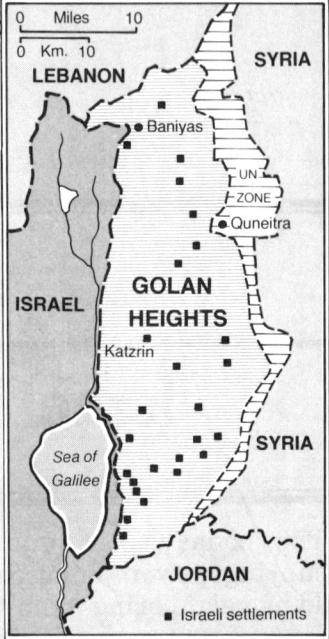

Israeli-occupied area

□ Settlements Israeli agreed to remove
■ Israeli settlements

MEDITERRANEAN SEA

GAZA STRIP

Gaza

Khan Yunis

Etam
Yamit
Rafah

SINAI

ISRAEL

0 Miles 10
0 Km. 10

MEDITERRANEAN SEA

ISRAEL

Haifa
Sea of Galilee
Tiberias
Nazareth

Jenin
Netanya
Tulkarm
Nablus

WEST BANK

Tel Aviv
Ramallah
Jericho
Jerusalem

Bethlehem
Hebron

Jordan River

Irbid

Amman

Zone D
Limited 4,000-member Israeli force with armored personnel vehicles; also, U.N. observers.

Gaza
GAZA STRIP
Rafah

Beersheba

Dead Sea

JORDAN

NEGEV DESERT

0 Miles 10
0 Km. 10

LEBANON

LEBANON

SYRIA

SYRIA

Baniyas

GOLAN HEIGHTS

UN ZONE

Quneitra

ISRAEL

GOLAN HEIGHTS

Katzrin

Sea of Galilee

SYRIA

JORDAN

■ Israeli settlements

Port Said

El Arish

Rafah

SUEZ CANAL

Ismailiya

Sinai after Israeli withdrawal
(Scheduled for 1982)

GIDI PASS

MITLA PASS

Suez

← Zone A → Zone B → ← Zone C → ← Zone D

Abu Rudeis

Gulf of Suez

EGYPT

El Tur

SINAI PENINSULA

Zone C
U.N. forces and Egyptian civil police.

Eilat
Etzion
Aqaba

Gulf of Aqaba

SAUDI ARABIA

Zone B
Egyptian border units with light weapons and up to 4,000 men.

Zone A
Egyptian force of up to 22,000 men with heavy weapons, tanks and armored personnel vehicles.

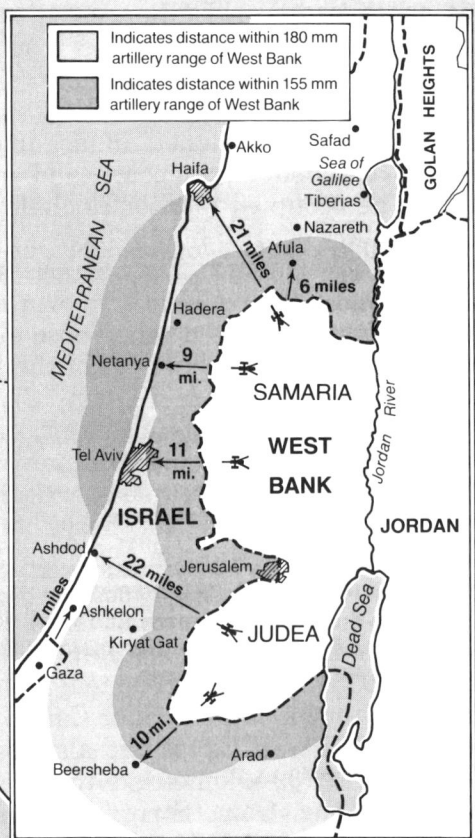

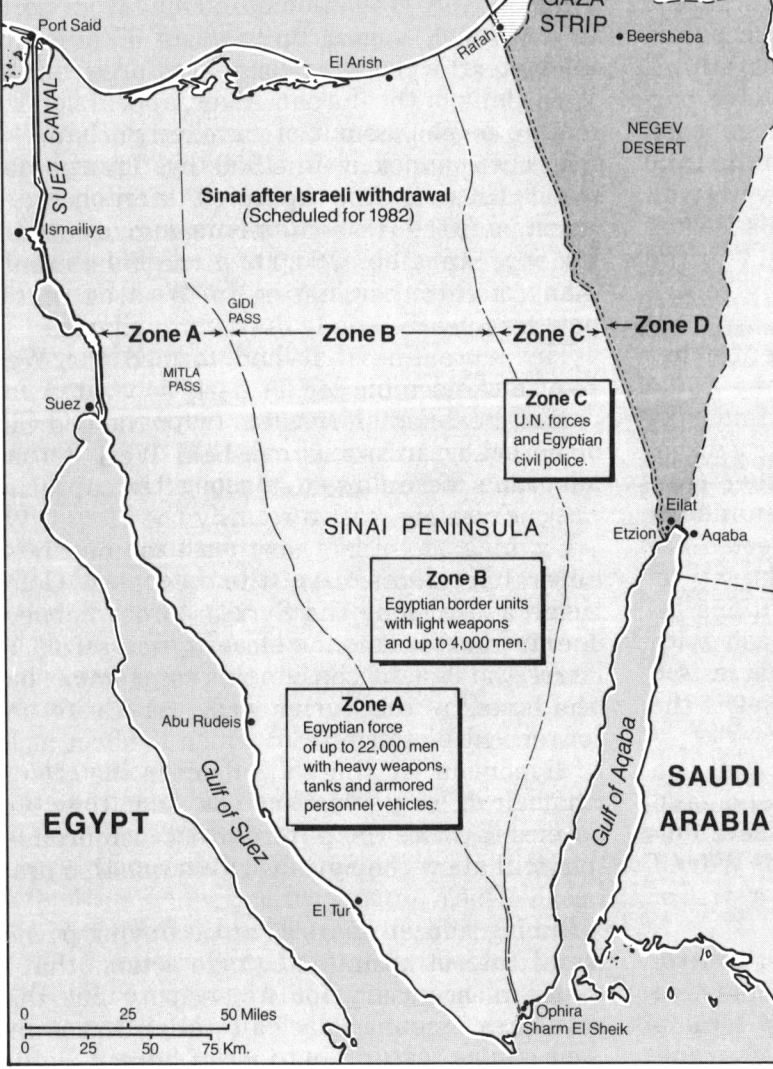

Ophira
Sharm El Sheik

0   25   50 Miles
0 25 50 75 Km.

Indicates distance within 180 mm artillery range of West Bank

Indicates distance within 155 mm artillery range of West Bank

GOLAN HEIGHTS

Akko
Safad
Sea of Galilee
Tiberias

Haifa
21 miles
Nazareth
6 miles
Afula

MEDITERRANEAN SEA

Hadera

Netanya
9 mi.

SAMARIA

WEST BANK

Tel Aviv
11 mi.

ISRAEL

Jordan River

JORDAN

Ashdod
22 miles
Jerusalem

7 miles
Ashkelon
Kiryat Gat

JUDEA

Gaza

Dead Sea

10 mi.

Beersheba
Arad

The peace treaty signed by Israeli Prime Minister
Menachem Begin and Egyptian President Anwar Sadat
March 26, 1979 required Israel to withdraw completely
from the Sinai Peninsula, the largest of the territories it
had occupied since the June 1967 war. The large map
shows the situation scheduled for the Sinai sometime in
1982, after phased Israeli pull-backs over a period of
about three years. Egyptian strength in Zone A may
comprise up to 22,000 men armed with field and antiaircraft artillery, surface-to-air missiles, up to 230 tanks
and up to 480 armored personnel vehicles. A lightly
armed Egyptian force of up to 4,000 men would be deployed in Zone B. "Only United Nations forces and Egyptian civil police will be stationed in Zone C." Zone D,
entirely on Israeli territory, would have U.N. observers
and "an Israeli limited force" of up to 4,000 men with
mainly light weapons. While Israel agreed to remove its
civilian settlements from the Sinai, it made no such
commitment about the extensive systems of settlements in the other occupied areas—the Gaza Strip, the
West Bank and the Golan Heights. The insert map of the
West Bank illustrates a major reason for Israel's desire
to keep this area: an enemy in the West Bank would be
right next-door to Jerusalem and within easy firing
range of most of Israel's other major cities—only 11
miles from Tel Aviv, for example.

rorists are blown up. The Israeli authorities rebuilt the Jewish section of the Old City of
Jerusalem, in which virtually all synagogues

BEGIN ON THE TERRITORIES

". . . [I]t was agreed upon [at Camp David] that
the question of sovereignty in Judea, Samaria
[the West Bank] and the Gaza Strip will be left
open. . . . [We] have a right and a claim to sovereignty over Judea, Samaria and the Gaza Strip.
But there are other claims. . . . The Palestinian
Arabs will have autonomy, full autonomy. And we
shall have security, mainly through the fact that
Israeli defense forces will be stationed in Judea
and Samaria and the Gaza Strip.
"—Israeli Prime Minister Menachem Begin
in *Time* magazine interview

and yeshivas (Jewish religious academies) had
been destroyed during nineteen years of Jordanian occupation. A tremendous Israeli construction boom in both sections (Arab and Jewish) of Jerusalem threatens to obliterate the
Arab character of the city, according to critics
of the Israeli regime. Archeological operations
are also attacked as menacing Islamic religious
shrines.

The development that evokes perhaps the
greatest opposition is the construction of Israeli
settlements in the occupied territories. As
many as 100 such settlements were started in
the four areas, according to a reliable estimate.
About half of them are in the West Bank. The
settlements are condemned as evidence of an
Israeli expansionist policy, and many Israelis
join in the denunciations.

But many other Israelis support the settlement policy, and some urge that the settlement
programs be enlarged. Among the latter, in
which Israelis of orthodox religious background
seem to predominate, are enthusiasts who in
several instances have attempted (sometimes
successfully, sometimes not) to erect settlements in areas that the Israeli government has
barred to Jewish settlement. In several cases
the Israeli armed forces were used to remove
unauthorized settlers.

Opponents of the settlement policy charge
that Arabs are sometimes evicted from their
homes to make room for Jewish settlers. They
claim that settlements are often constructed on
Arab-owned property. Even when settlements
are built on purchased land, critics say, they
constitute unwarranted provocation, they in-
trude in areas that should be reserved for Arabs
and they create obstacles to any eventual return of the territories to Arab control.

Supporters of the settlement policy—and those who would go beyond it—reply that Jews have a right to live in any part of the biblical Land of Israel. This right applies specifically to the West Bank, generally recognized (and referred to by spokesmen for this view) as biblical Judea and Samaria. This point of view also notes archeological as well as literary evidence that the Golan and Gaza (and much of Jordan) were among the lands assigned to the biblical Hebrew tribes. Many Arabs live in Israel, the argument continues, and it would be monstrous

Incident in Nazareth: baton-wielding Israeli troops run an Arab youth down street by his hair after catching him throwing rocks at security forces.

if only Jews were denied a parallel right to live in any part of their traditional homeland. As for the charge of stealing land, settlements supporters claim that the settlers use only land that was bought from the Arab owners (in some cases as far back as before the partition of Palestine) or land owned by the state.

In view of these attitudes, it was possible for Israeli Prime Minister Menachem Begin to agree at Camp David last fall to return the Sinai to Egypt. The Sinai, after all, is not part of the biblical Land of Israel. It was possible to agree to remove the Israeli settlements and other projects created in the Sinai at such tremendous cost to Israel (the figure has been put at more than $8 billion).

But Israeli leaders do not find it possible to agree to a complete Israeli evacuation of the West Bank, of Gaza and of the Golan. Recalling the nineteen years of Jordanian occupation of the Old City of Jerusalem, during which Jews were barred from their holy places there, Israeli leaders refuse to give up Israeli control of a reunified Jerusalem.

In regard to Jerusalem, the West Bank, Gaza and the Golan Heights, neither side is yet willing to compromise.

The U.S. F-15 jet warplane. In a controversial three-way package deal, the U.S. agreed to sell 15 F-15s to Israel, 60 to Saudi Arabia, less advanced aircraft to Israel and Egypt.

CHAPTER 45

Middle East Arms Race

After each round of war in the Middle East, the nations rebuilt and built up their armed forces.

Weapons were of the most advanced types—devastating anti-personnel cluster bombs; the small portable Soviet SA-7 anti-tank gun, highly lethal and easily handled; U.S. fighter aircraft, the F-15 and F-16; remotely piloted vehicles (RPVs).

With today's high-performance military aircraft costing about $20 million each, there is a growing interest in the use of RPVs for reconnaissance, electronic warfare, ground attack and air-to-air combat. The cost of a low altitude strike-reconnaissance RPV is about $500,000.

Using television cameras and data transmission, an RPV could be controlled precisely, and at a safe distance from the target area, by an operator either in a launcher aircraft or a ground control center.

Arms deals are inclusive—nobody is left out. In 1977, the U.S. signed contracts worth $8.16 billion with Iran, Saudi Arabia and Israel. Among the purchases: a $613 million helicopter base by the now exiled shah of Iran, a $420 million naval installation by the Saudis, and hundreds of millions of dollars worth of tanks, armored personnel carriers, and anti-tank missiles by the Israelis. The U.S., in a controversial package last year, sold fighter planes to Egypt,

163

The world's top four arms importers in 1976 were all in the Middle East. They were Iran, Iraq, Israel and Libya, the U.S. Arms Control & Disarmament Agency reported.

Photo by U.S. astronauts provides wide view of troubled area: Egypt, Israel, Jordan, Saudi Arabia, Lebanon, Syria, Iraq, Iran, Turkey, the Red Sea, the Dead Sea, the Sea of Galilee, the Mediterranian Sea, the Suez Canal, Sinai and the Gulf of Aqaba.

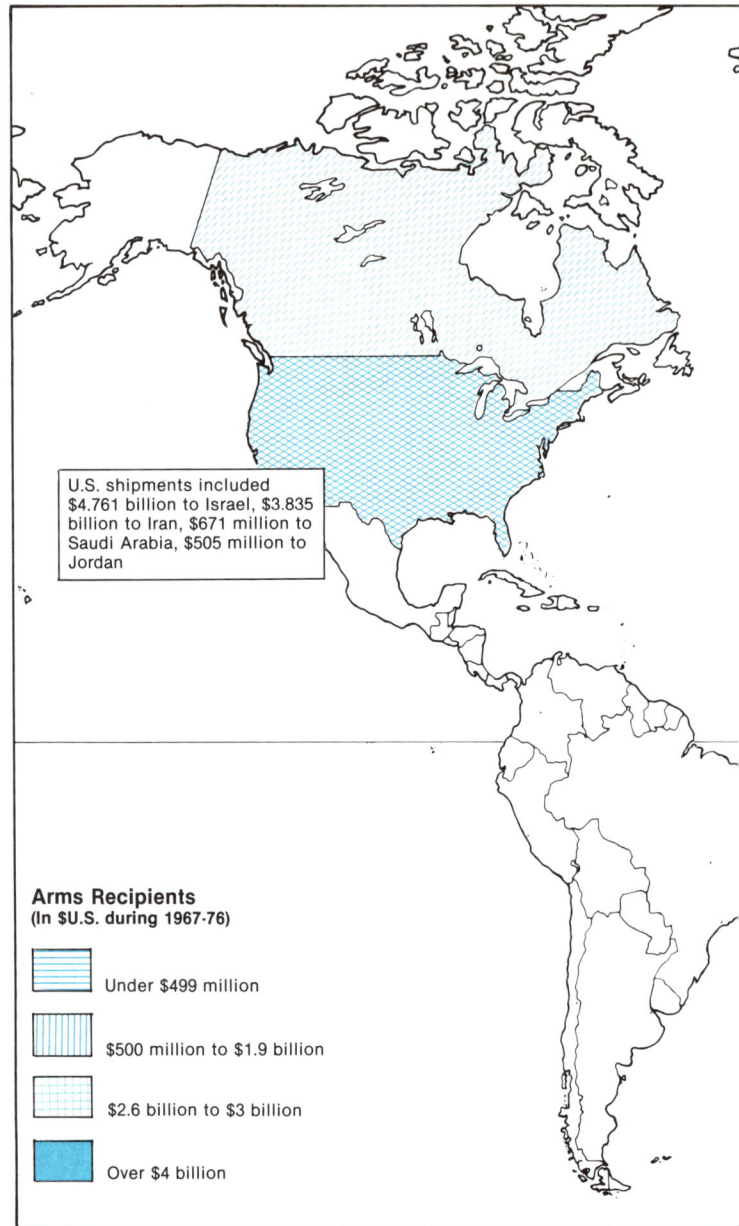

U.S. shipments included $4.761 billion to Israel, $3.835 billion to Iran, $671 million to Saudi Arabia, $505 million to Jordan

Arms Recipients
(In $U.S. during 1967-76)

Under $499 million

$500 million to $1.9 billion

$2.6 billion to $3 billion

Over $4 billion

Saudi Arabia and Israel. Syria, Libya, Iraq and Algeria received new weapons from the Soviet Union.

Other exporters of arms to the Middle East are France, Great Britain, Italy, the Netherlands, Spain, Switzerland and Yugoslavia. The market is "apparently unlimited," observes the Stockholm International Peace Research Institute (SIPRI).

In one no-holds-barred move, Iran bought 25 per cent of Krupp, the German arms manufacturer, wrote Mohamed Sid-Ahmed in *After the Guns Fall Silent: Peace or Armageddon in the Middle East.*

In another, Saudi Arabia hired a U.S. architectural firm to draw up plans for an arms manufacturing city. The city would be named Al Kharj; it would be located 60 miles (100 kilometers) southeast of Riyadh, the capital. Total cost of the city is estimated at $10 billion.

In general, the long-term plans of Saudi Arabia, Kuwait and some of the other so-called "oil states" include heavy investment in the joint Arab arms industry in Egypt, noted SIPRI. The Arab Organization for Industrialization, a pan-Arab arms industry with headquarters in Cairo, had been set up in 1975 with a starting capital of $1.04 billion. The original members included Egypt, Qatar, Saudi Arabia and the United Arab Emirates; Kuwait had made financial contributions. French and British weapons were to be produced under license.

Many recent arms contracts go far beyond the transfer of weapons. They include training,

Soviet shipments included $2.365 billion to Egypt, $2.015 billion to Syria, $1.795 billion to Iraq, $611 million to Iran

Chinese shipments included $15 million to Egypt

Major Arms Suppliers
(In $U.S. during 1967-76)

Under $100 million

$400 million to $1 billion

$6.9 billion to $9.9 billion

MIDDLE EAST ARMS RACE
Arms Recipients & Arms Suppliers

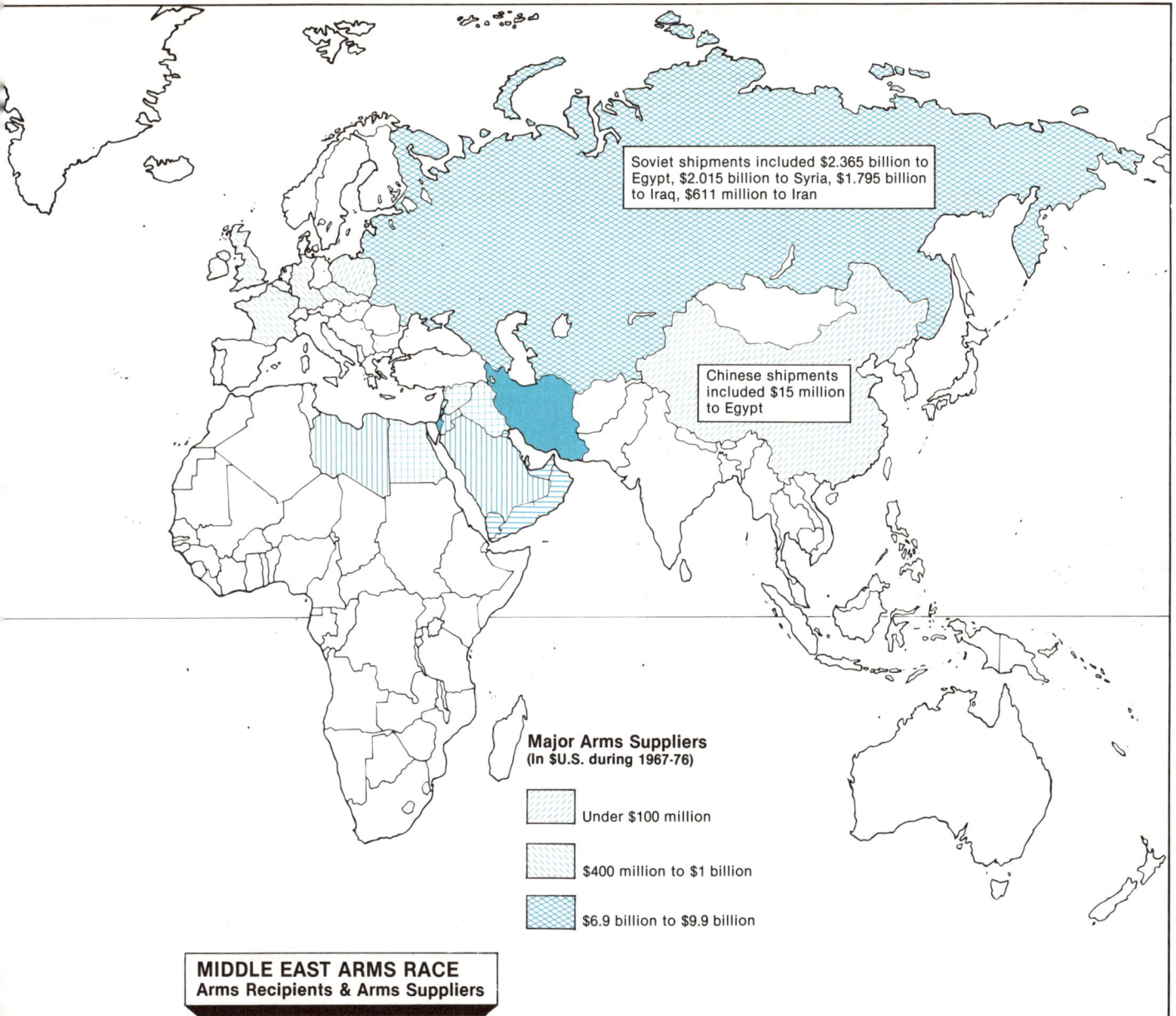

technical support, the establishment of maintenance and repair facilities in the purchasing country, and construction projects. By 1980, according to *U.S. News & World Report,* 50,000 to 60,000 American military technicians—maybe more—would have been needed to help maintain and operate the arms that Iran had acquired from the U.S.

A staff report to the House Committee on International Relations raised the question: "Why are these sales in our national interest and why are some of these states purchasing such quantities of military equipment and services?" Some of the replies that emerged cite regional security, availability of excess money, prestige factors, the British pullout east of Suez. Many states in the Arabian Peninsula and Red

Sea regions perceive threats to their security, the report said. In the case of Saudi Arabia, Iran and North Yemen, these perceptions are based on actual hostilities in the past. Continued poor relations with leftist governments in Iraq and South Yemen are another factor. "In all cases, issues of external security are closely related to . . . domestic security and ongoing threats to ruling authority."

That is part of the regional perspective.

The Arab-Israeli dispute is another matter, and viewpoints differ.

Opponents of last year's tripartite jet sale, for example, say it would imperil the special U.S. relationship with Israel.

Sen. Jacob K. Javits (R, N.Y.) asked, "What do we want to do with the Israelis? Sap their

ARMS SHIPMENT TO MIDDLE EAST
Recipients & suppliers 1967-76
(in current $U.S. millions)

	Total	U.S.	U.S.S.R.	France	U.K.	Czech.	China	Poland	Canada	West Ger.
Bahrain	1	0	0	0	0	0	0	0	0	0
Egypt	2,801	1	2,365	125	15	140	15	5	0	105
Iran	5,271	3,835	611	15	270	1	0	0	45	275
Iraq	2,451	0	1,795	95	5	125	5	15	0	35
Israel	4,941	4,761	0	105	35	0	0	0	0	5
Jordan	650	505	0	55	60	0	0	0	0	1
Kuwait	181	31	0	0	71	0	0	0	0	20
Lebanon	131	25	5	75	5	5	0	0	0	0
Oman	71	5	0	0	21	0	0	0	1	0
Qatar	5	0	0	0	5	0	0	0	0	0
Saudi Arabia	1440	671	0	225	451	0	0	0	0	11
Syria	2261	5	2015	5	5	140	1	21	0	35
United Arab Emirates	105	0	0	50	31	0	0	0	0	0
Yemen, North	80	1	35	11	1	0	0	0	0	0
Yemen, South	165	0	151	0	1	0	0	0	0	0
Total	2,0554	9,940	6,977	761	976	411	21	41	46	487

Source: U.S. Arms Control & Disarmament Agency

vitality? Sap their morale? Cut the legs out from under them? That's what this is about." Another opponent, Sen. Clifford Case (R, N.J.), cautioned that the sale would endanger Israel's security. "Will we risk destroying Israel by gradually eroding our support?"

Supporters of the sale argue that it would strengthen the position of moderate forces in the Arab countries. Saudi security is an issue. Sen. Thomas Eagleton (D, Mo.) contended that "it would be a catastrophe" if the Saudi oil fields were taken over by a hostile power. Oil—specifically the impact on the U.S. of the role played by the Saudis in the Organization of Petroleum

Exporting Countries (OPEC)—figured in the debate. Sen. Lloyd Bentsen (D, Tex.) pointed out that "for the past five years Saudi Arabia has been a force of moderation within OPEC on the question of oil prices." Bentsen continued, "The Saudis have steadfastly resisted efforts by some of our friends, Venezuela and Iran in particular, to raise oil prices even higher. . . . To discourage the sale would do incalculable damage to Saudi-American relations."

But the range and sophistication of the weaponry meant that should conflict break out, casualties would be substantially higher than in the last war.

CHAPTER 46

Population

The population problem is changing.

Looking at it one way, it is still a problem of numbers. Each number represents an individual person. The number of individuals taken together is the number of mouths to be fed, bodies to be clothed and housed.

Here are some of the numbers: The Population Reference Bureau told a FACTS ON FILE editor shortly before this book went to press that world population had reached an estimated 4.219 billion in mid-1978 and was increasing at a rate of about 1.7%—or some 73 million human beings every year. The United Nations Population Division told the same editor that world population was expected to rise from the estimate of 4 billion as of mid-1975 to about 4.4 billion in mid-1980.

China, India, the Soviet Union and the United States, in that order, are the most populous countries. Shanghai appears to be the largest city, with a population of 10,820,000. Tokyo, New York, Mexico City and Peking are next in line. (The definition of a city's boundaries varies from country to country, making it difficult to obtain internationally comparable figures of their size.)

Europe is the most urbanized region in the world, Africa, the least urbanized. Infant mortality rates continue to show a downward trend in much of the world. The highest life expectancy at birth is found in Sweden, where female infants could expect to live an average of 77 years; among males, the longest life expectancy also is reported in Sweden—72 years.

But the problem is shifting.

In Europe, 22 out of 34 countries or areas report population increases of less than one per cent annually; four countries—East and West Germany, Austria and Luxembourg—had birth rates too low to maintain the population level.

Great Britain experienced a demographic transition from high birth and death rates (before the industrial revolution) to a high birth and low death rate (during industrialization), to low birth and death rates (post-industrialization). Britain is approaching an equilibrium between births and deaths, a replacement growth level.

A great shift is taking place in Asia, where more than half of the world's people—2.391 billion persons, or 56.9 per cent—live and where from 1965 to 1975 the birth rate had fallen sharply. Growth rates are reported by the Popu-

POPULATION
(In Millions)

Region	1960	1965	1975	Growth Rate 1965–75 %
Africa	273	309	401	2.7
Nothern America	199	214	237	1.0
Latin America	216	247	324	2.7
Asia	1 644	1 824	2 256	2.1
Europe	425	445	473	0.6
Oceania	16	18	21	2.0
USSR	214	231	255	1.0
World	2 986	3 288	3 967	1.9

BIRTH & DEATH RATES, AREA & DENSITY

Region	Births per 1000 Population 1965–75	Deaths per 1000 Population 1965–75	Population Density per sq. km. 1975
Africa	47	20	13
Nothern America	17	9	11
Latin America	38	9	16
Asia	35	14	82
Europe	16	10	96
Oceania	23	10	3
USSR	18	8	11
World	32	13	29

Source: *World Statistics in Brief* (United Nations 1977)

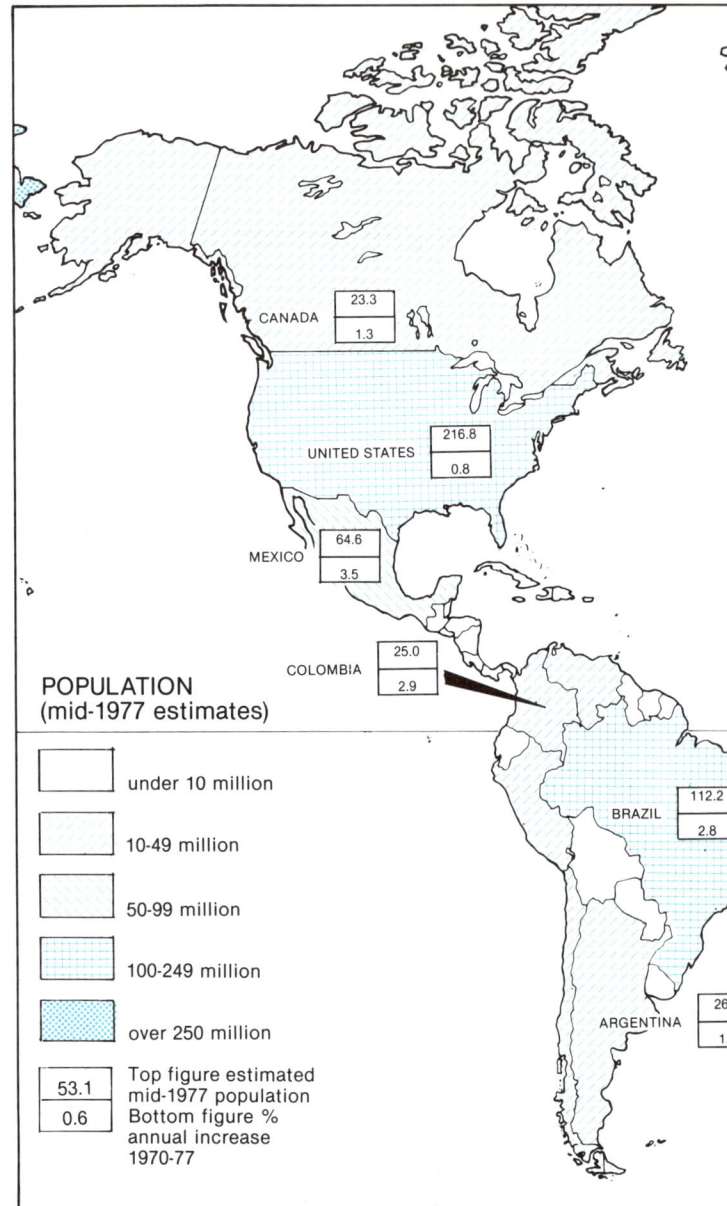

POPULATION
(mid-1977 estimates)

	under 10 million
	10-49 million
	50-99 million
	100-249 million
	over 250 million

| 53.1 | Top figure estimated mid-1977 population |
| 0.6 | Bottom figure % annual increase 1970-77 |

CANADA 23.3 / 1.3

UNITED STATES 216.8 / 0.8

MEXICO 64.6 / 3.5

COLOMBIA 25.0 / 2.9

BRAZIL 112.2 / 2.8

ARGENTINA 26 / 1.

Contrasts in population growth are displayed on the map. The annual rate of growth in the U.S., for example, is 0.8 per cent, in the Soviet Union 0.9 per cent. In China, the reported growth rate is 1.7 per cent, in Japan 1.3 per cent. The world's highest rates of growth are recorded in such countries as Mexico, 3.5 per cent; Algeria, 3.2 per cent; and Brazil, Nigeria and Thailand, all 2.8 per cent. Among the countries with the lowest rates of growth are West Germany, 0.2 per cent, and Great Britain, 0.1 per cent.

lation Council to have declined 32 per cent in South Korea, 30 per cent in Taiwan, 24 per cent in China, 23 per cent in Thailand and North Vietnam. The decline was brought about by active government policies, education in family planning and availability of birth control measures. Presenting population statistics in another way, the U.N. reported in 1977 that the birth rate in Hong Kong had decreased from 36.6 per 1,000 persons in 1960 to 19.7 in 1970; in Singapore, from 38.7 in 1960 to 22.1 in 1973; in Sri Lanka from 36.6 in 1960 to 29.5 in 1972.

Statistics are incomplete or unreliable in many countries. There are still some where no population census has ever been conducted, for example, Afghanistan, the Lao People's Republic, Oman, Qatar and Yemen. In others, data is not reported or published.

Birth statistics in India could be obtained through the civil registration, national sample surveys of the 1960s and the recent Sample Registration System, but "data given by the civil registration have not been reliable," the U.N. finds.

GREAT BRITAIN | 55.9 / 0.1
POLAND | 34.7 / 0.9
SOVIET UNION | 258.9 / 0.9
RMANY | 61.4 / 0.2
YUGOSLAVIA | 21.7 / 0.9
BANGLADESH | 80.6 / 2.4
FRANCE | 53.1 / 0.6
PAKISTAN | 75.3 / 3.2
JAPAN | 113.9 / 1.3
SPAIN | 36.4 / 1.1
TURKEY | 42.1 / 2.7
CHINA | 865.7 / 1.7
ALGERIA | 17.9 / 3.2
ITALY | 56.4 / 0.7
BURMA | 31.5 / 2.2
VIETNAM | 47.9 / 2.9
EGYPT | 38.7 / 2.2
PHILIPPINES | 45.0 / 2.9
NIGERIA | 66.6 / 2.8
AFGHANISTAN | 20.3 / 2.5
THAILAND | 44.0 / 2.8
ZAIRE | 26.4 / 2.5
ETHIOPIA | 28.9 / 2.3
INDIA | 625.0 / 2.2
INDONESIA | 143.3 / 2.6
AUSTRALIA | 14.1 / n.a.

POPULATION & POPULATION GROWTH

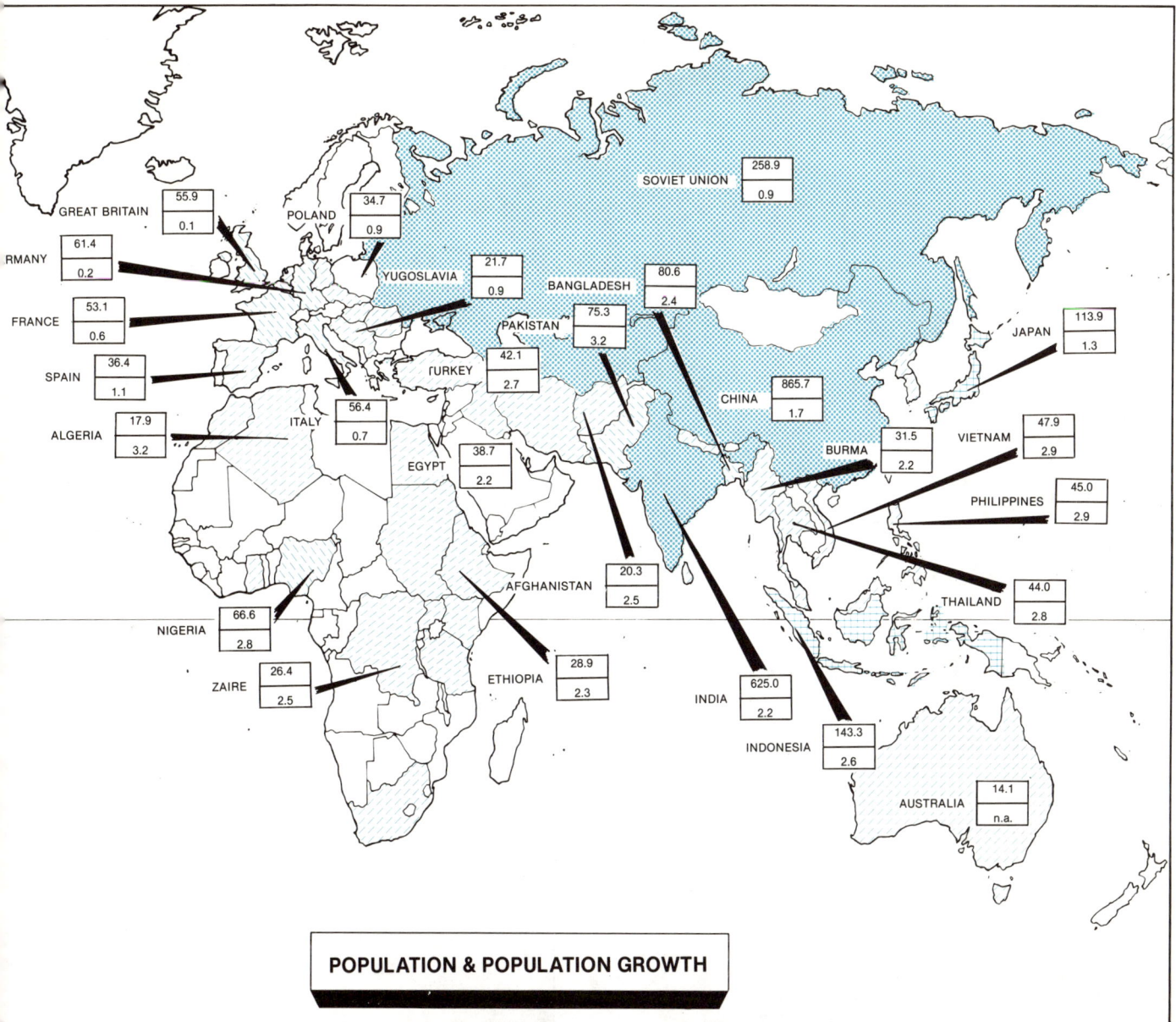

The last census in China was taken in 1953, when the population was reported to be 590,-194,715. Estimates of China's present population ranged from 750 million to 950 million. Its birth rate is not officially announced but is believed to have been reduced from 2.3 per cent in the 1950s to about 1.7 or 1.8 per cent. Japan's experience, however, has been carefully recorded; Japan's birth rate rose to 2.9 per cent following the Second World War, receded to 0.8 per cent in 1957 and then recovered to 1.1 per cent in 1971. A U.N. projection foresaw the Japanese birth rate declining gradually to the replacement level by the end of the century.

The most rapid increase in population is occurring in Africa, where growth rates are 2 to 3 per cent or more. What does this shift add up to? Overall, demographers conclude that the world's population is increasing more slowly than anticipated. The data suggests that it would rise to 5.4 billion by the year 2000 rather than the 6.5 billion previously forecast. The smaller increase would only give the world a breather.

IRAQ

IRAN

Ahwaz

Basra

Abadan

KUWAIT

Kuwait

KHARG I.

Persian Gulf

Bandar Abbas

Ras Tanura

Dhahran

BAHRAIN

Strait of Hormuz

OMAN

QATAR

Doha

GHAWAR

Gulf of Oman

Riyadh

Abu Dhabi

SAUDI ARABIA

UNITED ARAB EMIRATES

Muscat

OMAN

0   100   200 Miles

0   100   200   300 Km

TURKEY

U.S.S.R.

SYRIA

IRAQ

IRAN

AFGHANISTAN

EGYPT

SAUDI ARABIA

PAKISTAN

OMAN

Persian Gulf

INDIA

SUDAN

NO. YEMEN

SO. YEMEN

ARABIAN SEA

ETHIOPIA

SOMALIA

Areas of Soviet pressure

Norfolk

to Brega 4700 miles

Ras Tanura 8490 miles

Yokohama

1680 miles

Brega

Ras Tanura

to Bonny 4940 miles

Maracaibo

Bonny

to Ras Tanura 11,810 miles

to Yokohama 6580 miles

SEA LANES FROM SELECTED OIL FIELDS

Distances in nautical miles

Oil field

Oil pipeline

Refinery

Tanker terminal

THE PERSIAN GULF

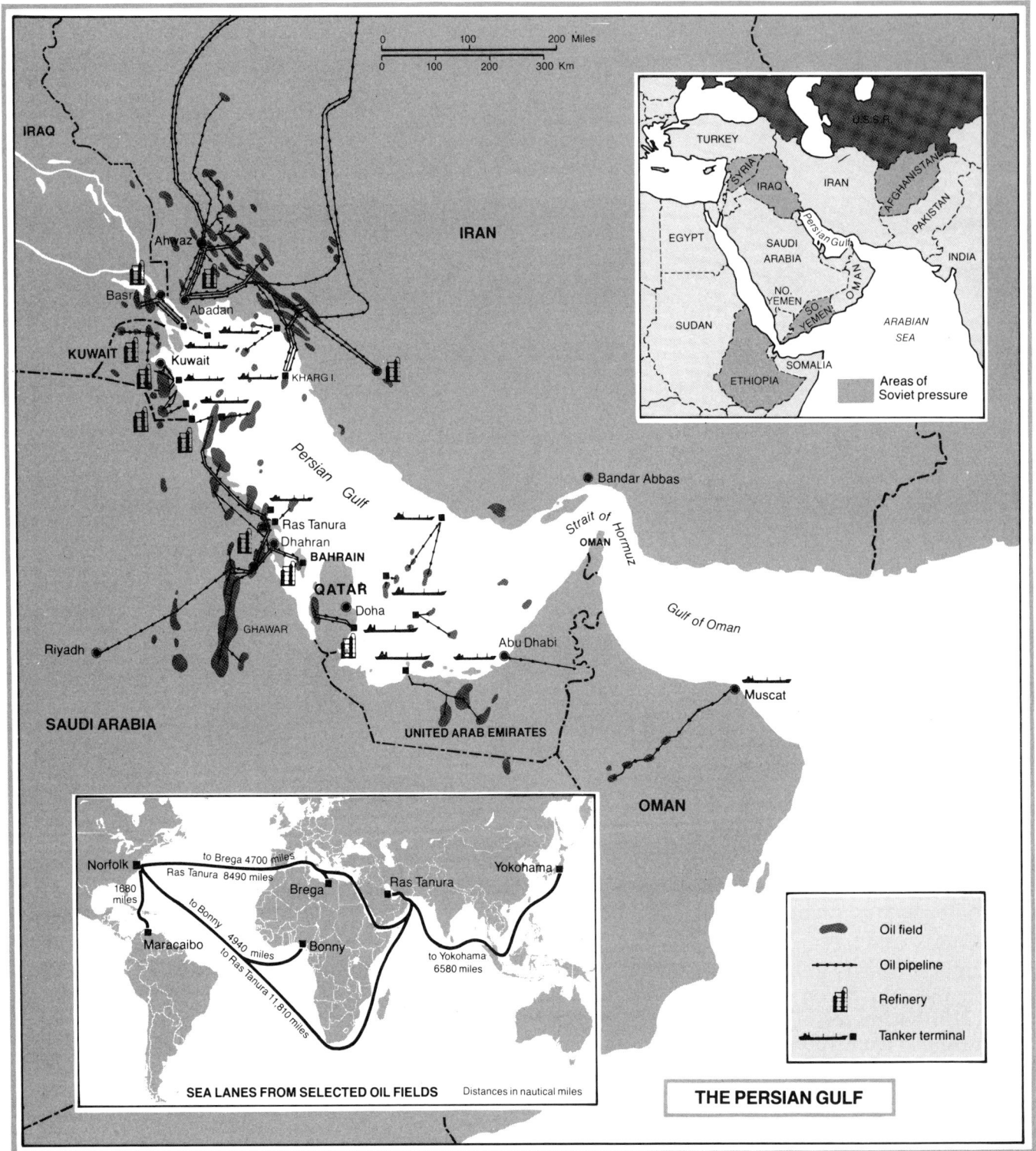

The great oil resources of the Persian Gulf produce conflict as well as wealth. The gulf's oil fields, pipelines, refineries and tanker terminals are located on the map. So are the areas in which Soviet pressure is being felt — Afghanistan, South Yemen, Iraq. The Iranian oil fields at the head of the gulf are said to be the richest in existence. With the revolution in Iran, the production of those fields and exports to Western countries were substantially reduced. The U.S. has indicated that if necessary it will act to protect its interests in the region.

CHAPTER 47

Persian Gulf

A drop of oil is worth a drop of blood.
—Georges Clemenceau

The Persian Gulf is a hot spot. Desert climate prevails throughout most of the area—aridity, long, severe summers, and an absence of ground water.

The gulf is an arm of the Arabian Sea between the Arabian Peninsula and Iran. It extends about 600 miles (970 kilometers) from the Strait of Hormuz to the delta of Shatt al Arab, a river formed by the confluence of the Tigris and Euphrates rivers. The gulf is shallow and has many islands, the largest of which is Bahrain. It is called the Arabian Gulf by the Arabs.

Oil was discovered in the gulf area in 1908, and major finds were made in the 1930s. More than half of the world's proven reserves are to be found today around the rim and beneath the bed of the gulf. Saudi Arabia, Iran, Iraq and Kuwait are the leading gulf producers, in that order; the Iranian oil fields at the head of the gulf are said to be the richest in existence. In 1975, 26 per cent of the oil imported by the U.S., 64 per cent of the oil imported by Western Europe, and 72 per cent of the oil imported by Japan came from the Persian Gulf. Imports of oil from the gulf are expected to rise over the next two decades.

The U.S. Congress has emphasized the vital character of the region's oil production, particularly that of Saudi Arabia and Iran, since the 1973–74 embargo by the Arab members of the Organization of Petroleum Exporting Countries (OPEC), six of which border on the gulf. The embargo, a report to the House Committee on International Relations pointed out, "allowed considerable leakage. Some tankers with false manifests found their way directly from the Persian Gulf to U.S. ports. Others took devious routes with full Arab knowledge. Nevertheless, that restrained effort showed how susceptible this country would be to renewed pressures."

". . . [O]ur oil supplies increasingly depend on the most remote and insecure areas," Deputy Assistant Secretary of Defense Roger K. Shields testified before the Senate Judiciary Committee. "The major oil loading ports of the Persian Gulf lie within 900 miles of the Soviet Union. The sea lanes from that area reach half way around the world. . . ."

The U.S. relationship with Saudi Arabia and Iran might be the "critical key for supply security from this region," the Senate Committee on Energy & Natural Resources said.

Stability is a goal of U.S. policy. "Special relationships" with Saudi Arabia and Iran are the instruments. The U.S. is Saudi Arabia's largest trading partner. The Saudis are reported to hold at least $35 billion in U.S. Treasury notes, home mortgage funds and other investments. Some 35,000 Americans live and work in Saudi Arabia; the number in Iran had reached 45,000 before the fall of the shah.

U.S. firms had been active in Iran, assembling cars, building a new port, installing telecommunications. From 1973 to 1977, Iran purchased more than $16 billion worth of military equipment from the U.S. Shah Mohammed Riza Pahlevi had been restored to power by the CIA in 1953 and sustained by the U.S. for the next 25 years. The U.S. was pledged under a bilateral security pact to use its armed forces if necessary and if requested by Iran to defend the country. But the virtual expulsion of the shah early in 1979 breached this U.S.-Iranian relationship.

Saudi Arabia and Iran were kingdoms. The former still is essentially a feudal absolute monarchy. The latter had been a modern authoritarian state. Saudi Arabia was the more stable. ". . . Political observers have, in fact, been predicting the end of the monarchy in Iran ever since the close of the 1940s," J. C. Hurewitz wrote in his pamphlet *The Persian Gulf: Prospects for Stability,* "and one of these years they may turn out to be right. . . ." The shah's regime was severely tested throughout 1978 by widespread violence, political and religious opposition and an oil workers' strike. The shah imposed martial law and appointed first a military

PERSIAN GULF STATES

Country	Population	Land Area (sq. mi.)	Crude Oil Reserves (billion barrels)
Saudi Arabia	9,240,000	873,000	153.0
Kuwait	1,030,000	7,780	71.0
Iran	33,900,000	636,363	65.0
Iraq	11,510,000	172,000	34.0
United Arab Emirates	230,000	32,278	30.0
Qatar	100,000	4,000	6.0
Oman	790,000	82,000	6.0
Bahrain	260,000	231	.3

Oil pipelines in Iran; waste gases are being burnt in the background.

government, then a civilian one. This didn't help, and he left the country in January for what observers concluded was a permanent "vacation."

In the shah's view—shared by the Saudis—the wealthy gulf states are "in the middle of a giant pincers movement being orchestrated by the Soviet Union," the *Christian Science Monitor* reported. "In this view, first came the leftist takeover of Iraq, next the Marxist government in South Yemen, then the Soviet and Cuban moves into Ethiopia, and, most recently, the Communist coup in Afghanistan.

"Color those areas red on the map and you see what looks like a giant nutcracker about to squeeze both Saudi Arabia and Iran."

Some observers consider the role of Islam, as personified by the Ayatallah Ruholla Khomeini, to be the dominant current factor in Iran.

Though Defense Secretary Harold Brown acknowledges that "we are as yet unsure of the utility of U.S. military power in Persian Gulf contingencies," the formation of a new elite three-division strike force is being considered. (Other trouble spots to which it might be sent are the Eastern Mediterranean and South Korea.) Its objectives in the gulf would be to seize oil fields and facilities intact, secure them and guarantee safe overseas passage for supplies and oil.

CHAPTER 48

Japan

The islands of Japan cover an area slightly less than the state of Montana—Japan, 143,574 square miles, Montana, 147,138 square miles. The population of Japan is 114,000,000, that of Montana 753,000.

In terms of size and population, these are striking comparisons, almost as compelling as Japan's postwar and current economic achievement. Defeated in war, Japan conquered the world economically, so to speak; it is now the world's third greatest economic power. The U.S. is first, the Soviet Union second. Comparative gross national products in 1977 were: the U.S., $1.874 trillion; the Soviet Union, $781 billion; and Japan, $642 billion.

Being an economic and population giant poses serious problems for a territorial midget. Japan must import 65 per cent of its oil and raw materials and 15 per cent of its food.

To import, Japan must export, and it does; its economy is built on a huge volume of exports. Japan is now in either first or second place in world exports of steel products, automobiles, ships, motorcycles, TV sets, radios and several high-grade synthetic textiles.

Moreover, Japan sells auto plants as well as autos, chemical plants, whole industrial plants and machinery. Twenty-five years ago, labor-intensive industries (textiles) made up half its exports, today, a tenth. Japan is shifting from growth industries (cars, electrical equipment) to "knowledge-intensive" industries (computers, precision equipment, special alloys and other sophisticated products).

Almost as remarkable as Japan's growth are some of the reasons for it—expert long-range planning by two famed government bodies, the Ministry of International Trade & Industry (MITI) and the Economic Planning Agency; the

design, performance and durability of its products; its competitive pricing policies; a smaller margin of profit than would be acceptable to U.S. firms; a traditional forty-eight-hour, six-day workweek. Japanese workers reportedly are reluctant to take time off. ". . . In order to help popularize the idea of taking summer vacations," writes Nobutaka Ike in *Japan: the New Superstate*, "both the Ministry of Labor and MITI have been putting pressure on their staffs to take vacations, with indifferent success. MITI has even taken to assessing fines on employees who fail to take time off. . . ."

Success thus also has its problems. In fact, there is no lack of problems. Everyone in Japan talks "economics and only economics," Peter F. Drucker observes in *Foreign Affairs*. ". . . Yet the basic issues facing Japan are not economic. They are changes in social structure and social values. Social policies that have served Japan superbly well . . . are rapidly becoming untenable. . . . Their very success is rendering them obsolete. . . ."

These policies include the seniority-wage system, under which incomes are determined primarily by length of service; the linkage of education to career opportunities; and the employee's commitment to one employer and one place of employment for a lifetime. Drucker contends that the six-per cent growth rate required for Japan to maintain its competitive position in the world is not sustainable on the basis of available manpower and existing retirement policy. The government is beginning to press for delayed retirement—at age 60 rather than 55. (Seventy-five years ago, the average life expectancy was 42 years. Fifty years ago, it was still only 53. Today it is 71.)

Japan's economic relationship with the U.S.

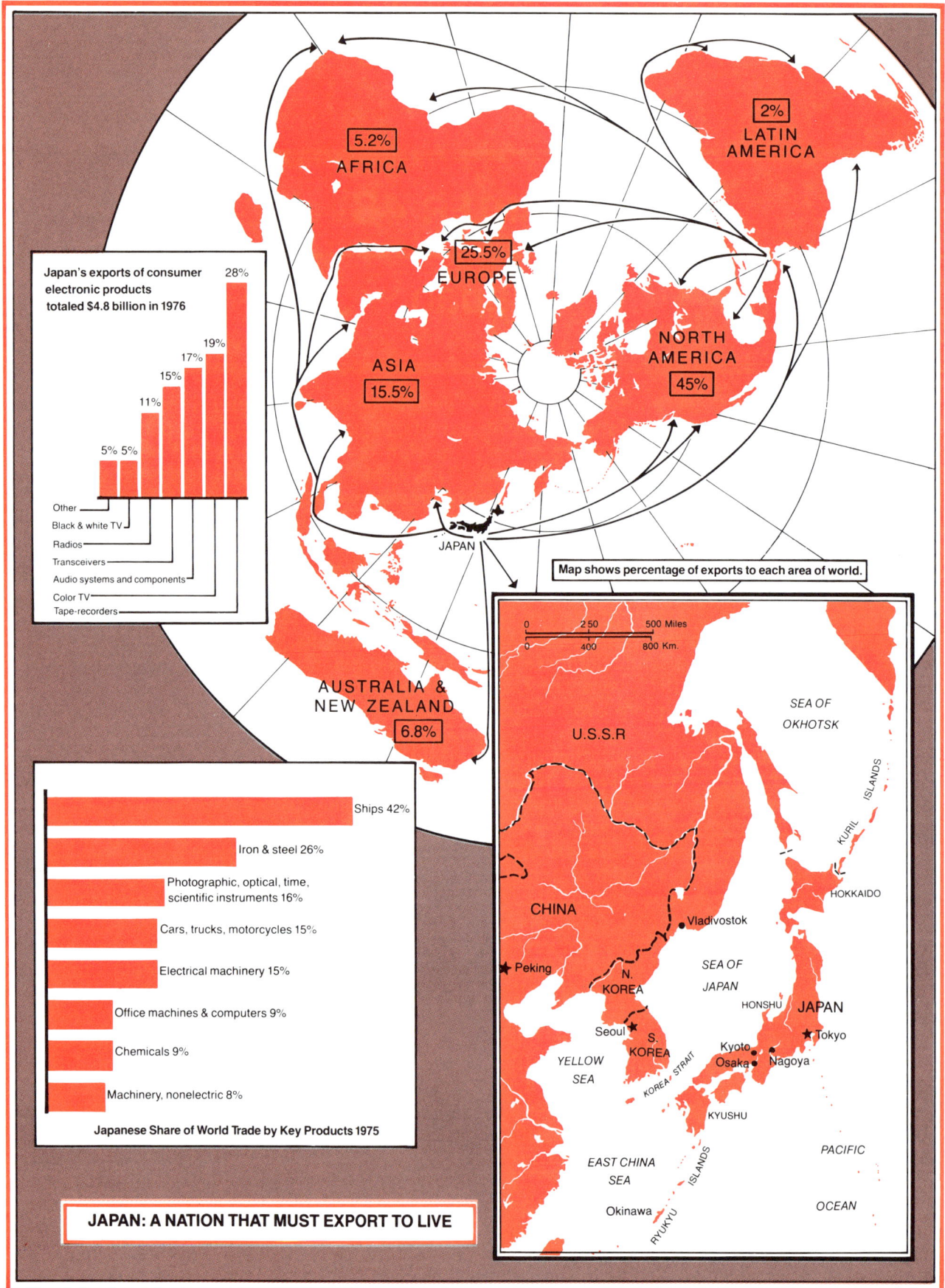

5.2%

AFRICA

2%

LATIN AMERICA

25.5%

EUROPE

NORTH AMERICA

45%

ASIA

15.5%

Japan's exports of consumer electronic products totaled $4.8 billion in 1976

28%

19%

17%

15%

11%

5% 5%

Other

Black & white TV

Radios

Transceivers

Audio systems and components

Color TV

Tape-recorders

JAPAN

Map shows percentage of exports to each area of world.

AUSTRALIA & NEW ZEALAND

6.8%

Ships 42%

Iron & steel 26%

Photographic, optical, time, scientific instruments 16%

Cars, trucks, motorcycles 15%

Electrical machinery 15%

Office machines & computers 9%

Chemicals 9%

Machinery, nonelectric 8%

Japanese Share of World Trade by Key Products 1975

JAPAN: A NATION THAT MUST EXPORT TO LIVE

0   250   500 Miles
0   400   800 Km.

SEA OF OKHOTSK

U.S.S.R

KURIL ISLANDS

HOKKAIDO

CHINA

Vladivostok

SEA OF JAPAN

Peking

N. KOREA

HONSHU

JAPAN

Seoul

S. KOREA

Kyoto

Tokyo

YELLOW SEA

Osaka

Nagoya

KOREA STRAIT

KYUSHU

EAST CHINA SEA

RYUKYU ISLANDS

PACIFIC

Okinawa

OCEAN

is particularly thorny. In 1976, Japan exported goods worth more than $15.5 billion to the U.S.; it imported American goods worth a total of $10.1 billion. Japan's overall trade surplus for fiscal 1977 was $20.5 billion—the highest ever recorded by any nation—and almost half of the total was in trade with the U.S. In fiscal 1977, Japan exported 1.89 million vehicles to the U.S. and imported from the U.S. about 15,000. Nippon Steel Corp. and four other major Japanese steel producers were accused by the U.S. in 1977 of dumping steel products on the American market at below-cost prices. After negotiations with Japanese officials, a trigger price system was established. The trigger price, based on Japanese costs of production, would serve as a minimum price level in the U.S.

The Japanese yen continues to rise against the U.S. dollar, while the U.S. marks up record trade deficits. The U.S. called on Japan to stimulate domestic demand for exports. MITI announced that it would promote imports through a liberalized government financing program. Japanese Premier Takeo Fukuda assured U.S. President Jimmy Carter that Japan would undertake to reduce its trade surplus. But, reports *The New York Times,* Japanese business leaders are openly critical of U.S. economic weakness, viewing American industry as noncompetitive and American workers as lazy. "In a sense, it was high time that someone gave voice to this undercurrent of vicious criticism," said a close associate of Kiichi Miyazawa, head of the Economic Planning Agency.

Aspects of modern and traditional Japan are united in photograph of high-speed train crossing bridge on Tokaido line below Mount Fuji.

Japan's remarkable economic achievement—it is the world's third largest economic power behind the U.S. and Soviet Union—is based on a huge volume of exports. It exports not only TV sets and tape recorders and cars and steel products but entire industrial plants. Japan's exports to the U.S. far exceed its imports from the U.S., resulting in a conflict between the two nations that trade negotiations have yet to resolve. The major Japanese exports are indicated, as are the country's trade routes and the areas to which it exports.

CHAPTER 49

China: New Paths

Be meticulous in organization and discipline.
—Hua Kuo-feng

Each family must have a bicycle, a sewing machine, a television set.
—Teng Hsiao-ping

China's revolutionary leaders—Mao Tse-tung and Chou En-lai—died in 1976.

Chou died Jan. 8. On Feb. 7, Hua Kuo-feng was named "acting" premier, succeeding Chou. Hua had been sixth-ranked deputy premier and public security minister. An agricultural expert, he had been the top Communist Party official in Hunan Province before he was elected in 1973 to the 21-member Politburo, the party's main decision-making body.

Hua's appointment was received with surprise by Western diplomats, who had expected senior Deputy Premier Teng Hsiao-ping to be named. Teng held key posts in the three critical areas—the party, the government, the military. It was speculated that radical opposition to Teng's so-called "moderate" line had emerged in party deliberations and had either forced him aside or caused him to withdraw. The choice of Hua was regarded as a compromise.

A wall poster campaign against Teng was launched by radicals. On April 5, an apparently spontaneous riot took place in Peking's Tien An Men Square. Widely interpreted as a response to the anti-Teng campaign, it was the first outbreak of violence between the two ideological wings of the Communist Party since the Cultural Revolution. (The Cultural Revolution had aimed at rekindling revolutionary fervor and eliminating tendencies to stray rightward from orthodox Marxism-Leninism.) Two days later Teng was deposed and Hua confirmed as pre-

mier and first deputy chairman of the Communist Party.

The "anti-rightist" drive spread. Posters demanded that Teng be put to death. Hua warned that "class enemies" had been engaging in "sabotage." His remarks followed reports that serious crime and unrest were increasing throughout China.

On Sept. 9, Mao died. Hua was named to succeed Mao as chairman. Mao's widow and three other leading party leftists—denounced as the "Gang of Four"—were arrested. A coup attempt reportedly had been crushed. Troops subdued unrest in Fukien Province and in the central provinces of Hupei, Honan, Shensi.

Early in 1977, wall posters appeared calling for Teng's rehabilitation. In July, he was reinstalled as deputy premier, chief of staff of the Army General Staff, member of the Politburo, and deputy chairman of the central committee's military commission.

Hua and Teng ruled China. Within eighteen months, Teng emerged as the more powerful figure.

Both men are described as "pragmatists," who emphasize the day-to-day work necessary to modernize and industrialize China; both had been proteges of Chou. Hua is 59, Teng 75. Hua speaks slowly and "so quietly that even his interpreters have a hard time following him," reports *Newsweek*. Teng has a blunt, no-nonsense style and a reputation as a technocrat-administrator. His "obvious disdain for ideological overkill . . . and his willingness to go down fighting against Mao's much-reviled widow . . . have made him extremely popular," said *Newsweek*. "So has his talk about the need for wage increases and more attention to consumer desires. . . ."

Street scene in Peking: bicyclists, vehicles and pedestrians.

Soon after Hua's and Teng's accession, a new constitution was adopted. It stresses discipline but also encourages more open discussion within the party. A new national anthem was approved. Its lyrics ("March on, brave people of our nation") are set to the music for the original anthem, *March of the Volunteers.*

Economic, scientific and educational goals were revised. A 10-year economic plan is now set. Farm output would be raised by an anual average 4 to 5 per cent and industrial production at a rate of 10 per cent. Factory workers and managers would receive gradual wage increases, provided that the production plan is fulfilled.

Science is to be given priority. China is "now lagging 15 to 20 years behind in many branches and still more in others." Research programs in such fields as laser development, space technology and high-energy physics were established.

Major educational reforms were announced. Colleges are to be required to give entrance examinations. Some high school students would be permitted to go directly to college without having to work several years in the countryside. Mao had endeavored to make the educational system more egalitarian and to eliminate what he regarded as useless academic practices.

The need to reevaluate Mao's ideas is pointed out by Teng. Mao's precepts should not be interpreted literally, he told a conference of army political commisars. "We must integrate them with reality, analyze and study actual condi-

tions and solve practical problems. If we just copied past documents word for word, we wouldn't be solving any problem, let alone solving any problem correctly."

Hua focuses on economic pragmatism. China must "learn from the advanced experience of other countries," he asserts. Among China's economic shortcomings, he says, are "low productivity, poor quality of products, high production costs, low profits and slow turnover of funds. A number of enterprises are still running at a loss." New practical policies are being followed. For example, Peking authorized the managers of the Bank of China and its 12 sister banks in Hong Kong to practice "capitalist methods." (The Bank of China in Hong Kong is Peking's principal foreign-exchange arm.) In addition, the banks were given authority to buy and sell stocks and bonds, gold, silver and other commodities, foreign currencies and real estate. Hua has expressed some misgivings about modernization, according to Victor Zorza of the *Manchester Guardian.* He seems to fear that it might endanger socialism, Zorza wrote. Teng is said to want to go much further in contact and trade with the West. The question is being debated by the Peking leadership in right-left terms.

Right-left, or moderate-radical—the choice of directions in which Chinese society is to advance and the pace at which it is to go—remain an issue. However, in foreign policy, there seems to be no such disagreement. ". . . The

**POST-MAO CHINA
A Change in Direction**

U.S.S.R.

MONGOLIA

Gobi Desert

U.S.S.R.

Amur River

Ussuri R.

Harbin

Changchun

Shenyang
Anshan

N. KOREA

Peking ★

Tientsin

Lüta

S. KOREA

Urumchi

Paotow

Taiyüan

Tsingtao

YELLOW SEA

Lanchow

Sian

Yellow R.

Nanking

Shanghai

H I M A L A Y A S

Lhasa

Yangtze River

Chungking

Wuhan

Nanchang

Changsha

Foochow

Taipei

TAIWAN
Tainan

INDIA

Canton

Hong Kong

Formosa Strait

BURMA

VIETNAM
LAOS

THAILAND

BAY OF BENGAL

SOUTH CHINA SEA

RESOURCES AND INDUSTRIES

Automobiles & trucks · Coal · Food processing · Machinery · Petroleum · Rubber products · Tool making · Bauxite · Copper · Iron & steel · Manufacturing · Porcelain & lacquerware · Shipbuilding · Textiles · Chemicals · Electrical equipment · Iron ore · Oil refining · Railroad equipment · Sugar refining · Uranium

With the death of Mao Tse-tung, China shifted from his ideological precepts to economic "pragmatism." The goals of its new leaders are modernization and industrialization, rapid increases in farm and factory productivity. A 10-year economic plan was adopted. The map shows the location of major resources and industries affected by this change in direction. Hua Kuo-feng and Teng Hsiao-ping emphasize the day-to-day work necessary to carry out China's economic, scientific and educational programs. Teng pointed out the need to re-evaluate Mao's ideas. "We must integrate them with reality," he said, "analyze and study actual conditions and solve practical problems." These changes in policy are among the factors that brought about the establishment of diplomatic relations between China and the U.S. at the beginning of 1979.

indications are that China's foreign policy in the post-Mao era," O. Edmund Clubb observed in *The Progressive,* "will be notable less for revolutionary campaigns than for a sober realism. . . ." The new leaders of China signed a peace and friendship treaty with Japan and eased up on talk of liberating Taiwan.

Last year, Hua made an unprecedented trip to Rumania, Yugoslavia and Iran—the first to Europe by a Chinese head of state since the founding of the People's Republic of China in 1949 and the first to a non-Communist country. At several points, he sharply criticized the Soviet Union, using the word hegemony to refer to Soviet domination. "In Asia, Africa, Latin America and Europe . . . hegemony stretches its hands, continually resorting to actions of infiltration, undermining, aggression and expansion in some countries," Hua declared at a state dinner in Bucharest.

Sino-Soviet hostility originally had been doctrinal, later related to questions of national interest, now takes several forms.

From Sinkiang to Manchuria, the two Communist antagonists deploy large border forces. Talks about disputed border areas are deadlocked. In the Northeast, for instance, the Soviet Union claim that the border is marked by the Chinese bank of the Ussuri River; the Chinese maintain that the border goes through the middle of the river.

Realpolitik also is tangled in Southeast Asia. Soviet influence in Vietnam is growing, while Vietnam and China quarrel over Hanoi's displacement of ethnic Chinese. Peking backed Cambodia because it was fighting Hanoi.

China's leaders apparently are more concerned about Soviet hegemony than about either Western capitalism or imperialism. They go shopping in the West for antitank guns and combat aircraft as well as technology. They advocated the normalization of relations with the U.S.; the U.S. initially responded with caution. Zbigniew Brzezinski, U.S. national security adviser, visited Peking and told Chinese Foreign Minister Huang Hua that the U.S. recognized and shared China's determination to "resist the efforts of any nation which seeks to establish global and regional hegemony." Soviet President Leonid I. Brezhnev denounced the U.S. for "attempts to play the 'Chinese card'" against the Soviet Union.

"The reasonable way to play the China card is to make our relationship with Peking as full and interlocking as our relationship with Moscow," commented Ross Terrill in *U.S. News & World Report.* "At the moment, it is not. This doesn't mean an American alliance with China. The list of items on which there can be positive cooperation between the two nations in the political sphere, I think, is rather short. The two societies are terribly different. Their values and ours diverge. But in a world where the Soviet Union is the only serious global contender against the United States, a good relationship with China—especially while China has a bad relationship with the Soviet Union—is a logical means of the United States maximizing its interests."

The U.S. and China formally established diplomatic relations Jan. 1, 1979. An agreement to "normalize" ties had followed several months of secret negotiations. Teng visited the U.S. shortly afterwards, conferred with President Carter at the White House and signed cultural and scientific pacts. Teng praised the agreements as "significant" but noted that "this is not the end but just a beginning."

CHAPTER 50

Indochina: The Continuing Conflict

The past, present and future are vivid issues in Indochina.

"The war is gone . . . planes come no more . . . do not weep for those just born . . . the human being is evergreen." John Pilger, who had covered the war in Vietnam for a decade, revisited the country last year and, at an orphanage in Saigon, heard a child singing the words of that song. In Hanoi, Pilger encountered a man, "an old nicotine-stained figure," who kept a daily vigil at the gaps in Kham Thiem Street. One night in 1972, bombs hit every third house on the street, killing 283 persons.

Writing in the *New Statesman,* Pilger recalled an American admiral, a jovial, obese man in a cap, on an aircraft carrier in the South China Sea. The "longest war game of the twentieth century" was coming to an end. " 'Well folks,' said he, 'that just about wraps up Vietnam. So let's all have a party and get outta here. . . .' "

DMZ, Quang Tri. Tet 1968. For Americans it was a TV war, atrocities, peace marches. The Vietnam War was the longest in U.S. history, almost 12 years. It cost 57,000 American dead, 153,000 wounded, $150 billion. Post-mortems were conducted in books and films, more than one dedicated to those who died in Vietnam. In some cases, the validity of wartime positions and decisions were reasserted; in others, the "lessons" of the war were examined. A number of works reflected the horrors of Vietnam and the anguish of the political divisions that grew with it.

Events—history—rushed on. Communist regimes took power in Laos and Cambodia. North and South Vietnam reunited in 1976 as the Socialist Republic of Vietnam. In 1977 Viet-

nam became a member of the U.N., the U.S. withholding its veto on Vietnam's third application; the following year Vietnam became a member of the Communist bloc's Council for Mutual Economic Assistance (Comecon).

Talks opened between Vietnam and the U.S. on "normalizing" relations. Tens of thousands of refugees fled Vietnam, Cambodia and Laos. The U.S. accepted 170,000 for resettlement, France took 42,000, Australia 10,000, Canada 7,000; some 95,000 remained in camps in Thailand.

"Paradoxically," Allan W. Cameron wrote in a prescient pamphlet in 1976, *Indochina: Prospects After 'The End,'* "the North Vietnamese victory exerts a profoundly destabilizing effect in Southeast Asia. Now the situation is more in doubt, the future harder to predict, than was the case when the fighting was in progress. . . . The end of the war . . . has left all concerned unsure, with few fundamental truths to serve as the touchstones of policy and action. . . ." Cameron noted the uncertainty of Vietnam's relations with its neighbors, the emergence of Vietnam as the strongest military power in Southeast Asia, and the respects in which Vietnam might find the Soviet Union a more attractive great-power ally than China.

Cameron was correct. Within a year, the "Parrot's Beak" was back in the news.

The "Parrot's Beak," a southeastern area of Cambodia, had been contested by Communist and U.S. forces. It jutted into Vietnam. Now, heavy fighting broke out between Cambodia and Vietnam in a border dispute that long predated America's Indochina war. By early 1979 Vietnamese troops were in Pnompenh. On the Thai-Cambodian frontier, too, clashes, ambushes, shellings, evacuations occurred as Cambodia claimed several border points and lent aid to Thai Communist guerrillas. There is tension also along the Sino-Vietnamese border. "... The border was fixed by two conventions in 1887 and 1895 between the French colonial power and the Manchu imperial court," *Le Monde* reports. "Today both Peking and Hanoi are trying to adjust the border, each to its own advantage. ..."

Peking accuses the Vietnamese of "persecuting" ethnic Chinese in Vietnam and compelling 70,000 to leave. Internationally, China backed Cambodia, and the Soviet Union supported Vietnam. Internally, still other issues, often bloody controversies—the Cambodian purges, internal resistance in Laos, the "long road" to socialism in Vietnam, large-scale population

shifts—block stability. To teach Hanoi a "lesson," Chinese troops invaded Vietnam.

What was it all about? "The situation is complicated, extremely complicated," Gen. Tran Van Tra, the conqueror of Saigon, tells Tiziano Terzani of *Der Spiegel*. "There is no way outsiders can get a full view of what is going on in Vietnam," says *U.S. News & World Report*. "... Oil, water and ideology ... have transformed ... traditional Vietnamese-Cambodian hostilities into a battle over what form progress will take in Indochina into the 21st century," writes Lowell Finley in *In These Times*. "... One must remain aware of the regional power struggle going on under the shadow of a worldwide competition among the Soviet Union, Shuck Jr. in *Current History*. It is *la condition humaine*.

Wall of a refugee camp hut in Thailand serves as bulletin board where pictures of missing family members are posted.

Scale: 0 — 100 — 200 — 300 Miles; 0 — 200 — 400 Km.

CHINA

Sino-Vietnamese border clashes 1978

Vietnamese and Laotian forces combat Meu guerrillas

Chinese troops invade Vietnam Feb. 17, 1979; withdrew about a month later

Hanoi

LAOS

Gulf of Tonkin

HAINAN

BURMA

Vientiane

• Rangoon

THAILAND

PARACEL ISLANDS

Refugees flee Vietnam, Cambodia, and Laos

Bay of Bengal

• Bangkok

Angkor (ruins)

Tonle Sap

SOUTH CHINA SEA

CAMBODIA

Mekong

Phnom Penh

• Ho Chi Minh City

Spratly Islands: Possibility of offshore oil spurs competing claims by China and Vietnam

SPRATLY ISLANDS

Gulf of Siam

Vietnamese troops and insurgent Cambodians capture Phnom Penh Jan. 7, 1979

MALAYSIA

• Kuala Lumpur

INDOCHINA: REGIONAL POWER STRUGGLE

SUMATRA

• Singapore

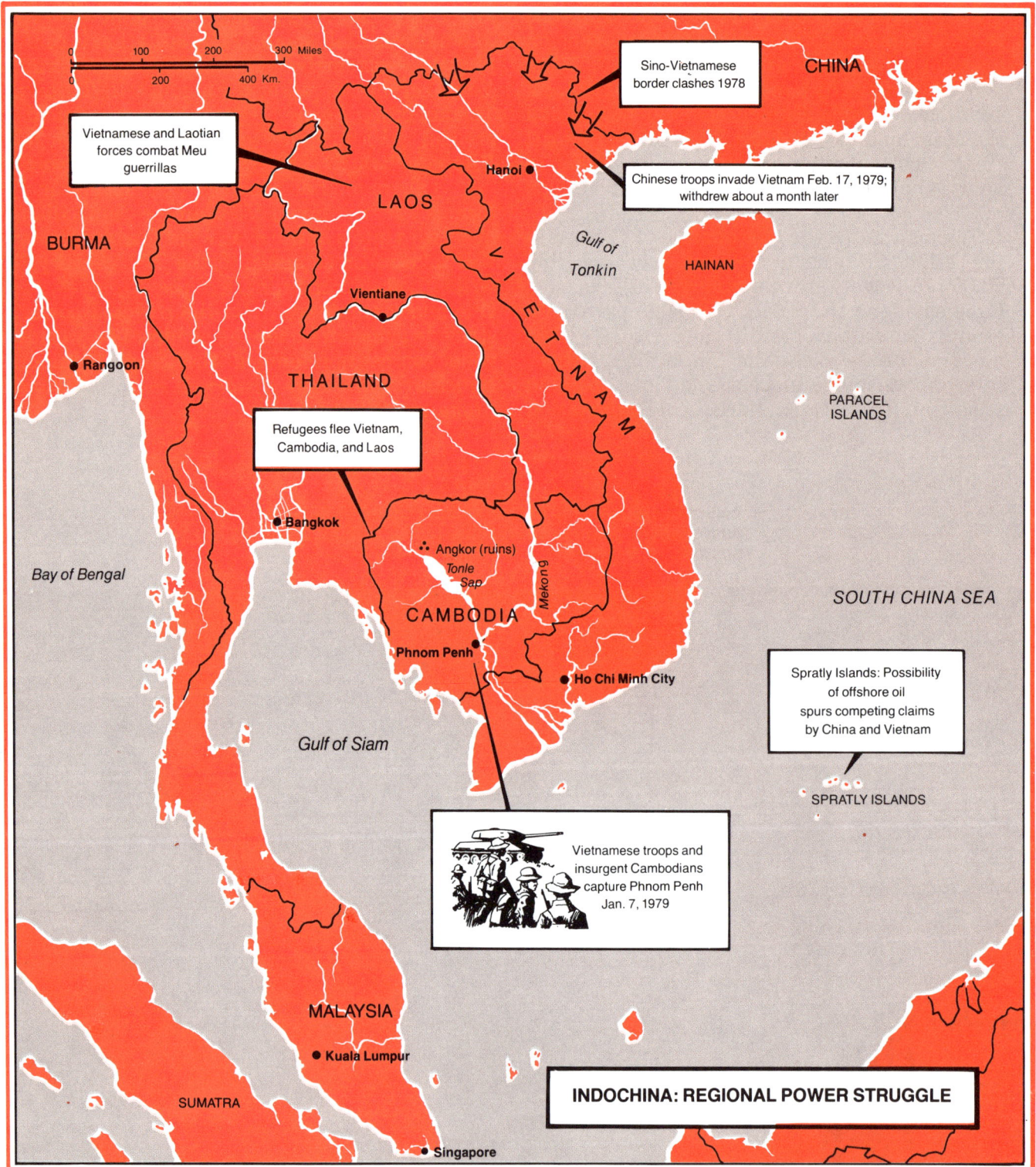

In Southeast Asia, conflict continues — China vs. Vietnam and Vietnam vs. Cambodia. One outcome is a very large number of refugees with camps mostly in Thailand. Recent episodes in the regional struggle are indicated on the map. Competition between the Soviet Union and China — and the struggle of these nations for world support — give the struggle a global dimension.

Index

Index